The Conversos and Moriscos in
Late Medieval Spain and Beyond

Volume One
Departures and Change

Studies in Medieval and Reformation Traditions

Edited by

Andrew Colin Gow
Edmonton, Alberta

In cooperation with

Thomas A. Brady, Jr., Berkeley, California
Sylvia Brown, Edmonton, Alberta
Berndt Hamm, Erlangen
Johannes Heil, Heidelberg
Susan C. Karant-Nunn, Tucson, Arizona
Martin Kaufhold, Augsburg
Jürgen Miethke, Heidelberg
M. E. H. Nicolette Mout, Leiden

Founding Editor
Heiko A. Oberman †

VOLUME 141/1

Converso and Morisco Studies

Edited by
Kevin Ingram

VOLUME 1

The Conversos and Moriscos in Late Medieval Spain and Beyond

Volume One
Departures and Change

Edited by

Kevin Ingram

BRILL

LEIDEN • BOSTON
2009

On the cover: Vicente Carducho, *The Expulsion of the Moriscos in 1609*, Prado Museum Catalogue no. D3055.

This book is printed on acid-free paper.

Library of Congress Cataloging-in-Publication Data

The Conversos and Moriscos in late medieval Spain and beyond : departures and change / edited by Kevin Ingram.
    p. cm. — (Studies in medieval and Reformation traditions ; v. 141)
    Conference papers.
    Includes index.
    ISBN 978-90-04-17553-2 (hardback : alk. paper)
    1. Marranos—Spain—History—Congresses. 2. Moriscos—Spain—History—Congresses. 3. Conversion—Christianity—History—Congresses. 4. Religious tolerance—Spain—History—Congresses. 5. Christianity—Spain—History—Congresses. 6. Nationalism—Spain—History—Congresses. 7. Spain—Church history—Congresses. 8. Spain—Ethnic relations—Congresses. 9. Spain—History—Ferdinand and Isabella, 1479–1516—Congresses. 10. Spain—History—House of Austria, 1516–1700—Congresses. I. Ingram, Kevin, 1956– II. Title. III. Series.

    DS135.S7C583 2009
    946'.004924—dc22

                                                                    2009009617

DS
135
.57
C583
2009
v. 1

ISSN 1573-4188
ISBN 978 90 04 17553 2

PRINTED IN THE NETHERLANDS

CONTENTS

ACKNOWLEDGEMENTS

First and foremost I would like to thank Saint Louis University and, in particular, Dr Rick Chaney, Vice-Provost of the Madrid Campus from 1992 to 2008, for supporting this project. My thanks also to the Plasencia city council and Spain's Higher Council of Scientific Investigations (CSIC) for sponsoring the 2005 and 2006 conferences, respectively. I also wish to thank Casa de America for allowing us the use of their elegant Cervantes room for the 2006 event. For their help in organizing the 2006 conference, I am grateful to Mercedes García-Arenal and Fernando Rodríguez Mediano. Finally, my thanks to Nicola Stapleton for her careful translations and to Marjory Hutchison and Jessica Nastel for their help in proofreading the essays in this collection.

Orientation Map

INTRODUCTION

Kevin Ingram

It is generally accepted that in the three decades following the 1391 pogrom against Spain's Jewish *aljamas* (neighborhoods), a third or more of Spanish Jews converted to Christianity. This mass conversion was repeated in 1492, when Spain's much reduced Jewish community was given the option of Christian baptism or expulsion. In this same year the Islamic Kingdom of Granada fell to the Christian forces and its Muslim inhabitants were soon presented with the same ultimatum: convert or leave the peninsula.

For the most part medieval Christian Spain viewed the expulsion or conversion of the two minority religions as a victory of the true faith over infidels, and this sense of triumph was nurtured during the next four centuries by clerical and secular authorities, who promoted the view that Spain was a morally and physically purer nation as a result of the 1492 catharsis. There were, of course, dissenting voices, like for example Charles IV's secretary of finance, Pedro Varela, who in 1797 recommended the return to Spain of the Jews, arguing that their business and intellectual skills would have beneficial effects on the Spanish economy; and José Amador de los Rios, whose *Judios de España* (published in 1876) attempted to reconcile his fellow countrymen to Spain's rich and influential Sephardic past. However, the prevailing view was that the Jewish and Islamic cultures had debased the peninsula and that Spain was a better place for their absence. As for the converts from Islam and Judaism, the Conversos and Moriscos,[1] the belief was that these formed small, insignificant minorities who had made little lasting impression on Spanish society: the Moriscos, those furtive, intransigent followers of Mohammed, had been ejected from Spanish soil in 1609 for their sins against Church and patria; while the Conversos, after posing some initial problems as secret heretics and impudent social climbers,

---

[1] The word *converso* is Spanish for convert. It is also used to describe Jewish converts to Christianity and their descendents. It will be written as "Converso" (with a capital C) throughout this compilation. The term *morisco*, meaning Islamic convert to Christianity, will be written "Morisco."

had been stifled (through the *limpieza de sangre* laws and Inquisition prosecutions) and ingested, without a trace, into mainstream (Old-Christian) society.

This historiographical interpretation was not seriously challenged until 1948, when Américo Castro published *España en su historia*, in which the historian and philologist accorded to the Jews and Conversos a central position in Spain's medieval and early modern intellectual environment. Castro's views were soon attacked by members of the Francoist academy, who preferred, for ideological reasons, to regard modern Spain as a pure Hispano-Catholic phenomenon. When other studies were published supporting many of Castro's claims, they were either dismissed as *Castrista* (a derogatory term meaning sensationalist or perverse) or, when it became impossible to refute them, flagrantly ignored. Thus, in the wake of Castro's study, an academic cold war developed between two rival schools. One school, comprised of émigré scholars, home-based academics on the margins of the Francoist academy and some foreign (mostly American) Hispanists, spoke of a Golden Age in which the Conversos and Moriscos were culturally significant; its antagonist, a Catholic-conservative group, made up of Francoist academics and a small but significant group of like-minded foreign scholars, emphasised an homogeneous Old-Christian Golden-Age culture in which the Conversos and the Moriscos figured as little more than Inquisitorial anecdotes.

This conflict was to begin with a very low-key affair. In the fifties and sixties Spanish history was still something of an academic backwater, generating little scholarship outside the peninsula; even Spain's Golden Age was approached mostly through subjects (American colonialism, Counter-Reformation, Price Revolution...) that were viewed to have important implications for the more historically attractive environments north of the Pyrenees. Indeed, it was largely as a result of this international academic indifference to Spain's Golden Age that old historiographical prejudices remained active for so long. Fortunately this situation began to change, albeit slowly, in the post-Franco era, promoted by a more liberal Spanish academic environment as well as by an increased interest in socio-cultural themes.

Today Spain's multicultural Middle Ages attracts an enormous amount of scholarly attention, engendering studies that continue to shed light not only on the Conversos and Moriscos but also on the related issues of individual and group identity, community violence, everyday resistance, passing and otherness, as the present collection of essays demonstrate. However, before turning to these studies, I think it appropriate to briefly situate the two communities within a broader historical context, beginning with the Conversos, who have, at least up until quite recently, generated most interest.

The Conversos

As I have already stated, the Converso phenomenon begins in 1391, when, throughout the peninsula, Christian communities rose up against the Jewish *aljamas*, forcing large numbers of Jews (how many is uncertain) to convert to Christianity. Naturally, few of these early converts sincerely embraced the Catholic Church or Christian society; indeed, most congregated in Converso neighborhoods, where the Sephardic culture continued to exert a strong influence on their lives. For its part, Christian, or rather Old-Christian, Spain, did nothing to entice Conversos to the fold. Old Christians remained antagonistic towards the new converts, whom they regarded (with some justification) as lukewarm Catholics, and this antagonism grew throughout the fifteenth century as a Converso middle sort, free from the social and commercial restrictions applied to the Jews, became increasingly prominent in business and professional activities.

Those Jews who converted to Christianity in the wake of the 1391 pogrom found themselves in an advantageous position vis-à-vis both the Jewish and Old-Christian communities. As New Christians they were no longer subject to the restrictions that had hampered Jewish merchants and professionals. As literate men (all Jewish males were required to gain a basic level of literacy in order to read the Torah), often with a sound knowledge of trade and finance, and with important contacts in Jewish financial and mercantile circles, they were able to compete at an advantage with an Old-Christian urban community. A number of these new converts accumulated large fortunes, which they used to advance their social positions within their cities. One method of social advancement was through the purchase of administrative offices within the church and local government; another method was to form marriage alliances with that other *arriviste* group, Castile's new nobility—families like the Ayala, Mendoza and Manrique, who, through wise political maneuvering, had risen rapidly to the top of Spain's fifteenth-century social hierarchy.

The Conversos' increasing commercial and social prominence in Castile's urban centers inevitably led to clashes with the Old-Christian community. One of the most dramatic confrontations occurred in Toledo in 1449, where a Converso agent of the crown, Rodrigo de Cota, was made responsible for collecting an extraordinary tax levied to aid Juan II prosecute his war against a French incursion into Navarre. Predisposed to see this tax as an example of Converso avarice and malice, the Old-Christian community turned on its New-Christian neighbors, looting and burning their neighborhoods. Ordered to put a stop to the violence, the *alcalde mayor*, Pedro Sarmiento, merely used his power to inflame anti-Converso feeling even further, and to introduce a statute, the *sentencia-estatuto*, prohibiting Conversos from occupying public office—that is to say from comporting themselves as nobles.

The Toledo statute (now recognized as the first *limpieza de sangre*, or pure blood, law) was soon followed by other similar legislation, preventing Conversos from entering city councils, cathedral chapters, universities and noble and religious orders on the grounds that they were of Jewish provenance and thus second class Christians. At the same time agitation grew for an inquisitorial body to investigate a Converso community suspected of being insincere neophytes. In 1480 the first tribunal of the Spanish Inquisition was established in Seville. Others followed in rapid succession, their task to root out Judaism from the New-Christian community.[2]

---

[2] One of the subjects most debated in Converso studies is the Catholic Monarchs' reasons for establishing their own Inquisitorial body (as opposed to utilizing the papal Inquisition council that had existed since the thirteenth century). Was the institution created to root out Judaizing or for other, more devious, reasons? Benzion Netanyahu, for example, believes that there were very few Crypto-Jews within the Converso community by the middle of the fifteenth century and that the Judaizing problem was used as a pretext to attack the Conversos as a whole, reducing their economic and political status. However, this argument is sustained only by ignoring or rejecting important documentation, not least of which are the fifteenth-century chronicles by both the Conversos' detractors and their sympathisers. It is instructive to note that while the Converso writers Alvaro de Palencia, Fernando de Pulgar and Juan Ramirez de Lucena berated the Inquisition for its inhumanity towards the New Christians, all three men recognized that Judaizing was prevalent in the Converso community, especially in Andalucía, where, Palencia noted, "the belief in the coming of the fallacious Messiah was widely extended among the Conversos." Fernando de Pulgar also indicated that Judaizing was widespread in the south of Spain, when, in attacking Inquisition brutality

A major obstacle in attacking this problem, or so it was believed, was the continuing presence of a large Jewish community in the peninsula, eager to entice the *anusim* (forced ones) back to the fold. And so in 1492 the Jews were ordered to convert to Christianity or leave Spain (Castile and Aragón) with whatever belongings they could carry. Some seventy or eighty thousand chose to leave; perhaps an equal number converted to Christianity. These unhappy converts now joined an older body of New Christians assailed by *limpieza de sangre* proscriptions and Holy Office persecution.

In the first forty years of Holy Office activity, it is reckoned that some three thousand Conversos were sent to the stake, accused of practicing the Jewish faith. Many thousands more were subjected to lengthy prison sentences and dispossessed of their property. However, after 1520 the rate of prosecutions declined quite considerably and this has led a number of historians to posit the view that the New Christian community had to a large degree been assimilated into the majority religion and culture by the mid sixteenth century. This view requires some qualification. For one reason or another, accusations of Judaizing declined after 1520, but this does not necessarily imply that the Conversos had become loyal subjects or good Catholics. It is noteworthy that all the major movements for reform in early modern Spain were either driven by Conversos or heavily supported by them. The *alumbrado*, or illuminist movement, which erupted in central Castile in the second decade of the century, was almost totally composed of Conversos who rejected Catholic dogma for mystical and quietist religious practice. The

---

and rapine, he wrote, "as the Old [Christians] are here [in Seville] such bad Christians, the New [Christians] are such good Jews...I believe that there are ten thousand girls who, because from birth they never leave their homes, neither hear nor know any other doctrine, but follow that [Judaism] which they observe their parents practicing indoors." There is no reason to believe that these chroniclers' views on Converso Judaizing were not shared by the Catholic Monarchs and that the royal couple saw the Holy Office as a means of eradicating an important religious problem. This is not to say, of course, that this was the only reason for the creation of a Spanish Inquisition. The Crown was also aware that Old-Christian antagonism towards the tightly knit Converso urban communities could, and did, lead to violent confrontations. Having gained power after a four year civil war, Ferdinand and Isabel were naturally sensitive to the issue of civil discord and saw in the Inquisition a means of institutionalizing and controlling an urban problem that was always in danger of escalating into disruptive civil uprisings. The measure undoubtedly created enormous distress within the Converso communities, attacked by rapacious and corrupt Inquisition officials. However, we should not jump too readily to the conclusion that this was the Catholic Monarchs' underlying intention in creating the Inquisition council.

Comunero revolt of 1521, an attack on a Crown that accrued political power at the expense of its nobility and urban patrician class, attracted a disproportionate number of Converso artisans and merchants to its ranks. Above all, Spain's Erasmian movement, which entered the peninsula with Charles I's Flemish court in 1517, was dominated by Converso professionals, both at court and in the universities, especially at the recently founded Complutense University, at Alcalá de Henares.

In assuming an Erasmian humanist mantle, Converso scholars were able to attack Catholic practice with a certain amount of impunity, at least at first, when the Flemish humanist enjoyed the support of powerful secular and clerical figures at court, including the Inquisitor General Alfonso Manrique. However, the Erasmists' situation deteriorated abruptly in the 1530s, as the Spanish monarch, now Emperor Charles V, became increasingly sensitive to the political dangers of a vociferous religious reform movement. With the Inquisition once more on the attack, the predominantly Converso Erasmian movement went underground, voicing its disquiet between the lines of humanist essays or through creative fictions, especially the picaresque novel, a particularly Converso genre.[3]

---

[3] When I say Converso genre, I do not mean merely that at its forefront were Converso writers, as this would hardly distinguish it from any other branch of Spanish Golden-Age literature (see note 11). What I mean is that picaresque fiction revolves around Converso, or barely disguised Converso, anti-heroes. The multiple misadventures of these marginal figures gave their creators an opportunity to paint a bleak picture of contemporary Spanish society, cynically attacking social mores and debunking Old-Christian pretensions to noble, honorable character. The works are laden with intertextual messages, aimed at what Mateo Alemán described as the "discreet reader," many of them allusions to the protagonists' Converso roots. While we have little biographical information on most of these authors (for obvious reasons), the information we do have usually points strongly to Converso backgrounds. It is particularly noteworthy that many of the authors were from medical backgrounds, as medical practice was virtually a Converso monopoly in early modern Spain. Mateo Alemán, author of *Guzmán de Alfarache* was from a well known Seville medical clan suspected of being Converso. Francisco López de Úbeda, author of *La pícara Justina*, was also a physician (from Toledo), as were Jerónimo de Alcalá Yáñez (*El donado hablador*) and Carlos García (*La desordenada codicia de los bienes ajenos*). García, from Zaragoza, moved to Paris early in his career, where he entered the circle of the Converso Elias de Montach, physician to Maria de Medici. Antonio Enríquez Gómez, author of *La vida de Gregorio Guadaña*, was not a physician. He was, however, a crypto-Jew who fled Spain for Amsterdam in 1636. The author of *Lazarillo de Tormes* (a work regarded as the first example of the picaresque genre) remains anonymous, although the text itself suggests that he was a Converso with strong Erasmian sympathies. Recently Rosa Navarro has compared the text with the *Diálogo de Mercurio y Carón* and *Diálogo de las cosas acaecidas en Roma* to make a convincing argument for the Converso humanist Alfonso de Valdés

Outside the Converso humanist elite, it is difficult to determine the character of Spain's Conversos in the sixteenth century. The view that the New Christians were divided into three groups, those who Judaized, those who were sincere Christians, and those who were neither (the apathetic, sceptical and atheistic) is often put forward by historians taxed with presenting a simple answer to the vexed question of Converso identity.[4] However, this is a singularly misleading taxonomy, because it implies an equal and rigid division that never existed. We have no idea what proportion of Conversos considered themselves Jewish, Christian or skeptics. We do know, however, that traumatized Conversos might make a number of religious border crossings as they searched for spiritual deliverance and/or social acceptability. As for the term "sincere Christians," this suggests a religious compliance that was far from the case. While many Conversos undoubtedly regarded themselves as Christian (by the sixteenth century, the majority), their brand of Christianity (hybrid, mystical, militant) was often a calculated affront to the Catholic Church, an act of subversion rather than conformism. Finally, the division implies a disjuncture within Converso communities that was, in fact, not so readily apparent. As the Inquisition records attest, those who Judaized, those who considered themselves sincere Christians, and those who were sceptics all interrelated in the same Converso neighborhoods and, frequently, in the same Converso extended and nuclear families.[5] Clearly, social and cultural ties were often much more important factors in deciding a Converso's sense of self than religious ones.

The diversity of the Conversos' responses to their peculiar sociocultural situation would seem to militate against categorizing them as a discrete group. Nevertheless, I believe the Conversos do share an important commonality: a feeling of resentment against an oppressive Old-Christian moral majority. This resentment is rarely overtly expressed;

---

as the author of the work. See Rosa Navarro Durán, *Alfonso Valdés, autor del Lazarillo de Tormes*, Madrid, 2004.

[4] This is the view of José Faur, *In the Shadow of History: Jews and Conversos at the Dawn of Modernity*, New York, 1992, ch. 3. Stephen Haliczer divides the Conversos into three broad groups, omitting the religiously apathetic group from his typology (Stephen Haliczer, *Inquisition and Society in the Kingdom of Valencia, 1478 to 1834*, Berkeley, 1990, p. 212.).

[5] The many different ideologies at play in Converso extended families is clearly presented by Pilar Huerga Criado, *En la raya de Portugal: Solidaridad y tensiones en la comunidad judeoconversa*, Salamanca, 1994, pp. 277–282.

rather, it takes a number of subtle forms, from the loaded subtext of picaresque novels to acts of everyday resistance, like those described by Leonor Zozaya in "A Thorn in The Community" (essay seven). The majority of sixteenth-century Spanish Conversos may not have been Judaizers, but it would be unwise to take for granted their assimilation or conformism. Certainly, there are grounds for arguing that many Conversos considered themselves both different from and superior to their Old-Christian neighbors, and that they believed this higher status was conveyed upon them by their Jewish background. They were, after all, the heirs of God's chosen people, who were authentic monotheists, not idol worshipers like their pagan (Gentile) counterparts.[6]

So far I have spoken only of the Converso phenomenon in Spain. In Portugal, the situation was somewhat different. It was here that the majority of Spain's Jews took up residence after the 1492 expulsion order, more than doubling the size of Portugal's own Sephardic community. At first the native Jewish community and the immigrants were allowed to practice their religion in peace. However, in 1497, under pressure from Spain's Catholic Monarchs, King Manuel of Portugal forcibly converted his Jewish subjects. It was a move he was reluctant to make, valuing, much more so than his Spanish counterparts, the Jews' economic potential. Thus, as an incentive to the neophytes to remain in his realm, he decreed a twenty year moratorium on investigations into their religious activities. It was during this period that many Converso traders became enormously wealthy through the booming spice and

---

[6] This point was made by the Converso writers Alonso de Cartagena (*Defensorium unitatis christianae*) and Diego de Valera (*Espejo de verdadera nobleza*), both writing in response to the 1449 *sentencia estatuto*. For Cartagena, Christianity was a redirection and a deepening of the Jewish faith: the Old Law had merely evolved into a more ideal form. Jews who embraced Christianity were embracing an evangelical spirit that had been present in their faith, in men like Moses and Aaron. The Gentiles did not have this foundation; none of their writings made reference to the coming of the Christ or to the Trinity. They were sons who after a long absence returned home; the Jews (for which read Conversos), were daughters who had never left the paternal house. In his *Espejo*, Diego de Valera writes: "If we are looking for authorities for Jewish nobility, we can find many, for it is written in the fourth chapter of Deuteronomy in speaking of the Jews: 'What other nation is as noble? As it says, not one.'" The Converso preacher Juan de Avila (later Saint Juan de Avila) echoed these thoughts on the Jews' superior status in his work *Audi filia*, written while he languished in the Seville Inquisition prison, accused on being an *alumbrado*. In this work Avila reminds his readers that Jesus preached only to the Jews. Later Christ's apostles took his message further afield, "and now the preaching of Christ's name is growing every day in distant lands, so that he is not only light for the Jews, who believed in Him, and to whom he was sent, but also to the gentiles, who were in blindness and idolatry far removed from God."

slave trades and used their wealth to maintain a powerful Converso lobby in the Vatican. Through this lobby the Portuguese Conversos were able to resist the establishment of an Inquisition council until 1534 and stifle its activities for yet another fourteen years thereafter.

It was thus not until the mid sixteenth century, over fifty years after the Spanish expulsion, that the Portuguese Converso community began to experience serious problems with the Holy Office. As a response to this increased vigilance, many Converso families opted to immigrate back to Spain, where they hoped to escape Inquisition attention. Unfortunately, their escape coincided with an increase in Spanish Inquisition activity, promoted by a Counter-Reformation monarchy ever more obsessed with socio-religious deviance. Suspected of crypto-Jewish activity, the Portuguese immigrants naturally attracted a great deal of Inquisition attention, as a result of which convictions for Judaizing escalated. Not all of those convicted were Portuguese, however. The Holy Office's increased sensitivity to crypto-Judaism led to the exposure of indigenous Jewish cells also, like that of Quintanar de la Orden, examined by Vincent Parello in "Inquisition and Crypto-Judaism: The 'Complicity' of the Mora Family of Quintanar de la Orden (1588–1592)," (essay eight in this collection).

While the Spanish Crown was well aware that most of the Portuguese Conversos were crypto-Jews, it was disposed, on occasion, to turn a blind eye to this heresy, in return for financial aid. In 1602 Philip III applied to Rome for a bull pardoning the past heresies of 6,000 Portuguese Converso families; in return for this munificence, a consortium of Portuguese businessmen paid the Crown the enormous sum of 1,860,000 ducats. Twenty-five years later, Philip IV brokered a deal with a new group of Portuguese businessmen, who were given licence to ply their trade in Spain and its dominions for another enormous sum of money. Many of these men now gravitated towards Madrid, where for two decades or more they dominated court finance. The architect of this deal was the king's *privado*, the Count-Duke of Olivares, a particularly fervent enemy of anti-Converso attitudes and legislation.[7] While the Count Duke remained in power, the Portuguese financiers were protected. However, on his fall, in 1643, the Inquisition took the offensive,

---

[7] Olivares was himself the great grandson of King Ferdinand's Converso secretary Lope Conchillos. Furthermore, his family belonged to the House of Medina Sidonia, a noble Andalucían clan that maintained close links with Seville's Converso patrician merchants.

prosecuting some of the court's wealthiest businessmen as Judaizers
and stripping them of their enormous fortunes. Faced with continuous
Inquisition attacks, many well-heeled members of the Portuguese business community chose to leave Spain for France and the Netherlands,
taking their financial expertise with them.

With Spain's wealthy Converso businessmen in exile, Inquisition
prosecutions for Judaizing slowly declined over the next century.[8] This
did not mean, however, that the Spanish obsession with the Conversos
followed suit. For this obsession was not only with Converso heresy;
indeed, that was the least of it. Spain was obsessed with the Conversos' Jewish essence. If this malady were allowed to reign unchecked, it
would, it was believed, infect the entire kingdom, impairing everyone's
virtue and honor. Even after the Inquisition ledgers ceased to record
accusations against Judaizers, even after the *limpieza de sangre* laws
became no more than a bureaucratic formality, this fixation with the
secret Jew remained.

For the majority of Spaniards, the Jews and the Conversos were the
embodiment of alien attitudes and beliefs, the corrupters of Spanish
tradition; and so, by some perverse inversion, everything foreign, different or innovative was liable to be labelled Jewish: the Spanish masons,
the Spanish Enlightenment, the First and Second Republics were all
associated with Jewish malfeasance; so too, in Américo Castro's view,
was capitalist enterprise and intellectual inquiry in general. According
to Castro, middle class activity was anathematized in Spain precisely
because of its association with the Jews and the Conversos, and this
rejection had grave consequences for the country's later development.
It is an intriguing view, although one that is difficult to validate, much
of the relevant evidence being locked up in a nation's psyche, beyond
the reach of social scientists' tools of measure. What cannot be denied,
however, is that the Jews and Conversos have remained a contentious
issue in Spanish culture up to the present day, as the recent academic
debate on their historiographical importance attests.[9]

---

[8] With the exception of the decade 1720 to 1730, which witnessed a last major wave
of prosecution.
[9] See my article in this collection.

The Moriscos

Sizeable Islamic communities existed in Christian Spain from the second wave of the *Reconquista* (in the thirteenth century) onwards. These communities were encouraged by a Spanish Crown eager to maintain the same infrastructure bequeathed to it by the retreating Islamic forces and to tap into the wealth and expertise of the Islamic society. Significantly, the Crown made no attempt to convert these Muslim denizens, known as *Mudéjares*, or change in any way their Islamic lifestyle. To do so would have run the risk of losing a valuable commodity to the Nasrid kingdom of Granada.

However, this policy of toleration towards the Muslims was seriously questioned after 1492, when the Granada stronghold fell to the combined forces of Isabel and Ferdinand. Having now destroyed the final remnants of Islamic rule on the peninsula, under the banner of "Holy Crusade," the Catholic Monarchs (a title bestowed upon the royal couple by the Pope for their crusading activity) could no longer justify their erstwhile relaxed attitude towards their indigenous infidels. Pressure now needed to be exerted on the Spanish Muslims, starting with the population of Granada, to convert to Christianity. But what form was this pressure to take? Was it to be a gradual but persistent process of proselytism and instruction, or was it to be a swift, radical act of enforced baptism? The first option was supported by Granada's civil governor, Íñigo López de Mendoza, Count of Tendilla, and its archbishop, Hernando de Talavera, who saw their task as one of pacification and accommodation. The second option was advocated by Francisco Jiménez de Cisneros, who as primate of Castile was in a position to make his hard line opinions felt.

In 1499, the rumor began to circulate in Granada and the surrounding territory that the Cisneros camp had triumphed and that the Catholic Monarchs were about to renege on the 1492 capitulations, allowing the Muslims liberty of religious practice. Street fighting now broke out in the *Albaicin*, the Muslim district of the city, and these disturbances soon escalated into pitched battles and open rebellion. By the time this insurrection was defeated, in 1500, the Catholic Monarchs had decided upon a policy of forced conversion, at least for the Muslim population of Castile, which now included Granada; for the time being the Muslims in Ferdinand's own kingdom of Aragón remained free to practice their chosen religion.

Quite why Ferdinand chose to delay implementation of the conversion order in his own territories remains open to debate; however, the fact that many of the Aragonese and Valencian Muslims were the vassals of powerful noble families certainly played a part in the king's decision. Any act that disturbed or threatened the equilibrium of this lucrative minority would inevitably have incurred the wrath of their noble landlords, and this was something the absentee monarch clearly wished to avoid. In the event, the Aragonese and Valencian Moriscos were not converted until 1525.

Meanwhile, the majority of Castilian Muslims took the baptismal waters. In theory they were given the choice of conversion or expulsion; however, the conditions under which they were allowed to leave the peninsula were so onerous that few took the latter option. It is clear that the majority justified their apostasy as an unavoidable necessity, and in this they were supported by their religious leaders, who counselled the converts to observe Islamic practice in secret.

In the circumstances, few of the converts chose to sincerely embrace Christianity, and somewhat surprisingly very little pressure was exerted upon them to do so. Once the Muslims were formally baptized they were left mostly to their own devices, at least during the first decades of the century, when the Inquisition was busy directing its attention towards the Converso community. Curiously, Castile's Judaizers were numerically far inferior to its crypto-Muslims. However, religion was not the Inquisition's only criterion for attacking neophytes; it was also moved by political and economic considerations, and patrician Converso merchants were a far richer prize than humble Morisco laborers. Thus for a time the Moriscos were let off the hook.

This situation changed, however, in mid century, when the Ottoman Turks began to threaten Spanish hegemony in the Western Mediterranean. As tension mounted, the Spanish Crown turned its attention to its Morisco subjects, who were now perceived as potentially dangerous fifth columnists. Particularly treacherous, or so the Crown believed, were the Granadan Moriscos (located closest to the Islamic regimes of North Africa), who, despite the 1502 conversion order and other legislation banning the use of Arabic language and dress, had made little effort to adopt Christian customs or religion.

In a new bid to acculturate this community, legislation reinforcing the earlier religious and cultural proscriptions was once again introduced. Again the legislation led to an insurrection, the Alpujarra War, which raged for two years and decimated the zone's Morisco communities.

At the end of the fighting, in 1570, those Moriscos who survived found themselves either enslaved or forcibly relocated to other communities throughout Andalucía and New Castile. Philip II undoubtedly viewed the break up and transfer of these communities as a necessary first step in their Christianization. But the harsh policy appears only to have steeled the dispossessed group in its resolve to remain Islamic.

And still there remained two hundred thousand Moriscos on the Valencian coast, many of whom were known to be in contact with the Islamic communities of North Africa. Should this community also be relocated? Or was the solution more drastic still: the expulsion of all the Moriscos from Spain? It was in this atmosphere of tension and uncertainty that a number of "ancient" lead books were discovered in the city of Granada, whose contents revealed that among Spain's first-century Christian evangelists were two converted Arabs.

The Lead Books were in fact recent forgeries by local Moriscos, who hoped to enhance their community's prestige by presenting Arabs, a people associated with Islamic iniquity, as founding members of the Spanish church. The implication was that Moriscos also had the capacity to be good Christians and worthy Spaniards (see Mercedes García-Arenal and Fernando Rodríguez Mediano, essay ten). However, it would be rash to consider this appeal for equality as the work of sincere assimilationists. The Lead Books affair was also a secret violation of Christian sacred history; an act of duplicity and defiance, through which we once again glimpse the New Christian's Janus face.

While the consensus of scholarly opinion is that the majority of Moriscos remained crypto-Muslims up until the expulsion order of 1609,[10] the paucity of preserved Islamic literature from sixteenth-century Spain has conditioned us to believe that this community was a modest, un-intellectual one. However, the lack of extant literature would appear to say as much about the hazards of literary production and preservation as it does about the intellectual resources of Spain's Moriscos. Recent studies of *aljamiado* literature (Castilian and Catalan writings in Arabic script) reveal a dispersed but active Morisco intellectual community,

---

[10] This assumption should, however, be qualified, and is being qualified in recent scholarly studies. Separated from their religious authorities, forced to observe Islam clandestinely, it was inevitable that the Moriscos' Islamic practice would undergo important changes in the sixteenth century. Furthermore, the Moriscos' increasing contact with Christian belief introduced them to religious tendencies that began to inform their vision of the Islamic credo, as the *aljamiado* literature attests.

whose devotional works were often influenced by *devotio moderna* and humanist views. They also introduce us to what appears to have been an extensive cultural resistance movement, anxious to preserve the Isamic faith and customs under extremely difficult conditions.

At the same time that scholars are re-examining *aljamiado* literature, they are also reassessing the "Moorish" novels and ballads. These works (the *Abencerraje* is perhaps the most famous), written in a period directly prior to the 1609 expulsion, present the Muslims not as villains but as noble and chivalrous heroes. Up until recently examined with little attention to its socio-historic context, this genre is now increasingly taken as evidence of a certain sympathy towards the oppressed Morisco within Spanish society. Both Barbara Fuchs' "Maurophilia and the Morisco Subject" (essay eleven) and William Childers' "Manzanares 1600: Moriscos from Granada Head a 'Moors and Christians' Fair" (essay 12) address the phenomenon of maurophilia in late sixteenth century Spain. Undoubtedly the matter will receive further attention in the next years, as we commemorate the four hundredth anniversary of the Morisco expulsion.

Converso and Moriscos Studies

It was in response to the ever growing historiographical debate on the Conversos and Moriscos that I began, in 2004, to organize an annual (now bi-annual) conference, examining Converso and Morisco themes. In staging this event, I had three aims in mind: first, to create an arena in which the Conversos and Moriscos were treated as related rather than separate socio-cultural phenomena; second, to bring together an interdisciplinary group of scholars to discuss Converso and Morisco themes from differing academic perspectives and approaches; and third, to provide a venue for Spanish scholars to exchange views with their non-Spanish counterparts, thus helping to establish much needed formal links between foreign and native Hispanists. These same goals have also guided the *Converso and Moriscos Studies* series, which will offer, periodically, selections of our conference papers, revised and expanded for publication.

In organizing volume one of the series, I have favored a loose chronological structure, in which the essays become episodes or vignettes in a longer, complex story. The volume begins with Francisco Márquez Villanueva's "On the Concept of *Mudejarism*," in which the author reflects on the problematic issue of *convivencia* (or coexistence). Márquez points out that in the Low Middle Ages, the Muslims, conscious of their limited military possibilities, established a cultural and religious pluralism which safeguarded Christian (Mozarab) communities in al-Andalus. With the Christian conquest of Toledo in the eleventh century, the Mozarab phenomenon became the Mudejar phenomenon, which guaranteed the continuity of the non-Christian minorities. The crucial problem of repopulation created a *de facto* tolerance that had nothing to do with the modern concept of liberalism, but rather with the practical necessity of group cooperation to avoid ethnic violence and chaos. This was far from an idyllic situation; nevertheless, *mudejarismo*, with all its problems, created an atmosphere of peace and prosperity during the High Middle ages. According to Márquez, its end was not brought about by an internal crisis in its system, but by the politics of violence inaugurated by Ferdinand and Isabel and perpetuated under Habsburg rule, creating serious consequences for the peninsula during the modern age.

It might well be argued, of course, that the Catholic Monarchs were merely late protagonists in a drama whose inevitable outcome had been determined in its first act, the late fourteenth century mass conversion of the Sephardic community. This pogrom created a large, embittered Converso community, the majority of whom, at least in the immediate aftermath of the violence, remained loyal to the Jewish religion and passed their beliefs down to their children. Many of these crypto-Jews were disposed to see their plight as a necessary preliminary to the Messiah's arrival, and thus were sensitive to any phenomenon that suggested cosmic change. For these secret Judaizers, the Ottoman Turk's capture of Constantinople in 1454 was loaded with Messianic portends.

In "Seeking the Messiah," Mark Meyerson examines the effects of this event on Rodrigo Cifuentes and his family, prosecuted in Valencia in 1464 for attempting to sail for the Ottoman Empire with the aim of returning to Judaism and awaiting the Jewish Messiah. Meyerson establishes the probable veracity of the inquisitorial accusations through an examination of the defendants' Judaizing, their contacts with Jewish merchants and kinsfolk in Valencia, and their messianic ideology. The author argues that the actions of the Cifuentes family are indicative of a wider, though limited, messianic movement among Valencian Conversos, essentially penitential in nature, sparked by the fall of Constantinople. The article concludes with a consideration of how the activities

of the Spanish Inquisition in Valencia and the expulsion of the Jews
created a more polarized religious milieu and contributed to a resur-
gence of Converso messianism at the end of the fifteenth century.

While it is certain that the majority of Jews who converted to Christianity in the wake of the 1391 attacks did so under pressure from their
Christian neighbors, it would be a mistake to assume that this pogrom
was perpetrated against a community united in its religious belief. A
number of Jews, especially prominent among the courtier elite, appear
to have long abandoned Jewish theology for an Aristotelian, rationalist
outlook. Although these wealthy and well-placed Jews had no interest
in Christian belief, they felt little compulsion to resist conversion. Once
baptized, they paid lip service to their new religion while maintaining
their rationalist credo in private, among a coterie of like-minded fellow converts. Gradually, their sceptical outlook filtered down into a
Converso rank and file, where it gained adherents among an educated
urban community, debilitated and assailed by religious doubts. In "'If
There Were God': The Problem of Unbelief in the *Visión Deleytable*,"
Luis Girón locates Alfonso de la Torre's fifteenth-century philosophical
compendium within this Converso rationalist milieu. The recent discovery of an early manuscript of the work in Hebraic *aljamiado* script
presents Girón with the opportunity to examine de la Torre's rationalist
vision and to advance the view that it was written by a Converso sceptic
for the edification of a distressed and disoriented Sephardic (Converso
and Jewish) intellectual community.

It should now be evident to everyone working on early modern Spanish culture that literary production during this period (both intellectual
and creative) was dominated by Conversos.[11] Unfortunately, many
scholars remain blind (sometimes perversely so) to this fact, and thus
continue to interpret texts without giving due consideration to shrill
undertones of Converso angst and anger. In "Converso Voices in Fif-

---

[11] The majority of Spain's great Golden Age literary figures were New Christians.
Spanish prose fiction was dominated by Converso writers: Cervantes, Alemán, Rojas,
Jorge Montemayor, Francisco Delicado, Luis Vélez de Guevara were all from Con-
verso backgrounds. Spain's great sixteenth-century mystics Teresa of Avila, Juan de
Avila, and Juan de la Cruz were also Conversos, as were Spain's foremost humanists,
among whom were Luis Vives, Juan and Alfonso Valdés, Juan de Vergara, Brocense,
Ambrosio Morales, Arias Montano, Luis de León and Juan de Malara. Conversos also
predominated in early sixteenth-century theater, as Elaine Wertheimer's essay indicates.
Indeed, where substantial information on a Golden-Age writer is available, the evidence
normally points to a Converso family background—unsurprisingly, given that most
writers came out of Spain's Converso-dominated professional middle sort.

teenth and Sixteenth-Century Spanish Literature," Elaine Wertheimer discusses Converso subtext in the works of six authors, writing in Spain, Portugal and Italy. Although the paucity of information available on these writers prevents us from determining their genealogies, a close examination of their written works reveal them to be New Christians, reacting to the proliferating *limpieza de sangre* laws that threatened all with the loss of honor and status.

Spain's *limpieza de sangre* laws divided society into pure Old Christians and tainted New ones. For a society obsessed with honor, this was a terrible stigma that affected both individuals and, on occasion, whole communites, as Juan Gil demonstrates in his essay "*Berenjeneros*: The Aubergine Eaters." This was the nickname given to the people of Toledo in allusion to their Jewish origins, the aubergine being associated with Sephardic cuisine. In their attempt to counter this "calumny," a number of Toledo's intellectuals (almost certainly Conversos), fabricated histories in which they presented the city as being founded by early Greek settlers, or by ancient (Old Testament) Jews, members of a pre-crucifixion Hebrew settlement that was totally divorced from the deicide, and thus untainted.

While the Inquisition vigilance and *limpieza de sangre* laws increasingly created problems for Spanish Conversos, their counterparts in Sicily (a Spanish dependency) appeared to have fared somewhat better. In "Sicilian Converts after the Expulsion," Nadia Zeldes examines this community's relationship with the island's Old-Christian majority. As Zeldes points out, unlike their Castilian and Aragonese brethren, the Jews of Sicily had not been subjected to mass conversion in the late fourteenth and early fifteenth centuries. Thus Sicily's Converso community barely existed before 1492, when many of the island's Jews converted to avoid expulsion from the Spanish realm. While these *neofiti* made little attempt to integrate into Christian society, they appear to have experienced fewer problems than the Castilian Conversos vis-à-vis the Old-Christian authorities. This situation gradually changed after 1500, when the Spanish Inquisition took a prominent role in Sicilian politics. An agent of the Spanish crown, the Holy Office now attempted to bring the *neofiti*'s situation into line with that of the New Christians of mainland Spain.

Leonor Zozaya's essay, "A Thorn in the Community," also examines inter-community relations between Conversos and Old Christians; however, this time in mid-sixteenth-century Castile. Zozaya's essay focuses on the Rodríguez family, who in the late fifteenth century had been prosecuted in Molina de Aragón as crypto-Jews. Fifty years later members of this family, Francisco Cortés and Diego López Cortés, were once again in trouble with the Inquisition for dubious religious views and activities. While the Cortés brothers do not appear to have been Judaizers, they were uncomfortable Christians, who antagonized their neighbors with their irreligious actions and remarks. Particularly scandalous, at least to some, was Diego's manipulation of a thorn which he claimed to be from the true crown of Christ. When the thorn began to take on popular cult status, the local religious authorities and the Holy Office stepped in, not to ban its use but to incorporate it into formal religious practice. "A Thorn in the Community" introduces us to the complexities and ambiguities of both Converso identity and local religious practice.

While many Spanish Conversos continued to resist orthodox Catholic practice for many generations after their ancestors had been baptized into the religion, few Converso families actually remained Jewish practitioners for such a long period. An exception (although certainly not the only one) was the Mora family of Quintanar de la Orden. In "The Complicity of the Mora Family," Vincent Parello offers a socio-religious profile of this family that was tried by the Inquisition in 1580 for Judaizing.

The attack on the Moras occurred in the period after the Tridentine Councils, when the Crown became more rigorous in its prosecution of religious non-conformism. One result of this harder line was the reloca-tion of the Granadan Moriscos within Castile. The aim was to divide this community into smaller, and thus less problematical, groups. However, the result was often the opposite of that desired, as the newcomers competed with Old-Christian natives for work and living space. One of the more fractious areas was the city of Seville, where in 1580 over six thousand Moriscos were congregated. In the summer of that year, in a time of famine and on the eve of the war with Portugal, popular sentiment in Seville ran against its Morisco population. It was in this extremely tense atmosphere that the Seville authorities announced that they had stumbled across a Morisco rebellion conspiracy, later known as "the Morisco uprising of Andalucía." Recently discovered sources, taken from the proceedings against the ringleaders of the uprising, allow Michel Boeglin ("Between Rumor and Resistance") to make a more precise evaluation of the nature and impact of this incident. Boeglin concludes that the "uprising" was blown up out of proportion by a city government perpetually suspicious of a group that remained both marginal and unified.

Almost a century after Spain's Muslims had been forced to convert to Christianity, their situation continued to deteriorate. More politically powerful and socially flexible, the Conversos' position was considerably better. However, even this group was continually challenged by *limpieza de sangre* legislation that cast it as alien and ignoble. Faced with this obstacle, most New Christians chose to take the path of least resistance and lie about their ancestry. Some, however, attempted to solve the problem by changing society's mentality towards honor. Spain's Converso humanists, for example, stressed the importance of education and ability, rather than ancestry, in conveying noble status, and they pointed to the great Romans Cicero and Seneca (the latter born in Córdoba) as men who gained respect and title through their own efforts. Others saw the solution to the Converso and Morisco problem in the reworking of Spanish historiographical fictions, especially its charter myths, to give Jewish and Arab groups a foundational role in early Christian society. In so doing, these falsifiers sought to change the society's attitude towards its New Christian minorities.

In "Jerónimo Román de la Higuera and the Lead Books of Sacramonte," Mercedes García-Arenal and Fernando Rodríguez Mediano examine the Toledan Jesuit Jerónimo Román de la Higuera, one of the principle falsifiers of Spanish historiography at the end of the sixteenth century, and his connexion with another major falsifier, Miguel de Luna, who perpetrated the Lead Books of Granada fraud in the same period. García-Arenal's and Rodríguez Mediano's study attempts to establish a parallel between both frauds, whose final objective, they believe, was to re-evaluate the role of the Arabs and Jews in Spain, promoting an historical vision that would facilitate the integration of the Converso and Morisco minorities into sixteenth-century Spanish society.

Like the false chronicles, the Moorish novels and ballads, which also began to appear at the end of the sixteenth century, appear to have been executed mostly by authors who wished to improve the image of the Morisco in Spanish society. Barbara Fuchs ("Maurophilia and the Morisco Subject") believes that the success of this genre cannot merely be explained by its exotic nature; rather, it appealed to a society that was still "hybridized" and thus receptive to Spain's multicultural past, despite its government's agenda of political centralism and ethno-cultural homogenization.

The theme of maurophilia is also explored by William Childers in "Manzanares 1600: Moriscos from Granada Head a Moors and Christians Fair." Childers' essay examines what might be described as an early version of the famous Moors and Christians fairs which became popular in the seventeenth century and have remained so up until the present day. However, whereas the later Moors and Christians fairs focus on the triumph of Christian forces over the Muslims, the Manzanares event, in which the Moors (Moriscos) are the chief protagonists, evokes an atmosphere of accord and accommodation. This attempt at integration was, however, frowned upon by Crown officials, appalled by the freedom granted to the town's Moriscos to bear arms and thus present themselves as men of noble bearing. Was the Manzanzares affair representative of a generalized grass roots rapprochement that ran against the Crown's own socio-political agenda, predicated more on division than inclusion? Like Fuchs, Childers invites us to re-examine our views on Old Christian/Morisco relations in the period immediate to the 1609 expulsion.

Undoubtedly the most famous example of maurophilia is Sancho Panza's brotherly embrace of his old friend Ricote in part two of *Don Quijote*. The question is: Did Cervantes sympathise with the Morisco Ricote as a man of liberal (humanistic) disposition, or did he empathise with him, as a fellow Converso? There are those scholars who would deny that this was New-Christian empathy on the grounds that there is no conclusive proof that Cervantes ancestors were Jews. However, I think most *Cervantistas* would now agree that the author's background (medical and mercantile) strongly suggests Converso provenance, and that this assessment is corroborated by his works, which reveal pro-Erasmian and anti-*limpieza* tendencies. There are already a number of studies which examine what I would call Cervantes' Converso-humanist credo. There are few studies, however, that suggest Cervantes was inspired on occasion by Jewish literary traditions, as Francisco Peña argues in "Sancho Panza and the Mimesis of Solomon."

In his essay, Peña explores the parallels between Sancho Panza and King Solomon in *Don Quijote*. Although a number of critics have already noted allusions to Solomon in Cervantes' masterpiece, as Peña states, no study has examined this subject in any depth. In his own study, Peña shows the rich inter-textual allusions to the relationship between the knight's squire and the Biblical king. To grasp these subtle allusions, Cervantes sixteenth-century readers would have required a knowledge of the numerous legends, of Jewish origin, concerning Solomon that circulated throughout the medieval and Renaissance periods.

In the final essay of this collection, "Historiography, Historicity and the Conversos," I examine the position of the Conversos in Spanish historiography since Amador de los Rios's seminal study, *Estudios históricos, políticos y literarios sobre los judíos en España*, published in 1848. I present the view that the Spanish academy's predilection for a pure or *castizo* Spain, genetically Celtiberian and spiritually Roman Catholic, has often militated against it recognizing the important contribution of the Conversos to Golden-Age culture. This failure, or reluctance, to admit the Conversos into the Golden-Age pantheon, deep rooted and pervasive during the Franco period, is still evident today, and is reflected in a mainstream history that shies clear of assessing the nature, extent and implications of the Conversos' involvement in sixteenth-century Spain's intellectual and artistic environment.

As the essays in this collection attest, the study of the Converso and Morisco phenomena is not only important for those of us focused on Spanish society and culture, but for academics everywhere interested in the issues of identity, nationalism, religious intolerance and the challenges of modernity. I hope that the *Converso and Morisco Studies* series will allow us to examine all of these subjects while addressing the two minority groups in question. Specifically, I hope it will give those of us caught up in Converso and Morisco issues the opportunity to address existing scholarship and to suggest fresh approaches to perennial concerns. To coincide with the first volume of the series, a website has been created (http://spain.slu.edu/Conversos), designed to provide information on the conferences and publications as well as to encourage scholarly debate on questions related to our theme.

CHAPTER ONE

ON THE CONCEPT OF MUDEJARISM

Francisco Márquez Villanueva*

The creation of *Mudejarismo* (Mudejarism), a concept which clearly integrated the Semitic element into the past of the Iberian Peninsula, is one of the great historiographical achievements of the second half of the twentieth century. What up until then had been a grudging recognition of limited contacts between the Christian and Islamic cultures on the Iberian Peninsula, now became a much deeper conceptualization of medieval Spanish history. The term itself is derived from the Arabic word *mudéjar* or "tributary,"[1] which medieval Castilian used to designate any Muslim who accepted non-Islamic sovereignty in return for guaranteed cultural and religious freedom. The term gained modern currency as a historiographical concept in the field of the visual arts as of 1859, when José Amador de los Ríos referred to it in his acceptance speech to the Real Academia de Bellas Artes de San Fernando,

---

* Translated by Nicola Stapleton.
[1] The etymology is disputed. It has been suggested it is derived from *mudayyan* "he who has been permitted to remain," as put forward by Joan Corominas-José A. Pascual, DCEH. Francisco Fernández y González proposed *dajala* and *mudejabat*, "to enter agreements and talks with others," and *mudegian* and *ahl ad dechm*, "people of permanence," in his *Estado social y político de los mudéjares de Castilla*, Madrid, 1866, pp. 3–4. Luis G. De Valdeavellano explains it as "like the Arab" and in a group sense, also designated *mu'ahidun* or "agreed" (*Curso de historia de las instituciones españolas. De los orígenes al final de la Edad Media*, Madrid, 1973, p. 642). From the passive participle of *mudayyan*, "domesticated, subdued, subject, he who has been allowed to remain," a term that was only frequent from the fifteenth century onwards, according to the study by Felipe Maíllo Salgado, "Acerca del uso, significado y referente del término 'mudéjar'. Contribución al estudio del medievo español y al de su léxico," *Actas del IV Congreso Internacional Encuentro de las Tres Culturas*, C. Carrete Parrondo ed., Toledo, 1988, pp. 103–112. From *mudadjian* or *ahl al-dadin*, the "Muslim left behind in Christian land" and both "left behind" and "tributary," according to Pedro Chalmeta, *The Encyclopedia of Islam*, New Edition, VII, 1991. For Leonard P. Harvey, it is a disparaging term for "domesticated," see "Límite de los intercambios culturales" in *Actas de la I Jornadas de Cultura Islámica. Toledo 1987: Al-Andalus, ocho siglos de historia*, Madrid, 1989, pp. 89–94 (p. 94).

entitled *El estilo mudéjar en arquitectura*.[2] In view of the material and obvious nature of the mixture or simultaneous acceptance of formal elements from East and West seen in the Spanish-speaking area from the Middle Ages until the early seventeenth century, the choice of name was only natural.[3] On Américo Castro's initiative, in 1948[4] Mudejarism came to mean the vast acculturating phenomenon which equally affected the fields of thought, literature, politics and life-styles throughout this period.[5] Moving onwards in the same direction, Juan Goytisolo[6] cleverly perfected the conceptual edifice of Mudejarism, making it one of the cardinal issues in his oeuvre.

In contrast to *Mudejarismo*, we have the term *Reconquista* (Reconquest), which also gained currency in the mid-nineteenth century, when it was accepted by the Real Academia de la Lengua as the designated expression for the eight-century struggle by Christianity to recover the territory lost to the Islamic military thrust in the eighth century.[7]

---

[2] For the reception and movement of ideas on the concept of Mudejar art, Manuel Valdés Fernández, "Arte de los siglos XII a XV y cultura mudéjar," in *Historia del Arte en Castilla y León*, t. IV *Arte mudéjar*, Valladolid, 1994, pp. 9–128 (p. 11). Basilio Pavón classifies Mudejar art as a "long and obsessive policy of reusing everything Islamic, either overtly or covertly," "'Qubba' y 'alcoba': síntesis y conclusión," *Revista de Filología Española* 60 (1978–1980), pp. 333–343 (p. 341). This is a topic that would merit a separate study and for which much valuable material and ideas are presented in the book by Ma. Elena Díez Jorge, *El arte mudéjar: expresión artística de una convivencia*, Granada, 2001.

[3] Thus, for instance: "El delicioso *Libre de Amich e Amat* es un ejemplo de mudejarismo literario," *España en su historia*, Buenos Aires, 1948, p 277. Francisco Márquez Villanueva, "Presencia judía en la literatura española," in *La sociedad medieval a través de la literatura española*, R. Izquierdo Benito y A. Sáenz-Badillos eds., Cuenca, 1998, pp. 11–26 (pp. 15–16).

[4] On the critical vicissitudes of the term as used by historians and art critics, see Manuel Valdés Fernández, "Arte de los siglos XII a XV y cultura mudéjar" in *Arte de Castilla y León. Arte mudéjar*, t. IV, Valladolid, 1994, pp. 9–128 (pp. 11–16). Also Gonzalo M. Borrás Gualis, *El arte mudéjar*, Teruel, 1990.

[5] Note the affirmation of the concept in even more vigorous terms than Castro's from a scholar ideologically remote from him like Guillermo Guastavino Gallent in "A propos du sens et des dimensions sociales du concept 'mudéjar' hispano-arabe," *Revue d'Histoire Maghrebine* 3 (1975), pp. 18–26. Míkel Epalza, "Nota sobre el concepto cultural euro-árabe de 'mudejar,' según Guillermo Guastivino," *Sharq al-Andalus*, 14–15 (1997–1998), pp. 342–351.

[6] *Crónicas sarracinas*, Paris, 1982.

[7] The verb *reconquistar* had already been used in the eighteenth century by such authors as Gaspar Melchor de Jovellanos and Leandro Fernández de Moratín, but was not accepted by the *Real Academia Española* until some time later. "Indeed, the very term 'Reconquest' has outlived much of its usefulness, except as the medieval canonist's synonym and justification for crusade against Islam in the East as in the West" (Robert I. Burns, *Muslims, Christians and Jews in the Medieval Kingdom of*

Reconquista was beaten out on the anvil of a nationalism tainted with religious fundamentalism in total contempt of complex historical realities. Suffice it to say that ideas like "a crusade lasting eight centuries" have now been refuted at the most basic level, because the great campaigns were undertaken by both sides, and took place intermittently, with considerable intervals between military engagements. Even a society organised for war,[8] like the Christian kingdoms of the High Middle Ages, lacked the technical means for anything other than short campaigns, which, despite their violent nature, were far removed from a genocidal project or even a religious war. By contrast, that was precisely what the *crusade* was all about. It was the radically innovative thesis of eleventh-century French monks, whose ignorance led them to equate Islam with the adoration of a trio of idols (a grotesque inversion of the Christian Trinity). As a result of this, ventures which originated on the other side of the Pyrenees always failed in Spain. In the last century, critics from outside Spain have always been disconcerted to find no echo in *El Cantar de mío Cid* of the Christian military exhortations inculcated, under the weight of other theses, by

---

Valencia. Societies in Symbiosis, Cambridge, 1984, p. 6). It is not difficult to gather a whole panoply of interpretative orientations from critics. These begin with the "genuine myth of a national epic" used by Isidro de las Cagigas, "Problemas de minorías y el caso de nuestro medievo," *Hispania* (1950), 506–538 (p. 507). No "normal exercise of a warring people but the formal demands of a given situation" for José A. Maravall, *El concepto de España en la Edad Media*, Madrid, 1954, p. 278. A "divinal" enterprise as Bishop Alonso de Cartagena would have it, but a very different concept from that of the Crusade, as Francisco Martín Hernández qualifies in "La Inquisición en España antes de los Reyes Católicos," in *La Inquisición española. Nueva visión, nuevos horizontes*, Madrid, 1980, pp. 11–28 (p. 25). The framework of the Reconquista is that of a "broadening of civilisations" which "cannot honorably continue to be considered a war of national independence against a foreign invader" for Antonio Linage Conde, "Las raíces medievales de la diferenciación española," *Religión y Cultura* 17 (1981), pp. 689–715 (p. 596). Nor is it of imperialistic design, but rather a process of colonising abandoned lands and kingdoms "whose population had to be preserved to prevent its ruin," is the view of Luis Suárez Fernández, "Tres humanismos: coexistencia árabe, judía y cristiana," *El Olivo* 10 (1986), pp. 133–143 (p. 134). It is only possible to talk about a Christian Reconquest from 1085 onwards, according to Oleg Grabar, "Una introducción a los cuatro primeros siglos de presencia musulmana en España," in *Al-Andalus. Las artes islámicas en España*, J. D. Dodds ed., New York, 1992, pp. 3–9 (p. 3). As Robert I. Burns notes, the concept of *Reconquista* is today no longer useful; see "Muslim-Christian Conflict and Contact in Medieval Spain: Context and Methodology," *Thought* 54 (September, 1979), pp. 238–252 (p. 242).

[8] Studied by Elena Lourie, "A Society Organized for War: Medieval Spain," *Past and Present* no. 35 (December, 1966), pp. 54–76.

Charlemagne in *La Chanson de Roland*.[9] The heroic Cid Ruy Díaz, the scourge of the African Almoravids, has an unshakeable friendship with the noble Moor Avengalvón, lord of Molina and with as much right as El Cid to call himself a son of the same land.

This manner of proceeding was unthinkable for Ultra-Pyreneans, and indeed continued to be so for a philologist like Leo Spitzer. The only exception to this was the last great abbot of Cluny, Peter the Venerable (1094–1156), whose position was very different from that adopted by the Cistercian monk St Bernard in his effort at propaganda promoting the second crusade. His visit to Castile in 1142 was decisive in enlightening him about Islam and led to his decision to support a translation of the Koran and other materials known collectively as the *Collectio Toletana*, which were the point of departure for medieval Islamology in the West.[10]

Under one flag or another, and to a greater or lesser extent, the Middle Ages incorporated a degree of religious tolerance of an inevitably practical nature for which there was no need for any explicit reference. From Tariq to Boabdil, Andalusi Islam stuck to a necessarily flexible policy of coexistence at the official level, which would only later experience intervals of *yihad* under the Almoravids and Almohads. These African invaders were ignorant of the land, its traditions and inhabitants, and consequently failed to put down roots, blowing through the region like a desert storm. It is worth noting that the fortunes of the foreign intervention favored by Cluny were no more successful on the Christian side than the Almoravids in Al-Andalus, which coincided with the same chronological period.

It is hardly surprising, given this state of affairs, that there was some—at times latent, at times overt—armed confrontation, with all the ensuing horror that war entails. It is equally true that within a couple of generations the border would turn into a no man's land which, given the ebb and flow of war and peace, could best be defined as in a situation of semi-permanent truce.[11] The border determined "a world of contacts,

---

[9] Thus Leo Spitzer, "Sobre el carácter histórico del Cantar de Mio Cid," *Nueva Revista de Filología Hispánica* 2 (1948), pp. 17–22. Edmund de Chasca, *The Poem of the Cid*, Boston, 1976, pp. 68–74.

[10] James Kritzeck, *Peter the Venerable and Islam*, Princeton, 1964. Francisco Márquez Villanueva, *Santiago. Trayectoria de un mito*, Barcelona, 2004, pp. 121–125.

[11] Thus characterized by Thomas F. Glick, "La frontera como imagen y creadora de paisaje," in *Cristianos y musulmanes en la España medieval (711–1250)*, Madrid, pp. 75–83. On the low-medieval period Andalucían borders, useful information is available

a channel through which subtle and not very well known processes of acculturation were taking place."[12] Here intermediate ways of life developed, including a law adapted to the circumstances, with institutions like the *alcaldía mayor* of the Christians (for disputes between Moors and Christians),[13] the *alfaqueques*[14] to rescue captives, the *enaciado*[15] or trusted man recognized by both parties, and even the *adalid*[16] or military chief who specialised in tracking and skirmishes, not to mention other methods of human contact and interaction. What was known as the *Extremaduras* was an unstable and volatile no man's land, but far from impermeable, in either real or figurative terms. No fixed frontiers, iron curtains or Maginot lines of any kind were recognized and the borders were therefore more an invitation to cross than anything else.[17] Scholars have reached a broad degree of consensus on defining the border as a constant and unique key to the history of Spain.[18]

---

in Juan de M. Carriazo, *En la frontera de Granada. Homenaje al profesor Carriazo*, 3 vols., Seville, 1971, vol. I. Teresa Pérez Higueras, "La frontera como agente de intercambio cultural," in "Al-Andalus y Castilla: el arte de una larga coexistencia," *Historia de una cultura. La singularidad de Castilla*, A. García Simón ed., Junta de Castilla y León, 1995, pp. 9–59 (pp. 35–46). María Martínez Martínez, "La cabalgada: un medio de vida en la frontera murciano-granadina," *Miscelánea Medieval Murciana* 13 (1986), pp. 51–62. Denis Menjot, "La contrebande dans la marche frontière murcienne au bas Moyen Âge," in *Homenaje al profesor Juan Torres Fontes*. 2 vols., Murcia, 1987, II, pp. 1073–1083.

[12] Manuel González Jiménez, "La frontera entre Andalucía y Granada: realidades bélicas, socio-económicas y culturales," *La incorporación de Granada a la corona de Castilla*, M. A. Ladero Quesada ed., Granada, 1993, pp. 87–145.

[13] Leonard C. Harvey, *Islamic Spain 1250 to 1500*, Chicago and London, 1990, p. 246.

[14] María C. Quintanilla Raso, "Consideraciones sobre la vida en la frontera de Granada," *III Coloquio de historia medieval andaluza*, Jaén: Diputación Provincial, 1984, pp. 501–519 (p. 516).

[15] Either Christian or Moor depending on the convenience of the moment, see B. Richard, "L'Islam et les musulmans chez les chroniqueurs castillans du milieu du Moyen-Âge," *Hesperis-Tamuda* 12 (1971), pp. 107–132 (p. 126). "Súbdito de los reyes cristianos españoles unido estrechamente a los sarracenos por vínculos de amistad o interés" (*Diccionario RAE*).

[16] Felipe Maíllo Salgado, "Función y cometido de los adalides a la luz de textos árabes y romances. Contribución al estudio del medievo español y de su léxico," *Actas del Congreso Internacional Encuentro de las Tres Culturas III*, C. Carrete Parrondo ed., Toledo, 1988, pp. 109–130.

[17] José García Antón, "La tolerancia religiosa en la frontera de Murcia y Granada en los últimos tiempos del reino nazarí," *Murgense* no. 57 (1980), pp. 133–143; the documented proportion of religious turncoats was two to one in favor of Islam (ibid., p. 143).

[18] "The key to the history of Spain," coinciding with Claudio Sánchez Albornoz and R. I. Burns, *The Crusader Kingdom of Valencia. Reconstruction on a Thirteenth-Century Frontier*, 2 vols., Cambridge, Mass., 1967, p. VII.

What occurred by osmosis and a more or less prudent proximity in the open country of the border area, also occurred through close proximity in the towns, where the three communities co-existed within the same city walls, legally recognized as such, but not necessarily segregated into ghettos. Christians, Muslims and Jews mixed together without losing their individuality because their underlying "laws" and beliefs were very firm in all three cases.[19] The conduct of war, captivity, domestic service, music and poetry, trade, sexuality (including prostitution) were the basic building blocks that would finally drive them all in a single direction, bringing people together in a material sense. Where women were concerned, for instance, female Moors visited Christian houses as gynaecologists, herbalists, pedlars and procurers,[20] and even acted as midwives at royal births.[21] This was just one kind of co-existence which the respective religious chiefs sought to prohibit, though to no avail, over the centuries.[22] It was not that Spain was so "different," but simply that it adapted to changing circumstances in its own way.

Was this *cohabitation, connivance or co-existence?*[23] The complexity of such a volatile state of affairs has led to the use of controversial terminology to reflect the serious difficulty of fitting this phenomenon into a historical model created by the French, British, Germans and Italians whose Middle Ages never experienced anything even remotely

---

[19] Robert L. Burns, "Muslim-Christian Conflict and Contact in Medieval Spain," p. 252.

[20] J. N. Hillgarth, *Los reinos hispánicos 1250–1516. Un equilibrio precario* 2 vols., Barcelona, 1979, I, p. 210. Marjorie Ratcliffe, "Adulteresses, Mistresses and Prostitutes: Extramarital Relationships in Medieval Castille," *Hispania* 67 (1984), pp. 346–350. Carmen Barceló, "Mujeres, campesinas, mudéjares," in *La mujer en al-Andalus. Reflejos históricos de su actividad y categorías sociales*, Madrid, 1989, pp. 211–217. Luce López-Baralt, Luisa Piemontese, Claire Martin, "Un morisco astrólogo, experto en mujeres (Ms. Junta XXVI)," *Nueva Revista de Filología Hispánica* 36 (1988), pp. 261–276.

[21] George Krotkoff, "The Arabic Line in the 'Cancionero de Baena,'" *Hispanic Review* 42 (1974), pp. 427–429. The custom is preferably documented in the Navarre dynasty (L. P. Harvey, *Islamic Spain 1250 to 1500*, p. 148).

[22] On the Christian side, at least since the Council of Coyanza in 1055. It also prohibits, for instance, the use of Moorish wet nurses after 1235, which is characteristically reiterated in 1258, 1335, 1386 and 1465; see Robert I Burns, "Mudéjar History Today: New Directions," *Viator* 8 (1977), pp. 127–143 (p. 137).

[23] Carlos Carrete Parrondo, "Relaciones sociales y culturales," in *Historia de una cultura. Las Castillas que no fueron*, A. García Simón ed., Junta de Castilla y León, 1995, III, pp. 55–85 (p. 56).

similar.[24] Today's Spanish speakers therefore find themselves faced with a twin problem, determined firstly by ideological motivations that were initially purist (*castizo*) and then (in the nineteenth and twentieth centuries) anti-liberal, and which eventually led to a mythification, like that of the aforesaid *Reconquista*. At the same time, however, they faced a resistance, influenced by both indolence and an inferiority complex, to abandon interpretative parameters imported from outside Spain and draw up their own new ones instead. In other words, they refused to tackle the slow and rather tedious, but highly productive, task in which we are collectively immersed today.

To start from the beginning, we have the problem the Arabs faced when Tariq's attack, which had previously been preceded by others that failed, finally put an end to Visigoth power in the year 711. This was not merely a raid or *razzia*, but rather was intended from the outset as a project of permanent settlement, the execution of which involved a deliberate strategy of civil order.[25] We should not lose sight of the fact that the triumph of the new owners was only possible as a result of the political disintegration of the Goth kingdom, already rent by internal strife which in the early seventh century reached critical point. The Arab chiefs now in charge of the Peninsula could not consider militarily effective occupation of the territory based on the expeditionary contingent[26] and had to opt for an alternative, benevolent, attitude towards the vanquished. Taking this one step further, and in his quest for an elusive veil of legitimacy, the first Emir Abd Al-'Aziz (714–716) promoted mixed marriages by taking the widow of King Rodrigo for a wife.[27] In line with an elementary political policy, dissidents from the

---

[24] It insists on the strong "individuality" of a Spanish phenomenon which "affects place, time, associative setting, and behavioural contexts," R. I. Burns, "Muslim-Christian Conflict and Contact in Medieval Spain," p. 244.

[25] We now have good information about the origin and execution of the 711 invasion thanks to Pedro Chalmeta's book, *Invasión e islamización. La sumisión de Hispania y la formación de al-Andalus*, Madrid, 1994.

[26] As the extremely partial Francisco Javier Simonet recognized, the Muslims "were neither strong enough to destroy the Spanish population, nor numerous enough to resettle the Peninsula," consequently, "the indigenous population was mainly protected by the capitulations and pacts agreed at the time of the conquest." (*Historia de los mozárabes de España*, Madrid: Real Academia de la Historia, 1897–1903, p. XXXIII). We should not forget here the military problem of the Omeya Caliphate, which was forced to depend on Berbers for its forces and even Slavs brought in from Central Europe.

[27] By so doing, he gave the subjugated Spaniards a pledge of affection and hope of protection, as F. J. Simonet romanticises in *Historia de los mozárabes de España*, p. 144. It was not a unique case, because, according to the author, the same occurred

internal regime, like Vitizanos and Jews were treated benevolently, and vast territorial regions like the semi-legendary Kingdom of Tudmir were permitted.[28] Above all, in keeping with the formula they had learned in the Near East with Christian sects persecuted by Byzantine Orthodoxy, the Koranic legal protection statute of *dhimmi* was extended to the Christian population (*ahl al-dhimma*) in religious, legal and linguistic matters.[29] Thus the *Mozarabs* emerged,[30] as a result of pacts (*suhl*) that enabled them to conserve their temples, monasteries and hierarchies, whilst the emirs and caliphs took on senior ecclesiastical roles and convened or presided over bishops' synods, just as Roman emperors and Visigoth kings had done before them.[31] The Church, in its quest for theological disarmament, responded in kind, with the subtle and clearly syncretic gesture of the adoptionist doctrine. By so doing, Eli-

---

with Lampegia, daughter of the Duke of Aquitaine and Munuza, and with Sara, grand-daughter of Witiza (ibid., p. 238). Even the political rise of Pelayo seems to have borne a relationship with the interest shown in his sister by the Arab governor of Gijón.

[28] C. E. Dubler, "Los defensores de Teodomiro (leyenda mozárabe)," *Études d'orientalisme à la mémoire de Levi Provençal*, 2 vols., Paris: Maisonneuve et Larose, 1962, I, pp. 111–124.

[29] Luis G. de Valdeavellano, *Curso de historia de las instituciones españolas*, Madrid, 1973, p. 639. Émile Tyan, "Gouvernés et gouvernants in Islam sunnite," *Recueils de la Société Jean Bodin pour l'Histoire Comparative des Institutions* (Brussels) 22 (1969), pp. 390–402 (p. 398). Fernando Díaz Esteban, "Los 'dimmíes' a nueva luz," *Anaquel de Estudios Árabes* 8 (1997), pp. 29–40. Despite its limitations, this situation is obviously a model of tolerance that is only equalled in the modern era, Leonard P. Harvey, "Límites de los intercambios culturales," p. 92. Differences between the *dhimma* dispensed to Christians and to Jews in Isidro de las Cagigas, *Los mozárabes*, 2 vols., Madrid, pp. 55–60.

[30] From the Arab *musta'rib*, "make similar to Arabs" in J. Corominas-J. A. Pascual, *DCECH*. Documented on the Christian side from 1024, but never used by the Arabs, who tend to prefer "barbarian" *achemíes*, "foreign" *naçraníes*, 'Christian' *rumíes*, 'polytheistic' *moxríques* or 'protected' *dimmíes*; see F. J. Simonet, *Historia de los mozárabes de España*, p. XIII. The ideological extremeness of Simonet is rather more moderate in Isidro de las Cagigas, *Los mozárabes*, 2 vols., Madrid, 1947–1948. Richard Hitchcock seeks to devalue the religious component of the concept, "¿Quiénes fueron los verdaderos mozárabes? Una contribución a la historia del mozarabismo," *Nueva Revista de Filología Hispánica* 30 (1981), pp. 574–585. Connection of the *dhimma* with the Islamic principle of not setting oneself up against the other revealed religions, but to come to complete them, in Mahmud Makki, "El islam frente a las minorías cristianas," *Actas de las I Jornadas de Cultura Islámica. Toledo 1987. Al-Andalus, Ocho Siglos de Historia*, Madrid, 1989, pp. 43–49 (p. 43).

[31] F. Simonet, *Historia de los mozárabes de España*, p. 360. Especially the synod convened in 852 by Mohamed I to put an end to the problem of the pseudo-martyrs of Córdoba (ibid., pp. 434–436), presided over, in his name, by the collaborationist metropolitan of Seville, Recafredo (I. de las Cagigas, *Los mozárabes*, I, p. 203).

pando, Archbishop of Toledo,[32] smoothed over the problem which the Trinity dogma represented for the two Semitic religions. There was no true resistance of either a political or armed nature to Arab power apart from the small *enragé* group of the martyrs of Córdoba (who were not in fact martyrs at all)[33] in the middle of the ninth century.

The Mozarabs, accepted as useful assistants to the administration and the army, were rapidly assimilated in terms of both language and intellectual life, to the extent that the lamentations on the matter in the *Indiculus luminosus* (854)[34] by Álvaro de Córdoba (still loyal to the Isidorian legacy) can be considered a classic text anticipating the concept of acculturation. Aside from the purely religious angle, the Mozarabs were strongly Arabised when, in the late eleventh and early twelfth centuries, they disappeared either by converting or by moving to Christian lands as much-needed re-settlers. This is why they have recently been described, in this final stage, as "a culturally disoriented group."[35]

The High Middle Ages began with the Christians completely cornered, although on the Arab side we cannot really refer to a concerted military policy until the reign of 'Abd al-Rahman I (756–788).[36] The Astur-Leonese monarchy lived under constant threat from devastating raids, which were perpetrated from time to time,[37] but were based neither on a policy of genocide nor permanent occupation. Apart from its pathetic weakness in the face of Muslim might, the monarchy was

---

[32] Studies by Dominique Urvoy, "La pensée religieuse des Mozarabes face à l'Islam," *Tradition* 39 (1983), pp. 419–432. Míkel de Epalza, "Influences islamiques dans la théologie chrétienne médiévale," *Islamocristiana* 18 (1992), pp. 55–72. Francisco Márquez Villanueva, "La controversia adopcionista" in *Santiago: Trayectoria de un mito*, pp. 65–70.

[33] His action was designed to cause legitimating repression but did not receive mass support. Many, if not most, were the children of mixed marriages which had proved uncontrollable and continued to be very common. As the offspring of a Muslim father, they were obliged to follow his religion because they would otherwise be considered apostates, a capital crime under Koranic law.

[34] F. J. Simonet, *Historia de los mozárabes de España*, pp. 505–507. Feliciano Delgado León, *Álvaro de Córdoba y la polémica contra el islam. El 'Indiculus luminosus,'* Córdoba, 1996, pp. 183–185, reproduced here in the appendix.

[35] T. F. Glick, *Cristianos y musulmanes en la España medieval*, p. 31.

[36] F. Simonet, *Historia de los mozárabes de España*, pp. 369 foll. On Álvaro (executed in 859) and his culture, Feliciano Delgado, "Álvaro de Córdoba," *Actas del I Congreso Nacional de Cultura Mozárabe*, Córdoba, 1996, pp. 73–88.

[37] A total of twenty can be calculated in the initial period of three centuries, according to Julián García y Sáinz de Baranda, "La ideología mahometana y su influencia en la invasión y conquista de España," *Boletín de la Institución Fernán González* 14 (1960–1961), pp. 251–257 (p. 256).

also riddled with severe internal problems and survived on occasion as a kind of protectorate of Córdoban power (for example, the reigns of Silo and Mauregato in the second half of the eighth century). Once again, we need to understand what this poorly named *Reconquista* really was. It began in an inhospitable landscape whose lands, even in the modern age, have proved unable to support their population. The more favored land of Catalonia and its more fortunate children did not show the same interest in expansion once their own borders were re-established with Frankish help. The Asturians, Cantabrians, Galicians and Navarre-Basques, however, had to be militarily organised, not only to avoid being overwhelmed, but also out of the necessity to take what they lacked from those who possessed it, namely the Muslims living south of the mountains. This advance on Muslim Spain was a tough and slow process which, by about the year 1000, had achieved no more than a rather precarious dominion over territory up to the right bank of the River Duero (*Extrema Durii*).[38] True, they were fighting to spread Christianity, but only as a means to an end under external pressure. El Cid Ruy Díaz reflects as much in his *Cantar*, when preparing to fight in Valencia against the fearsome Almoravid besiegers, recently arrived from Africa:

> My daughters and my wife will see me fight,
> in these foreign lands; they will see how we make our homes.
> well enough they will see with their own eyes how we earn our bread.[39]

And this urgent and unavoidable "earn our bread," or later "earn something against Granada,"[40] which was also used as a set phrase, are equivalent to a definition of the raison d'être and origin of Castile.

We should emphasise that this pattern is projected over a complex reality, which historiography has largely avoided tackling.[41] There are

---

[38] Claudio Sánchez Albornoz, *Despoblación y repoblación del valle del Duero*, Buenos Aires, 1966. Ramón Menéndez Pidal and others disagreed with his conclusions.

[39] Mis fijas e mi mugier ver me an lidiar,
en estas tierras agenas verán las moradas cómmo se fazen.
afarto verán por los ojos cómmo se gana el pan". (vv. 1641–43) N. Stapleton trans.

[40] José M. Cossío, "Cautivos de moros en el siglo XIII," *Al-Andalus* 7 (1942), pp. 49–112.

[41] María Rosa Menocal, "Pride and Prejudice in Medieval Studies: European and Oriental," *Hispanic Review* 53 (1985), pp. 61–78. In the nineteenth and part of the twentieth centuries, "this Northern historiography tended to dismiss medieval Spain as a quirky appendage to Christendom, a fusion of barely reconcilable Islamic and

documents from the earliest times of the presence of Muslim slaves
in the Christian kingdoms, as there were also Mudejars, about whom
as yet still little is known. It was mainly the Mozarab resettlers who
brought with them their Arabised lifestyles, as is very visibly apparent
in areas ranging from art to onomastics.[42] Another reality that is also
skated over is the frequency, on both sides, of apostasy. And not
just that of part of the Visigoth nobility,[43] but all kinds of turncoats,
converts or religious deserters, a recurrent theme in the *chansons de
geste* and legends like *Los siete infantes de Lara* and *Don Juan abad
de Montemayor.*[44] Christians converted to Islam at a considerable rate
throughout the Middle Ages; even in 1492 the so-called *elches* were
very common in Granada.[45] Anyone who considered himself dis-
honored or felt that had no future, even where this was the result of
a failed or imposed marriage, had the option of going to Moorish
territory and *liarse la manta a la cabeza*—a Spanish expression used
to mean tie a cloth around one's head—or, in other words, don a
turban and convert to Islam,[46] a term still used to denote radical or
desperate behaviour. Mixed sexual relations also occurred, though
forbidden by both sides, which only served to make it more tempting,

---

Christian values," as Robert I. Burns acknowledges in "Muslim-Christian Conflict and
Contact in Medieval Spain," p. 238.

[42] Mercedes García-Arenal, "Minorías religiosas" in *Historia de una cultura. Las
Castillas que no fueron*, A. García Simón ed., 3 vols.: Junta de Castilla y León, 1995,
III, pp. 9–53 (pp. 11–12).

[43] Primarily, in what today is Aragon, the case of the Banu-Qasi, who had a long
and eventful political history in al-Andalus (I. de las Cagigas, *Los mozárabes*, I, pp.
158–159*).

[44] Ramón Menéndez Pidal, *Leyenda de los Infantes de Lara*, Madrid, 1896; "La
leyenda del abad don Juan de Montemayor,'" in *Poesía árabe y poesía europea*, fifth
edition, Madrid, 1963, pp. 161–209.

[45] Antonio Luis Cortés Peña, "Mudejars et morisques grénadins: une vision dialec-
tique tolerance-intolerance. Grénade 1492–1493," *Du royaume de Grénade á l'avenir
du monde méditerranéen*. M. Aguilera y B. Vincent eds., Granada, 1996, pp. 109–122
(p. 116). Felipe Maíllo, "Diacronía y sentido del término 'elche,'" *Miscelánea de Estudios
Arabes y Hebraicos* 31 (1982), pp. 79–98. In particular, the Royal Nasrid Guard was
made up of *elches* (Luis Seco de Lucena Paredes, *Orígenes del orientalismo literario*,
Santander, 1963, p. 32). On the continuation of this phenomenon in the modern day
and age, see Bartolomé Bennassar, *Les chrétiens d'Allah. L'histoire extraordinaire des
renégats. XVIe et XVIIe siècles*, Paris, 1989.

[46] *Ponerse el turbante* ("Put on a turban") meant 'islamise'. Thus a character in
Fernando de Zárate-Antonio Enríquez Gómez's comedy, *Las misas de San Vicente
Ferrer*, refers to an apostate as "who put on the turban/and abandoned the true God";
see David M. Gitlitz, "La angustia vital de ser negro. Tema de un drama de Fernando
de Zárate," *Segismundo* 11 (1965), pp. 65–85 (p. 81).

as the Christian woman represented the same kind of erotic ideal for Muslims as the Moorish or Jewish woman for Christians. As faithfully portrayed in the Romance, men did not just go to "Moorish land" to fight but also, as the famous Don Bueso puts it, "to search for a female friend."[47] The caliphal harems of Córdoba are known to have included Christian women of royal blood[48] and Alfonso VI himself took a daughter-in-law of Seville's poet king Al-Motámid (Zaida, known afterwards as Isabel), first as concubine and then as wife, out of political expediency, proceeding in just the same way as any Muslim king would have done.[49] It was she who gave him his only male child, the Infante Sancho, who died at a tender age fighting the Almoravids. The same is true of the last claimant to the title of Córdoban caliph, the abominable Abd al-Rahman Sanchol or *Sanchuelo* (984–1009), known as such after his maternal grandfather, King Sancho Abarca of Navarre. For a time, a multireligious Spain could have been ruled by political leaders of mixed Christian and Muslim descent.

Intercultural contacts occurred constantly and through many channels. For example, in the early days of the Emirate, Christian kings travelled to Córdoba as semi-vassals. At the same time both kingdoms regularly took in political refugees from the other side.[50] El Cid is the most famous example of a political refugee, although there were many others. Side swapping was a frequent occurrence. It is noteworthy that

---

[47] Ramón Menéndez Pidal, *Flor nueva de romances viejos*, thirteenth edition, Buenos Aires: Espasa-Calpe, p. 211. On the transmigration of erotic stereotypes. Samuel G. Armistead and James T. Monroe, "A New Version of 'La morica de Antequera,'" *La Corónica* (1984), pp. 228–240 (p. 234). On the punishment and attempts to control all kinds of mixed unions on the Christian side, see Heath Dillard, *Daughters of the Reconquest. Women in Castilian Town Society (1100–1300)*, Cambridge, 1984, pp. 14–15 and 206–211.

[48] Dede Fairchild Ruggles, "La lengua materna: cultura y convivencia en al-Andalus" in *Américo Castro y la revisión de la memoria. El Islam en España*, E. Subirats coord., Madrid, 2003, pp. 145–174.

[49] Amidst discreet obscurities, the likelihood of initial concubinage prior to conversion and marriage is maintained by M. Fernández y González, *Estado social y político de los mudéjares de Castilla*, p. 48. Emilio Sola, "Historias de la frontera y oralidad: una cautiva que llega a Gran Sultana," in *Las Relaciones de Sucesos en España (1500–1750)*, Publicaciones de la Universidad de Alcalá-Publications de la Sorbonne, 1996, pp. 339–348. María Jesús Rubiera Mata disagrees in regard to Zaida, being more inclined to believe her the daughter of Al-Mamún de Toledo, "Los primeros moros conversos o el origen de la tolerancia," *Toledo siglos XII–XIII, Musulmanes, cristianos y judíos: la sabiduría y la tolerancia*, L. Cardaillac ed., Madrid, 1992, pp. 109–117 (p. 112).

[50] Robert I. Burns reviews this significant and often hidden aspect in "Renegades, Adventurers and Sharp Businessmen: The Thirteenth-Century Spaniard in the Cause of Islam," *American Catholic Historical Review* 58 (1972), pp. 341–366.

in Almanzor's famous raid on Santiago de Compostela in 999, a number of Leonese counts took part, and received rich pickings in return.[51]

So far I have been using the term Mudejarism to refer to intercultural contact between Christian and Muslim Spain throughout the medieval era. However, while Mudejarism can be understood as an underlying cultural macro-phenomenon in the Peninsula from the ninth century onwards, the term Mozarabism more appropriately applies to this phenomenon from the eighth to the eleventh centuries, whereas Mudejarism[52] refers to the period from the twelfth to fifteenth centuries, when subdued Muslim groups (*Mudejares*) began to form a part of Christian Spain. This process began in 1085, when Alfonso VI (1040–1109) took the city of Toledo. This was the first time that a great Islamic city fell into Christian hands, but it occurred in quite different circumstances from those prevailing in Jerusalem during the first crusade, just a few years later (one of the worst slaughters in history). The tables could only be turned on this occasion because of the collapse, also due to internal reasons, of the Córdoba Caliphate, fragmented as it was into small Taifa kingdoms (*muluk al-tawaif*) that were easy prey to the Castilian monarchs, from whom they had to buy their survival with the payment of huge sums in gold.

In the case of Toledo, the exceptional figure of Alfonso VI (1040–1109) was involved. He had taken refuge in the city, having been removed from the throne of León by his brother Sancho II. But thanks to the generosity of King Al-Mamún, who gave him shelter for nine months in 1072, Alfonso became acquainted with Toledo at a peak of its history, both as head of the most powerful and prosperous of the Taifa kingdoms and heir to the cultural traditions of an eclipsed Córdoba. Once re-established in his Castilian-Leonese kingdom, Alfonso subjected Toledo to a long siege, and it eventually fell to him on May 6, 1085. With exquisite tact, he then sought to ensure that its inhabitants should come to no harm and, to avoid any humiliation, entered the city as discreetly as possible through a secondary gate. He knew that victory lay not in the capture but in the preservation of a city that was the crown jewel of al-Andalus. Its government was placed in the hands of Sevilian renegade Sisnando

---

[51] Manuel Fernández Rodríguez, "La expedición de Almanzor a Santiago de Compostela," *Cuadernos de Historia de España* 43–44 (1967), pp. 345–363 (p. 158).

[52] Manuel Criado de Val insists on the distinction in "La tierra de Hita. El contorno mozárabe del 'Libro de buen amor,'" *Actas del I Congreso Internacional sobre el Arcipreste de Hita*, Barcelona, 1973, pp. 447–455.

Davídiz[53] to guarantee continuity, with minimal disturbance, of the *statu quo ante*. Each community was governed there by its own *fuero* or code of laws and *"fuero* was equivalent to freedom," whereas Toledo as a whole "was administratively a Muslim city."[54] From a conventional or conservative perspective, the inclusion of Toledo in Christian Spain can be considered no more than a pseudo or half-way conquest.

This unique incorporation of Toledo into the crown of Castile marked the launch of a politically mature Mudejarism which involved exploiting to the maximum everything that could be used from the Andalusi legacy. It was seen as superior, desirable and, above all, in keeping with the elemental and physical framework of life on the Peninsula. Alfonso VI's first aim was to preserve, at all costs, the Muslim population (now "Moors of Peace"), whose rights were guaranteed under what is known as the Mudejar settlement, probably resulting from a formal pact, whose text has not been preserved. The Mozarab population were linguistically and culturally assimilated to the point where their clerics glossed in Arabic the considerable difficulties posed by the Latin of their liturgical codices.[55] The fact is that Toledo continued to be a predominantly Arab-speaking city until well into the thirteenth century, whilst public documents continued to be written in Arabic for a further century after that.[56] The city maintained an Arabised way of life[57] and also preserved

---

[53] Ramón Menéndez Pidal, *La España del Cid*, Madrid, 1947, 2 vols, I, p. 92. "Sisnando's idea was to maintain the *status quo* in Toledo," Ramón Menéndez Pidal and Emilio García Gómez conclude in "El conde mozárabe Sisnando Davídiz y la política de Alfonso VI con los taifas," *Al Andalus* 12 (1947), pp. 27–41 (p. 32). For Luis Suárez Fernández, this was a process of colonization rather than imperialism, "Tres humanismos: coexistencia árabe, judía y cristiana," *El Olivo* 10, 24 (1986), pp. 133–143.

[54] Ramón Gonzálvez Ruíz, "La sociedad toledana bajomedieval (siglos XII–XIV)," *I Congreso Internacional de las Tres Culturas*, Toledo, 1983, pp. 141–155 (p. 153). Muslim administration (p. 154).

[55] Elie Lambert, "La civilización mozárabe," *Hommage à Ernest Martinenche*, Paris, 1949, pp. 34–45 (p. 37). F. Simonet quotes some in *Historia de los mozárabes de España*, p. 706.

[56] Ramón Ruíz Gonzálvez, "Las escuelas de Toledo durante el reinado de Alfonso VIII," *Alarcos 1195. Actas del Congreso Internacional Conmemorativo del VIII Centenario de la Batalla de Alarcos*, Cuenca, 1996, pp. 171–209. Francisco J. Hernández, "Language and Cultural Identity. The Mozarabs of Toledo," *Bulletin Burriel* 1 (1989), pp. 29–48.

[57] "Le goût pour le genre de vie musulman…demeurait vif dans dans la Tolède du XIIIe siècle, aussi bien, semble-t-il, dans les familles d'origine mozarabe que dans les familles issues de *populatores* castillans", states Jean G. Gautier, "A Tolède à la fin du XIIIe siècle: les enseignements d'un contrat de mariage et d'un testament," in *Economie et société dans les pays de la couronne de Castille*, London: Variorum Reprints, 1982, 15, pp. 183–198 (p. 198).

the libraries and system of schools (for the study of philosophy and sciences) introduced by its previous masters. Its continuing relationship with the Semitic culture[58] turned the city into the capital of translation and a crucial focus for Western intellectual progress over the next few centuries. Alfonso VI also promoted the immigration of Andalusi Jews (harassed by the Almoravids) and Frankish traders, making Toledo, as is recognized today, a "city of minorities and a city of liberties."[59]

After 1085, there were many other "Toledos," both large and small. The most striking was undoubtedly Murcia (another jewel) and its kingdom, subjugated by Alfonso el Sabio (the Learned) when he was still heir to the throne, in 1243. Initially Castilian dominion was exercised according to a formula close to that of a protectorate or trusteeship of the Taifa dynasty rather than a true occupation or conquest. However, it would be a mistake to equate this situation with modern liberal thinking, because rather than any kind of religious softening process, what we find in Spain is a tacit renunciation of group violence and, on the Christian side, of forced conversions. There were strong basic antagonisms and all were intolerant,[60] including Alfonso VI himself. For the Spanish monarchs, Mudejarism was the only sensible alternative to the imposition of peremptory order, because their kingdoms lacked the demographics, and economic and cultural resources, to get any benefit from their conquest. In the absence of the Islamic population and tradition to which it owed its grandeur and prosperity, Toledo would have been an unproductive empty shell, impossible to defend militarily.

---

[58] "Toledo was the natural point of departure for economic, diplomatic and military relations with the Muslim world," according to Ramón Gonzálvez Ruíz, "Las escuelas de Toledo durante el reinado de Alfonso VIII. Alarcos 1195," *Actas del Congreso Internacional Conmemorativo del VIII Centenario de la Batalla de Alarcos*, p. 171. The Toledan schools kept virtually up to date with Arab progress in philosophy and sciences in the late twelfth and early thirteenth centuries, as Miguel Cruz Hernández points out in "El averroísmo en el Occidente medieval," *Oriente e Occidente nel medioevo. Filosofia e scienze*, Rome, 1971, pp. 17–62 (p. 40).

[59] According to Ramón Gonzálvez, "Toledo is not only a city of minorities but a city of liberties," in "La sociedad toledana bajomedieval (siglos XII–XIV)," *I Congreso Internacional de las Tres Culturas*, Toledo, 1983, pp. 141–155 (p. 153). "Toledo symbolises living together. It is not a mere juxtaposition of religious groups," Míkel de Epalza concludes in "Pluralismo y tolerancia: ¿un modelo toledano?" in *Toledo, siglos XII–XIII. Musulmanes, cristianos y judíos: la sabiduría y la tolerancia*, L. Cardaillac ed., Madrid, 1992, pp. 251–261 (p. 256).

[60] As Robert I. Burns points out, medieval cultures "were intrinsically religious, with a stubborn exclusiveness," *The Crusader Kingdom of Valencia*, I, p. 9.

Over the course of a millennium, neither Christians nor Muslims could think of genocide, ethnic cleansing or crusades, owing to a simple shortage of inhabitants. What was needed was, on the contrary, to exploit human resources to the full, serving not an imperialistic but rather a colonising policy. In view of the difficulties they faced, the early Muslims soon gave up on the idea of direct occupation of the northern coastal fringe of the Peninsula, which, through lack of foresight, they believed would not bring political or economic recompense. The Christians then experienced great difficulties achieving effective domination of semi-desert lands north of the River Duero,[61] to which they nonetheless clung *usque ad unguem*. When, for reasons of military prudence, as occurred under Ferdinand III with his conquests of Córdoba and Seville, they chose to uproot the Muslim population, they faced problems they could not handle,[62] the consequences of which have continued into modern times. Spain was then to put all its energies into the American continent, whilst in Andalucía whole regions would be left abandoned. And it was not until the second half of the eighteenth century that the enlightened Peruvian Pablo de Olavide would resort to colonizing them with German and Swiss Catholics.

It is not hard to see that this Toledan Mudejarism is a carbon copy of the Mozarabism successfully adopted by Muslims since earliest times.[63] There was, however, an essential difference, because Mozarabism was in keeping with the Koranic doctrine of *dhimma*,[64] the protection extended to monotheistic religions "of the Book" (*ahl al-kitab*) and

---

[61] Fr. Justo Pérez de Urbel, "Reconquista y repoblación de Castilla y León durante los siglos IX y X," in *La Reconquista española y la repoblación del país*, Zaragoza, 1951, pp. 127–162.

[62] Ferdinand III's decision to expel the Muslim population after his conquest of Western Andalucía led to insufficient and disorganised resettlement which, in turn, led to an anachronistic feudalisation of both the south and the north of Castile. The kingdom thereby found itself suddenly plunged in a decisive demographic crisis and a devastating economic catastrophe that was not overcome for a very long time. See Teófilo F. Ruiz, "Expansion et changement: la conquête de Seville et la société castillane, 1248–1350," *Annales* 34 (1979), pp. 548–565. This problem of lack of adaptation and incompetence among the resettlers of the highly fertile Aljarafe of Seville is reflected by Alfonso el Sabio in one of his mocking poems studied by Francisco Márquez Villanueva, "El hiato literario de la conquista andaluza," *Studia in honorem Prof. M. de Riquer*, Barcelona, 1988, pp. 351–361.

[63] Henri Terrasse, *Islam d'Espagne. Une rencontre de l'Orient et de l'Occident*, Paris, 1958, p. 178. Mercedes García-Arenal, "Minorías religiosas," in *Historia de una cultura. Las Castillas que no fueron*, 3 vols., A. García Simón ed., Junta de Castilla y León, 1955, III, pp. 9–53 (p. 11).

[64] Henri Terrasse had already observed this in *Islam d'Espagne*, p. 178.

which opposed the other alternative of *jihad*. Even so, it should be understood that this was not a policy adopted for the occasion, far less a case of "religious tolerance" as we understand it today. Instead, it was "a religious law decreed by God and proclaimed by Mahoma, and as such was unmodifiable."[65] Compelled, however, by necessity, the Christians openly adopted it in total defiance of a Church which adhered to the Augustinian concept on the treatment of infidels and to the Canon Law which increasingly clearly and adversely upheld it.

Acculturation, for its part, operated in both directions. Whilst the Mozarabs practiced circumcision and refrained from eating pork, the Muslims joined in the New Year festivities (according to the Christian calendar) and *Ansara* or St John the Baptist Day.[66] Viewed from the other side of the Pyrenees, the resulting Spain was an absurdly confused land, where churches alternated with mosques and synagogues, and where Jews in particular were key players alongside monarchs and possessed considerable political influence. The French and the Italians abhorred this incomprehensible religious promiscuity: was this supposed to be a Christian country?[67] The peculiar physiognomy of medieval Spain knew no parallel in the Western world, but it was reproducing a multi-religious situation which, even now, is still familiar in much of the Islamic world. This state of affairs shocked the pontiffs in Rome, who officially reprimanded monarchs like Alfonso VI, Ferdinand III, *el Santo*, and his son Alfonso X, *el Sabio*, for the favorable treatment they gave the infidels, which was considered a scandal to Christianity.[68] The sovereigns, however, with no room for manoeuvre, could do no more

---

[65] Frank E. Peters, "En el nombre de la ley: cristianos bajo soberanía musulmana en el al-Andalus," in *Américo Castro y la revisión de la memoria. El Islam en España*, E. Subirats coord., Madrid: Ediciones Libertarias, 2003, pp. 103–113 (p. 106).

[66] The audacity of introducing non-Koranic religious practices of this kind is highlighted by Fernando de la Granja, "Fiestas cristianas en al-Andalus (materiales para su estudio)," *Al-Andalus* 34 (1969), pp.1–53.

[67] J. N. Hillgarth, *Los reinos hispánicos*, p. 187.

[68] This referred in particular to failure to comply with Lateran Decrees III (1180) and IV (1215) against infidels. At Ferdinand III's request, Pope Honorius III had to confer a bull of exemption from these decrees in favor of his Jews who otherwise threatened to leave for Muslim lands; see José Amador de los Ríos, *Historia de los judíos de España y Portugal*, 3 vols., Madrid, 1875–1876, I, pp. 361–362. In 1250, another dispute arose with Innocent IV for granting permission to build an impressive synagogue in Córdoba (Ibid., I, pp. 368–369). Nor was the papacy successful in making James I expel the Mudejars from his kingdoms (J. N. Hillgarth, *Los reinos hispánicos*, p. 121). "What should not exist but does" was tolerated (M. de Epalza, "Pluralismo y tolerancia: ¿un modelo toledano?" p. 257).

than weather the storm against Rome. There were also the cases of the military orders Santiago and Calatrava, which were created to sacralise the fight against Islam, and yet encouraged Mudejar resettlement in their dominions of the southern sub-meseta.[69] On a more personal level, we have the example of the Archbishop of Toledo, Rodrigo Ximénez de Rada (1180–1247), architect of the coalition (rather than Crusade) against the Almohads and the victory at Las Navas de Tolosa (1212), with the economic management of his vast archdiocese entrusted totally to Jews. Like virtually any educated Spaniard of his day, Ximenez de Rada knew Arabic. He also appears to have had a taste for Arabic material culture: he was buried in sumptuous Andalusí cloth.[70]

While it is not possible to examine here other aspects of Arabic influence, such as the adoption or continuity of legal and administrative institutions, it is nevertheless evident that Mudejarism was not something occasional, accidental or ephemeral.[71] The Iberian Peninsula was in fact composed of a *sui generis* society, which, unlike Christian Europe, divided into estates (*oratores, defensores* and *laboratores*), was formed of three religions (or "laws"), in which each group assumed, loosely, different a socio-economic function.[72] With the Christians fully devoted to arms, the Mudejars took on industrial tasks and the most productive agricultural jobs (irrigated crops), and the Jews assumed responsibility for scientific learning, administration and the economy. The consequences followed a logical sequence, but were particularly apparent in the field of culture, with the priest and his Latin losing out

---

[69] Leonard P. Harvey, *Islamic Spain 1250 to 1500*, pp. 70–71.

[70] Derek W. Lomax, "Rodrigo Ximénez de Rada como historiador," *Actas del Quinto Congreso Internacional de Hispanistas*, 2 vols., Bordeaux: Institut d'Etudes Iberiques et Ibero-Americaines, University of Bordeaux III, 1977, II, pp. 587–592 (p. 591).

[71] In the political terrain, we need only recall the oath of loyalty sworn by notables in recognition of the Crown Prince, still performed with Isabel II (L. G. de Valdeavellano, *Curso de historia de las instituciones españolas*, pp. 476 y 663). On another level, the survival, for instance, of the *almotacén* (inspector of weights and measurements) (Pedro Chalmeta, "El 'señor' del zoco en España: Edades Media y Moderna," *Madrid Instituto Hispano-árabe de Cultura*, 1973).

[72] Francisco Márquez Villanueva, "In lingua Tholetana," *El concepto cultural alfonsí*, corrected and extended version, Barcelona, 2004, pp. 283–302.

to the Muslim, or even the Jew, anchored in the Arabic language[73] and, subsequently, in Romance Castilian, as its disciple or heir.[74]

Legally speaking, Mudejarism depended totally on royal favor, which sought to preserve a *modus vivendi*, and it is unrealistic to expect that it would always work perfectly and be problem free. It is also important to understand that we cannot talk about "religious freedom" in a modern sense.[75] Once the danger of a surge in Islamism had been warded off, it was easier than ever to view Arabic culture as distant and different, but not as otherness, and its at times polar differences (in clothing, architecture, sexuality...)[76] could then begin to be seen as decidedly seductive. The Muslim was no longer a relevant enemy and was therefore able to colonise the intellectual and vitalistic sides of Christians, who were attracted by this more expansive view of life and more aware of what they lacked. Each of the three communities filled the gaps left by the others, even if, in keeping with their religious principles, they would all ideally have preferred to go it alone, which is precisely why serious problems at times arose. All sides understood, however, that the price of altering the *status quo* was impossible or too high to pay at a practical level. At the same time they were not formally required to relinquish their respective laws. It should be emphasised that this was no ideal situation and far from being idyllic, as some more naïve versions would have us believe.[77] It is not that problems did not occur, but simply that, even with them, Mudejarism worked effectively and,

---

[73] On the essential Mudejarism of the Jews, now living amongst Christians as they previously did amongst Muslims, see Eleazar Gutwirth, "Hispano-Jewish Attitudes to the Moors in the Fifteenth Century," *Sefarad* 49 (1989), pp. 237–262 (p. 239).

[74] We need to rein in excessively optimistic formulations such as those used by H. Terrasse when referring to "La dernière alliance de l'Orient et de l'Occident: l'âge mudéjar" (*Islam d'Espagne*, cap. V). "Alliance" is precisely something that never existed. What did exist was a clever way of sidestepping the intolerant effects of irreducible "laws," and that in itself was quite a lot.

[75] Marjorie Ratcliffe, "Judíos y musulmanes en la jurisprudencia medieval española, *Revista Canadiense de Estudios Hispánicos. Homenaje a Alfonso X el Sabio* 9 (1985), pp. 423–438. On the purely legal side is the issue of acceptance (like for the *Partida* laws compiled by Alfonso X) and compliance, quite apart from the even trickier issue of whether it would have been possible (given that these were Christian monarchs) to legislate on the unacceptable anomaly behind that religious situation.

[76] On the latter, see J. Goytisolo, *Crónicas sarracinas*, pp. 73–86.

[77] Serafín Fanjul accords a disproportionate amount of importance to these while avoiding basic critical issues in *Al-Andalus contra España, La forja del mito*, Madrid, 2000. All of this is subsequently repeated in what he terms *La quimera de al-Andalus*, Madrid, 2004.

overall, peacefully, at least until the arrival of the House of Trastámara in 1369, and it came to determine a precocious and often forgotten chapter in the history of human rights. Needless to say, the operation of this multi-religious period would not stand up (this should be emphasised) to analysis from the perspective of current-day liberalism, but its true significance can be gauged by the absence or extreme rarity of comparable examples outside the Peninsula. Above all, we should not lose sight of the fact that, in this respect, the problem of the Middle Ages was about the rights of communities and not individuals, which, politically speaking at least, did not exist as such before 1789.

Just as a microscope and a telescope allow us to reveal the imperceptible, so the concept of Mudejarism has made it possible to access historical facts that were either invisible or had been sidelined by old purist (*castizo*) ideologies.[78] In the visual arts terrain, emphasis today is placed on the fact that virtually all civilian and a substantial part of ecclesiastical architecture was the work of Mudejars. No thought is given to the fact that there was indeed no real need to give that architecture a special name, as with the equivalent phenomenon of levelling of usage and custom in everyday life.[79] Even the idea of "Arab" or "Oriental" art becomes debatable when everything has in fact arisen from an eclectic classical and Mediterranean vocabulary, albeit endowed with an exquisite ability to project Islamic spirituality, as Oleg Grabar shows in the case of Granada's Alhambra.[80] We could also highlight some "differential facts" of intrinsic significance, impervious to facile misinterpretations, yet often ignored by scholars. Examples include the caliphal title assumed by the Castilian monarchs from the capture of Toledo onwards, or their minting of gold coins with Arabic inscriptions.[81] The medieval

---

[78] "Although Mudejar art is the most genuine expression of medieval Spain, its historiographical evaluation has been strongly influenced in recent decades by an interpretation of Spanish medieval history which tends to reduce the weight of Islam and Islamic tradition." (Gonzalo M. Borrás Gualis, *El arte mudéjar*, 1990, p. 9).

[79] On this aspect and the Castilian monarchs' choice of an oriental style palace from Alfonso VII onwards, see María Teresa Pérez Higueras, "El mudéjar, una opción artística en la corte de Castilla y León," *Historia del Arte en Castilla y León*, t. IV, *Arte mudéjar*, Valladolid, 1994, pp. 129–222.

[80] *The Alhambra*, London, 1978. On the presence of Western Christian elements in it see T. Pérez Higueras, "La 'otra cara' del mudejarismo: influencias de los reinos cristianos en al-Andalus," *Historia de una cultura. La singularidad de Castilla*, pp. 54–59.

[81] J. Gautier Dalché, "Le rôle de la reconquête de Tolede dans l'histoire monetaire de Castille (1085–1174)," *Homenaje al profesor Juan Torres Fontes*, Murcia, 1987, pp. 613–622. Juan Ignacio Sáenz-Díez, "Toledo como emisor 'aljamiado' de moneda,"

tomb of Ferdinand III in the Seville cathedral, with inscriptions by his son Alfonso *el Sabio* in Castilian, Latin, Arabic and Hebrew is a further example.[82] The case of Rabbi Sem Tob is an example of a classic in both Hebrew and Castilian, in which the author tries to reproduce Semitic versification.[83] Another example is that of Ramón Llull, the only essential Spanish name in the history of medieval philosophy. Educated in the Moorish schools outside Scholasticism, Llull wrote his works in Arabic and Catalan, but not in Latin; furthermore, he referred to himself as "a Christian Sufi."[84]

We could, of course, devote one or more books to the Arabic influences on Spanish culture, in which we would include more than four thousand Arabisms still in use in Spain, vocabulary of construction and crafts, diseases and medication, clothing and culinary fair, not to mention legal institutions.[85] Has anybody given thought to the fact that the word *quinto* to designate a recruit continues the Koranic precept on legitimate fiscality?[86] We know that practical usage by Jews and Muslims acted as a catalyst in the direction taken by Castilian Spanish, from its

I Jornadas de cultura islámica. Toledo 1984. Al-Andalus, ocho siglos de historia, Madrid, 1989, pp. 160–172.

[82] Américo Castro, *La realidad histórica de España*, second updated edition, Mexico, 1962, p. 169. Francisco Márquez Villanueva, "Los epitafios plurilingües de Ferdinand III el Santo," *Diario de Sevilla*, September 10, 2002. Also Peter I, so well disposed to Moors and Jews, had epitaphs in Latin, Hebrew and Arabic, as H. Terrasse observes, *Islam d'Espagne. Une rencontre de l'Orient et de l'Occident*, p. 135.

[83] Emilio Alarcos Llorach, "La lengua de los 'Proverbios morales' de don Sem Tob", *Revista de Filología Española* 35 (1951), 249–309. Pedro Luis Barcia, "Los recursos literarios en los *Proverbios morales* de Sem Tob," *Romanica* 9 (1980), 57–92. For a look at all the medieval Spanish poems by Jewish authors, see Paloma Díaz-Mas, "Un género casi perdido de la poesía castellana medieval: la clerecía rabínica," *Boletín de la Real Academia Española* 73 (1993), pp. 329–346.

[84] Joseph S. Pons, "Réflexions sur le 'Llibre d'Amic e Amat,'" *Bulletin Hispanique* 35 (1923), 23–31, p. 23. Miguel Cruz Hernández, *El pensamiento de Ramón Llull*, Madrid, 1977, pp. 56 and 276–278; but Llull was not only acquainted with the Sufis, he also acted like one (ibid., pp. 120, 167–168).

[85] A huge step forward was taken in the study of this subject by Américo Castro, *España en su historia*, pp. 61–70. See "Los árabes y el elemento árabe en español," in Rafael Lapesa, *Historia de la lengua española*, eighth edition, Madrid, 1980, pp. 131–158. E. K. Neuvonen, *Los arabismos del español en el siglo XIII*, Helsinki, 1941. Felipe Maíllo Salgado, *Los arabismos del castellano en la baja Edad Media. Consideraciones históricas y filológicas*, second edition, Salamanca, 1991. Federico Corriente, *Diccionario de arabismos y voces afines en iberorromance*, Madrid, 1999. On the rich vocabulary of construction, see Fernando Martínez N. and Hamurabi F. Noufouri, *El diccionario del alarife (quinientos años después)*, Buenos Aires, 1994.

[86] On 'quintos' or *alajmás*, farmer settlers who paid taxes according to Islamic law, F. J. Simonet, *Historia de los mozárabes de España*, pp. 62–63.

earliest acceptance as an official language and even more so as a cultural vehicle, which had an integrating effect on a heterogeneous intellectual life; a Romance occurrence, of course, but incomplete if not considered as an intercultural phenomenon that is equally Mudejar.[87]

A number of other aspects of Mudejarism are worthy of treatment. Far from being unique, what happened in the Spanish Middle Ages was commonplace everywhere that Christians and Muslims had to live side by side. Similar phenomena began to occur in Sicily, though on a much smaller scale, while it was briefly dominated by Arabs,[88] or even the small marine republic of Amalfi during its brief period of commercial prosperity.[89] The aristocratic nuns of Las Huelgas de Burgos, for instance, built a mosque for their Muslim servants in the monastery,[90] like the one orthodox monks built for their loyal Bedouin defenders in Saint Catherine's on Mount Sinai, which still stands today. On a different level was the problem of *aljamiado* literature, written in Arabic or Hebrew characters which do not belong to it and which for many years was considered unique to the Peninsula. It has, however, since been documented in other areas and languages a great distance away, but which share similar cultural set-ups to the one that existed in low medieval Spain.[91] Finally, a consideration of crucial importance: Mudejarism, as an exponent of a Christian but multicultural society,

---

[87] Francisco Márquez Villanueva, "In lingua Tholetana," in *El concepto cultural alfonsí*, second edition, Barcelona, 2004, pp. 283–202.

[88] Keen to create a political entity able to oppose Byzantium, the Normans tolerated local minorities such as Greeks and Arabs; see Roberto Salvini, "Monuments of Norman Art in Sicily and Southern Italy" in *The Normans in Sicily and Southern Italy*, Lincei Lectures, Oxford: The British Academy, 1977, pp. 64–92. Henri Bresc studies parallel phenomena in "Mudejars du pays de la couronne d'Aragon et sarrasins de la Sicile normande: le problème de l'acculturation," *Jaime I y su época*. X Congreso de la Corona de Aragón, 5 vols. Zaragoza: Institución Fernando el Católico, 1980, pp. 51–60. The extensive adoption of Arab and Byzantine political institutions is studied by Giuseppe Galasso in "Social and Political Developments in the Eleven and Twelfth Centuries," *The Normans in Sicily and Southern Italy*, Oxford, 1977, pp 47–63 (pp. 50–60). The adoption of usage and custom by the Normans by in María R. Menocal, *The Ornament of the World. How Muslim, Jews, and Christians Created a Culture of Tolerance in Medieval Spain*, Boston-New York-London, 2002, pp. 119–122.

[89] Armand D. Citarella, "The Relations of Amalfi with the Arab World before the Crusades," *Speculum* 42 (1967), pp. 299–312.

[90] Peter Linehan, "Religion, Nationalism and Medieval Identity in Medieval Spain and Portugal," *Studies in Church History* 18 (1982), pp. 161–199 (p. 180).

[91] Studies shedding new light include O. Hegyi, "Minority and Restricted Uses of the Arabic Alphabet: the 'aljamiado' Phenomenon," *Journal of the American Oriental Society*, 92, 2 (1979), pp. 262–269; "Consideraciones sobre literatura aljamiada y los cambios en el concepto 'aljamía,'" *Iberoromania* no. 10 (1983), pp. 1–16. Luce López-

became securely rooted as the legal framework of a historical existence that was not without its tensions (because a society without tensions is a defunct society), but remained loyal for many years to an unspoken rule of agreed cooperation.[92]

A question I have often been asked, both in and outside the classroom, is how the more open Christian society could, in such a short space of time, have suddenly turned into the least tolerant of all. My answer is that this radical change in direction was not in the least bit spontaneous, nor did it originate from below. Rather it was violently imposed from above by Isabella and Ferdinand. We cannot talk here in terms of a crisis, because the loyalty of Mudejars and Jews was at that time guaranteed, so much so that both minorities even gave strong economic support for the conquest of the Nasrid kingdom.[93] But if Mudejarism arose with Toledo's capitulation to Alfonso VI, it died in November 1491 when Granada fell to the Catholic Monarchs. Shamelessly violated from day one,[94] it was then officially abolished by the pragmatics of the forced conversions of 1502, after the bloody Alpujarras revolt which so directly provoked the religious violence of Cisneros. The policy of religious-cultural autonomies that had proved beneficial first to Arabs and then to Christians, ended up in coercion and bloodshed. In the cultural sphere, a destructive hatred of anything "Moorish" led to the loss of countless monuments, an Inquisitorial ban on writing in any

---

Baralt, "Crónica de la destrucción de un mundo: la literatura aljamiado-morisca," *Bulletin Hispanique* 82 (1980), pp. 16–58.

[92] Nothing could be more illustrative than the condemnation of Christian historiography for truce violation which led to the death of the Infantes Juan and Pedro, Regents of Castile, in the campaign against Granada in 1319; see Diego Catalán Menéndez Pidal, "Ideales moriscos en una crónica de 1344," *Nueva Revista de Filología Hispánica* 7 (1953), pp. 570–582.

[93] Also the awarding by the monarchs of "assurances" in favor of Jewish communities angered by threats or unfair treatment until a time very close to the expulsion.

[94] Negotiated in bad faith by both parties in the view of L. P. Harvey, *Islamic Spain 1250 to 1550*, p. 313. This is reminiscent of the critique of M. Menéndez Pelayo of the capitulation of Granada as supposedly "impossible to fulfil" in Mahmud Ali Makki, "El Islam frente a las minorías cristianas," p. 49. This is scorned as pure "historical inertia" by Miguel A. Ladero Quesada, *Granada. Historia de un país islámico (1232–1571)*, Madrid, 1969, p. 151. Data is given on the mass non-application of the capitulations in José E. López de Coca Castañer and Manuel Acién Almansa, "Los mudéjares del obispado de Málaga (1485–1501)," *Actas del I Congreso Internacional de Mudejarismo*, Madrid-Teruel, 1981, pp. 307–347. The deliberate violation of the pact is covered in Ángel Galán Sánchez, "Notas para una periodización de la historia de los moriscos granadinos," *Actas del III Congreso de Historia Medieval Andaluza*, Jaén, Diputación Provincial, pp. 77–98 (p. 91).

non-Latin alphabet and even a campaign against lexical Arabisms, all of which were considered a kind of public obscenity.[95]

The die was cast. Mudejarism, the creative "solution" of the low-medieval political conscience, was turned, at that moment, into the Morisco "problem" of modern times. The breakdown in the policy of mutual respect and cooperation between the three communities, unequivocally marked by the establishment of the Inquisition in 1480 and the expulsion of the Jews in 1492, was determined by an extremely small and supreme circle. These senior members of the Christian community (not the people at large) felt sufficiently strong to become convinced that they no longer needed the other two groups, who from then on were considered an obstacle or burden that needed to be shaken off. It is pointless to speculate how the old Mudejarism would have worked or adapted to a modern world, but it is legitimate to wonder whether the conviction of these senior figures was not perhaps premature and even profoundly mistaken, and to wonder whether what really arose at that point was an ideal situation or simply a new source of trouble. Spain now entered this new age devoid of some of the members who could most have helped it in the times that lay ahead.

To conclude, we should add that Mudejarism—so solidly and deeply rooted over centuries—was attacked but not extinguished by the Catholic Monarchs, and this despite the aforesaid war on anything reminiscent of Moors or Jews, which led, for instance, to the walling up of books, thus saving *aljamiado* literature for posterity.[96] In the face of ferocious hatred, Jews and Muslims simply became Conversos and Moriscos, and the three laws or cultures were transformed into "castes" and reworked into the two opposing categories of Old and New Christians. In the future, the conflict would not be between "laws," but between two opposite ways of understanding Christian belief, as Bishop Alonso de Cartagena gloomily forecast in his 1449 *Defensorium unitatis christianae*.[97]

---

[95] Perhaps the most outstanding example (for the symbolism negating a historic past) was the destruction of the medieval tomb of Ferdinand III in the Royal Chapel of Seville Cathedral under Philip II. Its beautiful plurilingual tombstones (including Arabic and Hebrew) were hidden from the public eye in a place where they remain today, left forgotten in a pitifully dirty and neglected state.

[96] The same is true of the diverse Barcarrota materials whose discovery brought to light the unknown 1554 Medina del Campo edition of *Lazarillo de Tormes*.

[97] Guillermo Verdín Díaz, *Alonso de Cartagena y el 'Defensorium unitatis christianae,'* University of Oviedo, 1992. Earlier edition by Manuel Alonso, Madrid, 1943.

The centuries known as the Golden Age witnessed a mitigated version of Mudejarism. Intellectual responsibilities remained in Jewish terrain, now committed to a creative opening up to the modern world, whilst mechanical tasks (crafts and farming) continued visibly in crypto-Muslim hands. Yet, modern critics, influenced by the Inquisitorial myth of a homogeneous early modern Spanish society, have been reluctant to admit that Spain's Golden Age of thought, literature and religious sentiment was achieved thanks to the efforts of generations of men and women (Teresa of Avila) of officially tainted origin, who fought for an open and liberating Christianity to oppose Inquisitorial oppression. The list of names is long and glorious, even though this is not the place to review them. The problem of that complex Spain is brimming, to tragic proportions, with paradoxes which conventional Europeanism is incapable of deciphering. The vision of a monolithic culture preached by Menéndez Pelayo has been knocked down in view of the evidence of an intellectual life wrought with complex divisions and a society that became weak and paranoiac because it was at war with itself. And looming above us, the direct heirs of its glory and its misery, stands an immense task of study for scholars, for those engaged in deep reflection and for people of goodwill everywhere.

APPENDIX

The following passage is taken from El Indiculus luminosus, *written in 854 by* Álvaro de Córdoba. *In the extract the author attacks his fellow Mozarabs for adopting the Arab language and customs. I include it here as an early example of* Mudejarism.

All, indeed, welcome him [the Antichrist] on their brow or in the center of their heart or their hand, in other words, clumsily yearning for his actions, possessing his mark, going after pestilent sects of heathens, abandoning the customs of the saints and the very commendable habits of the Church. We even show his name on our brow when we use the gestures of the evildoer, forgetting the Sign of the Cross. For when performing circumcision—even with the pain felt by the body, which is not slight—to avoid the ignominy of reproaches, scorning the circumcision of the heart, which was the principal one that was commanded, what else are we carrying in our mind and on our member if not his very mark? And when we take delight in their verses and Milesian tales and pay a price to serve and be obliging to such wicked people, living with them and fattening our bodies, gathering greater riches with illicit service and a loathsome burden, or furnishing luxuries, perfumes, the richness of dress and other items for our own and our children and grandchildren's benefit for many years, speaking the name of the odious beast [Mohammed] with honor, as they do, with the accustomed plea, is it not true that by means of such displays of affection, we carry openly on our right hand the name of the beast? So too when we place criminal charges against our brothers before impious kings for the sake of temporal honours or extend the sword of cruel vengeance to the enemies of the Supreme God to kill the Lord's fold and we buy for money the power or service to exercise the same evil, what else are we doing but cruelly trading with the name and the mark of the beast and sinning with our purchases by exposing the sheep of the Lord to the teeth of wolves? So too when we inquire about his sacred institutions and learn about the doctrines of philosophers who are no more than defrauders of our souls, not to refute their errors but out of ingenious elegance, and when, with careful and brilliant expression, we abandon holy lessons and meet to discuss theirs, what else are we doing but placing within our dwellings the number of his name as if it were an idol? How many solicitous men among laymen today review the volumes of each of the doctors written in Latin devoted to the Sacred Scriptures? Which man remains kindled with love for the Gospel, the prophesies and the Apostles? Is it not true that all young Christians, of radiant appearance, eloquent, distinguished in their gestures and apparel, outstanding in their knowledge of the heathens, remarkable in their knowledge of the Arab language, take the greatest of care with the books of the Chaldeans, read them most attentively, discuss them ardently and, gathering them with great zeal, divulge them in a profuse and confident tongue, whilst ignoring the cleanliness of the tongue of the Church and scorning as vile the sources that flow from paradise. Oh pain! The Christians are ignorant of their own law and the Latins do not understand their own language. Indeed so much so that in the whole Christian community it is hard to find one in a thousand men who can correctly address a letter to a brother in Latin and yet there are countless multitudes who are able to explain the verbal bombastics of the Arabs, to the degree that, being more learned in metrics than these very peoples, and with more sublime beauty, they adorn their final clauses by shortening a letter, in keeping with the demands of expression in the Arab language, which closes all accentuated vowels with a rhythmic or even metric accent, which is suited to all the letters of the alphabet, by means of diverse expressions, and many variations are reduced to one and the same ending.[98]

---

[98] Feliciano Delgado León. El 'Indiculus luminosus,' Córdoba, 1996, pp. 183–185.

CHAPTER TWO

SEEKING THE MESSIAH:
CONVERSO MESSIANISM IN POST-1453 VALENCIA

Mark D. Meyerson

On 21 June 1464 Juan Sabastia, the inquisitorial prosecutor, and Bartolo-
meo Torro, the episcopal prosecutor, appeared before the Dominican
Juan Simo, the lieutenant papal inquisitor in the kingdom of Valencia,
and Guillem Ciscar, the episcopal Official, to indict the Conversos
Rodrigo Cifuentes, a functionary (*saig*) in Valencia's civil court, his
wife Elionor, their four daughters—Angelina, Aldonça, Gostança, and
Sperança—and two of their sons-in-law, both silversmiths and jewel-
ers, Juan Pardo, Angelina's husband, and Gonzalo Alfonso, Gostança's
husband. Their alleged crime was their attempted embarkation for
Constantinople or Valona (Vlorë, Albania) in Ottoman domains with
the aim of returning to Judaism and awaiting the advent of the Messiah.
Since they were apprehended in the port of Valencia, about to board
an eastbound ship, the defendants could hardly deny that they were
headed somewhere. They maintained that they were simply emigrating
to Venice to join Aldonça's husband, and Gonzalo's brother, Pedro
Alfonso, who was having great success in the jewelry trade there.

The existence of messianic longings, even movements, among Iberian Jews and Conversos before and after the expulsion is well known.[1]

---

[1] E.g., S. Sharot, *Messianism, Mysticism, and Magic: A Sociological Analysis of Jewish
Religious Movements*, Chapel Hill, 1982, pp. 62–85; M. Idel, *Messianic Mystics*, New
Haven and London, 1998, pp. 101–152; D. Ruderman, "Hope Against Hope: Jewish
and Christian Messianic Expectations in the Late Middle Ages," in *Essential Papers on
Jewish and Christian Culture in Renaissance and Baroque Italy*, ed. D. Ruderman, New
York, 1992, pp. 299–312; I. Tishby, "Acute Apocalyptic Messianism," in *Essential Papers
on Messianic Movements and Personalities in Jewish History*, ed. M. Saperstein, New
York, 2000, pp. 259–286; E. Gutwirth, "Jewish and Christian Messianism in Fifteenth
Century Spain," in *The Expulsion of the Jews and Their Emigration to the Southern Low
Countries (15th–16th c.)*, ed. L. Dequeker and W. Verbeke, Leuven, 1998, pp. 1–22;
C. Carrete Parrondo, "Messianismo/Sionismo entre los judeoconversos castellanos," in
Encuentros and Desencuentros: Spanish Jewish Cultural Interaction Throughout History,
Tel Aviv, 2000, pp. 481–490; and H. Beinart, "The Prophetess Inés and Her Movement

Indeed, the indefatigable Yitzhak Baer touched on this very case in his work. He did not, however, give the case a detailed analysis, probably because it is so lengthy (345 folios) and frustratingly incomplete. One cannot know if the trial resulted in a conviction, though there is good reason to think that it did or should have. The extant case file includes only the partially preserved accusations against the defendants and their responses to them, a brief rebuttal by the defense attorney, and the testimonies of twenty-two witnesses for the prosecution. Although the witnesses are anonymous—not just to the defendants, as per inquisitorial procedure, but also to historians—one can infer from internal evidence that the witnesses included, for instance, Venetian merchants and Conversos.[2]

Since Baer's fundamental exploration of this case, which includes transcribed snippets of some of the more evocative confessions and testimonies, other historians interested in the history of Jewish and Converso messianism have treated it.[3] They have not, however, dug any more deeply than Baer; content to rely on his transcriptions and limited comments, they have not examined the Inquisition record itself. Yet considering their specific interests, these scholars were probably wise not to bother with the trial record, for it reveals very little about the Conversos' messianic ideology. A thorough study of the case file

---

in Her Hometown, Herrera," [in Hebrew] in *Studies in Jewish Mysticism, Philosophy and Ethical Literature*, ed. Y. Dan and Y. Hacker, Jerusalem, 1986, pp. 459–506. The very terse statements about messianic ideas included in the trial record under consideration here make it impossible to offer a detailed analysis of the Valencian Conversos' messianic ideology or to locate it meaningfully in the intellectual and religious history of Jewish messianism. My approach here is necessarily that of a social historian, not of an historian of ideas or of religion.

[2] The record of the trial is Archivo Histórico Nacional (AHN): Inquisición (Inq.), legajo (leg.) 537, caja (c.) 1, número (no.) 5. Baer briefly treats the case in *A History of the Jews in Christian Spain*, 2 vols., trans. L. Schoffman, Philadelphia, 1961, 2: pp. 292–295; and transcribes some folios of the trial record in his *Die Juden im christlichen Spanien. Urkunden und Regesten*, 2 vols., Berlin, 1936, 2: pp. 437–443. See also his "The Messianic Movement in Spain during the Period of the Expulsion," [in Hebrew] *Me'asef Zion* 5 (1933), pp. 61–63; and R. García Cárcel, *Orígenes de la Inquisición Española. El tribunal de Valencia, 1478–1530*, Barcelona, 1976, p. 38. I have briefly touched on this case from a different perspective in "Milenarismo converso y morisco en el Reino de Valencia: Un estudio comparativo," in *XVIII Congrés d'Història de la Corona d'Aragó, Valencia-2004*, ed. R. Narbona Vizcaíno, 2 vols., Valencia, 2005, 2: pp. 1731–1740.

[3] See the works cited in n. 1; also, e.g., J. Genot-Bismuth, "Le mythe de l'Orient dans l'eschatologie des juifs d'Espagne à l'époque des conversions forcées et de l'expulsion," *Annales ESC* 4 (1990), pp. 823–827; and N. Zeldes, "Spanish Attitudes Toward *Converso* Emigration to the Levant in the Reign of the Catholic Monarchs," *Eurasian Studies* 11:2 (2003), pp. 252–257.

is nonetheless a worthwhile endeavor for historians concerned with Valencia's large and complex Converso community or, more generally, with the religious, economic, and social life of Iberian Conversos during the fifteenth century.[4] In this article, I intend to use the material in the case file to explore the lives and motivations of the defendants, and to shed a bit more light on the nature and extent of Converso messianism in Valencia after the fall of Constantinople to the Ottoman Turks in 1453. Although the evidence contained in this trial record does indicate the existence of a messianic movement among Valencian Conversos during the decade or so following 1453, what is perhaps just as striking about this one case from 1464 is the spectrum of Converso religious belief and practice it indicates and the religious and social fluidity among Conversos, Old Christians, and Jews it reflects. Valencian society in 1464 differed significantly from what it would become once the Spanish Inquisition set to work in the 1480s and once all of Spain's Jews were expelled in 1492. Despite, or, more accurately, because of the anti-Jewish measures initiated in the 1480s, messianic beliefs would remain vital among some of Valencia's Judaizers into the early years of the sixteenth century, as trial records of the Spanish Inquisition reveal.

The men on trial in 1464 were not, it seems, the sort of Conversos most likely to have been inspired by hopes for a Jewish Messiah. Rodrigo Cifuentes, the seventy-year-old patriarch, was of Andalucian origin; Jewish by birth but not knowing his parents, he converted voluntarily at around age 25 and moved to Valencia some five years later. One could well ask the rhetorical question Rodrigo posed to the notary Anthoni Lopiç when the latter asked him if the rumors about his imminent voyage to Constantinople were true: "'I've lived among you for forty years and more, and in my youth I did not leave; now in my old age...I'm going to depart to become a Jew'?"[5] What in fact

---

[4] On Valencian Conversos, see S. Haliczer, *Inquisition and Society in the Kingdom of Valencia, 1478–1834*, Berkeley, 1990, pp. 209–225; A. Garcia, *Els Vives: Una família de jueus valencians*, Valencia, 1987; J. Castillo Sainz, "De solidaritats jueves a confraries de conversos: entre la fossilització i la integració d'una minoria religiosa," *Revista d'Història Medieval* 4 (1993), pp. 183–205; and M. D. Meyerson, *A Jewish Renaissance in Fifteenth-Century Spain*, Princeton, 2004, pp. 184–224.

[5] AHN: Inq., leg. 537, c. 1, no. 5, 339v–340r (29 September 1464; witness no. 21). Lopiç: "'Compare, es ver lo que dien que vos ne anau en la nau que sen parteix para Gostantinoble per fer vos juheu'?" Rodrigo: "'Compare, quaranta anys e mas ha que vivo entre vosotros e en mi joventut no me'n so hido e agora en mi vellesa...me havia de hir per fer me judio? No lo creays.'"

roused Rodrigo to move his old bones was not just the Turks' conquest
of Constantinople but the urging of his sons-in-law.

One of them, Juan Pardo, was also born Jewish, probably in Portugal, and also converted voluntarily at age 25, in Lisbon, sponsored
by the Portuguese prince Pedro (Dom Pedro [d. 1449], the regent for
Afonso V, 1438–47).[6] However, the other two, the Alfonso brothers,
were the sons of Conversos from Córdoba. All three were motivated by
a deep and long-standing sense of penitence, a feeling shared by their
father-in-law. Both Rodrigo Cifuentes and Juan Pardo had regretted
their baptism and returned to some form of Jewish life years before.
Rodrigo's sixty-year-old wife Elionor, a Conversa of Valencian origin,
whose parents had been baptized in 1391, confided to one witness that
since marrying Rodrigo she had not lit a fire in her house on Saturday,
the Jewish Sabbath.[7] Rodrigo's unmarried daughter Sperança was proud
of her parents' Sabbath observances, and she was not shy about telling
another witness how her father made his own Passover *matzah*, which
unfortunately sometimes made her sick.[8]

Evidence from the case file suggests that the Jewish life of Rodrigo
Cifuentes and Elionor was enriched as a result of their daughters' marriages, unions over which they, as parents, had of course exercised some
influence. Indeed, marrying two of their daughters to the judaizing
Alfonso brothers and a third to the middle-aged Judaizer, Juan Pardo,
could not have been fortuitous but was a deliberate decision by Rodrigo
and Elionor to steer their family onto a particular religious course.
The professional circles in which their sons-in-law moved (see below)
must have heightened their profiles as both potential breadwinners and
committed adherents to Judaism. Rodrigo's work for the city's civil
court did not facilitate connection with the Jewish world to which his
sons-in-law had access, and his and Elionor's Jewish observances seem
consequently to have been quieter and less thoroughgoing than those
of their sons-in-law and daughters. In the event, it was Angelina and
Juan Pardo, and Gostança and Gonzalo Alfonso whom the episcopal
Official penalized for judaizing in 1460, not the parents. As penance

---

[6] AHN: Inq., leg. 537, c. 1, no. 5, 74v–75r (21 June 1464), from Pardo's response
to the inquisitors' questions.
[7] AHN: Inq., leg. 537, c. 1, no. 5, 282v (27 August 1464): witness no. 12 remembers
Elionor's words about her Sabbath activities; at 14v Elionor informs the inquisitors
about her lineage.
[8] AHN: Inq., leg. 537, c. 1, no. 5, 297r–298v, 299v–300v (witness no. 13).

the four had to purchase a large white candle to be used in the Mass at the parish church of Santa Catherina, and during Lent they were required to attend Mass every morning.[9]

From the perspective of the witnesses, the Jewish practices of Juan Pardo and Angelina were the most noticeable. Aldonça usually joined her sister and brother-in-law in their observances, apparently residing in their house in the absence of her husband, Pedro Alfonso. This was a logical living arrangement, since Juan and Pedro were the Cifuentes clan's guiding spirits in its long-range plan to return to Judaism abroad. Witnesses commented on the Pardo household's strict observance of the Jewish Sabbath. One, for example, noted that he had never seen them work on Saturday during the twelve years he had known them, though the women pretended to.[10] Instead, according to another witness, on Sundays they shut the doors of the house and polished corals.[11] Yet another witness provided a detailed account of Juan blessing the wine at the Sabbath table—making *"la barafa"*—and reading Hebrew prayers responsively with his wife and sister-in-law.[12] In keeping with his leadership role, Juan also ritually slaughtered meat for the entire extended family.[13] He forthrightly identified with the Jewish people, who, to his mind, included Conversos. He therefore refused to permit the burial of his baptized slave in the Conversos' cemetery, which he regarded as "sacred" ground.[14] Angelina shared Juan's boldness as well as his religious views. When the parish priest chided Angelina for the

[9] AHN: Inq., leg. 537, c. 1, no. 5: Gonzalo (71r, 170r–v), Angelina (124v–125r), Juan (150v), and Gostança (158r) all confess to this; witness no. 12 (268r) confirms it.

[10] AHN: Inq., leg. 537, c. 1, no. 5, 261v–262r (23 August 1464; witness no. 11).

[11] AHN: Inq., leg. 537, c. 1, no. 5, 213r–214r (26 June 1464): witness no. 2 recalls that on Sundays "aquelles tenien les portes tanquades e dins la casa de aquelles les dites dones e en Johan Pardo limaven corals."

[12] AHN: Inq., leg. 537, c. 1, no. 5, 271r–v, where witness no. 12 describes Pardo at the Sabbath table: "lo dit Pardo beney o dix oracio sobre huna taça en la qual havia vi e de aquell ne begue…e fon li dit que los juheus apellaven aquella benediccio del lo vi 'la barafa'." 275v–276r is her description of the responsive reading: "e aquell dit en Johan Pardo tenia hun libre en la ma en lo qual legia e fahia oracio ebrayqua, lo qual oracio ella dita testimoni no entenia, e les dites na Angelina e na Andolça responien a aquell sabadagant e aquelles deyen 'cados barafa, cados barafa'."

[13] AHN: Inq., leg. 537, c. 1, no. 5, 216r–217v (witness no. 2).

[14] AHN: Inq., leg. 537, c. 1, no. 5, 226r (witness no. 3): "e no permete [Pardo] que aquella fos soterrada en lo fossar dels conversos, lo qual es sagrat."

"reverence" she showed a Jew visiting her house, Angelina insulted the priest.[15]

This Jew was only one of many with whom the defendants were in contact, despite the fact that the city of Valencia had not housed a Jewish community, or *aljama*, since the 1390s.[16] The Alfonso brothers and Juan Pardo were enmeshed in a commercial network of Conversos and Jews that extended from Portugal through Castile to Valencia, and from there to Venetian and Ottoman outposts and ports in the Levant.[17] When interrogated, both Pardo and Gonzalo Alfonso admitted that they had a multi-faith clientele, including Jews; Pardo confessed to his friendship with a Castilian Jew whom he had come to know during his many trips to the fairs at Medina del Campo.[18] Witnesses went further, asserting that Castilian and Portuguese Jews frequently visited and even lodged in their homes. One of Pardo's neighbors observed that "no matter what part of the world a Jew came from, he was soon in the house of the said En Juan Pardo."[19] Jews entered the homes of the defendants "as if they were [their] brothers," noted another witness.[20]

If not brothers, some of the Jews were kin. That the willing adult converts Rodrigo Cifuentes and Juan Pardo had Jewish relatives is unsurprising; their persistent association with them, however, is remarkable. As late as 1463 Rodrigo was playing host to a Jewish physician, his relative. Two other Jews accompanied this physician to Rodrigo's

---

[15] AHN: Inq., leg. 537, c. 1, no. 5, 270r (witness no. 12): "e la dita muller del dit en Johan Pardo, per causa que lo dit mossen Bonet [vicar of the church of Santa Catherina] corregia a aquella per que feya reverencia al dit juheu, desondra al dit mossen Bonet e li dix altres injuries."

[16] J. Hinojosa Montalvo, "La comunidad hebrea en Valencia: del esplendor a la nada (1377–1391)," *Saitabi* 31 (1981), pp. 47–72; idem, *The Jews of the Kingdom of Valencia: from Persecution to Expulsion, 1391–1492*, trans. S. Nakache, Jerusalem, 1993, pp. 21–46, 258–268.

[17] On Jewish merchants in fifteenth-century Valencia, see Hinojosa Montalvo, *Jews*, pp. 193–212; idem, "Actividades comerciales de los judíos en Valencia, 1391–1492," *Saitabi* 29 (1979), pp. 21–42; L. Piles Ros, "Judíos extranjeros en la Valencia del siglo XV," *Sefarad* 7 (1947), pp. 354–360; and Meyerson, *Jewish Renaissance*, pp. 113–119, 132–137.

[18] AHN: Inq., leg. 537, c. 1, no. 5, 63v, 75v–76r: "dix que per raho de la fira de Medina a la qual ell confessant…anava sovint per vendre ses mercaderies e hague amistat ab lo dit juheu."

[19] AHN: Inq., leg. 537, c. 1, no. 5, 262v: witness no. 11 saw Jews many times "entraven, exien e muntaven en casa de aquell…e que no venia juheu que del cap del mon vingues que no fos tantost en casa del dit en Johan Pardo."

[20] AHN: Inq., leg. 537, c. 1, no. 5, 233r (29 June 1464; witness no. 5): "axi com si fossen jermans entrant e exint en les cases de aquells."

house, as did Pardo, who seems to have been the key figure organizing the Cifuentes family's re-entry into the Jewish world. Just a few
days before the failed embarkation, Pardo's seventeen-year-old Jewish
kinsman came to Valencia and in Rodrigo's house read to the women
of the family and other Conversas.[21] Even the born Converso Gonzalo
Alfonso concentrated on his Jewish lineage, cultivating memories of
his Jewish grandfather who, he assured one witness, had emigrated
to "Syria" where he died "as a Jew."[22] Whether the grandfather had
ever been baptized is unclear; what mattered to Gonzalo was his final
identification with Judaism.

The defendants' origins and their continual contacts with Jews,
perhaps especially Castilian Jews, are crucial factors to consider when
exploring their psychology. In contrast to Jews in the kingdom of
Valencia, whom the fall of Constantinople seems not to have deeply
affected—probably on account of their relatively optimistic economic
and social circumstances—some Jews in Castile were gripped by such
"eschatological enthusiasm" that they emigrated to Palestine.[23] One must
wonder what the defendants had been hearing since 1453 from their
Jewish commercial contacts, kin, and guests, or what Pardo's relative
read to the Conversas just before their failed flight. Yet perhaps more
important than any messianic ideas the Jews may have imparted to
them was the sense of frustration and inadequacy they experienced as
a consequence of their Jewish connections. The defendants were not
Conversos isolated in a crypto-Jewish world from which there was
no exit; they were all too aware of and plugged into the wider Jewish
world. Associating with Jews became a source of shame and reproach
for them; they felt that compared to what real Jews did, their private and
partial observance of Judaism was deficient and sinful. The Alfonsos'

---

[21] AHN: Inq., leg. 537, c. 1, no. 5, 285r–286v (witness no. 13).

[22] AHN: Inq., leg. 537, c. 1, no. 5, 223v. Witness no. 3 recounts his conversation
with Gonzalo in regard to rumors about his brother Pedro's return to Judaism in the
Levant. After answering that "Pedro de Cordova [Alfonso] era en Soria [Syria]," Gonzalo
elaborated: "que ja son avi del dit Pedro de Cordova ere stat en aquella part [Syria] e
alli era mort com ha juheu e que altre tal faria lo dit Pedro son jerma."

[23] B. Dinur, "A Wave of Emigration from Spain to Eretz Yisrael after the Persecu-
tions of 1391," [in Hebrew] *Zion* 32 (1967), pp. 161–174; and J. Hacker, "Links Between
Spanish Jewry and Palestine, 1391–1492," in *Vision and Conflict in the Holy Land*,
ed. R. Cohen, Jerusalem, 1985, pp. 114–125, with corrections to Dinur's dating of the
emigration. The phrase is from E. Lawee, "'Israel Has No Messiah' in Late Medieval
Spain," *The Journal of Jewish Thought and Philosophy* 5 (1996), p. 266; Meyerson, *Jewish
Renaissance*, for the situation of Valencian Jewry in the fifteenth century.

memory of their grandfather, who died Jewish in Syria, must have
gnawed at them and left them wondering if they could measure up to
his commitment to Judaism.

The Cifuentes clan's necessary practice of Catholicism exacerbated
their sense of being mired and trapped in iniquity. The defense attorney, of course, made much of their Catholic observances. The record
of their Catholic piety, however, was not terribly impressive, perhaps
no worse than that of many Old Christians but not such as to mark
them as devout. Their knowledge of the essential Catholic prayers
was mixed. Rodrigo's youngest daughter, eighteen-year-old Sperança,
knew scarcely any of the prayers, despite the efforts of her mother and
brother to teach her. Gostança could recite no more to the inquisitors
than the *Pater noster* and the *Ave Maria*, maintaining that she had
learning problems. Her parents could not do any better, with Rodrigo
apologizing that he did not "practice" the *Credo in deum*, though her
husband Gonzalo was able to show the inquisitors that he knew it
"well enough."[24] The defendants all attended Mass fairly regularly at
their parish churches: Sant Andreu, in the case of Rodrigo, Elionor,
and Sperança; and Santa Catherina for the married daughters and
sons-in-law. Occasionally Elionor and her daughters all went to Santa
Catherina together.[25] They all also confessed and took Communion with
a certain frequency. Rodrigo had the worst record; he admitted that he
had confessed only eight to ten times in the last forty years, and that
the last time he had done so was three or four years previously. All the
others, however, had confessed and taken Communion sometime within
the last two years.[26] Perhaps surprisingly, Angelina and Juan Pardo
made the most convincing demonstrations of Catholic knowledge and
observance, as if there was an inverse relationship between the intensity

---

[24] AHN: Inq., leg. 537, c. 1, no. 5: Sperança (10r–v, 107r–108v); Gostança (36r,
153v); Elionor (20v–22r, 114r–v); Rodrigo: "lo credo no'l pratichava" (57r–v, 136v);
and Gonzalo: "prou be" (68r, 165v–166r). This information on the defendants' Catholic
practices comes almost entirely from their responses to the inquisitors' questions and,
of course, from the arguments posed by their defense attorney (178r–179r, 183r–v,
184v–185r, 191r–192v). A perusal of *Visitas pastorales de Valencia (Siglos XIV–XV)*,
ed. M. M. Cárcel Ortí and J. V. Boscá Codina, Valencia, 1996, provides some sense of
the religious life of the Old Christian laity and its limitations.

[25] AHN: Inq., leg. 537, c. 1, no. 5: 11r, 20v–22r, 29r–v, 36r–v, 43v–44r, 58r–v, 68r–v,
80r–v, 114r–v, 121r, 229v–230r (witness no. 4).

[26] AHN: Inq., leg. 537, c. 1, no. 5: 12r–13r, 20v–22r, 29r–v, 36r–v, 43v–44r, 59r–v
(Rodrigo), 68r–v, 80r–v, 107r–108v, 121r, 128v–129r, 137v–138r (Rodrigo), 145v–146r,
154r, 165v–166r.

of inner commitment to Judaism and the energy expended in public displays of Catholic piety. Both knew more prayers than the others—all except the *Salve Regina*—and Angelina could even write them down. Both had recently confessed and taken Communion. Living across the street from the church of Santa Catherina certainly helped. Like a good Catholic master, Pardo also sought to have his slaves baptized, unsuccessfully in the case of a Muslim mother and daughter, and to have priests properly administer extreme unction to them when necessary.[27] Devotional paintings of Jesus, Mary, and the saints—described as "oratories"—were on display in the Cifuentes, Alfonso, and Pardo households. The defendants even brought some paintings aboard ship with them.[28] This façade of Catholic ritual and iconography might have shielded the defendants from the church authorities or from the ostracism of Old-Christian neighbors, but it could not prevent them from looking hard at themselves. The Turks' conquest of Constantinople and their openness to Jewish commerce and immigration created new options for the defendants and like-minded Conversos and the real possibility of ceasing to lead a double life.[29] Making excuses now became more difficult. The defendants recognized that one could escape from captivity among Christians and live unambiguously as a Jew.

This realization, however, dawned on the Cifuentes clan long before 1464. The mysterious Pedro Alfonso, the pivotal figure in this case, had sailed for Venice in 1457; he established himself in the trade in precious stones and pearls between Venice and Levantine ports, laying the groundwork for his family's move to the Levant. Venice, it is worth recalling, did not house an established Jewish community prior to the sixteenth century, though the city did permit the temporary residence of

---

[27] AHN: Inq., leg. 537, c. 1, no. 5: 28v–29v, 80r–v, 121r, 145v–146r for the Catholic prayers and practices of Juan Pardo and Angelina; 269v (witness no. 12) regarding the location of their house "davant la sglesia de Santa Catherina"; and 23r–v, 82v, 139r–141r, 148r–v, 156r–v, 167v–168r for Pardo's Christian treatment of his slaves.

[28] AHN: Inq., leg. 537, c. 1, no. 5: 9v, 19v–20r, 28r, 35v, 43r, 57r, 67v, 79r–v.

[29] On Ottoman Jewish policy, see H. Inalcik, "Foundations of Ottoman-Jewish Cooperation," in *Jews, Turks, Ottomans: A Shared History, Fifteenth through the Twentieth Century*, ed. A. Levy, Syracuse, 2002, pp. 3–14; D. Goffman, "Jews in Early Modern Ottoman Commerce," in ibid., pp. 15–34; J. Hacker, "The *Sürgün* System and Jewish Society in the Ottoman Empire during the Fifteenth to the Seventeenth Centuries," in *Ottoman and Turkish Jewry: Community and Leadership*, ed. A. Rodrigue, Bloomington, Indiana, 1992, pp. 1–65; and A. Shmuelevitz, *The Jews of the Ottoman Empire in the Late Fifteenth and Sixteenth Centuries: Administrative, Economic, Legal and Social Relations as Reflected in the Responsa*, Leiden, 1984.

Jewish merchants, and there were Jewish communities and merchants in
its various Levantine commercial outposts and colonies.[30] Pedro's New
Christian status would have facilitated his setting up shop in Venice;
his Jewish leanings would have helped him to deal with Levantine and
other Jews. In any case, Pedro soon acquired a favorable reputation
among Venetian merchants, such that they "recommended" him to local
ship owners whose vessels sailed to Levantine ports. According to the
Cifuentes family's defense attorney, Pedro became wealthy in Venice,
accumulating assets valuing 3,000 or 4,000 ducats.[31] Juan Pardo had
also worked in Venice for a time, selling jewelry in the plaza of San
Bartholomeo, but, declining the invitation of two local merchants to
relocate his family to Venice, he returned to Valencia.[32] Whatever the
precise dates of Pardo's residence in Venice—the trial record is unclear
about this—it seems that once the male heads of the Cifuentes clan
decided to return to Judaism abroad, they designated Pedro Alfonso
to make the necessary arrangements.

---

[30] The following works establish a context for, and the plausibility of, Pedro Alfonso's
commercial activities in Venice and in the Muslim Levantine ports where Venetians
traded, whether as a Christian or as a Jew in the latter cases: B. Ravid, "The Legal
Status of Jews in Venice to 1509," *Proceedings of the American Academy for Jewish
Research* 54 (1987), pp. 169–202; D. Jacoby, "Les juifs à Venise du XIVe au milieu du
XVIe siècle," in *Venezia centro di mediazione tra Oriente e Occidente (secoli XV–XVI).
Aspetti e problemi*, 2 vols., Florence, 1977, 1: pp. 163–216, esp. pp. 184–188, 199–205;
idem, "Les juifs vénetiens du Constantinople et leur communauté du XIIIe siècle
jusqu'au milieu du XVe siècle," *Revue des Études Juives* 131 (1972), pp. 397–427; idem,
"Venice and Venetian Jews in the Eastern Mediterranean," in *Gli ebrei e Venezia, secoli
XIV–XVIII*, ed. G. Cozzi, Milan, 1987, pp. 29–58; B. Cooperman, "Venetian Policy
Towards Levantine Jews in Its Broader Italian Context," in ibid., pp. 65–84; B. Arbel,
"Jews in International Trade: The Emergence of the Levantines and Ponentines," in *The
Jews of Early Modern Venice*, ed. R. C. Davis and B. Ravid, Baltimore, 2001, pp. 73–80;
H. Inalcik, "An Outline of Ottoman-Venetian Relations," in *Venezia centro*, pp. 83–90;
and E. Ashtor, "New Data for the History of Levantine Jewries in the Fifteenth Century,"
essay VIII in E. Ashtor, *The Jews and the Mediterranean Economy 10th–15th Centuries*,
London, 1983, pp. 67–102, esp. pp. 70–72, 80–84, 88–92. The intricacies of Venetian
Jewish policy and of the social and economic circumstances of the relevant Jewish
communities in the eastern Mediterranean cannot be elaborated on here.

[31] AHN: Inq., leg. 537, c. 1, no. 5, 180v: Pedro lives "opulenter emendo et vendendo
lapides preciosos, margalitas et alia jocalia adeo quia, ut fertur, est dives de tribus vel
quatuor milibus ducatis."

[32] AHN: Inq., leg. 537, c. 1, no. 5, 76v–77r: Pardo confesses, "es mercader e lapidari
e per quant es stat en altre temps en la ciutat de Venecia, en lo qual temps hi ha tengut
casa en aquella en la plaça de Sent Berthomeu venent joyes e obres domasquines, del-
liberava de anar a la dita ciutat de Venecia ab sa muller e tota sa casa e aço li consella[n]
micer Lois Lorida e micer Baltasar, mercaders Venecians, per praticar lo seu offici e
que alli se avançaria molt be."

By 1464 Pedro was no longer in Venice. He had converted to Judaism in some Levantine port. There was quite a buzz about this among Valencian Conversos. The source of their information was the Venetian merchants who regularly visited Valencia, some of whom testified in the inquisitor's court. Accounts are inconsistent about where Pedro converted. One witness mentioned Damascus or Beirut as possibilities; others spoke more vaguely of the "parts of the Turk" or "parts of the Levant," even while providing the significant detail that Pedro, after returning to Judaism, was "seen walking in a yellow headdress [i.e., turban] just as the other Jews are accustomed to do [in Muslim lands]."[33]

The most elaborate and apparently reliable accounts, however, specified Beirut and Constantinople as the sites of Pedro's conversion. One Venetian witness told the inquisitors the same story he had earlier recounted to Juan Pardo, who had wanted some information about Pedro's whereabouts. In 1459 the witness traveled from Damascus to Beirut upon learning that three Venetian galleys were approaching the port. As soon as the galleys anchored there, "a young man," who fit the description Pardo gave the witness, "went to the Jewish quarter (*judequa*) and there dressed himself as a Jew." The captain of the Venetian galleys then tried unsuccessfully to persuade Pedro to come back aboard ship and be reconciled to the Catholic faith. The witness believed that Pedro never returned to Venice.[34] Another witness, who had apparently heard the same story, added the detail that the Mamluk authorities arrested Pedro for having converted from Christianity to Judaism, instead of Islam.[35]

---

[33] AHN: Inq., leg. 537, c. 1, no. 5: 249v–250r (witness no. 8), Beirut or Damascus; 212r (witness no. 2), "se era tornat juheu en aquelles parts del Turch"; 321r–v (witness no. 17), "les parts de Levant." Witness no. 17's informant was a Castilian from Córdoba who told her that "lo [Pedro] havia vist anar ab tocha groga axi com los altre juheus acostumen anar."

[34] AHN: Inq., leg. 537, c. 1, no. 5, 240v–242r (witness no. 6; 30 June 1464). In Beirut the Venetian saw "hun jove [fitting the description given him by Pardo and a Converso surnamed Micero] lo qual era vengut ab les dites galeres e encontinent que fon en la dita ciutat sen ana a la judequa e alli se vesti juheu."

[35] AHN: Inq., leg. 537, c. 1, no. 5, 249v–250r. According to this witness (no. 8), when it was discovered that Pedro had been a Christian "e tornat juheu amagadament, per la dita raho fon acusat e ajutgat per catiu a la senyoria de la vila on lo dit en Pedro se atrobava, com segons la ordinacio de la dita terra los crestians que's tornen juheus amagadament son catius de la dita senyoria." A different witness (no. 5) also seems to refer to Pedro's arrest in a Levantine port, after a Venetian there denounced him: "lo acusa e dix que ell era crestia e sera tornat juheu, e per aço lo prengueren" (235r–v).

Pedro evidently managed to escape imprisonment or enslavement at
the hands of the Mamluks, probably because he was not a subject of the
sultan, and, notwithstanding the aforementioned Venetian's testimony,
was able to make his way back to Venice.[36] Valencian witnesses, who had
discussed the affair as recently as early June 1464 with two Venetians
visiting Valencia, informed the inquisitors about what Pedro did next.
Once back in Venice, Pedro used his connections among local merchants, presumably those who had not heard of his exploits in Beirut,
to secure passage for himself and a Castilian Converso companion on
a Venetian ship bound for Constantinople. When the two disembarked
in the now Ottoman city, they immediately returned to Judaism and
were then seen dressed like Jews. The Ottoman authorities proved
more welcoming to such New Christian converts to Judaism than their
Mamluk counterparts in Beirut had been. The chagrined patron of the
Venetian ship, who had given the highly "recommended" Pedro very
honorable treatment, told his merchant friend that he would have never
allowed Pedro and the Castilian aboard his ship if he had known they
would "become Jews."[37]

Full verification of the place and time of Pedro Alfonso's return, or
returns, to Judaism is impossible. Clearly Pedro performed his costume
and identity change more than once, moving back and forth between

---

[36] Whatever misgivings the Mamluk authorities may initially have had about such
reversions to Judaism in their domains seem to have evaporated soon enough. Zeldes,
"Converso emigration," p. 256, cites Rabbi Ovadiah de Bertinoro's praise, in 1488, of
some fifty household of repentant Conversos who were living in Mamluk Egypt following their return to Judaism there.

[37] AHN: Inq., leg. 537, c. 1, no. 5. In response to the questions of witness no.
10–identifiable from internal evidence as the silversmith Pere Chiquo–a Venetian
visiting Valencia's *argenteria* said that he had known Pedro well in Venice, and that
Pedro "sen era passat ab huna fusta en la ciutat de Gostantinoble ensemps ab un altre
companyo de aquell, als quals…lo patro de la dita fusta havia feta molta honor, e que
com la dita fusta fon junta en Gostantinoble lo dit en Pedro de Cordova [Alfonso]
hixque en terra e's torna juheu e que anava ab vestidures de juheu" (256r–v). Witness
no. 11 was with Pere Chiquo and heard the same story from the same Venetian, but
he could not remember the name of the port "en les parts de Levant" where Pedro
and his companion reverted to Judaism. He did, however, recall the chagrin of the
ship patron (259v–260v). Witness no. 18 spoke with a "ruddy Venetian" who had
lodged with Pedro in the home of a Venetian merchant in Venice, who happened to
be the brother of the ship patron who took Pedro and his friend to Constantinople.
The merchant, the witness recounted, "prega al dit son jerma, patro de la dita nau, que
per quant aquell dit Pedro e hun altre Castella companyo de aquell volien passar a la
ciutat de Gostantinoble que volgues haver aquells per recomanats." Upon returning
to Venice, "lo dit patro li [the Venetian merchant] dix que ell havia vist lo dit Pedro
juheu en Gostantinoble" (325r–326v).

Venice and various Muslim ports, and between Christianity and Judaism, until finally leaving Venice for good and staying as a Jew in Constantinople or some other Ottoman city to which he subsequently transferred. That Pedro converted in Mamluk Beirut before doing so in an Ottoman city seems odd, particularly in light of the Turks' role in the messianic dreams of Iberian Conversos and Jews. Yet the fact that Pedro's grandfather had ended his life as a Jew in Mamluk "Syria" probably made Beirut an especially attractive setting for his own return to Judaism, even if he planned finally to make his way to Ottoman domains. Indeed, according to one witness, Pedro's brother Gonzalo expected him to follow their grandfather's example in Syria.[38] A different witness, who mentioned Cairo as one of Pedro's several destinations, reported that Pedro dressed like a Jew in Mamluk lands so that he could travel more safely with his merchandise.[39] If this statement is accurate, this strategy would have assisted Pedro in gathering the wealth his family would have needed to move comfortably to the Levant. The difficulties that Pedro encountered in Beirut in 1459 were probably unusual.[40]

However circuitous Pedro Alfonso's route to the Ottoman empire may have been, the defendants' reported messianic yearnings leave little doubt that their ultimate destination was also Constantinople, or Valona, or some other city ruled by the Ottoman sultan, a key figure in the Conversos' imagined eschatological drama.[41] The defendants had endeavored to mislead acquaintances into believing that they were

---

[38] See n. 22.

[39] AHN: Inq., leg. 537, c. 1, no. 5, 234v–235r (witness no. 5).

[40] That Pedro would have devised such a strategy is hardly incredible, particularly in light of the experiences of many such Converso chameleons in the early modern Mediterranean and Atlantic worlds, on whom there is a large and growing bibliography.

[41] G. Veinstein, "Une communauté ottomane: les Juifs d'Avlonya (Valona) dans la deuxième moitié du XVIᵉ siècle," in Gli ebrei, 783–785, notes that Valona came under Ottoman control in 1417 and soon attracted Jewish immigrants from various Mediterranean regions, including Spain, especially Catalonia. The Jewish community in Valona seems to have disappeared in the 1440s, on account of Albanian revolts, but the immigration of Iberian and Italian Jews brought about its revival by the end of the fifteenth century. Veinstein cites the immigration of seventy Valencian Converso households—discussed below at n. 44 and transcribed by Baer, Die Juden, 2: 440—as the first evidence of the Jewish repopulation of Valona. Given the fragmentary evidence, one can only surmise that a number of Jews, including perhaps former Conversos, had already settled again in Ottoman Valona at some time between the later 1440s and 1464. It is hard to imagine Valencian Conversos deliberately leaving Iberia to revert to Judaism in a city without a Jewish community.

bound for Venice, but the ship on which they tried to embark was in fact sailing from Valencia to the Morea, and from there to the port of Beirut. They planned, the prosecutor asserted, to travel from Beirut to Damascus and then to make their way to Valona.[42] Pedro probably awaited them in Ottoman domains, though he may well have arranged to meet them in Damascus. An experienced traveler in these parts by 1464, Pedro could have advised them of, or guided them on, the safest route to Valona.

Prior to the defendants' attempted departure, Pedro and his wife Aldonça exchanged letters. These letters were read aloud by Juan Pardo and discussed by the family. Pedro first informed Aldonça of his conversion to Judaism. The news upset her and she wept, because Pedro, she realized, had taken the final, irreversible step. Aldonça experienced a crisis of confidence and wavered; her familiar and secure life in Valencia suddenly felt more appealing than the unknown and uncertain world of Turks, eastern Jews, and the Jewish Messiah. She wrote to Pedro, urging him to return to Valencia where he could be reconciled to the church. Pedro's response was unequivocal: the authorities would burn him if he returned to Valencia; the road East was open and he would send her money for the voyage. If she refused to join him, she should at least send him their son Jaume.[43] Juan Pardo and her parents must have stiffened Aldonça's resolve.

One of the arguments they could have used to encourage Aldonça was the fact that they would not be alone in their eastward migration. Other Conversos had already done or were doing the same thing, enough perhaps to allow one to speak of a "messianic movement." To strengthen their case against the defendants, the prosecutors pointed out that already "seventy households or families...of the present city...had

---

[42] AHN: Inq., leg. 537, c. 1, no. 5, 196r (23 August 1464) for the prosecution's claims. Witness no. 9 related that early in 1462 Juan Pardo had dissembled, telling him that he would be traveling to Venice, but that two or three days before the attempted embarkation Pardo revealed his true destination (or one of them), crying out, "'Compadre, datme la mano, que a Domasco me vo'" (253r).

[43] AHN: Inq., leg. 537, c. 1, no. 5, 265r–266v (witness no. 12). Aldonça's reaction to Pedro's letters: "feu molt dol e plora e...stava ab gran tristicia e sen congoxava molt de les dites letres." Pedro's response to Aldonça's suggestion that he "sen tornas en Valencia e que be's poria reconsiliar": "e aquell dit Pedro en la dita letra li dehia o scrivia que no'n faria, car si aquell era pres lo cremarien, mas en totes maneres del mon fes que li trametes son fill Jaume e si aquella dita na Andolça volia anar lla hon lo dit en Pedro de Cordova era que lo cami tenia ubert e que aquell li trametria diners per al viatge."

gone to the town of Valona and there became Jews." They also noted that there were many Jews living in Damascus and with them "many neophytes [Conversos] made Jews."[44] One witness asserted that "it is public knowledge in…Valencia that all the New Christians of this city who have departed for Constantinople…are going there only to become Jews."[45] Another witness related how men casually conversed in the governor's court "about some Conversos who went to Constantinople, they believed, to become Jews."[46] Converso emigration from Valencia to the East was clearly noticeable and a matter of public discussion. Some witnesses mentioned the names of other Converso émigrés, such as Benet de Pròxita and Pedro de Toledo.[47] Remarkably, two of the émigrés were the Old Christian wives of Converso tanners.[48] Such details undoubtedly horrified the ecclesiastical authorities.

While the fall of Constantinople excited and galvanized a good number of Conversos in Valencia, not all Conversos shared their enthusiasm. Among Valencian Conversos there was, after all, a spectrum of religious belief and practice and varying levels of identification with the Jewish people.[49] Conversos with different allegiances occasionally found themselves in uncomfortable social situations. The resultant tensions and bruised feelings must have left judaizing Conversos like Juan Pardo and the Alfonso brothers all the more desirous of moving to lands where they could live unashamedly as Jews, just as they impelled other

---

[44] AHN: Inq., leg. 537, c. 1, no. 5, 196v (23 August 1464): "LXX casati seu familie…LXX domorum de presenti civitate transiverant et iverant ad villam de Velona et ibi facti erant judei." In regard to the many Jews who "sunt et habitant" in Damascus, "plures neophiti facti judei."

[45] AHN: Inq., leg. 537, c. 1, no. 5, 315r–v (witness no. 16): "fama publica es en la present ciutat de Valencia que tots los crestians novells que de aquesta ciutat se parteixen per anar en Gostantinoble que aquells no'y van sino per tornarse juheus."

[46] AHN: Inq., leg. 537, c. 1, no. 5, 338v–339r (29 September 1464): witness no. 21 relates how he was in the Governor's court with some others, including the notary Anthoni Lopiç, "e parlaven de Gostantinoble, de alguns conversos qui sen eren anats, creyen, per fer se juheus." This discussion led to Lopiç's questioning of Rodrigo Cifuentes; see above at n. 5.

[47] AHN: Inq., leg. 537, c. 1, no. 5, 320r–321r (witness no. 17).

[48] AHN: Inq., leg. 537, c. 1, no. 5, 295v–296r. Witness no. 13 remembers the words of Sperança: "'Mirasseu a la muller de Johan lo sonador que era tota goya, la qual sen es passada en aquelles parts e tornada a la bona part, e axi mateix mirasseu a la muller de mestre Alfonso lo sonador que axi mateix era goya e en aquelles parts se es tornada a la bona part, que les tenen en palmes per esser stades goyes e tornades a la bona part.'"

[49] Haliczer, *Inquisition and Society*, pp. 209–225; Meyerson, *Jewish Renaissance*, pp. 184–224.

Conversos to embrace more firmly the religious and social values of the
Valencian society into which they were born and baptized.

The home of Rodrigo Cifuentes was the setting for one revealing
clash between Conversos with different religious leanings. In early
1461 Rodrigo hosted a feast celebrating the marriage of his wife's
niece, obviously a Conversa, to the Converso Anthoni Ferrada, the
son of an olive oil transporter or merchant (*traginer d'oli*). Most, if
not all, of the guests attending the celebration were Conversos. The
father of the groom, En Ferrada, took pains to have veal prepared for
the feast. When the rest of the guests happily sat down to eat the veal,
"which was not slaughtered by a Jew or according to rabbinic custom
(*rabinada*)," Juan Pardo, Angelina, and Aldonça refused to touch it.
Instead, they had a pair of chickens slaughtered in a *kasher* manner—in
all likelihood Pardo did it himself—and conspicuously proceeded to
eat them amidst the other guests dining on the veal. Accounts as to
what happened next vary. A Conversa witness recalled that when En
Ferrada saw what Pardo, Angelina, and Aldonça were doing, he cried
out that they were "'great Jews,'" adding that "'were it not for his love
for his son, he would want to denounce them [presumably to church
authorities].'"[50] En Ferrada himself, who testified for the prosecution,
emphasized the outrage of the other guests. The latter cursed "with
great anger" and said, "'these people—saying this of En Pardo, his
wife, and his sister-in-law—cannot eat here with us and they do not
[even] eat hidden in the room!'" These guests, in other words, were
fuming because the Judaizers seemed to regard themselves as too good
or too pious to eat with them and because they did not even have the
courtesy—or respect for the Catholic faith—to hide what they were
doing. Continuing his testimony, En Ferrada portrayed himself as
handling this volatile situation gracefully. He claimed that he stated,
"'Whether we're all Jews or all New Christians, it is fitting to perform
the [wedding] ceremonies.'"[51] Ferrada's rather lighthearted assertion is

---

[50] AHN: Inq., leg. 537, c. 1, no. 5, 273r (witness no. 12): "en les quales noçes apa-
rellaren vedella, de la qual per quant no era degollada per juheu o rabinada...feren
[Pardo, Angelina, and Aldonça] matar hun parell de gallines e aquelles mengaren en la
dita boda e no volgueren mengar de la dita vedella. E com aço vehes lo dit en Ferrada,
pare del dit novio, nols lexa de cridar que eren huns grans juheus e sino per amor de
son fill aquell los volia acusar."

[51] AHN: Inq., leg. 537, c. 1, no. 5, 310r–v (28 August 1464): "be es veritat que hoy
ell testimoni com alguns en la dita boda eren digueren ab molta fellonia, 'cul de tal
senyor'—dient ho de deu—'aqueixa gent'—dient ho den Pardo e de sa muller e de

telling. Even if the wedding ceremony itself was legitimate, there were, to his mind, two types of Conversos: "Jews" and "New Christians." The former, the fiercely committed Judaizers, were, especially after the earth-shattering events of 1453, more inclined to identify themselves as Jews without apology and thus to emigrate. The latter group would have included sincere Catholics, those who wavered between the two faiths, and even more circumspect Judaizers who were content enough to continue leading a double life—a course they could follow as long as the relatively lenient and unenergetic papal inquisitors were guarding the Catholic faith in Valencia. Such "New Christians" were not in any hurry to leave Valencia.

Nor was Jacme Rodríguez, the only son of Rodrigo Cifuentes. That there was not even unanimity among the Cifuentes clan is striking. Jacme adamantly refused to join the family on its journey to the Levant and he argued about it with his sister Aldonça a number of times. Once he told her: "'Because of you we have to endure bad things; we will not be well here because you have to leave [Valencia]. For s/he who does not serve God here will not serve Him there where you want to go.'"[52] Jacme approved neither of Aldonça's judaizing nor of the major changes she and her husband Pedro were causing the family to make.

Other Conversos from outside the family responded to news of its travel plans with a mixture of skepticism and derision. One Conversa witness who frequented Pardo's house laughed aloud at Angelina and Aldonça when they tried to persuade her to move east, convert to Judaism and thus save her soul. She added: "'God let me die in this city of Valencia, and when I am dead the bells of the church where my body will be buried will sound for me, and I will die in the Catholic faith.'" The inquisitors may have been impressed by this witness' declaration of faith but Aldonça had not been. She admonished her sister: "'You be careful of her [the witness]...she is *trefana* [unclean].'"[53]

---

sa cunyada—'no poden mengar açi ab nosaltres e no mengar en la cambra amagats'. E lladonchs ell testimoni dix, 'o tots siam jueus o tots cristians nous, cal fer cerimonies.'" Witness no. 15 is clearly En Ferrada, given his references to the groom Anthoni Ferrada as his son.

[52] AHN: Inq., leg. 537, c. 1, no. 5, 290v–291r (witness no. 13): "'Per tu...nosaltres...havem de haver mal; no siam be açi per que'us cal anar de fora, car qui no serveix a deu açi no'l servira lla hon tu...vols anar.'"

[53] AHN: Inq., leg. 537, c. 1, no. 5, 279v–280r (witness no. 12): "e les dites na Angelina e na Aldonça induhien a ella dita testimoni dient li que si ella dita testimoni sen anava en aquella part e's tornava juhia que ella testimoni hauria aquelles honors que a les altres que's tornaven juhies fahien e que salvaria la sua anima." The witness then "prenias a

Some Conversos who, like this witness, were keen to integrate and get ahead in Catholic society, regarded the phenomenon of Converso emigration more seriously than she did. They thought it embarrassing and feared that it would blacken the reputation of all Conversos. They did not want their Old-Christian neighbors to categorize them as Conversos intent on abandoning Valencia and the Catholic faith for Judaism. One witness, who had known the Alfonso brothers a long time and who thought they were "good Christians," was appalled when he heard rumors of Pedro's return to Judaism in the Levant and that his imprisoned relatives had intended to follow in his footsteps. His statement is full of antipathy for the defendants—and anxiety that all Conversos would be lumped together with them: "'If those said prisoners were going with that intention of becoming Jews, he who would spare them should have his throat slit. There should be no justice for them [the defendants], for when some do evil the others [Conversos] will be defamed.'"[54]

Not all Converso émigrés, or aspiring émigrés, were necessarily inspired by hopes for the Messiah's advent. For some, the ability to return to Judaism and to prosper in Ottoman domains probably provided sufficient impetus. Yet most Conversos eager to leave Valencia within a decade or so of 1453 must have been impelled by the powerful notion that the Ottoman conquest of Constantinople was part of the necessary upheaval that would precede the coming of the Messiah. The movement eastward and back to Judaism, moreover, was integral to the eschatology of such Conversos, who, as will be explained below, had much more in mind than their personal salvation. Of course, at this historical juncture, apocalyptic visions and messianic speculation were widespread on both learned and popular levels among Jews, Christians

---

riure" and said, "'Deu me lexe morir en aquesta ciutat de Valencia e quant sere morta sonen per mi en la sglesia hon lo meu cors sera soterrat les campanes e muyra en la fe catholica.'" Aldonça to Angelina: "'Guartat d'ella...que trefana es.'"

[54] AHN: Inq., leg. 537, c. 1, no. 5, 343r–344r (29 September 1464). The witness (no. 22), who described Pedro and Gonzalo as "bons crestians," knew that Pedro had gone abroad six or seven years ago but initially thought that Pedro was simply purchasing precious stones and jewelry "com en les dites joyes aquell [Pedro] se entenia be." After learning otherwise, "ell dit testimoni dix que si aquells dits presos sen anaven ab aquella intencio de tornar se juheus que degollat fos aquell qui'ls estalviaria; que no fossen justicia de aquells, car los huns feyen lo mal e los altres eren difamats." See also n. 72 for similar sentiments expressed by another Converso.

(New and Old), and Muslims.[55] In Valencia, for instance, the belief among Christians that in 1453 the struggle between Christendom and Islamdom had taken on new cosmic proportions precipitated the sacking of the local Muslim quarter in 1455.[56]

Ottoman victories over eastern and western Christians affected Conversos like the defendants so powerfully because the messianic age they presaged entailed the degradation of Christians, a status inversion in which not just Muslims but also Jews would lord it over them. The defendants resented Christians and Christianity. Unenthusiastic participants in the Mass, they reportedly neither prayed nor knelt during the service. Angelina and Aldonça asked one Conversa witness why she even bothered saying Catholic prayers, and spitefully commented that all the women who attended Mass were whores since they went only to see their lovers.[57] The sisters and Juan Pardo advised another witness, almost certainly a Converso, that when the Host was being raised "it was a sin either to say or to perform a [Christian] prayer; rather, [one should] curse the Christians." They also warned him of the penalty incurred by those—presumably of Jewish lineage—who

---

[55] For the effect of the fall of Constantinople on Jewish and Converso messianism, see Tishby, "Apocalyptic Messianism," pp. 259–262; Ruderman, "Hope Against Hope," pp. 299–304; Sharot, *Messianism*, pp. 76–77; Hacker, "Links," pp. 121–125; Lawee, "'Israel Has No Messiah,'" pp. 265–266; Genot-Bismuth, "Mythe de l'Orient," pp. 822–827. Gutwirth, "Jewish and Christian Messianism," pp. 9–13, presents evidence of Jewish and Christian predictions of the year 1464 being the beginning of the messianic process. Isaac Abravanel, for example, indicated the significance of 1464 in some of his exegetical works (see also Zeldes, "*Converso* emigration," pp. 256–257), as did certain Christian writers to whose works, Gutwirth believes, Castilian Jews and Conversos would have had access. The trial record under consideration here makes no reference to any textual sources for the messianic notions of the Cifuentes clan, nor does it include any references to the significance of 1464 in particular. Of course, the defendants could have heard about such predictions from the Jews with whom they dealt. The importance of Jewish-Converso contact in the dissemination of messianic ideas emerges clearly in Gutwirth's analysis, particularly in regard to New Castile, Andalucía, and the kingdom of Aragon.

[56] See M. Ruzafa García, "'Façen-se cristians los moros o muyren!'" *Revista d'Història Medieval* 1 (1990), pp. 87–110.

[57] AHN: Inq., leg. 537, c. 1, no. 5, 276v–277v (witness no. 12): After asking the witness "'guaya quina pressa per dir oracio'," the sisters said, "que totes quantes dones anen a missa eren bagasses per quant no'y anaven per altra cosa sino que aquelles poguessen veure sos enamorats e que en la sglesia se clohia lo matrimoni entre aquelles e sos enamorats." Witness no. 13 observed the four sisters and their mother at Mass: "quant levaven lo cors de Jhesu Crist, si ella testimoni era en loch que les pogues veure, veya que aquelles ni deyen ni fahien oracio alguna ni plegaven les mans ni agenollaven. E aço feyen aquelles tantes vegades quantes levaven lo cors de Jhesu Crist e de vespre sonaven la oracio" (302r–v).

said Christian prayers: God would not listen to their supplications for thirty days. None of this shocked the witness, since the three "were and lived like Jews."[58]

The defendants were sure that Christians would get their comeuppance at the hands of the Turkish "Antichrist," a figure from Christian eschatology to whom Conversos assigned a more positive role.[59] When a witness chastised Sperança for her family's bold and rather open observance of the Jewish Sabbath, concluding, "'Have you no fear of God or of the people? I'm surprised that our Lord God doesn't send fire down on your houses,'" Sperança retorted:

> The Gentiles (*los goys*) do not see us, for they are blind. They don't know that our Lord God has allowed us for some time to be subject to them, but now we will dominate them, for God has promised us that since we are going to those parts [the Levant], we will ride over them. Haven't you heard it said that Antichrist has to come? (saying that the Turk is that one [the Antichrist]). For he will destroy the Christians' churches and make them stables for animals, and he will do much honor to the Jews and their synagogues and show reverence to all those who go to those parts and return to the good side (*bona part* [Judaism]).[60]

It was Sperança, the youngest and still unmarried daughter, who spoke most to witnesses about the coming messianic age. The defense attorney thus claimed that she was "foolish" and "quasi-demented," but it is clear from the actions and words of her parents, sisters, and brothers-in-law that the entire extended family (save Jacme Rodríguez) was guided by messianic longing, and that Sperança was repeating the wisdom received from her elders. One witness heard about the family's messianic dreams from Juan Pardo and his in-laws Rodrigo and Elionor,

---

[58] AHN: Inq., leg. 537, c. 1, no. 5, 215r–v (witness no. 2): "quant levaven lo cors de Jhesu Crist o sonaven la oracio de la Ave Maria que era peccat de dir ni fer oracio sino malahir als crestians, e aça fahien...com aquells fossen e visquessen com ha juheus."

[59] B. McGinn, *Antichrist: Two Thousand Years of the Human Fascination with Evil*, San Francisco, 1994, pp. 178–199; idem, *Visions of the End: Apocalyptic Traditions in the Middle Ages*, New York, 1979, pp. 168–173, 230–233, 256–258, 270–276, 323 n. 13. The charismatic Valencian Dominican Vicent Ferrer (d. 1419) had preached about the Antichrist.

[60] AHN: Inq., leg. 537, c. 1, no. 5, 298v–299r. Witness no. 13 recalls her question to Sperança: "'Per que feu les dites coses axi descubertament, no haveu temença de deu ni de les gents? Yo'm maravella com nostre senyor deu no'us tramet foch en les vostres cases.'" See Baer, *Die Juden*, 2: p. 443, for a transcription of Sperança's reply.

another from Angelina and Aldonça, and yet another from Elionor and all four daughters or from Elionor alone.[61]

The source of the "truth that the Messiah was born" was "letters…from Constantinople." Their author was probably Pedro Alfonso, though perhaps other Conversos or Jews had written and sent them to Valencia. The Messiah, Sperança informed one curious witness, was a youth living on a mountain near Constantinople, a mountain like that "on which our Lord God gave the law to Moses." He would reveal himself only to circumcised and righteous Jews; no one else could see him.[62]

Hence it was crucial for the Conversos to travel to Ottoman, or even Mamluk, lands and convert to Judaism. The defendants envisioned a formal conversion and Elionor and her daughters described the ceremonies involved. For the men circumcision was, of course, essential. The women would take a ritual bath, where they would pray (*fahien lo tafilla*); then their hair would be cut, as well as their fingernails and toenails until they bled. Finally, "'the Jewish rabbis would give a benediction to both the men and the women, just as the chaplains do for the Christians [when] they baptize them'." Converso couples, furthermore, would be remarried with Jewish rituals and unmarried Conversas, Sperança thrilled, would be given Jewish husbands.[63] Even

---

[61] AHN: Inq., leg. 537, c. 1, no. 5: 211r–v (witness no. 2), 278v–280r (witness no. 12), 289r–290r (witness no. 13), 293r–v (witness no. 13). On 183v the defense attorney characterizes Sperança as "mentis fatua et quasi demens."

[62] AHN: Inq., leg. 537, c. 1, no. 5, 287r–288r (witness no. 13); Baer, *Die Juden*, 2: pp. 443, for a transcription.

[63] AHN: Inq., leg. 537, c. 1, no. 5, 288v–290r (witness no. 13): "que los homens se feyen juheus en aquesta manera: ço es quells circuncien; e les dones se feyen juhies en aquesta manera: ço es que entraven en hun bany e's lavaven be e aqui les fahien lo tafilla, e en apres quant aço era fet les lançaven aygua freda damunt ses persones e tallaven les les ungles de les mans e dels peus fins que'n exia sanch, e axi mateix tallaven los cabells. E que en apres los juheus rabins donaven axi als homens com a les dones la benediccio, axi com fan los crestians com los capellans los bategen, e que fet aço feyen nou matrimoni entre aquells qui eren marit e muller com eren crestians. E per ço aquelles dites na Elionor, na Angelina, na Aldonça e na Gostança, per lo novell matrimoni que havien de fer ab los marits que huy tenen, e la dita Sperança, per lo marit novell que havia de haver, sen portaven camises listades, joyes, robes e molts altres ornaments e areus de llurs persones." Witness no. 2 heard the Cifuentes clan discussing how "les fadrines donzelles que passaven de aquesta terra a la dita terra del Turch les donaven marits juheus e que ab aquells havien molt de be e riquees" (211v).

Old Christians, Elionor assured one witness, could go to the Levant and convert to Judaism, or "turn to the good side," to save their souls.[64]

The defendants did not elaborate on what the Messiah would do, but it is clear that they believed that the messianic age and this tumultuous time preceding it would involve wealth and domestic splendor for the Jews and the Conversos who returned to Judaism in the Levant. The defendants' dreams of an Ottoman paradise, as described in witness testimonies, were gender-specific, largely because almost all of the witnesses who got an earful about them were Old and New Christian women who interacted with the women of the Cifuentes clan at home. The latter imagined that after emigration and conversion they would be honored by the Turks, wear garments of silk and gold, and relax on comfortable beds with silk sheets while their husbands served them.[65] In this ideal world, the social, religious, and gender orders would all be inverted. That Converso males harbored precisely the same hopes about the new age is doubtful. In any case, women and men were both sure that the return to Judaism in the Ottoman Levant would guarantee the salvation of their souls.

Converso emigration to the East was, I have suggested, a penitential movement in important respects. The defendants' contrition may well have been fed, rather paradoxically, by the heightened penitential spirituality permeating Valencian Christian society, evinced in its vital Beguin movement, the enthusiastic popular reception of the preachings of the charismatic Valencian Vicent Ferrer and like-minded friars, and the municipal government's promotion of a civic culture of penitence.[66] Just as the defendants, and Conversos elsewhere, appropriated the Christian notion that the Ottoman sultan was the Antichrist and

---

[64] AHN: Inq., leg. 537, c. 1, no. 5, 293v–294r (witness no. 13): "E per ço aquells qui's trobaren circuncisos en les terres e parts della, encara que sien crestians de natura, puix se tornen a la bona part que no haver sino molt de be e salvacio de llurs animes, e los altres que no poden haver de algu ni salvacio de llurs animes."

[65] AHN: Inq., leg. 537, c. 1, no. 5, 278v–279r. When witness no. 12 was discussing with Angelina and Aldonça other Conversas who had departed Valencia to return to Judaism in the Levant, the sisters explained to her "que anaven en aquelles parts per tornarse juhies, que anaven vestides d'or e de seda e quels eren feta molta d'onor e que aquelles se staven en lits de repos cuberts de seda e los marits de aquelles les servien." Witness no. 2 heard most of the Cifuentes family describing similar scenes of splendor for the women, though no mention was made (perhaps significantly) of husbands serving their wives (211r–v).

[66] L. Woods, "Honouring the Body and Blood of Christ: the Development of Civic Religion in Valencia, Spain, 1300–1450," Ph.D. dissertation: University of Toronto, 2007, sheds much light on the formation of a penitential culture among Valencian Christians;

modified it for their own Jewish purposes—in effect, denying Christ the final victory over the Turkish Antichrist who, instead, would usher in the Jewish messianic age—they were also probably swayed by the pervasive Christian discourse of sin, repentance, and salvation, even though, for them, repentance required escape from the very society whence this discourse emanated. By converting to Judaism in the Levant they could atone for the sin of having lived as Christians and achieve their redemption.

As the time for departure—and the messianic age—drew nearer, the practice of Christianity became more intolerable for them. Sperança told one witness many times that since she and her family observed the Jewish Sabbath, there was no need for them to go to church to hear Mass; moreover, if they heard Mass, they would be "excommunicated"—that is, condemned according to Jewish law, as they understood it—"inasmuch as they would be observing what Christians observe."[67] Aldonça seems to have been preparing for the inevitable with more rigorous observance of Jewish fasts. She cut her nails and otherwise "cleansed" or "purified her person" so that "our Lord God would acknowledge and accept her fast." When a Conversa witness joked with her about her fasts, Aldonça became offended and retorted, "'Since you are unclean (*trefana*), from here on I'm going to keep away from you'."[68] The defendants were intent on dissociating themselves as much as possible from Christian religious practice and Christian society, including New Christians who did not share their world—and end-of-world—view.

Aldonça and Angelina explained to one witness that once the Conversos were living in the East as Jews, the men would wear black robes as a symbol of mourning for all those Conversos who still had not emigrated to escape Christian impurity and save their souls. The

---

see also R. Narbona Vizcaíno, *Pueblo, poder y sexo: Valencia medieval (1306–1420)*, Valencia, 1992, pp. 79–98, regarding one facet of this development.

[67] AHN: Inq., leg. 537, c. 1, no. 5, 297r–v (witness no. 13): "car si entraven en la sglesia per hoyr missa que eren scomunicats per quant aquells servaven ço que los crestians serven."

[68] AHN: Inq., leg. 537, c. 1, no. 5, 274v–275v (witness no. 12): "Encara ha vist ella dita testimoni que la dita na Aldonça se tallava les ungles axi dels peus com de les mans e denegava [sic?—netegava] la sua persona." When the witness asked Aldonça to explain her actions, she answered, "que per quant aquella havia de degunar e nostre senyor deu prengues e acceptas lo seu deguni, se tallava les ungles e netegava sa persona, e lo dit deguni aquella havia a fer le endema seria dijous." Aldonça's response to the witness' joke about her Thursday fasts: "'Puix sou trefana, de aqui anant yo'm guardare de vos'."

Conversos' return to Judaism in the Levant was part of the ingathering of the exiled Jews that would occur in the messianic age. The defendants thus pondered their voyage to Ottoman lands with a sense of urgency, and, not surprisingly, they tried to persuade other Conversos to join them.[69] The sooner they left the better, and the more Conversos who followed their path the better. Conversos like the defendants believed that they were ensuring not only their personal salvation but also the redemption of the entire Jewish people, which could not occur until all the exiles had returned from their captivity in Christendom.

The much shorter record of a case—only 27 folios—tried just a few years after the prosecution of the Cifuentes clan, yields corroborative evidence as to the beliefs and behaviors of Conversos in post-1453 Valencia. The defendants, the hosier Jaume Tori and his wife Tolosana, were Judaizers who of course knew and performed the essential Catholic prayers and rituals. According to their former and probably Conversa maidservant Johana, the couple attempted, in the summer of 1465, to persuade her "to go with them to that land where the others have become Jews, for she would do very well there and they would make clothing of silk for her." The inquisitors assumed that the "land" in question was "Turkey."[70] Like members of the Cifuentes clan, Tori had at least one Jewish contact—a Jew named "Calatayu" who sewed stockings for him—and he knew about and could name other Conversos who had emigrated and returned to Judaism.[71] Yet Tori himself seems

---

[69] AHN: Inq., leg. 537, c. 1, no. 5, 279r–v (witness no. 12): "e aquells dits marits [of Conversas in the East] portaven les robes sobiranes de seda negra e lo davall les dites robes de brocat, e la dita roba de seda negra denotava e significava que aquells portaven dol per los qui no anaven en aquelles parts per ferse juheus, e que aquells tals qui's tornaven juheus salvaven llur anims." Angelina and Aldonça then tried to "induce" this same witness to travel to the Levant and convert to Judaism (279v–280r). See also A. Hillel Silver, *A History of Messianic Speculation in Israel: From the First through the Seventeenth Centuries*, Boston, 1959, pp. 117–130; and S. Regev, "The Attitude Towards the *Conversos* in 15th-16th Century Jewish Thought," *Revue des Études Juives* 156 (1997), pp. 122–128.

[70] AHN: Inq., leg. 538, c. 2, no. 42, 3r (1 July 1466): "E no res menys lo dit en Tori e sa muller induhien a ella testimoni be pot haver hun any que sen volgues anar ab aquells en aquella terra hon los altres se son tornats jueus, car li faria molt de be e li farien vestidures de seda." The inquisitors' subsequent interrogation of Tori on 12 July show that Turkey was the *terra* in question: "Fuit interrogatus si ell confessant hauria induhit a persona alguna que sen anas ab aquell en la Turquia o en altre part de infells per abnegar la fe" (5r–v). At 4r Tori displays his knowledge of some Catholic prayers and asserts that he confessed and took Communion.

[71] AHN: Inq., leg. 538, c. 2, no. 42, 13v–14r (15 June 1469): Tori maintains that he gave work to the Jew at the request of the Converso Manuel Bou, but that the Jew

never to have done much more than muse about returning to Judaism abroad, and he apparently was not gripped by the messianic excitement that seized the likes of Pedro Alfonso and Juan Pardo. The ongoing inquisitorial investigation must have dampened his enthusiasm, such that in 1469 he could voice the opinion shared by other Conversos who had to stay and survive in Valencia: the flight of "some" Conversos to become Jews in the East has "in this land [Valencia]" resulted in "much denigration to the reputation of the Conversos."[72] Jaume and Tolosana abjured their errors and escaped with only a light penance. They would not be so lucky when the tougher Spanish Inquisition came to town in 1482 and discovered that they had since reverted to their Jewish ways.[73]

The investigations of the Spanish Inquisition also revealed that a strain of messianism, and a concomitant desire to emigrate, persisted among Valencian Conversos during the years preceding the new institution's advent. Yet in light of the masses of evidence that the inquisitors gathered on the Conversos' Jewish beliefs and practices, messianism motivated only a minority of Valencia's Judaizers. One such Converso was Alfonso, the brother of Angelina, the wife of Berthomeu de Leo. At the age of seventeen he traveled to the Levant, reverting to Judaism in Jerusalem circa 1472. Later, dressed as a Jew, he visited his sister in Valencia and gave her a black stone from the Temple in Jerusalem.[74] Another apparently messianic Converso was the linen merchant Jaume Ferrer. Desiring penitence, he allegedly said many times, "that the Conversos were in captivity for their sins...deeming the said Conversos, for living among Christians, to be in captivity like the Jews." But despite his wearing of *zizit* (a fringed garment; see Numbers 15: 38), his study of Torah with a Jew, and having circumcised his own son, he was not a Jew and was thus, to his own mind, irredeemable.

---

neither ate nor slept in his house. In his earlier confession, on 12 July 1466, he spoke of the Conversos who had left to return to Judaism: "dix que...li han dit que en Bernat de Proxita e hun castellan qui stava al mercat e Dalmau se eren tornats jueus e aço ha hoyt dir una e moltes vegades" (4v).

[72] AHN: Inq., leg. 538, c. 2, no. 42, 15r: "dixit que alguns que son anats a fer e tornarse juheus han salpiscat e jaquit en aquesta terra molta denigracio a la fama dels conversors [sic]."

[73] AHN: Inq., leg. 538, c. 2, no. 42, 26r–27r (1 July 1469) for the sentence of Jaume Tori and Tolosana. García Cárcel, *Orígenes*, p. 299, records that the Spanish Inquisition condemned them to death in 1493 and 1504, respectively.

[74] AHN: Inq., leg. 541, c. 1, no. 8, 26r–v, 28v (1484–85); Meyerson, *Jewish Renaissance*, p. 201.

His solution, then, "in order better to perform...Jewish ceremonies" was "to go to Constantinople to become a Jew, saying that he had a paternal cousin in Constantinople, a rich Jew, who had written to him that he should go there."[75]

If the messianic excitement that the Ottoman conquest of Constantinople had sparked among Valencian Conversos gradually diminished over the years, it was certainly rekindled by the Spanish Inquisition's extensive prosecution and punishment of Judaizers and by the expulsion of the Jews in 1492.[76] Again, serious hopes for the coming of the Jewish Messiah cannot be said to have been entertained by a majority of Valencian Conversos. Still, the records of the 1500 trial of Joan Liminyana, a Converso apothecary from Oriola (Orihuela) who had moved to Valencia in 1498 shortly after abjuring his Jewish beliefs before the inquisitorial tribunal in Murcia, show that a sizeable minority of Judaizers in Valencia and Oriola was enthusiastically discussing "prophesies" concerning the Jewish Messiah's advent and even emigrating to Naples, in order to practice Judaism more safely, or to Constantinople, in order to return to Judaism completely.[77]

Liminyana himself, after his arrival in Valencia, quickly became associated with the circle of Judaizers headed by Miquel Vives and his mother Castellana. The latter described her son Miquel as a "second Abraham" for knowing so much about the "law of Moses" without having received formal instruction, and herself as another "Queen Esther" for her leadership. Miquel used the Book of Psalms to demonstrate to Liminyana that the Messiah had not yet come and that God was going "to redeem the people of Israel." Clearly Liminyana and the Vives, as well as many of the other Conversos with whom Liminyana pon-

---

[75] AHN: Inq., leg. 539, c. 1, no. 8 (1486) records the sentence of Ferrer condemning him to be "relaxed" to the secular arm. Ferrer allegedly said many times "que los confessos per sos peccats estaven en captivitat y que deu se recordaria de la captivitat dells, tenint los dits confessos per star entre cristians esser en captivitat com los jueus" (104r). "E lo pigor es per fer millor a son plaer les dites çerimonies judayques, tenia deliberat de anarsen a Constantinoble per tornarse jueu, dient que tenia un cosin jerma en Constantinoble, jueu, molt rich, el qual li havia escrit que anas alla" (105r).

[76] Tishby, "Apocalyptic Messianism"; Idel, *Messianic Mystics*, pp. 132–140; Carrete Parrondo, "Messianismo/Sionismo," pp. 484–488; Beinart, "Prophetess Inés"; and R. Levine Melammed, *Heretics or Daughters of Israel? The Crypto-Jewish Women of Castile*, New York, 1999, pp. 45–72.

[77] AHN: Inq., leg. 541, c. 1, no. 10 (24 March 1500). This case file contains the extensive confessions of Liminyana regarding his dealings and discussions with many Conversos in Valencia. He was "relaxed" to the secular arm for execution in 1503 (García Cárcel, *Orígenes*, p. 271).

dered the messianic "prophecies," regarded themselves as part of this "people."[78] Thus Liminyana admonished the daughters of the Converso Gabriel Vives not to become romantically involved with or to marry Old-Christian suitors, "because if they married Old Christians (*crestians de natura*), their mixing their blood with those who are contrary to His law would much displease our Lord God."[79] Like the Cifuentes family, Liminyana and his fellows perceived those who did not have Jewish blood—and probably those Conversos who did not share their Jewish beliefs—as impure and inimical to God. Witnessing both the Inquisition's condemnation and punishment of judaizing Conversos and the expulsion of the Jews heightened their sense that they and the Jews shared not only the same blood and belief but also the same destiny and ultimate redemption through God and His Messiah.

Jews and Conversos, as discussed above, had interpreted the fall of Constantinople to the Turks as part of the upheaval that would precede the Messiah's coming. Yet they were not the main players in the dramatic events of 1453, merely interested observers of this clash of Christian and Muslim civilizations. With the Spanish Inquisition's offensive against the Judaizers and the 1492 expulsion, however, Conversos and Jews viewed themselves as the principal sufferers of the tribulations that would usher in the messianic age and, as Valencian Conversos put it, their eternal bliss (*benaventurança*). Psalm 44, with its description of the Jews' hardships and hopes for divine redemption, proved to be crucial for how Liminyana and his fellows understood the current afflictions of their people. While reading "some Psalms of

---

[78] AHN: Inq., leg. 541, c. 1, no. 10, 1v (25 March 1500), where Liminyana describes the preaching of Miquel Vives: "E lo dit Vives tambe li mostra alguns salms del saltiri en los quals li donava a entendre a ell confessant lo sobredit que deu havia encara a redemir la pobla de Yrael [sic], entenent el confessant que haun tenia de venir lo mesies de lo qual demana misericordia." At 29r, Liminyana recounts Castellana's description of herself and her son. For more on the Vives family and its circle, see Garcia, *Els Vives*, pp. 83–211.

[79] AHN: Inq., leg. 541, c. 1, no. 10, 33r–v (15 May 1500): Liminyana describes how he "parla ab les dites donzelles dient lis que elles devian guardar sa castedad e virginitat pera que poguessen casar e deven molt pensar com era molt odios a nostre senyor deu que los seus mesclassen sa sanch ab los qui heren de altra condicio, ço es crestians de natura, specialment sens matrimoni, e que guardant sa virginitat elles se porien casar ab persones que fossen de sa condicio que fossen conversos e no crestians de natura, per que si se casavan ab crestians de natura desplauria molt a nostre senyor deu per mesclar sa sanc ab sos contrariis en la sua ley." On the growing anxiety about blood and lineage, see D. Nirenberg, "Mass Conversion and Genealogical Mentalities: Jews and Christians in Fifteenth-Century Spain," *Past and Present* 174 (2002), pp. 3–41.

the Psalter" to several Conversas, "he [Liminyana] showed them that Psalm 44, making the said women understand that in that Psalm all the tribulations of the Conversos are included." He also cited it when explaining to two Conversos why they should emigrate to Naples: "there...they could rest their heads, away from the danger of the Inquisition and from being like sheep for the slaughterer, just as that Psalm of the Psalter, namely 44, says [specifically at ll. 23–24]."[80]

If inquisitorial persecution were not enough, the expulsion of the Jews convinced Conversos that "this time is approaching that our Lord promised us." The Converso dyer Rafael Simó—a "great *biblista*," according to Liminyana—elaborated: "'Consider the expulsion of the Jews from Spain and with how much loyalty and steadfastness they [the Jews] have wished to die at sea in order to go to serve God...and we see the road that they take for our salvation.'"[81]

Of course, not all of Spain's Jews had chosen the path of exile; some had remained and received baptism. Some of these *tornadizos*, as Liminyana referred to them, had settled down in Valencia. Despite what Liminyana's label *tornadizo*, or "turncoat," implied, these newly baptized Jews only strengthened the conviction of other Conversos that their adherence to Judaism would ensure the coming of the Jewish Messiah. Thus, just as Miquel Vives assured his followers that if they maintained their covenant with God and observed His Commandments and Sabbath, God would send them the Messiah, so Master Franco, the

---

[80] AHN: Inq., leg. 541, c. 1, no. 10, 12r (31 March 1500): "e algunes voltes a les dites dones [the sister and daughters of Miquel Maurrana] el confessant lis mostra alguns salms del saltiri entre les quals lis mostra aquell salm de quaranta quatre, donant les ha entendre a les dites dones que en aquell salm se comprenian totes les sues tribulacions dels convessos en que estaven e que encara tenien de haver moltes mes tribulacions, e per ço desigava de esser fora desta terra." His discussions of Psalm 44 with a relative surnamed Boyl and the Converso Francesc Cases: "E que ja alla en Napols tendrian son cap reposat fora de perill de la Inquisicio e de estar com a ovelles al degollador segons diu aquell salm del saltiri ques lo quaranta quatre" (16r). In their discussions of Psalm 44, Liminyana and other Conversos were drawing on a long-established Sephardic tradition. See J. Hacker, "'If We Have Forgotten the Name of Our God' (Psalm 44: 21): Interpretation in Light of the Realities in Medieval Spain," *Zion* 57: 3 (1992), pp. 247–274 [in Hebrew], especially pp. 268–272 for interpretations of the psalm in relation to rabbinical views of the Conversos, both positive and negative.

[81] AHN: Inq., leg. 541, c. 1, no. 10, 29r–v (14 May 1500): "les dix moltes paraules lo dit Rafael Simo en favor de la ley de Moyses, dient que moltes coses [hole] veyem clarament per hont conexiam que aquest temps [hole] se apronpicava del que nostre Senyor nos havia promes e dient 'mirau, si'us pensarra lo desterro dels jueus de Spanya e ab quanta costancia e fermetat han volgut morir en les mars per anar a servir a deu...e vehem lo cami que lleven pera la bonaventurança nostra'."

tornadizo silversmith, discussed with Liminyana and other Conversos "some signs and prophecies…and all this that they were teaching was considered to be in favor of the Old Law, and it seemed to the confessant [Liminyana] that everyone [there] desired the coming of the Messiah."[82]

In the minds of these Conversos, such prognostications of the Messiah's advent were validated by the conflict and calamity Spain was currently experiencing. They spoke specifically, and expectantly, of Spain's wars with France and of the Muslim rebellions in the recently conquered sultanate of Granada. Spain, the Conversos felt, was getting its just deserts (though its defeat of France in Italy and its suppression of the Muslim revolt would later prove otherwise). Interpreting recent history for a group of Conversos to whom he was reading the Bible, Liminyana compared King Fernando to King David. He asserted that if God condemned the people of Israel for the sin that King David had committed with the wife of Uriah, then "it would not be a surprise that for the merits of the king [Fernando] in persecuting this generation of Conversos, Spain would experience great conflicts, for he [Liminyana] had always heard it said that our Lord God will take revenge on all those peoples who have persecuted this generation."[83]

Liminyana and like-minded Conversos were as unclear about the form that this divine vengeance would take as they were about the precise time and place of the Jewish Messiah's coming. Still, they believed—as had the Cifuentes clan—that Ottoman victories over

---

[82] AHN: Inq., leg. 541, c. 1, no. 10, 19v, 30r for the encouraging words of Miquel Vives. At 30v Liminyana describes how in the presence of "mestre Franco, argenter tornadizo" and three other Conversos he "comença a praticar e pratica de aquestes juhins e profecies, e lo dit mestre Franco dix alguns juhins e profecies e que tot aço que praticavan se sguardava en favor de la ley vella e que segons el parer del confessant tots desigaven el adveniment del mesies." In another Converso gathering at which Liminyana and another unnamed *tornadizo* were present, they all discussed "coses de Constantinoble e de com estaven alla be los jueus e altres coses en favor de la ley dels jueus" (27v). According to Liminyana, this discussion prompted some sixteen Conversos, whose names are listed, to attempt to return to Judaism in Constantinople, although apparently some of them traveled only as far as Naples.

[83] AHN: Inq., leg. 541, c. 1, no. 10, 11v (31 March 1500), where Liminyana discusses the significance of "les guerres de França y'ls moros com se son llevats." At 35v–36r, it becomes clear that he was referring to the Muslim revolt in "les Alpuxarres." He then continued, "que havia oyt dir que per lo peccat que lo rey David havia fet ab la muller de Ories comdepna lo poble e que no seria maravella que per los merits del rey [Fernando] per perseguir aquesta generacio dels convesos rebes Spanya grans encontres, que tots temps havia oyt dir ell confessant que tots los pobles que havian perseguir aquesta generacio que nostre Senyor ne havia pres vengança."

Christendom were somehow part of the divine plan for the redemption of the people of Israel. Liminyana recounted how three Conversos went to Valencia's commercial exchange (the *Lonja*) "seeking news of the Turk." They said "that Venice and Rome had to be destroyed [by the Turks] and that thus the salvation of this people [Jews and Judaizers] had to come."[84]

Even if the Turks did not succeed in destroying the capitals of Christian Europe to set the stage for the Messiah's coming, the Conversos were sure that the Turks were welcoming Jewish and Converso immigrants. They could wait for the Messiah—perhaps until the afterlife—but they could not wait to escape Spain and return to Judaism. Indeed, as suggested above, they probably saw the latter as a process inextricably bound up with the former. Therefore Liminyana argued with other Conversos that they could not simply sit passively in Spain until God delivered them from captivity; they had to do their utmost to emigrate so that they could practice Judaism and properly serve God. When Francesc Coscolla and his wife responded to Liminyana's impromptu preaching with the contention "that they were not obligated to leave this land [Spain]" because God, having put the Jews in captivity, "had promised to gather them in from the four parts of the world and grant them eternal bliss," Liminyana would have none of it. He countered:

> You are much deceived in this, because you know that our fathers and mothers were not put in this land [Spain] as Christians but were forcibly made Christians and against their will, and we are thus like a Christian in a Muslim country who is made a Muslim by force. Consider this: such a one [the converted Christian] is indeed obligated to leave the Muslim country in any way that he can and to put himself in danger of death in order to serve his God. Therefore we are required to go, in whatever way we can, to seek a place or localities where we can serve God and keep the Sabbaths and His Commandments as He commands.[85]

---

[84] AHN: Inq., leg. 541, c. 1, no. 10, 30v (14 May 1500): "Castell lo berreter e Miquel Sánchez corredor e hun son companyo anaven per la longa fent correts e buscant juhis parlaven noves del Turch que si noves hi ha en la longa entre ells se trobaven, dient que havia de ser destruyda Venecia e Roma e que axi havia de venir la benaventurança de aquest poble."

[85] AHN: Inq., leg. 541, c. 1, no. 10, 32r (15 May 1500): "que havian [the Coscollas] oyt dir que puix deu los havia posat en cativeri, quel havia promes de replegar los de las quatre parts del mon e donar lis la benaventurança...que no eran obligats de exir de aquesta terra fins que deu los replegas puix los havia promes. Y el confessant [Liminyana] respos: 'molt vos enganau en aço per que sabeu que nostres pares e mares no foren llançats en aquesta terra cristians, que hans se son tornats cristians forçadament e contra lur voluntat, e som axi com hun cristia que en terra de moros se torna moro

For Liminyana, forced conversion had created new circumstances and placed new demands on the converted and their descendants, especially when the End Days seemed to be approaching. Conversos were not quite the same as the Jews whom God had scattered in the Diaspora, however much they identified with them. Their secret, inner longing for and adherence to Judaism were no longer enough. A more active and perilous penitential return to Judaism and the open practice of it were essential for ushering in the messianic age and the redemption of Israel. Forcibly baptized Jews should no more deny their true religious allegiance than should Christian captives coerced to embrace Islam in Muslim lands. The battle lines in the Mediterranean were now clearly drawn between Muslim forces, headed by the Ottoman Turks, and Christendom, represented by the Catholic Monarchs, Isabel of Castile and Fernando of Aragon. Conversos had to take their place among the Jews. The Spanish Inquisition's persecution of Judaizers and the Catholic Monarchs' expulsion of the Jews from Spain were additional signs and prods in the process initiated by the Ottoman Turks in 1453: the movement of Conversos eastward to return to Judaism and await the Messiah.

The 1464 trial of the Cifuentes clan does not lend itself to drawing radical conclusions about fifteenth-century Converso experience. That the Ottoman conquest of Constantinople in 1453 excited a segment of Valencia's large Converso community there can be no doubt. If the inquisitorial prosecutors were not exaggerating in their claim that seventy Converso households, out of a Converso population of some 3,000, had left Valencia to return to Judaism in Valona—which would amount to around ten percent of the Converso community—then one may legitimately speak of a 'messianic movement' among the Conversos of Valencia, a movement in which the Cifuentes clan was swept up. Whether adult voluntary converts of non-Valencian origin, like Rodrigo Cifuentes and Juan Pardo, were typical of the Conversos moved by messianism is difficult to say, though one can imagine that their penitential anxiety was higher than that of second- and third-generation Conversos. Also, and just as importantly, the trial record

per força; mirau aquest: tal si es obligat exir de terra de moros en totes maneres que puga e metres al perill de la mort per servir a son deu, axi nosaltres som obligats a anar en qualsevol manera que puxam a cerquar loch o habitacions ont puxam servir a deu e guardar los dissaptes e los seus manaments com ell mana', les quals coses playan molt als dits Coscolla."

reveals a broad spectrum of Converso religious belief and practice, and a fluidity of relations among Conversos, Jews, and Old Christians often ignored by historians of fifteenth-century Spain. One finds Old Christians viewing the Jewish practices of Conversos with minimal concern or animosity, assimilating Conversos mocking Judaizers for their different observances and messianic notions, Old-Christian women following their Converso husbands to the Levant, Conversos mingling freely and easily with Jews in a city without a Jewish community, and so on. So much was possible, and without much explosive religious conflict. Within twenty years of this 1464 trial the Spanish Inquisition was operating in Valencia and relative fluidity was giving way to rigidity; in 1492 the Jews were expelled from Spain. More upheaval, more anxiety, more hope for the Messiah's coming, and more reason for the judaizing Conversos whom the Spanish Inquisition had not arrested to go abroad. As civilizations clashed and messianic prophecies circulated, Conversos like Joan Liminyana became ever more convinced that they must live among Jews and as Jews. Truly Jewish Conversos could no longer reside, after 1492, in a Spain without Jews. The Ottoman sultan and the Catholic Monarchs had made religious ambiguity an impossibility, and God and His Messiah required more of the Conversos than dissimulation.

CHAPTER THREE

"IF THERE WERE GOD":
THE PROBLEM OF UNBELIEF IN THE *VISIÓN DELEYTABLE*

Luis M. Girón-Negrón*

Several years ago, Benjamin Richler and Malachi Beit-Arié, from the Hebrew University of Jerusalem, made public a Hispano-Jewish manuscript which they had discovered in the Biblioteca Palatina in Parma (Ms. 2.666): a codex of great interest for students of the medieval philosophical tradition in Spain.[1] This manuscript dates from the fifteenth century (its filigree work places it between 1457 and 1477, and what may be a colophon at folio 137v gives the date of February 1, 1468). The codex contains a handful of Castilian texts transcribed into Hebraic *aljamía*, of which the following are of particular interest:

- Two Spanish-Hebrew/Hebrew-Spanish vocabulary lists of philosophical terms (together with a third Hebrew-Spanish dictionary of philosophical terms taken from Maimonides's *Millot ha-Higgayon*);
- A new version of *La Danza de la Muerte* (at present being studied and edited by María Morrás and Michelle Hamilton);
- A collection of *Proverbs* attributed to Seneca;
- A Hispano-Jewish poem;
- A short fragment—barely the index—of an *ars memoriae*; and, the subject of our present interest,
- An almost complete version of the *Visión deleytable*: the great "Maimonidean cento" composed by Alfonso de la Torre.[2]

---

* Translated by Nicola Stapleton.

[1] See María Morrás and Michelle Hamilton, "Un nuevo testimonio de la 'Danza de la muerte': hacia la version primitive," in *Actas del VIII Congreso Internacional de la AHLM (1999)*, Margarita Freixas and Silvia Iriso eds., Santander, 1, pp. 1341–1352, for the story of its discovery (esp. Pp. 1342–1343). Description of the contents of the manuscript in Malachi Beit Arié and Benjamin Richler, *Hebrew Manuscripts in the Biblioteca Palatina in Parma: Catalogue*, Jerusalem, 2001, pp. 370–371, no. 1343. I consulted the manuscript *in situ* in March 2005.

[2] The text of the *Visión* fills folios 1r–96v, corresponding to pages 104–294 in the Jorge García López edition of 1991, but it includes neither the prologue nor the final

This *aljamía* version of the *Visión deleytable* is a valuable addition to the fifteen fifteenth-century manuscripts (one of which, in Catalan, was discovered only a few years ago),[3] four incunabula and other early editions which bear witness to the work's extraordinary popularity and widespread dissemination in late medieval Spain.[4] It is a particularly revealing discovery in the light of what we already know about this fifteenth-century encyclopaedia of religious philosophy.

Composed probably towards the middle of the fifteenth century, the *Visión deleytable* is the most important work written by the phi-

---

chapters. See Beit-Arié and Benjamin Richler, *Hebrew Manuscripts*, pp. 370–371 and Morrás and Hamilton, "Un nuevo testimonio," pp. 1342–1343 for a complete list of the philosophical-didactic works it contains. Finally, the Hispano-Jewish poem has been edited and translated by John Zemke; cf. "In Memoriam Charles Cook, Mentor of Samuel G. Armistead" in *Spain's Multicultural Legacies. Studies in Honor of Samuel G. Armistead*, eds. Adrienne L. Martin and Cristina Martinez-Carazo, Delaware, 2008, pp. 333-347.

[3] Cf. Gemma Avenoza, "El manuscrito catalán de la Visión deleitable: un códice recuperado," in *Actes del VII Congrés de l'Associació Hispànica de Literatura Medieval*, Castelló, 1999. My 2001 book had already gone to press when I became aware of this reference.

[4] In the prologue to his critical edition of the *Visión* (vol. 1, pp. 11–96), García López describes the manuscripts, incunabula and early editions of the work. A summary of this, updated, is found in his article about Alfonso de la Torre for the extensive philological dictionary of Castilian medieval literature edited by Alvar and Lucía Megías. See Jorge García López, "Alfonso de la Torre, *Visión deleytable*," in *Diccionario filológico de literatura medieval española. Textos y transmisión*, eds. Carlos Alvar and José Manuel Lucía Megías, Madrid, 2002, pp. 128-133. Salinas Espinosa and I also briefly examine the history of the work's various manuscripts and editions, with additional information and clarifications. See Concepción Salinas Espinosa, *Poesía y prosa didáctica en el siglo XV: la obra del bachiller Alfonso de la Torre*, Zaragoza, 1997, pp. 176–183; and Luis M. Girón Negrón, *Alfonso de la Torre's 'Visión deleytable': Philosophical Rationalism and the Religious Imagination in 15th Century Spain*, Leiden, 2001. I would like to make use of this footnote to put right an incorrect piece of information about editions of the work which all three of us have included in our respective studies. Contrary to what García López (1: p. 32), Salinas Espinosa (p. 158) and I (p. 213) have stated, the Jewish Theological Seminary in New York does hold a copy of the important Ferrara edition of 1554 prepared by Abraham Usque (cf. Yosef Hayim Yerushalmi and José V. Pina Martins eds., *Consolação às Tribulações de Israel. Ediçao de Ferrara, 1553*. 2 vols. Lisbon, 1989: 1: pp. 120–121; Herman Prins Salomon, *Deux etudes portugaises = Two Portuguese Studies*, Braga, 1991, pp. 57–61). Salinas Espinosa and I took our information from García López, who in turn followed information supplied by Vicente Salvà (*Catalogue of Library of Vicente Salvá*, 1872: no. 2435) that no surviving copy of the said edition existed. Recently, García López ("Alfonso de la Torre," p. 132) has rectified this oversight, including the copy in a new list of surviving printed versions, although he does not state its whereabouts in New York. I am greatly indebted to Dr. Herman Salomon who wrote to me personally to draw my attention to this omission.

losopher and poet Alfonso de la Torre. According to the *incipit* in the introduction, the work was commissioned by Juan de Beamonte, royal chamberlain at the Navarran court of Prince Charles of Viana. It takes the form of an allegory and is written in a didactical prose of exquisite precision and even literary excellence. Its author—almost certainly a Converso—examines the fundamental concepts of the liberal arts and all the classic themes of pre-modern religious philosophy (particularly problems of metaphysics, physics and moral philosophy). To do this, he selects from Jewish, Christian, Islamic and Greek sources, and brings them together within a rationalist framework of Maimonidean inspiration (the *Visión* is, amongst other things, a mosaic of diverse passages taken from the *Moreh ha-Nevukhim*—the center of gravity for Hispano-Jewish philosophy in the late Middle Ages). He takes his liberal arts from Isidore, but he uses Al-Ghazzali to teach logic; he demonstrates the existence of God with the help of Maimonides, but turns to Albertus Magnus to support his argument for the immortality of the soul. His cosmogony is also Maimonidean, but it is peppered with magical-astrological traditions of Kabbalistic flavor, inconsistent with the refined naturalism associated with the Córdoban philosopher. Most importantly, the rationalist vision of human perfectionism which he defends is rooted in the *Guide for the Perplexed*, but it is reached in roundabout fashion via Aristotle's *Nichomachean Ethics*, pausing en route at Aquinas' moral psychology and pseudo-Senecan gnomic literature.

This sober and comprehensive exposition of a rationalist *Weltanschauung* in Castilian established the pre-eminence of the Maimonidean tradition as a first-class philosophical source in fifteenth-century Christian Spain. In fact, it took the tradition further, both geographically and chronologically. Translated into Catalan and Italian, quoted in Hebrew sources (e.g. the *Shebet Yehudah*) and reprinted on numerous occasions, the *Visión* enjoyed widespread literary success both inside and outside Spain in the fifteenth, sixteenth and seventeenth centuries, becoming a veritable bestseller among Jews and Christians in the Peninsula, as well as Jews and Conversos living in the Sefardi Diaspora in Italy and the Low Countries.[5]

---

[5] The sources, content and success of the *Visión deleytable* are discussed at length in Girón Negrón, *Alfonso de la Torre's 'Visión Deleytable,'* with particular emphasis on how it was inspired by Maimonides. The work is also examined in detail in an all-embracing study of De la Torre's prose and poetry, Salinas Espinosa, *Poesía y prosa*

An exceptional number of medieval editions of the *Visión* have survived (a real *avalanche de richesse* when compared with the paucity of manuscripts of other pre-modern literary classics). Even so, the recently discovered Palatina version stands out from its fellows for various reasons. Firstly, it is the earliest unequivocal proof we have that this philosophical manual was being read in strictly Hispano-Jewish spheres. The fact that *aljamía* is used in this codex in effect confirms that, shortly after its composition, the *Visión* was already circulating in manuscripts aimed exclusively at Jews or Conversos (i.e. virtually the only people able to understand Spanish transcribed into the Hebrew alphabet). The manuscript fits within the cultural sociology of Spanish Jews who were beginning to affirm their emerging identity as an ethnic-religious minority by using *aljamía* to transcribe their literary output in Castilian, first in late medieval Christian Europe and then in the Sefardi Diaspora.[6] The other texts found alongside it suggest that this manuscript was almost certainly prepared for study purposes. The *Visión* comes complete with auxiliary tools to improve understanding and appreciation of its philosophical content. The *ars memoriae* which accompanies it, for instance, (of which only a fragment survives) would have facilitated study of the book by helping readers to memorise the text (this would support Concepción Salinas' thesis, which suggests that the attention paid to architectonic spaces in the allegorical framework of the *Visión* may also have served a mnemonic purpose).[7] The inclusion of a Spanish-Hebrew dictionary in this Judeo-Spanish manuscript also invites speculation about the kind of fifteenth-century student at whom it might have been aimed. In all likelihood, this would have been a Jew or Converso interested in studying Maimonides (or other Jewish thinkers),

---

didáctica, pp. 9–190—cf. our review in Girón Negrón, "Un avance crítico sobre *La Visión deleytable*," *La Corónica*, 28/2 (2000), pp. 169–178.

[6] Although writing about the Moriscos and their *aljamía* literature, Omar Hegyi's sociocultural observations and Vincent Barletta's important contributions are also relevant in the case of Spanish Jews. These contributions are inspired by cultural anthropology, new philology and performance theory. See Omar Hegyi, "Minority and Restricted Uses of the Arabic Alphabet: the Aljamía Literature," *Journal of the American Oriental Society*, 99/2 (1979), pp. 262–269; and by the same author, "Una variante islámica del español: la literatura aljamiada," *Homenaje a Álvaro Galmés de Fuentes*, Oviedo-Madrid, 1, pp. 647–655. See also Vincent Barletta and María Palmar Álvarez Blanco, "'El nacimiento del Profeta': textualidad y performance entre los moriscos aragoneses," *SIGNO. Revista de historia de la cultura escrita*, 12 (2003), pp. 7–30; and Vincent Barletta, *Covert Gestures: Crypto-Islamic Literature as Cultural Practice in Early Modern Spain*, Minneapolis, 2005.

[7] Concepción Salinas Espinosa, *Poesía y prosa didáctica*, pp. 157–176.

but prevented from doing so, either because of the intrinsic difficulty of philosophical Hebrew or because of insufficient knowledge of the sacred language. Unable to understand the original Hebrew (let alone Judeo-Arabic) sources, he would have acquired not only the *Visión* in Castilian, but also other texts which might allow him more direct access to Hebrew philosophical literature. But what might our student have gained from a manual of philosophy like the *Visión deleytable?* What interests or concerns might have been addressed by studying this work? This is not the place to examine in depth the intellectual directives which gave rise to its conceptualisation, or the multiple purposes which it served. Let us limit ourselves instead to a few broad observations based on a specific passage from the *Visión*, a section which tackles an uniquely nettlesome issue for medieval philosophers with an unprecedented explicitness and more than a tinge of unease. It is the question of religious unbelief.

According to Jacques Le Goff, in medieval Christian Europe, openly professing unbelief was a phenomenon which was, if not non-existent, then certainly insignificant (at least until the thirteenth century and even up to the dawn of Modernity).[8] In the case of Spanish literature, it is no easy task to glean examples of pre-fourteenth-century authors or works which openly cast doubt on the certainties of collective faith, much less deny it altogether. It is, for example, quite startling to come across Ibn al-Muqaffa's prologue to his translation into Arabic of *Kalilah wa-Dimnah*, which has been expurgated or falsified in some medieval translations—though not in the Alphonsine version in Spanish—and to note the lack of religious enthusiasm of the semi-Islamised Mazdeite who confesses his inability to be fully convinced by any of the religious laws or confessional creeds:

> And I decided to give the benefit of the doubt to the sages of each Law and their beliefs, and see what they would say that could help me tell apart truth from falsehood, and select and give credence to one over the other; and, once I had learned the truth, to devote myself to it completely, and not believe what contradicted it, nor pursue that which I did not understand. And I did this, and asked questions, and pondered, and found no-one who could tell me anything more than that I should praise him and his law and insult someone else's. And I clearly saw that they sought after what was pleasing to them and that they were working for what pleased them rather than for what was right. And in none of them

---

[8] Jacques Le Goff ed., *The Medieval World.* Trans. Lydia Cochrane, London, p. 3.

did I find a reason which was either true or right, nor any that a wise man would believe and that a wise man would not refute with reason. And after seeing this, I could find no way to follow any of them. And I knew that, if I believed that which I did not know, I should be like the cheated thief who talks in the tale.[9]

However, despite Le Goff's assertions, literary treatment of radical unbelief did begin to take root in pre-modern Spain, and it did so within a contemporary intellectual tradition which was deeply rooted in the Peninsula: the rationalist philosophical tradition of the Muslim and Jewish Aristotelians. The Arabised Aristotle, whose Latin translations gave rise to Christian Scholasticism across the Pyrenees, was the immediate stimulus for an intellectual earthquake which brought to the fore the thornier implications of Greek science for medieval religious faith: the pre-modern debates about such dilemmas as the nature of divine Providence, the immortality of the soul or eternity versus the creation of the world. In some cases, these debates culminated in the great conciliatory efforts of a Thomas Aquinas or a Maimonides. In others, such attempts at synthesis were harshly disputed (and even condemned): e.g. the famous list of 219 heterodox Aristotelian propositions (in particular those deemed Averroistic) denounced in 1277 by the Parisian bishop Etienne Tempier.[10] As Francisco Márquez Villanueva argues, the most radical interpretations of the Aristotelian corpus were even crystallised in sceptical or anguished postures, many deeply rooted in popular lore, such as deploring how we "are born and die

---

[9] "Et tove por bien otorgar a los sabios de cada una ley sus començamientos et ver qué dirían por razón de saber la verdat de la mentira, et escoger et anparar la una de la otra; et conosçida la verdat, obligarme a ella verdaderamente, et non creer lo que non cunpliese, et nin seguir lo que non entendiese. Et fize esto, et pregunté, et pensé, et non fallé ninguno dellos que me di[x]ese más que alabar a sí et a su ley et denostar al agena. Et vi manifiestamente que se enclinavan a sus sabores et que por su sabor trabajavan et non por el derecho. Et nin fallé en ninguna dellas razón que fuese verdadera nin derecha, nin tal que la creyese omne entendido et non la contradixiese con razón. Et después que esto vi, non fallé carrera por donde siguiese a ninguno dellos. Et sope que, si yo creyese lo que non sopiese, que sería atal commo el ladrón engañado que fabla en un enxenplo." José Manuel Cacho Blecua and María Eugenia Lacarra eds., *Calila e Dimna*, Madrid, 1987, pp. 108–9. For more on the prologue containing this passage, see R. J. González Casanovas, "The Mirrors of Wisdom in the Prologues to *Calila e Dimna*: Reception Models from Bidpai to Alfonso X," *Romance Languages Annual*, eds. J. Beer and C. Ganelin, Purdue Research Foundation, 1993; and Fernando Gómez Redondo, *Historia de la prosa medieval castellana. I. La creación del discurso prosístico: el entramado cortesano*, Madrid, 1998, pp. 189–195.

[10] See Roland Hissette, *Enquête sur les 219 articles condamnés à Paris le 7 mars 1277*, Louvain, 1977.

like beasts."[11] Numerous heterodox assertions of this nature crop up in inquisitorial proceedings and are a recurring theme in Old Spanish literature, from the *Libro del cavallero Zifar* or the *Libro de buen amor* to the *Cancionero de Baena* and *La Celestina*. These assertions are sometimes praised, sometimes rejected and sometimes compared one with the other: the distinguished Hispanist links these assertions to a home-grown Averroism which, he claims, was singularly popular among Crypto-Jews and other Conversos in fifteenth-century Spain.

The *Visión deleytable* fully engages this philosophical-literary tradition. Within a Maimonidean framework, its author systematically collects, analyses and refutes the wide-ranging repertory of heterodox naturalist doctrines which fuelled the radical scepticism of their presumed readership. Nor does he limit himself to an abstract debate on the premises of unbelief, but rather brings out its human dimensions through his allegorical interlocutors. Maimonides, for example, gave a very precise description of his ideal student in the prologue to his philosophical guide: the observant but perplexed Jew, perturbed by the apparent incompatibility of the Torah with the naturalistic premises of Aristotelian science (the *ha'irin* o *nebukim* of the title beautifully expressed in Spanish as "desarrados" ("disoriented": lit. "in disarray") in a gloss to Pedro of Toledo's fifteenth-century translation).[12] Alfonso de la Torre also gives a voice to these poor "disoriented" people. He uses his allegorical student as a mouthpiece for the deeply-buried anxieties which inspire these philosophical debates, and which are shared by the disoriented; this mass of doubt and confusion which will be dispelled by

---

[11] Francisco Márquez Villanueva, "'Nasçer e morir como bestias' (criptojudaísmo y criptoaverroísmo)," in *Los judaizantes en España y la literatura castellana del Siglo de Oro*, ed. Fernando Díaz Esteban, Madrid, pp. 273–293.

[12] "It is true that '*More*' means 'Guide', but what he says about "turbados" (perturbed, perplexed) is not correct, for he translates another word which is used in Hebrew, *hanebochim*, as 'turbados', when in fact the Hebrew word *nebochim* means 'desarrados' (disoriented), and not as he has translated it, for the Hebrew for 'turbados' is *njbhalim* or *mebohaljm*; but this is only of temporary relevance, as we shall see later." ("Verdad que '*More*' lo que quiere dezir es 'mostrador,' mas non esto que dize delos turbados, que otro vocablo que dize en ebrayco *hanebochim*, aquel dize 'los turbados,' e aun enla verdad *nebochim* en ebrayco 'desarados' quiere dezir, non commo el lo traslado, que el ebrayco de 'turbados' es *njbhalim* o *mebohaljm*; mas esto pasadero es, segunt lo que tenemos en que entender adelante": Lazar 1989: 3, a). See Márquez Villanueva on the subject: "*La Celestina* y los 'desarrados,'" in *Siglos dorados. Homenage a Augustin Redondo*. 2 vols., Madrid, 2004, vol. 2: pp. 889–902. This debate concerns the first Spanish translation of Maimonides "Guide of the Perplexed," which in Spanish was rendered "Mostrador e enseñador de los turbados."

his wise tutors. The passage which best illustrates this is the immediate
prologue to De la Torre's lessons on metaphysics. When Intellect—his
alter ego—reaches the top of the sacred mountain and, accompanied by
Reason and Nature, enters the house of Wisdom, it is in the following
way that he expresses to his teachers the inner anguish which brought
him to her door:

> "You do not know how much joy is in my heart," said Intellect, "because
> we are surrounded by those who understand us." And with the tall maid-
> ens at his sides and all the wise men at his feet, Intellect spoke in this
> manner. "Do not think, by chance, ladies and gentlemen, that it is lack of
> sense and ignorance which have caused me to doubt man's purpose, or
> whether God exists in the world. Rather, you should think the opposite:
> for reasons of great importance have brought me to this position, and
> they are these: that I have reflected that, if there were God, as Reason
> has stated, then all things would be done well, both on high and down
> below, and yet we see the opposite: that the first confusion on earth was
> in the angel and in other intelligent beings; and of the stars and heavens
> we see that they do many bad things, for Saturn often corrupts the air and
> causes people to die, both the just and the unjust, yet if there were God,
> this would not happen, but rather he would preserve the good and slay
> the bad. Also, we see the sun dry up some regions with extreme heat, so
> much so that those lands become unpopulated and uninhabitable. When
> the elements combine, they often cause lightning, thunder and other
> storms, which destroy fruits and animals. Sometimes both the seas and
> the rivers rise and flood neighboring settlements, destroying houses of
> prayer along with all the other houses, and earthquakes bring down the
> house of the poor old holy woman. And we see the righteous shepherd
> praying while his sheep are being devoured by the wolf, yet if there were
> God, it would not have done this. And we see the just man giving alms
> and thereby becoming poor himself, yet good sense tells us, if there were
> God, he would have made him rich. And we have seen the holy man
> pray to God for the health of his children, and the children die, yet the
> opposite should happen. Of men it cannot be said that some complain to
> God about the injustices they receive, yet God never avenges them, but
> rather proceeds at once to do them more harm. These things and other
> similar occurrences have led me to this opinion, and I have said in my
> heart: surely, everything is uncertain and susceptible to change, and this
> plunges the world into disarray, and there is no other ruler or governor,
> and man was made for nothing other than to die, and after death there
> is nothing." And when he had said this, he spoke no more.[13]

---

[13] "No sabeys quánta alegría está en mi coraçón—dixo el Entendimiento—porque ay
alderredor quien nos entiende." E estando las donzellas altas en sus estados e todos los
sabios en torno a los pies suyos, el Entendimiento fabló en esta manera. "No por ventura

This extraordinary soliloquy has barely any precedents in pre-modern Ibero-Romance literature. Comparable perhaps to Metge's *Lo Somni*, it is the first rhetorical discourse on unbelief in the Spanish language, a litany of philosophical doubts, an *enumeratio* of absurdities, throughout which runs the anaphoric reiteration of the if-clause "si Dios ovyese" ("if there were God"), calling into question the existence of divinity. Unlike the utterance in the famous verse from El Cid (¡Dios, qué buen vasallo, sy ovyesse buen Señor!), Intellect's "ovyesse" is clearly conditional. There is no attempt to mitigate the doubts Intellect places before his interlocutors or to attenuate the seriousness of the matter. It is not—he tells us—"lack of sense and ignorance" which has brought him to ask these questions: "reasons of great importance have brought me to this position." His catalogue of "reasons" is a desolate description of tragedies, infinite variants of the same problem: Lactantius's *unde malum*. If there were order in the world and it were ruled over by a just and merciful God, "he would preserve the good and slay the bad." And yet, we are all exposed to the same avatars of fortune: we suffer the same mishaps, and are abandoned to the mercy of unforeseeable accidents, and to a blind, cruel, merciless nature which assails both

---

penséys, señoras e sennores, que synrazón e ynorançia me ha movida a dubdar del fin del omne e de aver Dios en el mundo, antes devéys pensar el contrario, ca grandes razones me han movido a aquesto, e son éstas: que yo he pensado que sy Dios oviese, como la Razón ha dicho, que serían todas las cosas bien fechas, asy en lo alto como en lo baxo, e veemos el contrario, que la primera desordenança del mundo a seydo en el ángel e en las otras ynteligençias; e de las estrellas e çielos veemos que fazen mucho mal, ca muchas vezes Saturno corronpe el ayre para que muera la gente, e tanbién los justos como los ynjustos, que sy Dios oviese non se devía fazer, ante guardaría los buenos e mataría los malos. Yten, veemos el sol desecar tanto unas regiones con destenplado calor, que despuebla aquella tierra e la faze ynabitable. En los elementos veemos muchas vezes por la comystura de aquéllos fazerse rayos, tronitus e otras tenpestades, las quales destruyen los frutos e los animales. A las vezes cresçen tanto las mares e los ríos que destruyen las poblaçiones çercanas, e tanbién se pierden las casas de oraçión como las otras, e fázense torromotos que derruecan la casa de la vieja santa e pobre. E ya veemos al pastor justo fazer oraçión e en tanto comerle el lobo las ovejas, que sy Dios oviera non lo oviera fecho. E ya veemos al justo fazer limosnas e fazerse pobre por aquello, como de buena razón, sy Dios oviera, lo oviera fecho rico. E ya vimos al omne santo rogar a Dios por la salud de los fijos e morírseles, lo que devyera ser lo contrario. En los omnes non cale dezir, que algunos se querellan a Dios de las synrazones que resçiben e nunca Dios les da vengança, antes de contyno les recresçe más daño. Estas cosas e otras semejables me traxieron en esta opinyón, e dixe en mi coraçón: çiertas, todo es caso ynçierto e ventura mudable, la qual trastorna las cosas, e non ha otro regidor nin governador, e el omne non se fizo synon para morirse, e después de la muerte non ay cosa alguna." E esto acabado de dezir fizo fyn." *Visión deleytable* 1,17—García López edition, vol. 1, pp. 153–4.

the righteous and the sinner indiscriminately. A river bursts its banks and destroys, we are told, "houses of prayer along with all the other houses"; an earthquake brings down "the house of the poor old holy woman"; the "righteous shepherd" in vain prays as the wolf devours his sheep; the air polluted by Saturn slays "both the just and the unjust"; the righteous man begs for alms; the "holy man" prays to God for the sake of his children, and yet they die. The overwhelming weight of evidence—evoked plainly and graphically with heartrending impressionism—drives the perplexed Intellect to his painful confession: "These things and other similar occurrences have led me to this opinion, and I have said in my heart: surely, everything is uncertain and susceptible to change, and this plunges the world into disarray, and there is no other ruler or governor, and man was made for nothing other than to die, and after death there is nothing."

There can be no doubt that this discourse has a didactic purpose. Intellect's questions provide a framework, in the form of a *disputatio*, for Wisdom's exposition about the two canonical themes of this philosophical tradition: on the one hand, the Aristotelian demonstration of the existence of God and the syllogistic derivation of His attributes—His unity, His incorporeality, His omnipotence and His goodness; on the other hand, the nature and *telos* of man and his position within the universe. These questions in turn connect with other classic problems, set out later on by Nature herself, which also play a part in the drama of theodicy. These include questions about nature and the order of the cosmos, the world as created or eternal, the importance of Providence, and, of course, the immortality of the soul. The enigma of the righteous who suffer in particular prepares the ground for the fervent defence of the Maimonidean theodicy set out in *Moreh ha-Nebukim* 3:12. De la Torre will argue, for instance, that suffering is inherent to the imperfection of matter here on earth, but that it is overcome by God's goodness and His creation, and the author systematically re-examines each of the accusations made by Intellect in his soliloquy:

> Now behold what kind of a thing man is with respect to the angels and all other created things. What happens to them, with regard to the whole universe, is what would happen to ants if they thought that all the world were made for them, the very presumption of which is absurd. And basing their beliefs on this false supposition, they attribute all things to themselves, saying that they are evil, and they believe that Saturn is evil because, in conjunction with other planets, he causes pestilence, and they

do not stop to consider that, in this ever-turning world, he has reigned for hundreds and thousands of years, and is the source of wisdom, truth, justice and peace, just as in their greatest exaltation, natural philosophers steeped in magic discover deeply buried, dormant secrets. And they believe fire to be evil because it burnt down the house of the holy woman, yet they do not consider the good that fire does in the world, for example lighting up the night, for some people live in parts of the earth where it is night for six months of the year, and they survive thanks to the light of the fire; and think what a benefit it is to you to constantly have fire to illuminate the nights, and to warm you when it is cold, and for cooking and roasting raw foods, and other countless things. And they also say that rain is evil because it ruined the tiles that the poor tiler had put out in the sun, yet they do not consider that the rains nourish vegetables, as well as the trees and other plants, and they cause the animals to exist, for without water there would be no springs, or rivers, or any life on earth. And they say that the air is evil because sometimes it is polluted or it is so strong that it uproots trees, and they do not consider that, without air, no animal could live and fire would suddenly consume all the sea and the earth. And if you say these things to the *voluntarios*, they reply that God could accomplish all these things without these obstacles, and they do not see that God did everything in the best possible way, in the most fitting order and present things in the best way he could. And neither air nor fire nor rain could discern whether the house, or the tree or the tile were of a rich or poor man, just or unjust…[14]

---

[14] "Pues vey tú qué cosa es el omne en respecto de los ángeles e de las otras cosas criadas. A ellos contesçe, en respecto de todo el universo, lo que contesçería a las formigas sy pensasen que toda la tierra era fecha por ellas, e esto escarnio es sólo presumirlo. E de aqueste yrróneo fundamento fecho, atribuyendo todas las cosas a sy, dizen que son malas, e consyderan que Saturno sea malo porque en alguna conjunçión cabsa pestilençia, e non consyderan cómo en el mundial rebolvimiento, él regnante por çentanales de años e millares, es cabsa de la sabieza, de la verdad, e de la justiçia e de la paz, cómo en su ensalçamiento alcançan los naturales mágicos amagados e muy ocultos secretos. E consideran qu'el fuego sea malo porque quemó la casa de la muger santa, e no consyderan los bienes que faze en el mundo, asy como el alumbramiento en las noches, ca ya ay tierra poblada donde seys meses del año es noche e biven con la lunbre del fuego, e a vosotros quánto benefiçio es el contynuo que del fuego resçebís en el alunbrar de las noches, e en el escalentar de los fríos, e en el cozer e asar de las cosas crudas, e otras cosas ynnumerables. E tanbién dizen que sea mala la pluvia porque desató las tejas que avía puestas al sol el tejero pobre, e non consyderan que las pluvias son causa del nodrir de los vegetales, asy como árboles e yerbas, e son cabsa del permanesçer de los animales, ca syn agua nin avría fuentes, nin ríos, nin sería poblada la tierra. E dizen que el ayre sea malo porque algunas vezes se corronpe o es tan rezio que derrueca los árboles e non consyderan cómo, sy no oviese ayre, non bevirían ningunos animales e súbita mente el fuego quemaría toda la mar e la tierra. E sy les dizes estas cosas a los voluntarios, dizen que Dios bien lo podría fazer syn estos ynconvinientes, e non veen que Dios lo fizo en la mejor manera que ser pudo, en la

The *Visión deleytable* reconceptualises Maimonidean philosophy as a *sensu latu* theodicy: a philosophical defence of God in the face of the terrifying option of unbelief. It is an important addition to the considerable body of fifteenth-century treatises which debate with obsessive insistency the reasoning of unbelievers from other philosophical-theological perspectives. And it does so with a fine sense of drama and great pedagogical skill. In other words Intellect's soliloquy in part has a merely didactic objective: it forms a prologue to the Maimonidean approach to which De la Torre subscribes. This does not, however, lessen the rhetorical power of his questions or mitigate the anxious uncertainties reverberating in each one. On the contrary, even though it was conceived to be refuted, we know that this deeply moving apology *pro incredulitam suam* made a number of its readers extremely uncomfortable. The soliloquy appears in its entirety in the *aljamía* version found at Parma (ms. 2666, fols. 26v–27v), but the Seville edition of the *Visión* prepared by Jacobo Cromberger en 1526,[15] an edition based in turn on Fadrique of Basle's already corrupted incunabulum (Burgos 1485),[16] omits it completely. García López, the great modern editor of the *Visión deleytable*, noted this curious lacuna.[17] In his critical edition, he suggests that the folio containing the soliloquy may already have been missing from Fadrique of Basle's incunabulum. At the same time he accepts that it might have been a deliberate omission by a careless editor who considered it to be "a pointless scene within a strict economical narrative." In effect, its absence does not strike us as accidental. But nor do we believe that it was simply an act of stylistic pruning. Any discerning reader could quite easily grasp what lay beneath the surface: namely, the rhetorical plausibility which the author confers on a cast-iron scepticism, in particular for a reader unconvinced or unimpressed by De la Torre's philosophical refutation of the soliloquy. We should not be surprised that, by 1526, with the Inquisition firmly in place, the passage was expurgated due to religious scruples: a deliberate act of editorial censure. We need only recall that, in 1525, barely a year before the first Sevillian edition of the *Visión* appeared, Álvaro de Montalbán, the

---

orden más convenible e en la mayor perfecçión que las cosas resçebir sabrán e podrán. E non puede ser ayre, nin fuego, nin pluvia que diçernyese si la casa, o el árbol o la teja, sy era de omne pobre o rico o bueno o malo..." *Visión deleytable* 1,23—García López edition, vol. 1, pp. 169–171.

[15] See a description of this in *Visión deleytable*, García López ed., vol. 1, pp. 31–2.

[16] Cf. García López, vol. 1, p. 29.

[17] Ibid. vol. 1, p. 78.

father-in-law of Fernando de Rojas, was tried by the Holy Office for having indiscreetly let slip: "Let me be well off down here, since I don't know if there's anything beyond [Acá toviese yo bien, que allá no sé si ay nada]," a pronouncement also made by Intellect in his soliloquy.[18] De Montalbán's famous son-in-law, who himself possessed an incunabulum of the *Visión* (probably the 1494 Tolosa edition),[19] also had a profound understanding of the problem faced by De la Torre—*La Celestina* echoes his doubts, but not his solutions, against which the play rants and rebels furiously and bitterly.

Again it is worth noting that the omission of the provocative soliloquy is not the only lacuna in the Burgos incunabulum. Also missing, from the previous chapter (1.15), is the list of philosophical luminaries reclining at Wisdom's feet, venerable *auctoritates* with "faces inflamed" by his wise words, including "the modern thinkers…Al-Farabi, Al-Ghazzali, Avicenna and Moses the Egyptian (Maimonides)."[20] Once again, under the glare of the Inquisition, which had been set up only five years earlier, it is not surprising that an editor should be wary of including this open profession of faith by Muslim and Jewish scholars, in particular the explicit invocation of Maimonides as a philosophical basis with which to refute the extreme accusations that sent so many Conversos to the dungeons or the stake. Failure to mention Maimonides by name would not have prevented De la Torre's immediate readership from recognising his Hispano-Jewish source of inspiration: we need only recall how Francisco Cáceres, when retranslating Domenico Delphini's Italian version of the *Visión* back into Castilian in the 1626 Frankfurt edition, does not hesitate to omit the only two chapters with explicitly Christian content (2.23 and 2.24). Indeed, as late as the eighteenth century, the *Visión* was still circulating among Jews and Conversos in Italy, Germany and the Low Countries who held it to be an authorised synthesis of Maimonidean thought in Castilian.

In short, the philosophical problems tackled by De la Torre are all classic themes in the medieval Aristotelian tradition—for Jews, Christians and for Muslims. Strictly speaking, none of these themes is new. But this was the first time in our literature, aside from Metge, that so

---

[18] Stephen Gilman, *The Spain of Fernando de Rojas*, Princeton, 1972, p. 82.
[19] Cf. F. Lersundi del Valle, "Testamento de Fernando de Rojas, autor de 'La Celestina,'" *Revista de Filología Española* 16, 1929, pp. 366–388, and Luis Girón Negrón, *Alfonso de la Torre's 'Visión Deleytable,'* pp. 252–253, n. 119.
[20] *Visión deleytable*, García López ed., p. 150.

much importance had been placed on the plausibility of unbelief and on the abandonment of the idea of Providence as an unavowed backdrop to the medieval philosophical project. And it is from this perspective that the *Visión* was particularly well received in certain circles, both Jewish and Converso, in fifteenth-century Spain: the feasibility of unbelief became particularly significant under the overwhelming burden of anti-Semitic hatred and the unflinching gaze of the Inquisition.

CHAPTER FOUR

CONVERSO "VOICES" IN FIFTEENTH- AND SIXTEENTH-CENTURY SPANISH LITERATURE

Elaine Wertheimer

What do we mean by "Converso voice"? Do we hear this "voice" in the work of a known convert with a specific point of view, or in that of a spokesperson for Conversos, who advocates equal treatment for them? Is it perhaps the voice of a writer of suspected Jewish origin, whose work reflects Converso concerns? This study contends that all of the above are valid Converso voices. In fact, the variety of their responses proves that no single element can denote the Converso, nor exemplify his voice. Francisco Márquez Villanueva advised us of this when he stated: "Converso activity involves so many facets that it is almost imposible to make a judgement on them as a group."[1]

Ronald E. Surtz and Ángel Alcalá also caution against trying to find a single characteristic to define the Converso author. As Surtz writes: "One of the problems that arise when we define the principles of the literature written by Conversos is that the Converso as such does not exist, only Conversos exist, as there was no one way of being a New Christian."[2] Alcalá asks: "...is it not incorrect to speak of the *conversos* as a 'world' in themselves, as a 'collective community' as if they all shared a common denominator? Each *converso* responded to the situation as a person, individually, from his or her own experiences."[3]

---

[1] "Conversos y cargos concejiles en el siglo XV," *RABM*, t. LXIII (1957), p. 532: "La actividad de los conversos envuelve tal cantidad de facetas que hace casi imposible la emisión de juicios de conjunto."

[2] "Características principales de la literatura escrita por judeoconversos: algunos problemas de definición," *Judíos, sefarditas, conversos: la expulsión de 1492 y sus consecuencias*, ed. Angel Alcalá, Valladolid, 1995, p. 547: "Uno de los problemas que surge en el momento de definir las características principales de la literatura escrita por judeoconversos es que el converso como tal no existe, solamente existen los conversos, ya que no había un modo único de ser cristiano nuevo."

[3] "From Dislike to Disguise: Jews and Conversos in Spanish Literature at the Time of the Expulsion (1474–1516)," in *Jews and Conversos at the Time of the Expulsion*, ed. Yom Tov Assis and Yosef Kaplan, Jerusalem, 1999, p. 109.

With these cautions in mind, I consider six writers, whose works span the period from the mid-fifteenth to the mid-sixteenth centuries. Writing in Spanish but living in Spain, Portugal and Italy, their works reveal the variety of the Converso voices. The authors selected: Antón de Montoro, Juan del Encina, Lucas Fernández, Diego Sánchez de Badajoz, Bartolomé de Torres Naharro and Gil Vicente, each in his own way reflects the hopes, fears and anxieties of Conversos of his time and place.[4]

The earliest of these authors, Antón de Montoro, was a known convert who was ever mindful of his Jewish origin. Concerning the lineage of the others, we are on less certain ground. Although all are suspected Conversos, the truth of their heritage can perhaps never be conclusively proved documentarily. What we can show is that concerns arising from Converso problems did lead to their taking a literary stand on the question of the value of a person, of his honor and of the relationship which they hoped could be established among all Christians, Old and New. Their work also has a darker side, reflecting the fear of *malas lenguas*, (evil tongues) the terror of a sudden denunciation, the shadow of the Inquisition—all elements of their life situation.

Their work is set against the background of a social revolution that was brewing in Spain, based on the statutes of blood purity (*limpieza de sangre*), first enacted in Toledo in 1449.[5] This legislation had a profound effect on the concept of honor in Spain. Previously the two main sources of honor had been noble birth and deeds of valor. With the growing concern for blood purity, New Christians were held in low esteem even if they were of noble birth, since there was no way to expunge the stain of their Jewish blood. A complete inversion of values was threatened when those who prided themselves on their unmixed blood, even if they belonged to the lowest social classes, claimed superiority.

Resonances from the *limpieza* statutes are not yet present in the work of Antón de Montoro, the first author considered. A poet and also a tailor, Montoro was known as "el Ropero de Córdoba." Born around 1404, he probably converted to Christianity as an adult[6] and apparently never took his conversion seriously, since his sense of his Judaism colors

---

[4] For a fuller treatment of the pre-Lope dramatists, see Elaine C. Wertheimer, *Honor, Love and Religion in the Theater before Lope de Vega*, Newark: DE, 2003.

[5] Albert A. Sicroff, *Les controverses des statuts de "pureté de sang" en Espagne du XV au XVII siècle*, Paris, 1960, pp. 32–36.

[6] We deduce this from poem #79, entitled "Montoro a un caballero que le mando un puerco y envio por el y no gelo quiso dar diciendo que aun apenas era cristiano": "Muy mas bondado de fe/que no de fojas el guindo;/no sabéis como gané/carta de

all of his work. Throughout his long literary career—encompassing the reign of three kings—Montoro sought the protection of high-placed patrons, as did most of the poets of his time. We know that he was favored by the Señores de Aguilar, and that he took refuge with don Alonso de Aguilar after the anti-Converso uprising in Córdoba of 1473. In spite of the exile of all Conversos from the city, decreed by don Alonso after the massacre, Montoro must have returned to Córdoba, since it was there he made his last will and testament, on March 31, 1477. It was generally assumed that he died later that year;[7] however, in 1984, Manuel Nieto Cumplido published documents proving that Montoro was still living in December of 1482, three months after the naming of inquisitors for the city of Córdoba.[8] From this time on, it must have been impossible for the *Ropero* to speak so openly, and in fact there is no record of works addressing the concerns of Conversos that can be dated after 1474.

The first printing of his work was in the *Cancionero General* of Hernando del Castillo in Valencia in 1511. Other poems appeared in the *Cancionero de obras de burlas provocantes a risa* in Valencia in 1519.[9] Montoro never forgot his Jewish origin, nor did he allow anyone else to forget it. Since the majority of his works were written before the establishment of the Inquisition,[10] he could express himself with an audacity that was not seen again. He frequently engaged in polemics with other poets, as was usual at the time, and often reminded other Converso poets of their common heritage, evoking furious insults from

cristiano lindo?" (Marithelma Costa, *Antón de Montoro Poesía completa*, Cleveland, 1990, p. 166). All citations from Montoro's work are taken from this edition.

[7] Rafael Ramírez de Arellano, "Antón de Montoro y su testamento," *RABM*, t. IV, (1900) pp. 484–9. Also see S. Mitrani-Samarian, "Le sac de Cordoue et le testament d'Antón de Montoso," *REJ*, t. LIV (1907), pp. 236–40.

[8] *Corpus mediaevale cordubense*, 1984, p. 288. Cited by Marithelma Costa, *Bufón de palacio y comerciante de ciudad*, Córdoba, p. 17.

[9] Hernando del Castillo, *Cancionero General* 1511, ed. Antonio Rodríguez Moñino, Madrid, 1958; Hernando del Castillo, *Cancionero general nuevamente añadido* 1520, New York, 1967; *Cancionero de obras de burlas*, ed. Luis Sánchez, Madrid, 1841. Modern editions of Montoro's works are Emilio Cotarelo y Mori, ed. *Cancionero de Antón de Montoro (El Ropero de Córdoba) Poeta del siglo XV*. Madrid, 1900; *Antón de Montoro Cancionero*, ed. F. Cantera Burgos y C. Carrete Parrondo, Madrid, 1984; *Antón de Montoro Cancionero*, ed. Marcella Ciceri y Julio Rodríguez Puértolas, Salamanca, 1990; and the aforementioned edition of Marithelma Costa.

[10] We do not know if Montoro came to the attention of the Inquisition. However, documents show that his wife Teresa Rodríguez was burnt at the stake as a heretic sometime before April 4, 1487. "Archivo general de Simancas," *Registro general del sello*, Valladolid, 1958, n. 298, p. 45. Cited by Marithelma Costa, *Anton de Montoro*, p. xi.

those anxious to erase all traces of their lineage. One such poet was Juan Poeta, also known as Juan de Valladolid, a suspected Converso. Montoro apostrophized him thus:

> Por ser vos y yo judíos
> vuestros enojos son míos
> y mis daños todos vuestros (*Poesía* #40, p. 100)

> [Since you and I are Jews
> your anger is mine
> and my hurt is all yours]

When Juan Poeta rejected the relationship violently, Montoro replied caustically:

> Mal trobador, importuno
> desavido y desgrasciado,
> aveys de mi publicado
> lo que non sabe ninguno
> ....
> al que azotan en la calle,
> que gelo digan en casa,
> non paresce desonralle (*Poesía* #104b, p. 239)

> [Bad troublesome
> misguided and miserable troubador
> about me you have disclosed
> what no one knows
> ....
> for the man who is whipped
> in the street
> what they say in his own house
> does not appear to dishonor him.]

The *Ropero* was no less bold when engaging in literary combat with the *Comendador Roman* and with Gómez Dávila, corregidor de Córdoba, who were Old Christians and men of rank and privilege. They consistently insulted him with epithets like "vil judío, retajado, deicida, vil escopido marrano" and waxed indignant that a man of low origin, a Jew and a tailor, should dedicate himself to the noble art of poetry.[11] Montoro never denied his ancestry. In an extremely audacious poem, he uses his Judaism as a weapon to strike against his opponent:

---

[11] *Cancionero de obras de burlas*, p. 87.

Porque el linaje que es visto
de grand fuerza y de valor,
que pudo con Iesu Christo,
podríe con corregidor. (*Poesía* #110, p. 252)

[Because the lineage in question
is of such great strength and worth
that it could triumph over Jesus Christ
so can it triumph over a *corregidor*]

It must have been stanzas like these that elicited from Amador de los Rios the comment that Montoro "seemed to be boasting of his sambenito."[12]

Montoro's work gives us a clear picture of the Converso situation in 1473 and 1474, when rioting broke out in Carmona and Córdoba, leaving death and devastation. The *Ropero* directed himself to King Enrique IV, lamenting the fate of the victims, and assuring the King that he would weep to see their pitiable condition:

Si vuestra alteza mirara,
el corazón vos manara
gotas de gran piedad. (*Poesía* #19, p. 45)

[If your highness could see this
his heart would pour out
tears of great pity.]

He begs the King for justice for them:

digolo por la pasión
de esta gente convertida;
que sobre las ascuas anda
con menos culpa que susto,
que los que muy menos mandan
cient mill veces les demandan
aquella muerte de Justo. (*Poesía* #19, p. 43)

[I say this with regard to the Passion
of the converts;
who are on tenterhooks
not with guilt but fear,
for those who are least to blame

---

[12] *Historia crítica de la literatura española*, t. VI, Madrid, 1865, p. 151: "parecía hacer gala del sambenito." The sambenito was a penitential garment worn by those who the Inquisition found guilty of heretical acts.

100,000 times are accused of
that death of the Just One.]

In the midst of his earnest plea, he cannot resist a sly taunt at the
Christians by using the disrespectful term "aquella muerte" (that death)
in referring to the Crucifixion.

In a poem addressed to Queen Isabel, Montoro complained that he
was now 70 years old but could not erase the epithet of *confeso*, even
after a lifetime of Christian practices.

¡Oh Ropero, amargo, triste
que no sientes tu dolor!
Setenta años que naciste
y en todos siempre dijiste:
"Inviolata permaniste";

y nunca juré al Criador.
Hice el credo y adorar

Ollas de tocino grueso
torreznos a medio asar
oir misas y rezar
santiguar y persinar
y nunca pude matar,
este rastro de confeso. (*Poesía* #98, p. 202)

[Oh bitter, sad Ropero,
that feels no pain1
seventy years ago born
and all that time you maintain:
"immaculate remained";

and never did I swear to the Creator.
I followed the credo and worshipped

Pots of fatty pork
half cooked bacon
listened to mass and prayed
crossed and crossed myself
and never could I slay
that trace of Converso.]

According to Montoro, in the eyes of Old-Christian Spain he remained
a Jew, even after hearing Mass, crossing himself, and "worshipping" pots
of fat, greasy bacon. In spite of his exaggerated complaint, we know
that he had not devoted himself to Christian practices all of his life,
nor had he exerted himself much to remove the traces of his lineage.

In one of his last poems[13] Montoro takes pride in the fact that many of his family successfully resisted the pressures to convert to Christianity and remained true to the faith of their ancestors:

> que tengo hijos y nietos
> y padre pobre y muy viejo
> y madre dona Jamila
> y hija moza, y hermana
> que nunca entraron en pila. (*Poesía* #151, pp. 339–40)

> [I have children and grandchildren
> and a poor old father
> and mother, doña Jamila
> and a young daughter, and sister
> that never entered the font]

A bold and fearless spirit, Montoro openly expresses his needs and problems, his confidence in his own poetic talent, and, especially, his concern for his people. Although a convert to Christianity, Judaism still burns within him. Despite being aged and worn down with troubles, he continues to exhibit the same freshness and daring which characterized him throughout his long poetic career.

Juan del Encina, the next author under consideration, presents us with an entirely different reaction to the Converso situation. The Inquisition was well established by his time, and it was no longer possible for anyone to speak with the audacity we see in Montoro. Born around 1469, Encina studied law and theology at the University of Salamanca and graduated with the degree of *bachiller* and with minor orders up to the deaconate. Like Montoro, Encina sought the protection of high-placed patrons, and served the Duke of Alba as director of theatrical presentations. In order to consolidate his position at the House of Alba and to demonstrate his superiority over the other poets in the Duke's employ, Encina published in 1496 a *Cancionero* of his collected works: poetry, essays and eight dramatic compositions.[14] In imitation of Virgil's Eclogues, he gave the name of *églogas* to his theatrical works.

---

[13] Based on the line referring to don Alonso de Aguilar as "He that helps the poor" ("aquel de pobres abrigo"), a gloss on the line "He that helps the good" ("aquel de buenos abrigo") of Jorge Manrique's *coplas* on the death of his father. Don Rodrigo Manrique died in November, 1476 and the *Coplas* were written shortly thereafter.

[14] For biographical data, see Rafael Mitjana, "Nuevos datos relativos a Juan del Encina," *RFE*, I (enero–marzo, 1914), pp. 275–88 and Ricardo Espinosa Maeso, "Nuevos

Although we cannot know for sure whether Encina was *ex illis*, we can show that concerns arising from the Converso problem did condition his point of view. In his first *Écloga*, presented at the palace of the Duke and Duchess of Alba, Encina claims a place for himself in high society on the basis of his poetic talent. He thus gives his own name to the shepherd who will represent him. According to the introductory summary, the shepherd Juan "in the name of Juan de Encino presents a hundred folk songs to the duchess during this fiesta."[15] He is opposed by "the other shepherd called Mateo in the name of the detractors and slanderers."[16] Mateo challenges Juan for his audacity, since his lineage does not allow him to appear in a palace:

> ¿Cuydas que eres para en sala?
> No te vien de gerenacio.

> [Hey, are you going to enter the hall?
> You don't come from the same stock]

Juan's response is to berate Mateo for questioning his ancestry, and to point out Mateo's base character:

> ¿No me viene de natío?
> Calla, calla ya, malsin
> que nunca faltas de ruyn. (*Eglogas*, p. 25)

> [I am not from the nation?
> Shut up, shut up, mischief maker
> Never lacking in bad intention]

It is significant that Juan does not deny Mateo's allegation, but accuses him of being a slanderer (*malsin*). Encina here takes the first step in denying the importance of ancestry. He also reveals the fear of the tale-bearer, the *malas lenguas* (evil tongues) which presented such peril to Conversos. In the play, Juan convinces Mateo that his talent constitutes a valid form of honor. Then Encina takes the next step, con-

---

datos biográficos de Juan del Encina," *BRAE*, VIII, 8dic. 1921, pp. 640–56. Editions are: *Teatro completo*, ed. M. Cañete y F. Asenjo Barbieri, Madrid, 1893 (reprinted 1969 Greenwood Press); *Cancionero*, ed. facsimil, ed. Emilio Cotarelo, Madrid, 1928; *Obras completas*, ed. Ana María Rambaldo, Madrid, 1978–1983, 4 vols; *Obras completas*, ed. Miguel Angel Pérez Prieto, Madrid, 1996; *Eglogas de Juan del Enzina*, ed. H. López Morales, New York, 1968. All citations are taken from this edition.
[15] *Eglogas*, p. 23: "en nombre de Juan de Enzina llegó a presentar cien coplas de aquesta fiesta a la señora duquesa."
[16] Ibid.: "el otro pastor llamado Mateo en nombre de los detractores y maldicientes."

necting honor based on a new form of nation (*natío*) to the possibility of equality for all Christians, Old and New. This theme represented the fondest hope of the New Christians. Thus, in the second eglogue, the shepherds Juan and Mateo, together with the shepherds Lucas and Marcos, representing the four Apostles, receive the news of the Birth. Lucas asks Juan what it means:

> Y tu, Juan de buen asseo
> ¿que dizes que estas calando?

> [And you, Juan of good character
> What tell me do you make of this?]

Juan answers:

> Miafe, digo que lo creo
> que ya estava yo en oteo
> de luengo tiempo esperando. (*Eglogas*, p. 34)

> [By my faith, I do believe
> that I am witnessing
> what for so long we have been awaiting]

It must be noted that the word "esperar" (to wait) carried a heavy weight of symbolism in Spanish, since it denoted the Jew still waiting for the Messiah.[17] Here the Advent of Christ fulfills the promises of the Old Testament for which Juan, representing Encina, has been waiting. Juan then asserts that Christ the shepherd has come to liberate his flock and to bring unity and harmony to all Christians:

> Nacio nuestro Salvador
> Por librar nuestra pelleja.
> ¡O, que chapado pastor
> Que morira sin temor
> Por no perder una oveja! (*Églogas*, p. 35)

> [Born was our Savior
> To set us free
> Oh, golden shepherd
> Who will die without fear
> So that no sheep will be lost!]

---

[17] Edward Glaser "Referencias antisemitas en la literatura peninsular en la edad de oro," *NRFH*, VIII (enero–abril 1954), #1, p. 57.

This Shepherd extends his love to all and dies in order to save all of his flock. Here Encina emphasizes the all-embracing love which includes all Christians, Old and New, a theme which will recur frequently in Converso writings.

Up until now, we see a confident Encina, sure of the good name to which his talent entitled him, happy in the prospect of harmony among all Christians; however, later he becomes disillusioned. We are not sure what events in Encina's life precipitated this change. We know that he moved frequently, from one city to another and from one clerical position to another, and was never well received wherever he went.[18] His later Eclogues, published in 1507, show that hopelessness and despair have succeeded the happier times. In Eclogue IX, the *Egloga de Cristino y Febea*, Cristino wants to live the life of a hermit. Cupid, the god of love, decrees vengeance on him for trying to escape Love's dominion, and sends the nymph Febea to tempt him. The preoccupation with rumor and denunciation, which could so tragically affect Conversos lives, surfaces here. Speaking soothingly to him, Febea asks:

> Deo gracias, mi Cristino
> ¿do te vino
> tan gran desesperacion,.
> que dexasses tu nacion
> por seguir otro camino? (*Églogas*, p. 168)

> [Good God, my Cristino
> from whence did it come
> such a great depression
> that you leave your nation
> to follow another path?]

This is one of the most suggestive citations, indicating that the Converso problem lurks in the background of Encina's writing. The shepherd Cristino has left his own people to follow another path. Cristino's greatest concern seems to be for his own reputation, rather than for his convictions, when he answers:

> Si agora yo renunciasse
> o dexasse
> la religion que escogi,

---

[18] Rafael Mitjana, "Nuevos datos relativos a Juan del Encina," *RFE*, I (enero–marzo, 1914), pp. 279–85.

yo soy cierto que de mi
todo el pueblo blasfemasse. (*Églogas*, p. 170)

[If now I renounce
or abandon
the religion I chose,
I am certain that
all my country will blaspheme me]

When Cristino finally succumbs to the charms of Febea, he laments
to his friend Justino:

Amigo mio, Justino
¡ay mezquino!
¿qué diran en el aldea?
que tornar es cosa fea; (*Eglogas*, p. 175)

[My friend, Justino
how miserable!
what will they say in the village?
When changing back is such a base thing;]

Cristino's reconversion, exacted in the name of Love, earns him a bad
name in society. He has no defense against the *malsines* who he fears
so greatly. The hope of harmony and unity has been frustrated. Since
it would have been too dangerous to attack the insufficiency of divine
love, Encina transposes his complaints to the mythological realm and
inveighs against the pagan god Cupid.

In sum, Encina reacts to the stresses of his society by challenging
traditional values and expressing unaccustomed ideas about human
dignity and equality among all Christians. Yet later the reality of his
situation seems to have overwhelmed him and his works reveal his
disillusionment and bitterness. Perhaps the Christian *caritas*, of which
Encina had expected so much, had failed him by this time.

Encina's contemporary, Lucas Fernández, also a poet, dramatist and
musician, was born in Salamanca in 1474. His mother belonged to the
family of Cantalapiedra, a name which often appears on Inquisition lists
of suspect Christians.[19] Lucas studied arts and music in the University
of Salamanca, and gained a post with the Duke of Alba. He also served

---

[19] In 1572 the Hebraist Martin Martínez de Cantalapiedra was imprisoned, along with
Fray Luis de León, for his Judaizing tendencies. Martínez de Cantalapiedra was, like
members of Lucas Fernández' family, closely associated with Salamanca University.

as *cantor* in the Cathedral of Salamanca. By 1507 he was an ordained priest. In 1514, he published his *Farsas y eglogas al modo y estilo pastoril y castellano* in Salamanca.[20] Emilio Cotarelo notes that Fernández' dedication to arts and letters did not prevent him from procuring rents and benefices which constantly improved his comfortable financial position. He also took an active part in the reforms and economic affairs of the University of Salamanca until his death in 1542.[21]

Obviously Fernández lived a comfortable life. We see in his work, however, the reaction against the growing social revolution caused by the pure blood statutes. In his plays, Fernández ridicules the rustics' claims to social status, based on the purity of their blood, and creates burlesque genealogies in order to satirize them. In the play *Comedia en lenguaje y estilo pastoril*, the shepherd Bras Gil wants to marry the shepherdess Beringuella. To further his suit, he sets forth his fine ancestry to the girl's grandfather, asserting that these are his cousins who come from his land:

> Papiharto y el Cancudo
> son mis primos caronales
> Y Juan de los Bodonales
> y Anton Prauos Bollorudo
> Brasco Moro y el Papudo
> también son de mi terruno. (*Farsas*, p. 70)

The use of comic names, with their undertones of physical ugliness, such as *Papiharto* (Fatcheeks), *el Papudo* (Doublechinned) and *el Çancudo* (Longshanks), increase the satirical effect. The claim of high lineage is reduced to absurdity. John Lihani comments that the shepherd's paradoxical pride in his humble background was a piece of dramatic irony that was used as a comic device to entertain the noble audiences who witnessed his plays at the House of Alba.[22] Francisco Márquez, however, points out the destructive intention underlying all this humor: the desire to "reduce completely the social status of the laboring class."[23]

---

[20] Ricardo Espinosa Maeso, "Ensayo biográfico del maestro Lucas Fernández," *BRAE*, t. X, Cuad. XLIV, (Oct. 1923) p. 392. The Real Academia Española published a facsimile edition of the princeps in 1929 with a prologue by Emilio Cotarelo.

[21] Prologue, p. xiii to the facsimile edition.

[22] "Lucas Fernández and the evolution of the shepherd's family pride in early Spanish drama," *HR*, xxv (1957), p. 252.

[23] *Fuentes literarias cervantinas*, Madrid, 1973, p. 71: "rebajar a todo el estamento de labradores."

Another way that Fernández scorns the rustics is to make fun of their ignorance. In his *Auto o farsa del nascimiento*, the shepherds comment on the alterations in the sky and the changes in the animals on the night Jesus is born. They ask each other what might have caused such disruptions in the natural order. One shepherd says that Benito Sabidor will know the answer. When another asks: "Tan terrible es su sabencia?" ["So great is his knowingness?"], the first replies:

> A la he, tiene huerte sciencia;
> qu'el a, b, c te dira,
> que lletra no errara. (*Farsas*, p. 143)

> [Without a doubt he has great knowledge;
> he'll tell you the abc
> without erring in a letter.]

Fernández, an educated man and very likely a Converso, a member of a social group which had always held learning in high esteem, undermines the ludicrous claims to value status of those who consider knowledge of the alphabet evidence of "*huerte sciencia.*" However, Fernández' theater is not all negative. Along with his scathing portraits of rustics, he advocates peace and equality among all Christians, a common theme, as I have previously noted, in the work of Conversos. In his *Auto o farsa del nascimiento*, the shepherd Gil asks the hermit Macario if the Birth will bring a new law to the world.: "Y otro ley ay, digo o ¿que?" Macario replies:

> Ya dos leyes son pasadas;
> la una fue de Natura,
> y la otra sus pisadas
> quió por sendas holladas
> de la Sagrada Escriptura;
> de Gracia es la tercera ley
> más verdadera,
> la qual este sancto Rey,
> como Amador de su grey,
> os nos dio con paz entera. (*Farsas*, p. 131)

> [Now two laws have passed;
> one of nature
> the other whose steps
> were guided by paths
> of the Holy Scripture;
> based on Grace the third law
> is the more truthful

in which this holy King
Lover of his flock,
grants us total peace]

The idea expressed here echoes that of a famous fifteenth-century treatise, *Lumen de revelationem gentium*, in which the author, Alonso de Oropesa, himself a Converso, sustains the view that religion has always been one and the same. He traces the historical process of perfecting the religion from Adam to Jesus. In this process, he points out three stages through which religion developed: under the law of nature, under the written law of the Old Testament, and finally under the law of grace of Jesus. Oropesa claims a place for the Conversos in the community of the faithful under the perfect law of grace.[24] We cannot know whether Fernández is directly using Oropesa's work, but he is certainly making use of an idea which was current in Old versus New Christian polemics. The novelty here is that he is presenting in dramatic terms the case for religious equality for all Christians, regardless of whether they descend from Gentiles who lived under the law of nature or from Jews who lived according to the written law of the Old Testament. Thus, in his advocacy of peace and harmony among Old and New Christians, and in his scorn for the peasants' claim of superiority based on the purity of their unmixed blood, Fernández tries to find a place for the Converso in the society of his time.

Like Lucas Fernández, Diego Sánchez de Badajoz, a poet, dramatist and priest, uses his work to advocate harmony among Old and New Christians. We do not know the date of Sánchez' birth, but from the investigations of José López Prudencio, we learn that he earned the degree of *bachiller*, probably from the University of Salamanca, and that he was ordained as a priest in 1533 and served in the church of Talavera until his death in 1549. His literary career spanned the years of 1525 to 1547,[25] but his work was not published until after his death, when his nephew Juan de Figueroa collected his plays and published them in Seville in 1554, with the title *Recopilación en metro*.[26]

---

[24] Albert A. Sicroff, "Anticipación del erasmismo en el Lumen ad revelationem gentium de Alonso de Oropesa" NHFH, 30, 2 (1981), pp. 315–38.
[25] *Diego Sánchez de Badajoz: studio crítico, biográfico y bibliográfico*, Madrid, 1915, pp. 32 and 66.
[26] A facsimile edition of the princeps was published in 1929 by the Real Academia Espanola. Other editions are those of Barrantes, *Libros de Antano*, tomos XI and XII, Madrid, 1882–1886 and Frida Weber de Kurlat, *Diego Sánchez de Badajoz, Recopilación en metro*, Buenos Aires, 1968. All citations are taken from this latter edition.

Sánchez wrote only religious *farsas*, and his fundamental didactic purpose was to teach the message of unity of all Christians, Old and New, who have been saved by the Passion of their Redeemer. Thus his *Farsa de Ysaac* ends with a *copla* showing how the two distinct groups will be harmonized and blessed by the divine love.

Ya no falta bendición
a nosotros y a vosotros
pues después de su passion
mora Dios entre nosotros;
ya los unos y los otros
festejemos por mil modos
pues que Dios combida a todos.
(*Recopilación* p. 402)

[Now we are blessed
both us and you
because after his passion
God resides in us;
now the two of us
celebrate in a thousand ways
God uniting everyone]

In his *Farsa de Santa Barbara*, the virgin martyr, he defends virtuous converts but also graphically presents the horrors of false denunciations which lead to torture and death, a clear picture of the atmosphere in which Conversos lived. In this play, Sánchez questions the value conferred on a person by birth, since it is no guarantee of nobility of character. Here the young saint, although born of pagan parents, is so dedicated to her new faith that she will not recant her beliefs, although the flesh of her breasts is torn with pincers. The moral is that high birth does not guarantee merit. In fact, often it is quite the opposite:

¡Dios! que de linage astrosa
salen hombres muy rebuenos,
vellacos ni mas ni menos
de linaje generosa;
Sancta Barbola preciosa,
anque de gente rruyn,
hu muy buena: en fin, en fin,
del espino sal la rrosa. (*Recopilación* p. 164)[27]

---

[27] This recalls the *Proverbios Morales* of Rabi Sem Tob de Carrión who used the same image of the rose born from thorns a century earlier: "Por nacer en espina/la rrosa/yo no siento/que pierde…" Edition of Guzman Alvarez, Salamanca, 1970, pp. 46–7.

[My God! from what low lineage
comes good men,
and rogues and nothing more,
from noble lines;
dear Saint Barbara
although from base family
so very good: and thus, and thus,
from the thorn comes the rose.]

With all of the hagiography at his disposal, Sánchez de Badajoz has chosen to dramatize the life of Saint Barbara to show that one should not scorn the convert, since he/she is often a truer believer than the born Christian. To underscore his message, he introduces a humorous comment by the shepherd, who contrasts the martyrdom of the Saint with the frivolity of the young girls of the day who would never have the courage to suffer for their beliefs:

Dezi a las mozas de agora
que andan hechas gallaretas
que corten por Dios las tetas,
diros han: "Anda en mal hora"
(*Recopilación*, p. 164)

[Say to the girls today
who walk around like peacocks
that they cut their breasts for God
and they tell you: "Go to blazes!"]

In the *Farsa de Tamar*, Sánchez' moral outrage is directed toward the crime of denunciation, which in his scale of values weighs heavier than incest.[28] In Sánchez' play, neither Judah nor Tamar is punished for their crime, but the shepherd who reveals their secret is condemned to torture for being a *malsin*. In a trial scene which bears a strong resemblance to an Inquisitorial procedure, the wretched prisoner moans:

Guay del que no tien fauor
de padrinos y dinero.

[Woe to him who has no support
of godparents and money.]

Judah answers pitilessly:

---

[28] The story is told in *Genesis*, XXXVIII: 6–26.

Mas quay del necio parlero
te cabe dezir major.
tu mala lengua te obliga.

[Woe to the stupid talker
you should have said.
Your evil tongue has caught you.]

The scribe who has been transcribing the proceedings adds:

Lengua diz y cuerpo paga. (*Recopilación*, p. 261)

[Tongue speaks and body pays]

In his call of harmony and unity for all Christians, in his defense of the good convert, and in his depiction of the horrors of denunciations, Sánchez reflects Converso concerns of the time.

Bartolomé de Torres Naharro, a Spanish poet and dramatist who lived and wrote in Italy, was able to treat the Converso problem openly and ironically. We know little of Torres Naharro's life, and even less of his family background. Menéndez y Pelayo surmised that he attended the University of Salamanca, that he served as a soldier of the *reyes católicos*, and that he spent some time in Valencia. From there he sailed for Rome but was captured by Turks. After being ransomed, he continued his journey. He served different patrons in Rome and Naples, and, at some point, was ordained as a priest. In 1517, he published a collection of poetry and dramatic works, which he entitled *Propalladia*.[29]

In Torres Naharro's *Comedia Jacinta*, the problem of blood purity arises when Pagano, Precioso and Jacinto, three men traveling from different points, converge in Rome. Precioso relates the news of how Rome has gathered to herself the Conversos fleeing persecution in Spain:

Pues en Roma a la sazon
mas nuevas no se dezian
sino que algunos huhyan
de la Sancta Inquisicion. (*Propalladia*, II, p. 358)

[And so in Rome in that time
there was no news

---

[29] Marcelino Menéndez y Pelayo, introduction to his edition of the *Propalladia*, Libros de antaño, X, Madrid, 1880–1900. Cited by Joseph E. Gillet, *Propalladia and other works of Bartolomé de Torres Naharro*, Bryn Mawr, 1956, 4 vols. All citations are taken from this edition.

but that of those who fled
the Spanish Inquisition.]

Pagano immediately suspects that Precioso is one of these converts
and asks if he is fleeing also. Precioso answers ironically that he is not
completely Jewish, only three quarters so. If he were completely Jewish,
he too could be rich like the other *marranos*.[30]

Sabe Dios que me ha pesado
por no ser marrano fino
que por faltarme vn costado
biuo pobre de contino. (*Propalladia*, II, p. 359)

[God only knows my troubles
in not being a real marrano
for by lacking one branch
I remain constantly poor.]

Pagano, the *villano*, secure in the purity of his own blood, reacts haugh-
tily against the *hidalgo* who is by no means above suspicion:

Pues no te burles, hazino
que muchos y muy vfanos
dizen mal de los marranos
y ellos no comen tocino.[31] (*Propalladia*, II, p. 359)

[Don't joke, neighbor
for many very proud people
speak ill of the marranos
and they themselves don't eat bacon.]

Torres Naharro's bitter humor is unusual, but living and writing in the
freer atmosphere of Italy, he obviously felt that he could make these
ironical comments without fear of reprisal.

Another recollection of the Converso situation is seen in the *Comedia Calamita*, where the shadow of the Inquisition hovers over the
two servants Phileo and Jusquino. When Phileo boasts of his ability to

---

[30] A term meaning "swine," *marrano* was applied to converts who were suspected of
continuing to practice their old religion. Precioso is telling his assailant, in a roundabout
way, that he is not a Judaizer.

[31] Following this line, we come to Quevedo insulting his rival Góngora by saying:
"Yo me untaré mis versos con tocino/para que no me los muerdes, Gongorino." accusing him of plagiarism and Judaism in just two lines. Cited by Sanford Shepherd, *Lost
lexicon Secret meaning in the vocabulary of Spanish literatura during the Inquisition*,
Miami, 1982, p. 90.

foresee the future, his remark is twisted into a reference to those who still foretell the coming of the Messiah:

> O Jusquino,
> par Dios que para adeuino
> valgo más que pesar puedo.
>
> [O Jusquino,
> by God I am worth more as a fortune-teller
> than I can measure.]

Jusquino warns him that he may be denounced as a Jew:

> Por otro tanto en Toledo
> Quemaron un mi vezino
> enemigo del tocino
> capital
>
> [For such a trifle in Toledo
> they burnt my neighbor
> an enemy of Pork
> to the death]

Phileo states emphatically:

> No moriré d'esse mal
>
> [I won't die of this ill]

But Jusquino is not convinced:

> Quiça te viene de casta. (*Propalladia*, II, p. 416)
>
> [Maybe you come from the Jewish caste.]

These plays show Torres Naharro's preoccupation with *malas lenguas*, in an atmosphere charged with the threat of secret denunciations. From the safety of his Roman haven, he can afford to treat the fearsome situation in Spain with irony. No one writing inside Spain after Montoro's time could afford to express himself this clearly.

Another overt literary expression of the Converso situation is found in the work of Gil Vicente. A poet, dramatist and goldsmith who lived in Portugal, Vicente's rich and varied literary production encompasses religious *autos* and secular *farsas, comedias* and *tragicomedias*, written in both Spanish and Portuguese.

We are not sure of Vicente's date of birth. We know that he moved in Portuguese court circles and enjoyed the favor of two kings, don Manuel, *el venturoso*, and, later, his son don João III. He was also the protégé of Queen Lianor, the sister of King Manuel. His first dramatic work, the *Auto de la visitacion* of 1502, was composed in honor of the birth of prince João, who would later become his patron. For the next thirty years, in his capacity as official dramatist and organizer of dramatic entertainment, Vicente accompanied the Court in its travels to Lisbon, Almeirim, Coimbra and Evora, writing works for various occasions. Only one of these works was published during the dramatist's lifetime.[32] His complete works were not published until 1562, when two of his children, Luis and Paula Vicente, revised, edited and published them in five volumes as the *Copilaçam de todalas obras de Gil Vicente*.[33]

Vicente's stand on the Converso question is presented in a sermon he wrote for Queen Lianor in 1506, as well as by his plays portraying Jews or Conversos. In 1506, riots against New Christians in Lisbon lasted for three days, resulting in several hundred deaths. Only by accepting baptism were Jews able to save their lives. Vicente contended that it was useless to expect Jews converted under those circumstances to be good Christians in their hearts:

> Es por demas pedir al judío
> que sea cristiano en su corazon;
> es por demas buscar perfeccion
> adonde el amor de Dios está frio.
> También está llano
> que es por demas al que es mal cristiano
> doctrina de Cristo por fuerza ni ruego.
> (*Obras*, ed. Braga, VI, p. 195).

> [It is pointless to ask a Jew
> to be a Christian at heart;
> it is pointless to look for perfection
> where the love of God is cold
> it is also evident

----

[32] Aubrey F. G. Bell, *Gil Vicente*, Oxford, 1921, p. 6. A *folleto separado* of the *Barca do inferno* is in the Biblioteca Nacional de Madrid.

[33] *Obras completas de Gil Vicente*, reimpressão facsimilada da edição de 1562, ed. José Maria Rodrigues, Lisboa, 1928. Since Vicente belongs to both Spanish and Portuguese literature, there are many editions of his works, among them: *Obras completas*, ed. Marques T. Braga, Clasicos Sa da Costa, Lisboa 1986, 6 vols. (from which all Portuguese citations are taken); *Gil Vicente*, ed. Jack Horace Parker, New York, 1967; *Farces and festival plays*, ed. Thomas R. Hart, Univ. of Oregon, 1962; *Teatro*, ed. Antonio José Saraiva, Sintra, 1984; *Autos portugueses de Gil Vicente y de la escuela vicentina*, ed. Carolina Michaëlis de Vasconcelos, Madrid, 1922; and *Obras dramáticas castellanas*, ed. Thomas R. Hart, Madrid, 1962, (from which all citations from the Spanish plays are taken).

that it is pointless for the bad Christian
to worship Christ by force or plea]

In these verses he dares to censure the King's policy of requiring a technical conversion. Since King Manuel was reputedly ill-disposed to criticism, Vicente's courage is shown in this, his first official position statement on the Converso problem.[34]

A sympathetic portrait of a Converso appears for the first time in Vicente's Portuguese play, *Juiz da Beira*. Here we meet Alonso López, shoemaker and converted Jew, who mourns the general worsening of his financial situation since he emigrated from Spain.

> Cuando eramos judios
> dolor del tiempo pasado
> ciento y veinte y um ducado
> tenia en ducados mios,
> sin le faltar un cornado
>
> Agora que soy guayado
> y negro cristianejo
> andome a calzado viejo,
> desnudo, desfarrapado,
> el mas triste del concejo.
> (*Obras* ed Braga, V, pp. 286–7)
>
> [When we were Jews
> a painfully long time past
> a hundred and twenty one ducats
> I had of my own
> not counting pennies
>
> Now I am a broken
> unhappy Christian
> walking in old shoes,
> naked, ragged
> the most abject of the council.]

López has come to the court of the Judge of Beira to file a complaint against Ana Diez, a *cristiana vieja*, who arranged a meeting for a *caballero* with López' virgin daughter Marina. The Judge refuses to punish Ana Diez, and the shoemaker leaves the courtroom cursing all

---

[34] No criticism of the monarchy was allowed or contemplated, according to Damião de Gois, *Chronica do Felicisimo Rei D Manuel*, Coimbra, 1926. Cited by Laurence Keates, *The court theater of Gil Vicente*, Lisbon, 1962, p. 28.

concerned with the trial and ranting that he deserves a black old age if he does not convert back to Judaism:

> Pascoa mala de Dios al Juez,
> y mala pascoa al Portero
> y negra pascoa al herrero,
> y al Juez otra vez
> y mala pascoa a Ana Diez
> y a mi negra vejez
> me de si christiano muero.
> (*Obras*, ed. Braga, V, pp. 293–4)

> [Unhappy Easter from God to the Judge
> and unhappy Easter to the gate keeper
> and a black Easter to the smith
> and to the Judge again
> and unhappy Easter to Ana Diez
> and to me a black old age
> if I die a Christian.]

López rails against his Old-Christian antagonists, hoping that the Passion of their Redeemer will not avail them. In his study of honor in Spain and in Spanish literature, Américo Castro stated: "It was unthinkable that a New Christian could appear on stage attentive to his honor."[35] Certainly that was true of Spanish plays, but here we see one clearly portrayed in a Portuguese play. The shoemaker's concern with his family honor, destroyed through the action of Ana Diez and with no possibility of remedy through the courts, is especially noteworthy since it shows the distance between Gil Vicente's overt treatment of the problem and the oblique manner in which authors in Spain expressed their concerns. Vicente's dramatic presentation of Alonso López' troubles is an eloquent plea for tolerance for New Christians. There is nothing comparable in any Spanish play of the time.

We hear a variety of Converso voices here: Montoro boasting of his Jewish heritage, attacking his detractors and seeking sympathy and aid for his people; Encina claiming a new form of honor based on a person's merits instead of his ancestry, to find a place for Conversos in the society of his time; Fernández ridiculing the pretensions of the *gente menuda* to a nobility based on the purity of their blood; Sánchez showing how the true convert can be nobler than the born Christian;

---

[35] *Da la edad conflictiva*, Madrid, 1963, p. 40: "Era impensable que apareciese en escena un cristiano nuevo con cuidados de honra."

Torres Naharro, living in Italy, satirizing the obsession with Conversos in Spain; Vicente, in Portugal, giving a human face to a *cristiano nuevo*; and all of them expressing their dearest hope for unity and harmony among all Christians, Old and New, a hope that would never be realized.

CHAPTER FIVE

BERENJENEROS: THE AUBERGINE EATERS

Juan Gil*

It is common knowledge that the life of a Converso was subject to a host of dangers and uncertainties. But perhaps worst of all was having to put up with daily insults: any trifling matter, any trivial conversation, could suddenly be diverted on to the dangerous subject of ancestors, leading to a reproach against anyone—however important—for their Converso origin. I shall dwell no further on something so obvious, except to refer to a more unusual and less familiar case: the generalisation of an insult which was extended to an entire city. Such generalisations more commonly refer to other nations: they are the channel for chauvinism and xenophobia. The earliest examples date back to Classical Antiquity. Phocylides's ironic distich on the subject is well known: "The Lerians are wicked, not one, but every one; all except Procles; and Procles is a Lerian."[1] For their part, the Cretans were branded out-and-out liars.[2] In a curious chapter entitled *De proprietatibus gentium*, the *Crónica Albeldense*[3] labels the Greeks as wise, the Goths as courageous, the Romans as arrogant, the Britons as irascible, the Scots as lustful, and so on and so forth. In the Renaissance, the Germans had a reputation for being drunkards, the Italians effeminate...[4] Need we go on?

---

* Translation by Nicola Stapleton.
[1] Frg. 1 Diehl; He was aped by Demodocus (Frg. 2, 3 Diehl) and afterwards mimicked by Porson in a famous epigram: "The Germans in Greek are sadly to seek; all, save only Hermann, and Hermann is a German", an epigram which Wilamowitz still recalls with certain bitterness (*Euripides. Herakles*, Darmstadt, 1959, I, p. 233).
[2] The saying goes back to Epimenides (Frg. 1), and is recalled by St Paul (Tit. 1, 12).
[3] VI (p. 155 Gil).
[4] Wilibald Pirckheimer fiercely ridiculed this mutual fame in an atrocious epigram: the Germans obviously came out on top here as there was no law to punish inebriation, whereas the penalty for homosexuality was death at the stake. His verses read as follows:
Germanos Bacchus, te par iuuat, Itale, sexus,
   Itale, quem gelide blanda puella mouet

Moving from the national to the local level, we note that when people speak of cities, they often make false comparisons between their inhabitants, as in the following examples: "A quien Dios quiere bien, en Sevilla le dio de comer; y a quien Dios quiere mal, en Córdoba le dio un lugar" ["He who God loves very well, gets fed in Seville; he who God loves not at all, in Córdoba gets a home"]; "En Ciudad Rodrigo, damas; en Cáceres, caballeros, y en Plasencia, dineros" ["In Ciudad Rodrigo, ladies; in Cáceres, gentlemen; in Plasencia, money"];[5] or "En Hervás, judíos los más; en Aldeanueva, la judería entera; en Béjar, hasta las tejas; en Baños, judíos y tacaños" ["In Hervás, mainly Jews; in Aldeanueva, Jewry in its entirety; in Béjar, full to bursting; in Baños, Jews and misers."][6] The inhabitants are sometimes attributed a virtue or failing that obviously has little to do with reality:[7] thus, recently,

---

Nec alterna manet concors et honesta uoluptas.
    Te, pedico, rogus sub Phlegetonte manet.
Nulla lege meri Caesar condemnat amantem.
    Lex damnat pathicos sulphure, pice, rogo.
"German, you like your wine and you Italian, your own sex. Sweet maidens leave you cold and women give you no honest or harmonious pleasure. For you sodomite, the fire awaits you under the Phlegethon. Caesar does not condemn wine-lovers with the law. Sodomites though are punished with the law, by sulphur, pitch and the pyre" [N.S. trans.] (E. Reicke, *Willibald Pirckheimers Briefwechsel*, Munich, 1940, I, pp. 50–51). In another letter addressed to Antonio Kress (Nuremberg, September 22, 1501) Pirckheimer branded the Italians cowards in another hackneyed cliché: "Cuperem sumopere congredi Italis, qui, ut scis, nos contempnunt solumque uerbis et uentositate militant perpessique sunt totam Italiam subiugari a uix decem milibus Gallorum, cum tamen totum mundum se excepturos iactarent. Sed tandem et temeritatis et superbiae meritas, ut spero, poenas luent" (ibid., I, p. 138). Pirckheimer was not a good Latin poet: in *pice* and *Itale* he incorrectly lengthens the first vowel sound.
    [5] A reference to Plasencia's large Jewish population.
    * Translator's note: The Spanish rhymes cannot always be rendered into English.
    [6] José Ramón y Fernández Oxea, "Nuevos dictados tópicos cacereños," *Revista de Estudios Extremeños*, V (1949) p. 398 foll.
    [7] I list a few such sayings: "Alcalá de Henares, mucho te precias y poco vales"; "Alba de Tormes, llena de putas más de ladrones"; "Badajoz, tierra de Dios, que andan las putas de dos en dos"; "Benavente, buena tierra y mala gente"; "Hijos de Madrid, uno bueno entre mil"; "Hijos de Sevilla, uno bueno por maravilla", "Los de Peñaranda, lo que dicen a la noche no lon cumplen a la mañana", "Orense, buen pan, buen vino y mala gente"; "Pancorbo, Briviesca y Belorado, patrimonio del diablo"; "Salamanca, a unos sana y a otros manca y a todos deja sin blanca." ["Alcalá de Henares, highly you think of yourself but little are you worth"; "Alba de Tormes, full of whores and thieves galore"; "Badajoz, God's land, where whores walk in twos, hand in hand"; "Benavente, a good land unlike the people"; "Sons of Madrid, do what you would, only one in a thousand is good"; "Do what you would, sons of Seville, a good one is a miracle"; "What those in Peñaranda say today, tomorrow it has gone away"; "Orense, fine bread, fine wine and wicked people"; "Pancorbo, Briviesca and Belorado, the devil's legacy"; "Salamanca, heals some and cripples many but leaves them all without a penny."]

jokes about people from Lepe were all the rage, with the people of this Spanish town in the province of Huelva mocked as boorish, brainless yokels. What I intend to deal with here is the history of a generic insult aimed at the noble and imperial city of Toledo. But before I begin, I would like to consider the circumstances in which, to the best of my knowledge, the insult first emerged.

It is the year 1480, just before the vital *Cortes* convened in Toledo. According to the royal chronicler Alonso de Palencia, the solemn oath to be sworn by Crown Prince Juan had been postponed and in the intervening interval the well-known dispute for prelacy arose between the procurators of Toledo and León. On home turf, supported by a local crowd, the Toledans believed they could mount a challenge for the title of premiere city of the kingdom of Castile, held by Burgos. Indeed, their arguments seemed solid and consistent. There had been kings who, in their official documents, had entered their titles in this order: King of Castile, of Toledo, of León etc.,[8] owing to the grandeur, antiquity and power of a city which the Goths had called "imperial." Moreover, to serve their argument, they used some bronze plates which declared that the Romans had considered Toledo worthy to be placed before every other city in Hispania Citerior; these were glorious titles for which the Leonese could offer nothing comparable.

In reply the Leonese stated that the Toledans were stirring up age-old feuds that were long since settled. It was poor reasoning to ground one's pleas in antiquity, when even a dullard knew that the entire Visigoth kingdom had succumbed to the rise of Islam, outside the narrow valleys of Asturias and Vasconia. The first to put right this national disaster was the See of León, long before Burgos—which now bore the honor "premier city"—was even founded. It had been a King of León and Castile, namely Alfonso VI, who had recaptured Toledo, which had previously posed such a threat to Christians in view of its grandeur. Before that, even the Toledans themselves had been unable to expel the Muslims and incapable of helping the Leonese to embark upon a war on their behalf. While one king, swayed by Toledan flattery, had

---

[8] In this case, the Toledans were right in part: e.g., Alfonso VIII often gave himself the title *regnans in Castella et in Toleto* (one example will suffice: J. González, *El reino de Castilla en la época de Alfonso VIII. Colección documental*, Madrid, 1960, III, doc. 846 [p. 485]); but this was because Alfonso IX ruled in León.

chosen to put the vanquished before the victors,[9] it was ultimately justice that had triumphed at the moment when the Leonese had bluntly and mordaciously set down their terms for withdrawal from Toledo.

What were these "terms for withdrawal" that the procurators of León referred to? It is here that the problem arose, for it all depended on the interpretation of Alonso de Palencia's Latin text, which read as follows: *ab oratoribus Legionensibus prolatum est in publico concilio Legionenses, quamquam inuictos, iniuriae antelationis Toletanae nunquam obluctaturos, dummodo reges Castellae et Legionis insignia a Legionensibus accepta dimitterent et melangenam Toletanis carissimam loco leonis admitterent.*[10] The great Spanish humanist López de Toro translated this text rather hurriedly and obviously without revising his work. His Castilianized version of Alonso de Palencia's document ran as follows: "The delegates of León declared that they would never fight against the unfair preference for Toledo, provided the monarchs of Castile and León replaced the insignia on the flags accepted by the Leonese, and instead of the lion of León placed a man of black race like those so dear to Toledans."[11] However, the errors of López's translation are immediately obvious. Firstly, it clearly does not refer to "the flags accepted by the Leonese", but rather to the "emblem received from the Leonese." The greatest difficulty, however, lies in the meaning attributed to the surprising term *melangenam*.

Painstaking searches in Latin usage dictionaries are all to no avail: *melangena* simply does not exist. Thus it seems obvious that López de Toro opted to treat the word as a compound. In the first part, he looked for Greek etymology (*mélas* meaning 'black'), whilst the second part he treated as a Latin suffix (*gena* meaning 'born'). But how could "a man of black race" possibly fit into this context? Was it a reference to the darker skins of the "Moors" who were associated with the city, in Islamic hands until 1085? The real answer, I believe, is much simpler. Despite its horrific appearance, the word *melangena* is nothing other than an 'eggplant' or 'aubergine', known today by the scientific name of *solanum melongena* and in Spanish as "berenjena". All Alonso de Palencia did was to Latinize the Italian word *melanzana* (a word which, in an interesting circle, appears to come in turn from Castilian).

---

[9] A reference to Alfonso VIII, who placed Toledo before León in his list of titles. See previous note.

[10] XXXVI 1 (pp. 165–66).

[11] II, p. 194.

Having clarified the meaning of the term, let us move on to the
next question: What have aubergines got to do with Toledo and why
should the Leonese sarcastically suggest that the aubergine become the
royal emblem if Toledo were to get the prelacy? The solution is provided by the great Doctor Andrés Laguna in his thoroughly charming
comment on Dioscórides. This is what he has to say: "The plant that
produces aubergines, both the leaves and the stalk, are very much like
burdock... In France and in Germany, it is extremely rare. In Castile
it is copious, especially in Toledo, which has exposed the Toledans to
much mockery and derision."[12]

"Mockery and derision"? This, indeed, was the case. A shameful
proverb in everybody's mouth at that time, ran as follows: "Toledan,
ahó, berenjena. Ya no las como que soy de Llerena" ["Toledan, *aho*,
aubergine. I don't eat them any more for I am from Llerena"]. M. Frenk
Alatorre records another version of the saying with a similar meaning: "Toledano, alzó, berengena. Yo no las como, que soy de Llerena"
[Toledan, *alzo*, aubergine. I don't eat them, I'm from Llerena].[13]

Sebastián de Horozco y Covarrubias, a Toledan who loved his native
city, sought to put a positive slant on this adage, although he acknowledged unwillingly, its wicked satire. (It comes as no surprise to learn
that, as well as a Toledan, he was also a Converso).

> This proverb [writes Horozco] is used because they call the Toledans
> "berengeneros" [aubergine-eaters]. This means that in Toledo there are
> many aubergines and therefore they eat a great many of them; and the
> word 'aho' is used because in Toledo, when singing to children and show-
> ing them how to eat their food, they give them aubergines saying "aho,
> the aubergine."[14] But the man of Toledo answers maliciously saying "I
> no longer eat them, I'm from Llerena." And that is because in Llerena
> and even in a lot of other places in these kingdoms, they grow and eat
> many more than in Toledo; and so to say "I don't eat them for I am from
> Llerena" means that the people from Llerena are really the ones who eat
> them and it is to them—the people of Llerena—that the term "*aho* the
> aubergine" should apply, because the people from Llerena eat many more

---

[12] *Pedacio Dioscórides Anazarbeo, acerca de la materia medicinal y de los venenos
mortíferos*, Salamanca, 1566, p. 425.

[13] *Corpus de la antigua lírica popular hispánica (siglos XV al XVII)*, Madrid, 1987,
n° 1044, p. 496.

[14] Pace Covarrubias explanation, it would seem evident that the *aho* (or *alzo* in
other versions) is a corruption of *ajo* [garlic], another vegetable associated with the
Conversos. The corruptions may imitate a Toledan or Jewish idiomatic use and thus
add to the derision of the saying.

aubergines than the Toledans; and we could even say the same for the
people of Seville, where there are even more and where they eat more
aubergines than in ten Toledos, and where they are bigger and worse-tast-
ing, because in Toledo, there are only a few and those are of very good
stock, medium sized and they keep very well. And they are eaten not only
by the converted—just in case that is what the saying refers to—but even
more so by the Old Christians, hidalgos and knights, clerics and laymen,
in all manner of different ways. Thus the aubergine of Toledo is not just a
delicacy for Jews, nor for this reason can the Toledans be labelled converts,
as fools believe. And it can be assumed[15] that another reason why this
saying "Toledan, *aho* the aubergine" may be used and is used is that it
refers to bruised faces and black eyes which are also called "aubergines"
So "Toledan, *aho* the aubergine" means that the Toledan knows how to
give other people black eyes and bruised noses from a very early age, but
he never gets hurt or has to sustain any blows himself.[16]

The lexicographer Diego de Covarrubias, on the other hand, was more
cautious, taking care not to include any references to Conversos in his
grand vocabulary. "In Castile," he noted, "there are copious amounts
of [aubergines], particularly in Toledo, and because their flesh is used
in different dishes there, they are called 'aubergine-eaters,' and there
is a proverb that says "Toledano, *aho* aubergine."[17] Covarrubias also
emphasised the poor qualities of the plant: "they are insipid and of
poor substance, because they produce melancholy, sadden the spirit,
and cause headaches and other damage, their poor quality appears in
the face, rendering it livid and dark green in color."

The aubergine's bad reputation, however, was not really due to the
fact that it supposedly produced sadness or melancholy, or for the
poor color of the complexion of those who ate it frequently. Rather,
it came from the fact that it was a vegetable that had been introduced
into Spain by the Muslims, that it was a must on the Jewish table and,
ultimately, in the diet of Conversos.[18] In Doctor Laguna's commentary

---

[15] I correct here the word "prosupuesto" [meaning 'of course'] as used by Weiner,
with "presupuesto" [meaning 'assumed'], and remove the period which the editor
places after "llaman berengenas" [called aubergines].

[16] *Libro de los proverbios glosados*, ed. Jack Weiner, Kassel, 1994, pp. 482–83.

[17] *Tesoro de la lengua castellana o española*, Madrid, 1611, see entry on "berenjena."

[18] This was already noted by M. Ciceri, based on examples from fifteenth century
lyrical poems, in an excellent article: "La 'berenjena': un cibo connotante" in Mª Grazia
Profeti (ed.), *Codici del gusto*, Milan, 1992, pp. 92–93. I would like to express my sincere
gratitude to Prof. Ciceri for his kindness in providing a photocopy of his work which
I received through Prof. P. Botta's helpful mediation.

on the aubergine, part of which is quoted above, the scholar added that "the aubergine...adapts easily to any dish, like the pumpkin. After cooking in water, they [the Toledans] fry it with oil and spices, and finally they eat it with walnut sauce." In other words, it is cooked in a typically Jewish fashion, with olive oil and pungent condiments.[19] The Converso poet Rodrigo Cota, in a burlesque celebration of the son or nephew of the famous moneylender Diego Arias, lists the delicacies served at the wedding feast as follows:

> En la boda desta aljama
> No se comió peliagudo
> Ni pescado sin escama,
> Con quanto el marido pudo,
> Sino mucha berengena
> Y açafrán con acelguilla.
> ¡Quien 'Jesú' diga en la çena
> Que no coma alhondiguilla![20]

> [At the wedding of this *aljama*[21]
> Nothing thorny was eaten
> Nor fish without scales,
> As much as the husband could eat,
> But plenty of aubergine
> And saffron with beet.
> And anyone who says 'Jesus' in the hall
> Won't be eating, not even a meat ball!]

The *Coplas del conde de Paredes a Juan Poeta en un perdonança de Valencia*, contain a huge indictment of the Converso Poeta who taints the Christian religion with his Judaism:

> No dexemos la patena
> A que la boca llegastes,
> Que luego que la besastes
> Se dize que la tornastes
> Caçuela de berenjenas.[22]

---

[19] Christians did not share the Jews and Muslims taste for spices, nor did they cook in olive oil, preferring lard (pig fat).

[20] R. Foulché-Delbosc, *Cancionero castellano del siglo XV*, Madrid, 1915, nº 967, 37–38, p. 590 b.

[21] *Aljama* is the Arabic term employed by the Spanish for Jewish quarter.

[22] V. 31 foll. in *Cancionero general de 1511*, f. 222v (B. Dutton, *El Cancionero del siglo XV*, Salamanca, 1991, V, p. 514 a).

[We won't let the communion plate
Reach your lips,
For after you kiss it
They'll say that you had turned it
Into a pot of aubergine stew.]

In Francisco Delicado's *Lozana andaluza*, the Convero heroine Aldonza
boasts about her talents as a cook, and in so doing reveals her Jewish
provenance: "And do I know how to make *boronía**? Wonderfully!
And aubergine casserole? To perfection. And casserole with a nice bit
of garlic and cumin, and a nice dash of vinegar. None could find fault
with anything I made!"[23]

As a prelude to his *Lusitania* (1532), the Converso playwright Gil
Vicente offers us a kind of *entremés* (or short, one act play) involving
a Jewish family. In one scene, one of the family's daughters attempts to
sweep the family store while being wooed by a nobleman so highborn
that he claims to be descended from the lineage of Aeneas, although
to gain the maiden's favor, it would have been better if his line had led
to Abraham. In an effort to keep her suitor at bay, the girl invites him
to eat "*pinhoada*, or apple casserole". This is not, however, the food
that awaits her father, a tailor by profession.[24] When he returns from
his morning walk, he inquires of his wife:

[Levantaram-se os meninos?
O mantâo mandei guardar.
Que temos para jantar?]

[Are the children up?
Tell them to put away the blanket[25]
What do we have to eat?]

To which she replies:

Berenjelas e pepinos
E cabra curada ò ar.[26]

---

* Translator's note: A savoury pudding made with aubergines, cheese, breadcrumbs and honey.

[23] Mamotreto II, p. 39 Damiani.

[24] The work is full of sub-textual references to the family's Jewish origin. Tailoring, for example, was a profession associated with Jews and Conversos.

[25] The word blanket or *mantao* (*manta* in Spanish) was often employed as a euphemism for the *sambenito*, or sackcloth, worn by penitents convicted of Judaizing by the Inquisition.

[26] *As obras de Gil Vicente*, Lisbon, 2002, II, pp. 386–87. Here, air dried goat is undoubtedly an allusion to the Jewish practice of hanging animals to drain the blood.

[Aubergines and cucumbers
And air-dried goat.]

Another writer of Converso lineage, Baltasar del Alcázar, ironically celebrates the virtues of the aubergine in a quatrain of his humorous poetry:

Tres cosas me tienen preso
De amores el corazón:
La bella Inés, el jamón
Y berengenas con queso.[27]

[My heart is a prisoner
In love with three things:
Beautiful Inés, ham
And cheese with aubergines.]

The same mixture of opposites—pork and aubergines—also appears in a saying quoted by Juan Lorenzo Palmireno: "Fresh pork and aubergines, who can keep their hands off them?"[28]

There is no need to add that the word "Berengena," or aubergine, was a disparaging nickname for Jews and Conversos. For example, the Inquisition records reveal that a Pedro Ruyz, a Converso from Almodavar del Campo, was the son-in-law of an "Aubergine."[29] In the 1508 census of the San Pedro de Carmona district of Seville, a woman is nicknamed "The poor Aubergine."[30] And, in *Don Quixote*, the reckless but logical Sancho confuses Cide Hamete Benengeli with Cidi Hamete *Berengena*, "for…the Moors"—and we might add, the Jews—"are very fond of aubergines."[31]

This is a suitable point at which to discuss the malevolent references to aubergines made by Francisco Quevedo in his picaresque novel *El*

---

[27] 201. The Converso ancestry denoted by the eating of aubergines is alluded to in *Los Conversos y la Inquisición sevillana*, Seville, 2001, III, p. 105; cf. also V. Núñez Rivera, *Baltasar del Alcázar. Obra poética*, 2001, pp. 101–02.

[28] J. Mª Sbarbi, *El refranero general español*, Madrid, 1874–76, I, p. 282. Another variation on the proverb is: "A pies de puerco y cabeza de barbo, ¿quién tendrá quietas las manos?" ["Pork trotters and head of barbel, who can keep their hands still?"].

[29] F. Cantera – P. León Tello, *Judaizantes del arzobispado de Toledo habilitados por la Inquisición en 1495 y 1497*, Madrid, 1969, p. 78: "Pedro Ruyz, son-in-law of Aubergine."

[30] Professor M. González gave me a copy of this census for which I am deeply grateful.

[31] *Don Quixote*, II, 2. (Translation taken from Penguin Classics, first published 1950, p. 485).

* Translator's note: paste made with pine seeds.

Buscón (*The Swindler*). Here one of the main character's fellow students boasts about throwing "two aubergines at his mother when she was a bishop,"[32] in other words when she wore the cone-shaped hat associated with penitents in the auto de fe.[33] In an earlier scene, the Swindler himself receives an avalanche of aubergines and turnips as he proudly struts around the streets of Alcalá de Henares, as if he were a king. Recalling his ordeal, he confesses that, "as I had feathers in my hat, I realised they had mistaken me for my mother, and were throwing them at her as they had done before."[34] As the Swindler, Pablos, has already informed the reader, his mother "was suspected…of not being an old Christian";[35] furthermore, she was considered a witch—a crime for which the Inquisition of Toledo later threw her into jail.[36] Like her, all those condemned for witchcraft were hailed with aubergines by uncharitable souls when they were forced to parade in their pointed hats to the auto-de-fe: hence, they were "thrashed" and "hailed" with vegetables. Quevedo himself gives us a further example of the same jeering in a picaresque ballad where a woman complains about what happened to her own mother:

> Pues sin respetar las tocas,
> Ni las canas, ni la edad,
> A fuerza de cardenales
> Ya la hicieron obispar.
> Tras ella, de su motivo,
> Se salían del hogar
> Las ollas con sus legumbres:
> No se vio en el mundo tal.
> Pues cogió más berengenas
> En una hora, sin sembrar,

---

[32] I 2 (*BAE* 23, p. 487 b). Translator's note: People found guilty of witchcraft were paraded in a cone-shaped hat, often called a mitre for its resemblance to a bishop's hat, and vegetables were thrown at them.

[33] The same metaphors (cone-shaped hat = mitre = bishop) are found again in the *Vida del Buscón* [*Life of a Swindler*], when some rogues are laughing at an old bawd and witch: "One looked at her and said: 'How well this mitre will suit you, mother, and how gladly I would see you consecrating three thousand turnips to your service!' And another: 'Their Excellencies the Mayors have already chosen some feather so you cut a dash when you come in.'" (II 8 [p. 522 a]).

[34] I, 2 (p. 488 a and b).

[35] I, 1 (p. 486 a).

[36] I, 7 (p. 498 a).

Que un hortelano morisco
En todo un año cabal.[37]

[For with no respect for hats,
Or grey hair, or age,
With bruises
They made her bishop.
Following her, for this reason,
They brought out of the house
Pots with their vegetables:
You never saw such a thing.
For they picked up more aubergines
In an hour, without planting them,
Than the Morisco gardener
In a whole year.]

This barbaric custom goes back at least to the fifteenth century. In one vulgar poem, Íñigo de Estúñiga imagines the Converso poet Juan Alfonso de Baena "forced to flee from the blows of aubergines (*berengenadas*)."[38] Thus the Spanish term 'berenjenada' was used to define the action of mortifying, not just witches, but also Conversos; although initially, of course, the hail of aubergines was reserved exclusively for Jews.[39]

Berenjenero was, then, a generic insult used against Toledans in an attempt to hit them where it hurt most, namely alluding to their tainted condition. Cervantes' hero, Don Quijote, himself makes reference to the nickname, indicating that it was a term that caused some distress among

---

[37] *El Parnaso español*, 336 (*BAE* 69, p. 99 b). Note that the aubergine is planted by a Morisco. [Translator's note. This is my own translation. The English is unable to render the puns used here by Quevedo.]

[38] *Cancionero de Baena*, 418 (in B. Dutton, *El cancionero del siglo XV*, Salamanca, 1991, III, p. 262 a). In Baena, the birthplace of its compiler, Juan Alfonso "they take care to plant plenty of good aubergines, which they consider a delicacy" (ibid., 424 [p. 263 a Dutton]). The satire cannot help but remind us more of Toledo than of Baena.

[39] In this context, it seems very likely that the firing of this fruit and vegetable projectiles gave rise to the Spanish expression "*meterse en un berenjenal*" [literally, get into a field of aubergines], which is defined by the Spanish Academy as "getting into complicated or difficult affairs or business." The first example I know of its use, however, is by the Archpriest of Talavera (Archpriest of Talavera, *Corvacho*, I 35) and does not enable us to draw any definitive conclusions. The term is used by an angry man: "Fie upon that whore, that daughter of a whore! Making scornful gestures at me or signs with her eyes and doing this and that…making signs at me with her eyes and pushing me with her hand. For…it was perhaps the devil got us into this *verengenal* [predicament].

the city's inhabitants. However, in this instance, Quijote, that great righter of wrongs, recommends restraint on the part of the insulted.

> This being so, then, that one man alone cannot insult a kingdom, a province, a city, a commonwealth, or a whole population, there is clearly no need to go out and take up the challenge for such an insult, for it is not one. It would be a fine thing for the people of the *Clock Town* to be perpetually at drawn swords with anyone calling them by that name, or for the *Heretics* [of Valladolid] either, or the *Aubergine-eaters* [of Toledo], the Whalers [of Madrid, also disparagingly referred to as "cats"],[40] the Soap-boilers [of Seville], or others whose names or nick-names are for ever on the tongues of the boys and the riff-raff! It would be a fine thing, indeed, for all these famous towns to be enraged, and take vengeance, and perpetually go about with their swords out like gutting knives in every petty quarrel![41]

It is more than likely that Cervantes was well acquainted with the meaning of each of these insulting nick-names, but he remained discreetly silent on the matter. In the case of the "Soap-boilers," the name was apparently intended to brand the people of Seville "Moors," because the production of soap—a product which was sold in the city for the astronomical price of fifty to sixty thousand arrobas, according to A. Morgado[42]—was generally in Muslim hands. Even today, some villages in the North of Spain, confident of their own blood purity and no less proud of the eminence of their race, refer to Andalucíans as "Moors." The foolishness of such insults infuriated Cervantes, quite justifiably. But let us leave this subject and move on to a second and no less interesting question.

How did the Toledans defend themselves against this insulting label? The royal chronicler Alfonso de Palencia himself tells us something about the matter: they collated ancient inscriptions and old parchments singing the praises of an age-old Toledo; moreover, they brought out bronze plates apparently inscribed in Latin, which heaped more glorious titles on their city. In other words, they looked back to a kind of paradise lost, a beautiful but imaginary golden age, conveniently discarding

---

[40] Cf. F. Márquez Villanueva, *Investigaciones sobre Juan Álvarez Gato*, Madrid, 1960, p. 52.

[41] *Don Quixote*, II 27 (Penguin Classics, first published 1950) Trans. J. M. Cohen. p. 649.

[42] *Historia de Sevilla, en la qual se contienen sus antigüedades, grandezas, y cosas memorables en alla acontecidas, desde su fundación hasta nuestros tiempos*, Seville, 1587, f. 52r.

the misfortunes, and very real stains left by recent history. Such subtle sophism and elegant invention immediately brings to mind the origin of that other great fraud, indeed, the most famous forgery of the sixteenth century, the deception of the Plomos [Lead Books] of Sacromonte. Inscriptions in bronze, inscriptions in lead; this kind of falsification, as we shall see, was deeply rooted in the history of Spain.[43] The most curious thing about it is that, in both cases, the subterfuge was conducted with the very specific aim of washing away the stains that stigmatised a religious minority.

Labelled Jews, and thus second class Spaniards, it was natural that the Toledans should be sensitive to slights to their city's noble status. One such "attack" occurred in 1492, when the recently conquered city of Granada was placed before Toledo in the royal titulature. In that year the Toledan Canon Alonso Ortiz was sent to Granada to congratulate the royal couple on their triumph and to present the protests of both the city council and the cathedral. Toledo deserved "primacy over all cities in Spain by virtue of her antiquity and nobility," Ortiz's memorial stated.

> This is the royal See from which the monarchs who came before you dominated all of the Spains and large part of France, with all of Tangier in Africa. This See sends out the laws; from this See, all the provinces learned their language and customs, here was the primacy and the head of Divine Worship and of the Churches of Spain, here were the Holy Councils over which monarchs presided with its primates, here are the royal tombs, here the emblems and arms that ruled, here the signs and the standards of the victories of your predecessors, and here the true flags and arms that commemorate your first victory are placed as an example for those that come after you, glorious prince and princess.[44]

King Alfonso VI was already known as King of Castile when he conquered Toledo and could therefore not change his titulature and start the list of his lands with Toledo. "Nevertheless, he placed it before the

---

[43] The taste for falsification shared by another Converso, the great Fray Antonio de Guevara, is also interesting.

[44] Ortiz's text can be read in a codex belonging to Sebastián de Orozco: Madrid, Biblioteca Nacional, ms. 9175, f. 114v and foll. (council letter) and f. 120v and foll. (letter from the Cathedral chapter) or in Jerónimo Román de la Higuera, *Historia eclesiastica de la ymperial ziudad de Toledo y su tierra* (Madrid, Biblioteca Nacional, ms. 1291 [vol. VII], f. 74v foll.). The letters were also printed in Seville, at the printers run by Three German Partners, a year after they were presented to the Catholic Monarchs (1493).

city of León…, although a short time ago, as this was not upheld, we had to complain many times for having altered and, to be more precise, perverted the ancient order of your royal titles, placing León first in contravention of a three hundred year old custom." The loss of this honor caused by the new situation would have been unbearable in every respect. In addition to this, how could the vanquished city be placed before the victor? The kingdom of Granada should therefore have been the last of the royal titles. How could temporal and civil might prevail over ecclesiastical power so that Toledo ranked lower than a city that was spiritually subordinate to it?

Ortiz argued that the city was willing to defend its rights to the hilt. But there was no time to revive old laurels. The issue was settled immediately: on March 20, 1492, the monarchs replied that they had placed the kingdom of Granada first because they had included it in their coat of arms, but that they had no intention of in any way harming Toledo, which they would always give precedence over Granada in any of their courts, together with other councils which would be celebrated from that point onwards.[45] Faced with this reply, the Toledans could only swallow their indignation in silence, with no opportunity for further boasting, either rightfully or wrongfully.

There remained, however, the insult of Judaism.[46] The chroniclers of Toledo—a city which has never been short of panegyrists—sought to shake off this ignominy in every possible way. The first subterfuge was to obscure its origins, submerging the birth of the Toledan synagogue in a dim and distant past. Thus, its very antiquity exonerated its members from any charge that might be brought against the Jewry of Palestine for their active participation in the crucifixion of Jesus. This is an argument found in a "summa" written against the Jews by Doctor Honorato Figuerola, Canon of Valencia,[47] a document I have not

---

[45] Jerónimo Román de la Higuera, *Historia eclesiástica de la ymperial ziudad de Toledo y su tierra* Madrid, Biblioteca Nacional, ms. 1291 (vol. VII), f. 77r.

[46] It is interesting that, in his youth, Juan Ginés de Sepúlveda, should have been annoyed that the members of the House of Alba referred to themselves as "from Toledo" rather than "Toledans", as classical rules dictated (*Cato Vticensis* rather than *Cato ab Vtica*): it was an invention, he added, to try to distinguish their family from the common people ("discrimen…ad claritatem ipsius familiae a ciuibus quibusque Toletanis uelut lato clauo distinguendam excogitarunt" [*Ioannis Genesii Sepulvedae opera omnia*, Madrid, 1790, III, p. 365]). Is this not an indirect reproach that the Alba family should have tried, in this way, to shrug off any Jewish blemish?

[47] Figuerola, a passionate supporter of the Inquisition, also made some addition to the treatise *De haereticis* by Zanchi Ugolini, which were published as notes in the

been able to handle myself and which I am acquainted with thanks to a quotation from Pedro Antonio Beuter:

> They also say another thing worthy of note: that when the Jews came to Spain during the persecution of Babylonia, they founded a synagogue in Toledo; and afterwards, when they were free to return to Jerusalem and build the temple, when those who were here were called back, they did not want to return, and said that they knew from the prophets that the second temple that was being built would also be destroyed, and so they stayed here; and that the Synagogue of Toledo that remained from that time was blessed by our St Vincent Ferrer of Valencia, and it was called Our White Lady. This is what the Jews said, though we do not know if they told the truth. It may have been the case.[48]

While some of Toledo's apologists attempted to demonstrate the innocence of the Toledan's ancient Jewish community, others, of a humanist bent, preferred to ignore the Jews altogether and concentrate on the city's links to the Greeks. Indeed, the arrival of the Greeks in Spain was documented by venerable sources. Was not the name of the city Tuy (Tude) in Galicia derived from Tydeus? Why, then, could the same not be true for Toledo? In 1549, a scholarly and highly readable work appeared written by the Toledan Canon Blas Ortiz which exalted the grandeur of the Toledo Cathedral. Ortiz sought to ennoble his See by endowing it with a Hellenic origin. This, he claimed, was what its etymology suggested, for Toledo came from *ptoliethron*, meaning "city."[49] This supposed Greek foundation was just the thing to rid the city of its stain of Jewish origin, an aim shared, as we shall see, by other writers.

A native of Toledo, Pedro de Alcocer is full of praise for his native city, "imperial city, known in the histories as head of the Spains" (I 4 [f. 10r]).[50] According to him, it was founded by the Greek astrologer Pherecius, who, after abandoning Amphilochus in Galicia, had established

---

margin in *De haereticis D. Zanchini Ugolini Senae Ariminen. i.c. clar. Tractatus aureus,* Rome, 1579. The cover shows *breues ac perutiles notae in margine è regione singularum disputationum D. Honorati Figuerolae, patricij Valentini, Iuris Vtriusque doctoris.*

[48] *Primera parte de la Corónica general de toda España, y especialmente del reyno de Valencia,* Valencia, 1546, Chap. XXIV, f. 78v.

[49] "Toletum enim e Graeco nomine ptoliethron, quod oppidum urbemque significat, deductum esse coniicio" (*Summi templi Toletani descriptio, Blasio Ortizio iuris pontificii doctore eiusdem templi canonico Toletanique dioecesis uicario generali auctore,* Toledo, 1549, f. 8r).

[50] In his book *Historia, o descripción de la imperial cibdad de Toledo. Con todas las cosas acontecidas en ella, desde su principio y fundacion,* Toledo, 1554. I have quoted by book, chapter and folio in the text.

a city called Taigeto, a name that had since been corrupted to Toledo
(I 6 [f. 11v foll.]). This was another *ad hoc* fable. And Alcocer goes on to
say that even in the days of the Roman conquest "this city was praised
with titles of honor, even though writers did not write of these" (I 16
[f. 19r]). Also thanks to this false testimony, endorsed by the primacy
(the Cathedral housed books that had been adulterated for the greater
glory of the See), it was possible to prove that Toledo had been magni-
fied by the visits of both Pope Sixtus II ("they say that Pope Sixtus, the
second to go by this name, came to this city to celebrate council in it in
the year of Our Lord 253": I 21 [f. 21r]) and of Emperor Constantine
("which proves in the testimony of a very ancient book that this Holy
Church possesses, where it is written that Emperor Constantine came
to Spain 24 years into his reign": I 20 [f. 20v]).[51]

Up until that moment, by singing the dithyramb of the city and
its inhabitants, their condition of "aubergine-eaters" was concealed.
Alcocer, however, could not deny the existence of Jews in Toledo;
his only escape route was to rewrite history, replacing reality with
imaginary accounts: the same trick that had previously been used, as
we have seen, for the Toledan Synagogue. Alcocer therefore assumes
that King Pyrrhus (= Nebuchadnezzar) brought a large contingent of
Hebrews to Toledo at the time of the Babylonian captivity. The excellence and nobility of these Jews was considered to have left its mark
on the toponymy: Maqueda, Escalona (from Ascalón), Noves (from
Nobe), Yepes (from Jope), Aceca and *Collis Aquile* (Cerro del Aguila).
We shall return to this later. It should be added here, however, that by
that stage another incredible fraud had also been designed: the famous
inscription of Murviedro which referred to Adoniram, King Solomon's
tax collector, who died on Hispanic territory whilst carrying out his
business (I 10 [f. 14r] and foll.).[52]

Leaving aside impossible etymologies of the city that were no less
fantastic than their medieval counterparts,[53] it might be said that the

---

[51] Note that Alcocer opts, where possible, for a Roman rather than a Muslim origin. Thus, for instance, he claims Bisagra to be derived from *via Sacra*, the name of a
famous street in Rome, explicitly rejecting its Arab etymology (I 16 [f. 19r]). Chapter
I 32 defends that the primacy of the Hispanic Church was always in Toledo, undoubtedly in an attempt to ward off the claims of the See of Seville.

[52] On this aspect, cf. my article "Judíos y Conversos en los falsos cronicones," in
A. Molinié – J. P. Duviols, *Inquisition d'Espagne*, París, 2003, pp. 21–43.

[53] I would here like to recall just one thing which can be read in a manuscript
which falsely imitates Gothic writing and style. Tarcos King of Ávila married his only

doctrine expounded by Alcocer on the Hebrew origin of some Toledan place names, enjoyed virtually universal acceptance. Even the Iberian Peninsula's greatest Bible editor, Arias Montano, accepted it as valid, although he too undoubtedly had ulterior motives for doing so. The list of supposedly Hebrew place names given by Montano, which is identical to the one that appears in Pedro de Alcocer's work, follows almost exactly the same order, thus making it possible to correct the errata that disfigure the original Latin text (its publisher, the Frenchman Christopher Plantin, did not understand Spanish, and the print setter even less so):

> *Azeca* in Latin means "ditch," in Spanish "the Hole." There is still a city of this name in the country of Toledo, given this name by the Jews who populated this region in antiquity, and who gave Hebrew names to other places in the same stretch of countryside, like Matreda (= Maqueda),[54] Ascalona (= Escalona), Icuene (= Noves), Iope or Iopea (= Yepes).[55]

---

daughter to Rotas, a King of the Indies, and great astrologer, who had come to Spain "tired of the peoples of that land" and who, before he got married, lived in a cave in Toledo with a huge bear. The marriage produced two children called Tolo and Ledo who built two towers "on the two highest parts of the hill, one of which is now the Fortress of Toledo and the other the tower of Saint Román, near Saint Clement and Saint Peter the Martyr; and they gave their name to Toledo. Afterwards, many years later, it was destroyed because of the great drought that Spain suffered, and it did not rain in thirty-seven years, which was in the time of King Pyrrhus, who succeeded King Hispan in the realms of death, and was uninhabited until the arrival of the Almonids who threw the Greeks out of Spain. These settled in Toledo and Córdoba and made a place named after them called Almonazir near Toledo" (Madrid, BN ms. 3346, f. 280r). Rodrigo Jiménez de Rada had assumed that the name of Toledo came from Consuls Tolemon and Brutus, its foundation being dated 108 years before the arrival of Julius Caesar, in the time of Ptolemy Euergetes (*De rebus Hispaniae*, I 3); and this is the doctrine Renaissance historians usually accepted (cf. Tarafa, *Chrónica d'Espanya*, Barcelona (Claudio Bornat), 1563, ff. 34r–34v, who adds "Ptolemy says that before it was called Cerezola"). According to *Historia Pseudoisidoriana*, 5 (Mommsen, *Chronica minora*, II, p. 380), it was Augustus who built the city; and his name came from '*Tolle lectum tuum', quia ibi requieuit*; as ever, this chronicle comes as a surprise.

[54] Before, without Alcocer's help, I had thought of Méntrida (cf. *Arias Montano y su tiempo*, Exhibition catalogue, Badajoz, 1998, p. 105).

[55] *De optimo imperio, siue in lib. Iosuae commentarium*, Antwerp, 1583, p. 449: "*Azecha* Latinè fossam, Hispanicè uerò redditur *la Caua*. Cuius nominis oppidum in Toletano agro etiam nunc est ab Israelitis, qui illam regionem olim habitauere, impositum, à quibus et loca alia nominibus patrijs appellata sunt in eodem agro, ut Matreda, Ascalona, Icuenes, Ioppe siue Ioppes".

The well-worn story of the conquest of Hispania by Nebuchadnezzar comes from a text by Megasthenes quoted by Josephus[56] and Strabo.[57] If we are to believe the Greek historian, by the third century B.C., the Assyrian king had taken most of Africa and Iberia, thereby surpassing even the glorious feats of Hercules. Iberia is an ambiguous term, for it may refer to the Spanish Iberia or the Iberia of the Caucasus; but expansion throughout Africa suggests that Megasthenes was referring to Hispania. We can therefore also assume that part of the Babylonian troops consisted of Jews who had been brought into the war either willingly or by force. This was certainly the view of some, including Tarafa, who even gave a date for this unprecedented event, recording in his annals Nebuchadnezzar's renunciation in favor of his successors: "before the coming of Jesus Christ .Dlxxj., and having ruled for nine years, he gave it to the Carthaginians."[58]

According to Esteban de Garibay, the Jews—"one of the most prominent nations which came in the armies of Nebuchadnezzar"—"founded a settlement on the banks of the Tagus on a naturally strong position on a high hill, which in their Hebrew language they called Toledoth, which means 'generations,' for all the generations of the ten tribes of Israel contributed to its settlement and foundation."[59] However, while Garibay presented the Jews as ancient inhabitants of the city, he deemed totally fictitious the view held by some, "that the Jews of this city, being so ancient, and for not having consented either for themselves or their messengers the imprisonment and death of the Redeemer of the world, were later exempted and freed from certain kinds of taxes which the other Hebrews in other regions paid to their princes."[60] The spotlight was once again on the Jews of Toledo, whose provenance, although ancient, did not separate them from the Synagogue of Jerusalem or the death of Christ.

Garibay, on the other hand, did attribute great significance to the Jews who had supposedly come to Spain in the "second dispersal," in other words, the diaspora resulting from the capture of Jerusalem by Titus in A.D. 70. Garibay suggested that it was these settlers who had

---

[56] *Antigüedades judaicas*, X 227.
[57] *Geografía*, XV 1, 6 (cf. my book *La India y el Catay. Textos de la Antigüedad clásica y del Medievo occidental*, Madrid, 1995, pp. 180–81).
[58] *Chrónica d'Espanya*, Barcelona (Claudio Bornat), 1563, ff. 29r–29v.
[59] *Los XL. Libros del compendio historial de las Chrónicas e universal historia de todos los reynos de España*, Amberes, 1571, V 4, p. 129.
[60] Ibid., p. 132.

named the city of Granada, the etymology of which was Garnat, "the Pilgrim" in Hebrew. Reginaldo González de Montes also attributed the arrival of the Hebrews on the Iberian Peninsular to the destruction of the Second Temple, "as its most ancient annals relate."[61] However, the idea of descending from such recent Jewry, and, in particular, Jews who had come from Palestine after the Crucifixion, did not seem dignified or even decent to other Spanish historians who were always concerned about their honor, because these Jews—either themselves or their relatives—may have been precisely the ones who condemned Jesus. Hence even a serious chronicler like L. del Mármol Carvajal, whilst accepting the etymology proposed by Garibay, predated the settlement of the city to the first wave of Jews, in other words, to the mythical times of Nebuchadnezzar.[62]

It should be noted, moreover, that there was even mention of a third diaspora, caused by the Jewish war in the time of Hadrian. For Yosef ha-Kohen,[63] this was the origin of "the emigrants of Jerusalem who are in Spain today," those who had been banished and whom the Prophet Abdias had promised a glorious destiny.

Garibay's lucubrations met with an angry response from an atypical Toledan: the renowned Jesuit impostor, Jerónimo Román de la Higuera. In his long-winded—and as such never published—history of Toledo, Román de la Higuera could not emphasise enough that he had no idea about the distant origins of the city, although he did scoff rather wittily at Garibay's fantasies:

> This would be very well put if it had any grounds for truth or were based on anything but conjectures, these being neither appropriate nor well refined. And it would be reasonable that anyone who takes on the task of great history should look and consider that what he puts his name to really is history and not more legend or fabrication than anything else; and it is outrageous to write about uncertain things with little foundation with the licence and confidence of someone writing the conclusions or mathematical demonstrations of Euclid.[64]

---

[61] Nicolás Castrillo Benito, El "Reginaldo Montano": primer libro polémico contra la Inquisición española, Madrid, 1991, p. 168.

[62] Rebelión y castigo de los moriscos de Granada, I 4 (BAE 21, p. 129 b).

[63] 'Emeq ha-Bakha (El valle del llanto), p. 52. I was unable to find a similar passage in Usque's Consolaçâo.

[64] Historia eclesiástica (Madrid, BN ms. 1285 [vol. I], f. 36).

Román de la Higuera would have done better to apply the same caustic criticism he aimed at Garibay to his own work, for his own histories often plummeted to the same dark depths. According to the Jesuit, the Jews did not come to Spain with Nebuchadnezzar's army, although Toledo was indeed founded by the Assyrian king who gave it the Chaldean name of *Toledoth*.[65] This saved it from its Jewish origin. So when did the Hebrews first reach Spanish soil? Román accepts the opinion of Beuter: after Babylon was destroyed, Jews came with the fabled Pyrrhus to Spain.[66] We need hardly add that he then goes on to speak about the burial of Adoniram and the fleets sent by Solomon to Tartessus, in other words, to Tarsus and Ofir.[67] Centuries later, the Jewish apostles (St James, St Peter and St Paul) also came to Spain to preach the gospel, and it was in Toledo that their seed flourished.

Let us now see how Román de la Higuera treated another of these delicate subjects: the capture of Toledo by the Muslims in 711. After weighing up opinions on the surrender of the city, the Jesuit eventually accepts that, before its conquest, siegers and besieged took part in fierce fighting (underling the bravery of Toledo's inhabitants): "so it seems more likely to me that this city was besieged for a long time and that great feats took place during the siege."[68] However, the weight of tradition was too strong to deny that, when they saw that the siege was continuing without any possibility of salvation, the Jews—"despicable and cowardly people, accustomed to similar vile deeds"—made a pact with Muza and handed over the city to him on April 9, when the Christians were celebrating the feast of Saint Leocadia.[69]

---

[65] *Historia eclesiástica* (Madrid, BN ms. 1285 [vol. I], f. 39v).

[66] In reality, Figuerola's opinion, as quoted above. Interestingly, Beuter shied away from tackling the antiquity of Toledo: he did not even mention its etymology.

[67] *Historia eclesiástica* (Madrid, BN ms. 1285 [vol. I], f. 47v foll.).

[68] *Historia eclesiástica* (Madrid, BN ms. 1286 [vol. II], f. 236r). It is interesting to note how Román excuses the flight from the invaders of the Metropolitan Sinдеredus, whom the *Crónica mozárabe* dubbed a "mercenary" for this unseemly action: "Moreover if we consider the operation attentively, what benefit could a pastor divested of his office and name of pastor have done for his sheep, or the sheep already infected with mange?" The Metropolitan was said to have gone to Rome to defend his just cause against the tyrannical intrusion of Oppas in his archbishopric (ibid., f. 229v). The blame for this huge disaster lay, according to Román, as in the medieval chronicles, with "the sins of the Goths, who brought down the just revenge of Heaven upon them" (ibid., f. 228r).

[69] *Historia eclesiástica* (Madrid, BN ms. 1286 [vol. II], ff. 236v–237r). This is the low medieval tradition described by Alonso de Espina in his *Fortalitium fidei* (Third book, Seventh consideration, Third point, First example).

It was this legend of the Toledan Jews' treachery that Pedro Sarmiento focused upon in 1449, when he led an attack on the city's Converso population and introduced the infamous *sentencia-estatuto*, now recognized as Spain's first *limpieza de sangre* legislation. In that document, Sarmiento emphasised the Conversos' congenital malfeasance:

> ...according to the old chronicles, when the city was surrounded by our enemies the Moors under Tariq their leader, after the death of King Roderic, [the Jews] sold out the city and its Christian population, allowing the said Moors to enter, after which 306 old Christians were put to the sword and more than 106, among whom were women and children, great and small, were removed from the Cathedral and the church of Saint Leocadia and taken prisoner. And this treachery is continued by Conversos, descendents of the Jews, who through great deceit have taken and robbed great and innumerable quantities of maravedi and silver from our lord the king and from his rents and rights and taxes, and have destroyed and ruined many noble ladies, knights and hidalgos...[70]

However, unlike Sarmiento, Román de la Higuera, writing in the late sixteenth century, was keen to separate the city's Converso population, or at least the majority of them, from an earlier Jewish treachery. He thus notes in his *Historia* that the 1449 insurgents

> only attacked nineteen people [for corruption], which is very significant in this imperial city,[71] which boasts a population of four thousand Jews and where the total inhabitants number one hundred thousand; and that these [nineteen converos] were falsely accused can be seen by the events of thirty years later when numerous members of this caste [the Conversos] were reconciled [by the Inquisition] without any of these names, it seems, being present, who came from families that were converted by Saint *** in this city; and I have known descendants of theirs who have not been punished by the Holy Office, and have shown every sign of being as good Christians as could be wished for, and from parents and grandparents of great purity.[72]

In other words, the Toledo population of Conversos could be divided into two groups, old and new. The old Conversos were those who came from Jews converted in antiquity by an apostle—interestingly, Román de la Higuera leaves out the name—and had a long and impeccable tradition of Christianity, so none of them had been reconciled by the Inquisition. To this clean and pure caste there belonged nineteen

---

[70] Eloy Benito Ruano, *Toledo en el siglos XV*, Madrid, 1960, pp. 193–194.
[71] The words "*no se*" have been removed from the Spanish text.
[72] *Historia eclesiástica* (Madrid, BN ms. 1290 [vol. VI], f. 227v).

regidores and officials who were, according to Román de la Higuera, wrongly accused by Sarmiento and expelled from all public posts. At the same time, new Conversos—although this is not clearly stated—came from Jews who arrived in Spain after the Passion, Jews who were stubborn and obstinate in their faith and only converted to Christianity at a very late stage. In this way, the Toledan lineages of those patrician Conversos stigmatised by Sarmiento, and whose names Román de la Higuera knew well and kept quiet about, became even more splendid than the Old Christians themselves, because their Christianity was from an earlier age, uncorrupted by secular temptations.

Roman de la Higuera, that great falsifier of history, did his best to contest the Toledans tainted (Converso) image. The Toledo presented by him in his false chronicles was an illustrious city whose inhabitants, even those of Jewish provenance, were both honorable and pious. However, as the chronicler wrote his hagiographies, celebrating the city's glorious past, Toledo was already in steep decline, its nobility, wealthy merchants and bureaucrats having followed the royal court to Spain's recently established capital, Madrid. It is noteworthy that among these elite exiles were numerous members of the city's influential Converso community. Ironically, when the vilified aubergine eaters left Toledo, in the late sixteenth century, the great city sank.

CHAPTER SIX

SICILIAN CONVERTS AFTER THE EXPULSION:
INTER-COMMUNITY RELATIONS, ACCULTURATION
AND THE PRESERVATION OF GROUP IDENTITY

Nadia Zeldes

The first indication of the presence of a significant number of Conversos, or *neofiti* in Sicily comes from a letter that Pope Sixtus IV wrote in 1483 to Queen Isabella, who on her marriage to Ferdinand received the large fief of Syracuse and its environment as a marriage gift.[1] The letter mentioned the growth of false conversions that "had spread like a plague in Sicily."[2] Conversions in that period may have been the result of intensive preaching by mendicant friars (such as the Dominican Giovanni da Pistoia, who was active between 1463–1467),[3] or perhaps a result of the riots of the summer of 1474 that spread throughout the island and hit the Jewries of southern Sicily, in the counties of Modica and Noto, particularly hard.[4] As yet, however, there is not enough

---

[1] In 1470 King John II of Aragon gave Princess Isabella the "Camera reginale", traditionally given to the Aragonese queens since the fourteenth century: J. Vicens Vives, *Fernando El Católico, Principe de Aragon, Rey de Sicilia 1458–1478*, Madrid 1952, p. 430. Thus, not only Ferdinand, who inherited the kingdom, but also Isabella had interests in Sicily.

[2] Sixtus's letter: "Quantum vero attinet ad negotium neofitorum, quod solum inquisitoribus deputatis demandari velles…Conati semper fuimus, miserti illorum insanie, tam pestifero morbo oportuna remedia adhibere. Sentientes etiam huiusmodi pestem in Sicilia invaluisse, iam pridem per varias bullas nostras adversus tam perfidum et scelestum genus hominum istuc transmissas provideramus" S. Simonsohn, *The Apostolic See and the Jews*, Toronto 1991, Vol. III, No. 1023, p. 1291. The political circumstances surrounding this correspondence are discussed by L. Suárez Fernández, *Politica internacional de Isabel la Católica*, Valladolid 1965, Vol. I, pp. 225–258. The letter: ibid. vol. II, p. 183ff.

[3] On the activities of Mendicant Friars in Sicily, see: M. Bevilacqua Krasner, "Re, regine, francescani, domenicani ed ebrei in Sicilia nel XIV e XV secolo. Potere politico, potere religioso e comunità ebraiche in Sicilia", *Archivio Storico Siciliano* XXIV (1998), pp. 61–91. N. Zeldes, "Sicilian Converts in the Contemporary Mediterranean Context (1400–1492)," *Guglielmo Raimundo Moncada alias Flavio Mitridate. Un ebreo converso siciliano. Atti del Convegno Internazionale Caltabellota 23–24 ottobre 2004*, ed. M. Perani, Palermo, 2008, pp. 33–47.

[4] On the pogroms of 1474, see: G. Modica-Scala, *Le comunità ebraiche nella contea di Modica*, Modica 1978, pp. 215–227; G. Giarrizzo, "La Sicilia dal cinquecento all'unità

documentation to determine the extent of conversions that occurred before the 1492 expulsion.

A large number of conversions occurred during the period of the expulsion, in part as a result of the persuasive tactics of the Sicilian authorities. On the 6th of July 1492, less than a month after the publication of the edict of expulsion, the Viceroy of Sicily, Don Ferrando de Acuña, published a letter promising the Jews who wished to convert that they would not be harmed and that they would be treated in the same way as Christians, and he had the letter read in the synagogues. The letters from the Portuguese Jew, Abraham Hayyiun, who witnessed the expulsion, confirm this.[5] In certain cases, Jews who had already sold their property in order to depart changed their minds and converted.

Another wave of conversions occurred after 1494, this time among the Sicilian Jews who had migrated to the kingdom of Naples. The death of King Ferrante I in January 1494 and the invasion of the French army, headed by Charles VIII, destabilized the country and riots broke out against the Jews, resulting in mass conversions. The presence of large numbers of converts in the Kingdom of Naples is attested to by a variety of sources, among them contemporary Jewish chronicles and the *Capitoli* (pleas) presented to King Federico d'Aragona, king of Naples in 1498. The latter mention "the New Christians who converted since the coming of the French to this place [i.e. the kingdom of Naples]."[6] Of the conversion of the Sicilian Jews in the Kingdom of Naples we have only indirect evidence. An agreement between King Ferdinand the Catholic and a converted Sicilian Jew, the physician Fernando de Aragona, promised the converted exiles that they would be allowed to recover the property they had left in Sicily, deducting 40% of its value in favor of the king's treasury. In another agreement concluded in 1497, the percentage was increased to 45%. The treasury expected to collect 65,000 Sicilian florins from this transaction and the fact that this sum

---

d'Italia," in V. D'Alessandro, and G. Giarrizzo, *La Sicilia dal Vespro all'Unita d'Italia*, Serie Storia d'Italia, ed. G. Galasso, Torino 1989, Vol. 16, p. 110; G. Palermo, "New Evidence about the Slaughter of the Jews in Modica, Noto and Elsewhere in Sicily (1474)," *Henoch* XXII (2000), p. 263.

    [5] J. Hacker, "Some Letters on the Expulsion of the Jews from Spain and Sicily," *Studies in the History of Jewish Society in the Middle Ages and in the Modern Period, Presented to Prof. J. Katz*, Jerusalem, 1980: pp. 64–97, (Hebrew).

    [6] B. Ferrante, "Gli statuti di Federico d'Aragona per gli ebrei del regno," *Archivio Storico per le Provincie Napoletane* XCVII (1979), p. 147.

was collected by 1508 indicates that a large number of converts had indeed returned to Sicily.[7]

Considering that the first notice of large scale conversions comes from 1483, and since we know that the rest occurred during the period of the expulsion and in the decade that followed, it appears that most Sicilian *neofiti* were first generation converts. By the time the Spanish Inquisition began investigating them in earnest, from 1500 onwards, it was in fact acting against a population that had had very little time to adjust to the changes in their religious and social status. Moreover, these neophytes did not have the time to become integrated into Sicilian society or create an identity of their own. For this reason and for others that we shall address presently, they were easily recognized by the surrounding society and treated as "former Jews" rather than good or bad Christians.

Distinctive legal status is expressed in a series of documents concerning the taxation of the property of Sicilian converts. The first agreement, concluded in 1495 between King Ferdinand the Catholic and the Sicilian convert Ferrando de Aragona, allowed the returning converts to recover property they had left in Sicily, but only after ceding a certain percentage to the royal court. It is significant that the term used to designate converts in that document is "the former Jews of this kingdom" (*los que se fueron judíos desse reyno*). A subsequent agreement, concluded in 1497 between King Ferdinand and Ferrando de Aragona, stipulated that the latter had been empowered to act as the "general procurator of all the Jewish and convert community of the said realm in all matters pertaining to property, elected in the kingdom after the general expulsion of those Jews from the kingdom" (*generalis procurator totius universitatis neophitorum et iudeorum regni predicti de bonis, et electus in regno post ipsorum iudeorum generalem expulsionem a regno*).[8] This tendency to regard converts from Judaism as a separate group that was given a distinctive legal status, may have been a long standing legal tradition that had had its roots in the south of Italy.[9]

---

[7] N. Zeldes, "The Extraordinary Career of Ferrando de Aragona: A Sicilian Convert in the Service of Fernando the Catholic," *Hispania Judaica Bulletin* 3 (2000), pp. 97–125; Idem, *The Former Jews of this Kingdom. Sicilian Converts after the Expulsion (1492–1516)*, Leiden, 2003, pp. 27–42 and Appendix II, No. VIII.

[8] Zeldes, "Ferrando de Aragona," pp. 97–125; Idem, *The Former Jews of this Kingdom*, Appendix, Doc. No. VIII.

[9] In Southern Italy groups of converts were designated as a legal entity in certain documents, and in a document from 1511 the notary used the term "*universitas*

It is possible that the converts themselves were aware of their collective status, namely that they were, as a group, entitled to protection
by the authorities. Geronimo de Galiono, a rich merchant-banker of
Sciacca who feared the violence of debtors in his hometown, pleaded
with the viceroy to grant him a royal safeguard (*salvaguardia regia*),
arguing that "all New Christians have [a royal safeguard] as they are by
order under royal protection..."[10] Since this petition had been issued
and signed by the highest officials of the Sicilian administration, his
argument can be interpreted as an acknowledgement of the status of
neofiti as a protected group. Thus, legal status and formal designation
in official documents meant that in practical terms the New Christians
remained a distinctive minority group in Sicilian society.

Popular attitudes towards the converts also reflect their treatment as a
separate group. When in 1499 the city of Trapani negotiated the taxation
of property that remained after the expulsion, it referred to the "assets,
debts, silver, gold, jewels, and other things of the said former Jews, at
present baptized" (*li dicti tunc iudei et a lu presenti bactati*).[11] This was
no slip of the tongue, nor was the expression confined to returning
exiles from Naples. A chronicle written in Catania in the second half
of the sixteenth century also used the word "*vactiati*" (baptized) to
denote Jewish converts to Christianity.[12] Furthermore, a dictionary of
the Sicilian dialect compiled by a Spanish humanist, Lucio Cristoforo
Scobar, and published in 1519–1520, lists the term ("*bactiatu*" (*vactiatu*):
conversu, neophitus),[13] indicating that it was in common use in Sicily.[14]

---

neofitorum." I have discussed the use of this term in Sicily and in southern Italy in
my lecture at the VIII Italia Judaica convention held in June 2003, *Ebrei e giustizia in
Italia dal Medioevo all'Età moderna*: "Universitas Neofitorum: aspetti giuridici delle
conversioni di massa nell'Italia meridionale e nella Sicilia" (unpublished paper).

[10] The safeguard accorded to Geronimo Galiono of Sciacca also quotes his own plea:
"vostra illustrissima signoria comu iustissima si digni concedirili salva regia guardia
in forma actento maxime chi tucti cristiani novi ex regia protepcione et mandamento
la tenino," ASP Conservatoria di Registro reg. 89 c 276r–277r, 7/10/1503: Zeldes, *The
Former Jews of this Kingdom*, Appendix no. VI.

[11] ASP Protonotaro del Regno reg. 191 cc 115r–117r, 8/11/1499, Zeldes, *The Former
Jews of this Kingdom*, Appendix, No. I.

[12] *Cronaca siciliana del secolo XVI*, eds. V. Epifanio e A. Gulli, Palermo 1902, pp.
59–60.

[13] Here I refer to the modern publication: *Il vocabolario siciliano-latino di Lucio
Cristoforo Scobar* (moderna edizione a cura di Alfonso Leone), Palermo 1990, p. 41.

[14] Scobar was a student of Antonio Nebrija, the Spanish humanist. He later studied in
Sicily and Italy and therefore his work reflects the speech and usages of the first half of
the sixteenth century (see the Introduction to the *vocabolario*). The dictionary had been
published originally as two separate works: *Vocabolarium Nebrissense, ex latino sermone*

The term "baptized" is in a way worse than "New Christian" (*cristiano nuevo*), the most common designation in the Iberian kingdoms and one that was rarely used in Sicily. Whereas the term "New Christian," like the Greek derived word "*neofita*" (*neophytos*, newly planted), indicates a new beginning that entails obliteration of the former religious identity, the term "baptized" looks backward, to the convert's Jewish past. It is perhaps significant that "*neofiti*" is the official term found in letters issued by the royal administration and in notarial acts, whereas "baptized" appears to have been in common use by townspeople who did not trouble themselves with legal niceties. The persistence of this term indicates that even second generation converts, almost thirty years after the expulsion, continued to be regarded as a group apart.

An examination of the Conversos daily life also suggests that they formed a discrete group in Sicilian society. Notarial contracts and inquisitorial records show that in most cases converts retained the occupations and professions they had practiced as Jews (artisans, blacksmiths, shopkeepers, traders, brokers, and physicians). According to property lists made by the Spanish Inquisition in Sicily, most of the houses owned or leased by converts were in the former *Giudecca*. The *Giudecca* was usually situated in the oldest part of the city, sometimes very crowded. Nevertheless, after the expulsion the New Christians did not take advantage of their new status to move to other neighborhoods. They lived, therefore, in the same physical environment as they had as Jews, occupying the same houses and shops, in close proximity to the same neighbors. A notarial act from Sciacca, written in 1500, illustrates this point. It lists several property leases paid by converts who still lived close to each other in the former Jewish quarter:

> And twenty tari are paid every year by Franciscus Sichilianus the neophyte for that building situated in the said city (Sciacca) in the Cada quarter [the Jewish quarter, a term derived from the Catalan: call, calle] near the building of the monastery of Santa Maria de Ytria on the south-eastern side…and one tari owed by Franciscus Grecu the neophyte for a shop situated in that city in the street of the iron mongers close to the shop of

---

in sicilensem et hispanicum denuo traductum. Adiunctis insuper L. Christophori Scobaris viri erudissimi reconditissimis additionibus, Venezia, per Bernardino Benaglio, 1520 and the other, *Vocabularium Nebrissense ex siciliensi sermone in latinum L. Christophoro Scobare bethico interprete traductum*, Venezia per Bernardino Benaglio, 1519.

Joannes Antonio de Grignanu the neophyte on the northern side, and near the shop of Joannes Calandrinus the neophyte on the southern side.[15]

The Giudecca, however, was not a ghetto. Within the Giudecca, even before the expulsion, Jews and Christians lived in close proximity, and the same is true for converts and Old Christians. Frequently the house of a convert was attached to the house or shop of an Old Christian. Sometime they even lived in the same courtyard. A faith trial held in Mazara in 1494 provides us with a glimpse of this environment.

In 1494 the Inquisition—in this case, the old episcopal inquisition[16]—accused Caterina, wife of the blacksmith Pietro Monteverdi, of Judaizing. In the course of the trial the witnesses called to testify describe the everyday life of this family of artisans.[17] When Caterina gave birth to a boy, an Old-Christian midwife, Jeronima "la mammana," ministered to her. The baby, however, was found to have been circumcised, and this discovery led to the accusation of Judaizing. Caterina claimed to have done nothing, saying that the baby had been born already circumcised. The midwife also swore that he had been born this way. Strangely, her statement was not contested, and the court apparently accepted the testimony of expert witnesses (probably physicians) that such an occurrence was possible.

Of greater interest are the relations between the accused couple and their neighbors. One witness described how one evening, at the time of prayer, while the neighbors knelt in the courtyard reciting "Ave Maria,"

---

[15] "et quolibet anno solvendos hoc est tarenos viginti per Franciscum Sichilianus neophito in et supra quodam palaciocto sito et posito in dicta civitatis in quarterio Cade secus domus monasterii Sancte Marie de Ytria ex parte orientis meridiei…et tarenum unum debitum per Franciscum Grecu et neophita supra quadam apoteca sita et posita in dicta civitati in cursu ferrariorum secus apoteca magistri Joanni Antonio de Grignanu neophiti septentrionis secus apoteca Joanni Calandrini neophiti ex parte meridiei," Archivio di Stato di Sciacca, Notai Defunti (ND), Notaio Pietro Buscemi reg. 37 c 561v (unpublished manuscript).

[16] At the time Mazara belonged to the queen of Naples and was therefore not subject to the Spanish Inquisition, which had been formally established in Sicily already in 1487.

[17] The trial protocol was published by A. Rizzo-Marino, "Gli ebrei di Mazara nei secoli Quattordicesimo e Quindicesimo," *Atti della Società Trapanese per la Storia Patria* ed. G. Di Stefano, S. Costanza, Trapani 1971. It is the only record of a trial against Sicilian Judaizers that survived, since all the dossiers of the Spanish Inquisition were destroyed in 1783, when the Inquisition was abolished in Sicily: V. La Mantia, *Origine e vicende dell'Inquisizione in Sicilia*, Palermo 1977, pp. 102–115. On the Spanish Inquisition in Sicily, see also: F. Renda, *L'Inquisizione in Sicilia. I fatti. Le Persone*, Palermo, 1997; R. Canosa, *Storia dell'inquisizione spagnola in Italia*, Rome, 1992.

Caterina refused to kneel and her husband Pietro hit her with his fists. The testimony reveals a scene of public piety that called for a certain code of comportment; moreover, it shows that the couple's behavior was constantly scrutinized by the neighbors. One can interpret the husband's actions as those of a sincere Christian shocked by his wife's behavior, or perhaps those of a prudent man. In view of the fact that Pietro supported Caterina throughout her trial, I am more inclined towards the second possibility. In the same trial, another witness told the court that Pietro de Monteverdi shared half a slaughtered pig with a neighbor and that he asked the neighbor to render the fat and prepare sausages. Caterina, however, was accused of giving the meat to the dogs and of intentionally burning the sausages. The couple was also accused of refusing to share meals with their neighbors. The accusations of Judaizing are not unusual: refusal to eat pork, cooking with olive oil instead of lard, refusal to eat birds that were not slaughtered according to the laws of Kashrut, etc.

Some of the testimonies suggest that Catarina's and Pietro's neighbors deliberately spied on the couple in a bid to discover errant behavior. One of the witnesses for the prosecution, a neighbor named Margarita, occasionally forced herself into Catarina's house. Margarita told the court that Caterina, lacking a ritual bath for washing herself according to Jewish custom, washed once a week in the house tub completely naked (*et non potendu haviri bagni di lavarisi a modu Judaicu, si lava intru la pila di la casa, totam nudam*).[18] The same witness also accused Caterina of bathing in the same manner a month after the birth of her child, revealing a knowledge of Jewish ritual cleansing.[19] It would seem that this knowledge was shared by the Old-Christian community as a whole; some years earlier, before the expulsion, the Old-Christian population

---

[18] Ritual bath: Rizzo-Marino, "Gli ebrei di Mazara," p. 51.

[19] Margarita may, nevertheless, have been mistaken about Catarina's ritual cleansing. First, in order for the immersion to have been valid according to the Halakha, it should have been done in running water or in collected rainwater, and the house tub did not fulfill this requirement. Moreover, it should have been a monthly immersion instead of a weekly one. It is possible, however, that in Sicily some women did not perform their immersion strictly according to rabbinical law. See R. Ovadiah de Bertinoro's criticism of Palermitan Jews: E. Horowitz, "Towards a Social History of Jewish Popular Religion: Obadiah of Bertinoro on the Jews of Palermo," *Journal of Religious History*, 17 (1992), pp. 138–151. For further discussion of this topic see: J. D. Cohen, "Purity, Piety, and Polemic Medieval Rabbinic Denunciacions of 'Incorrect' Purification Practices," *Women and Water: Menstruation in Jewish Life and Law*, ed. R. R. Wasserfall, Hanover-London, 1999, pp. 82–100.

of Mazara had argued against the Jews' attempts to transfer the ritual
bath inside the city walls for the following reason:

> And it so happens in this city that the water of the wells flows by means
> of subterranean conduits from one well to another, and thus does all the
> filth of their menstruation flow with the water from one [well] to another.
> And it is the opinion of many learned and intelligent persons that for this
> reason, and because of that bath, many suffer from leprosy and diseases
> of the eyes and other sickness.[20]

It might also be argued, however, that Margarita's accusation against
Caterina was formulated not by her but by the prosecutor, the priest
Bartholomeo de Marchioso, and patterned on standard accusations
of judaizing. This premise is often advanced by scholars who reject
inquisitorial proceedings as a source of information on Converso
customs and daily behavior.[21] However, the particular circumstances
of the Mazara trial do not lend themselves to such views. First, there
was not yet an established tradition of Inquisitorial procedure against
Judaism in Sicily. Second, and most important, they were acquitted,
which militates against the idea that the Inquisition had coerced witnesses to gain a conviction.

Pietro and Caterina Monteverdi may have owed their acquittal to
the favorable testimonies of local priests Bartholomeo de Cremona and
Paolo de Casalichio. Cremona testified that during Lent the couple
came regularly to Mass and partook of the Eucharist, while Casalichio
stated that they came to confession and received Holy Communion
like all Christians. The chaplain, Giovanni Caruso, corroborated this
testimony and added that the couple gave alms and fasted on fast days.

---

[20] "Et la cita predicta et cussi li acqui di li puzzi vanno da l'uno a l'altro per li vini
sutta la terra et cussi tutte quelle loro bruttizzi de li loro mestrui si vanno con li acqui
l'uno e l'altro unde la opinioni di multi valenti et intelligenti persuni che per quista
causa e quisto bagno multa genti di lepra e di l'occhi malati et altri morbi patino,"
Rizzo Marino, "Gli ebrei di Mazara," pp. 43–44. At a trial conducted in Modica in 1471,
a witness ironically referred to a Jewish woman of dubious reputation as a "virgin"
describing her thus: "she is a virgin, as they say, and goes neither to the water nor
to the river" (esti vergini, secundu dichinu, et non va ne all'aqua ne a lu fiumi). This
ironical remark shows that knowledge of Jewish customs was fairly well-spread among
the gentile population of Sicily.

[21] B. Z. Netanyahu, Marranos of Spain, New York 1973; Idem The Origins of the
Inquisition, New York, 1995; António José Saraiva, Inquisiçao e cristiaos novos, Lisbon
1985, and more recently, The Marrano Factory. The Portuguese Inquisition and its New
Christians, translated, revised and augmented by H. P. Salomon and I. S. D. Sassoon,
Leiden, 2001.

However, perhaps the key figure in the trial was Antonio de Ballo, the jurist presiding over the proceedings. He urged everyone to take into consideration that the accused were "neophytes" and that they now lived as good and sincere Christians, despite the short time that had elapsed since they had been baptized.[22] Ballo's statement demonstrates that the court's main consideration was not punishment of transgressions committed by the accused, but primarily the integration of these baptized Jews into the Christian community. The Spanish Inquisition, however, saw things differently and in 1525 the bones of Pietro de Monteverdi were exhumed in order to burn him as a heretic. There is no record of Caterina's ultimate fate.

Despite physical proximity and even reasonably good relations between Old and New Christians, there is little evidence of social integration between the two groups. Since inquisitorial records usually provide information on the spouses of condemned converts, it is relatively easy to find out how common mixed marriage was. Out of several hundred names listed in the account books of the Spanish Inquisition in Sicily, only twenty-seven couples were mixed. An analysis of the data reveals that intermarriage became more frequent in the second generation, that is, after 1530. Generally speaking, endogamy is a good criterion for gauging the extent of assimilation even after conversion. One of the accusations brought against the *neophyti* of Southern Italy who had remained there after the mass-conversions of the thirteenth century was that they continued to marry only among themselves as late as the middle of the fifteenth century, thus maintaining their separate identity.[23]

---

[22] "Itaque considerata et maturius pensata qualitate tam ditti magistri Petri ejusque uxoris prout plene probatum est de eorum fide et observantia religionis xpistiane et considerato quod sint neophite et quod tam brevi tempore firma radice radicati vivunt religiose et fideliter ut ceteri veters et antiqui xpistiani...," Rizzo Marino, "Gli ebrei di Mazara," p. 75.

[23] Simonsohn, *The Apostolic See*, 1, p. 365; J. Starr, "The Mass Conversion of Jews in Southern Italy," *Speculum*, 21 (1946), pp. 203–211; S. Grayzel, *The Church and the Jews in the Thirteenth Century (1254–1314)*, Vol. II, ed. K. Stow, New York—Detroit, 1989, pp. 187–189. Similar observations have been made by Haim Beinhart regarding the Conversos of Ciudad Real. H. Beinart, *Conversos on Trial. The Inquisition in Ciudad Real*, Jerusalem 1981, pp. 234–235. An enduring example of endogamy is that of the Chuetas of Mallorca, who continued to marry almost exclusively within their own group up to the twentieth century. K. Moore, *Those of the Street. The Catholic Jews of Mallorca*, University of Notra Dame, 1976, pp. 174–175.

Some Sicillian Conversos did, however, marry into Old-Christian families, with a view to improving their social status (just as Old Christians sometimes married Conversos as a means of improving their financial situation). In 1491 Aloysio Sánchez, an Aragonese Converso who fled Saragossa to settle in Sicily, married two of his children to the offspring of Pietro Augusti, *magistro razionale* of the Sicilian treasury.[24] As a result of one of these unions, Aloysio's elder son, Ludovico, became *Prothonotaro* of the kingdom, one of the highest officials in the judicial system of Sicily, responsible for the appointment of judges and notaries, and Secretary of the Royal Council.[25]

More typical of the Sicilian experience, however, was marriage between offspring of merchant families and members of the petty nobility or the urban bourgeoisie. In 1496 a merchant, Antonio Compagna, promised to marry the younger daughter of a widow from a noble family from Randazzo (near Catania). The girl's family offered a very modest dowry, listing only the essential items. The groom's father promised 25 ounces, not a large sum, but not a negligible one either (this was the cost of a modest house).[26] Another marriage contract, from 1513, gives the details of an agreement between the daughter of one of the wealthiest merchants among Sicilian converts, one Paris Damiano of Sciacca, and the son of a well-known musician, the member of an Old-Christian family of that city. The father of the bride gave 200 ounces as a dowry and also promised to pay for her upkeep for three years. Now, 200 ounces was a huge sum and it stands to reason that the groom's

---

[24] The "maestro razionale" dealt with all the financial and fiscal affairs of the Royal Court, the administration of the royal demesne and all transactions between the treasury and private persons: A. Baviere-Albanese, "Diritto publico e istituzioni amministrativi in Sicilia," *Archivio Storico Siciliano* Ser. III 19 (1969), pp. 484–485. For the marriage contract: ASP ND Notaio Domenico di Leo reg. 1405 c 62v–66r, 18/9/1491 and C. Trasselli, "I banchi delle città minori del Cinquecento siciliano," *Nuovi Quaderni del Meridione* 8 (1970), p. 130. See also N. Zeldes, "Doña Eulalia Tamarit Sánchez: The First Victim of the Inquisition in Sicily—The Migration of a Distinguished Converso Family from Spain to Sicily," *Peamim* 69 (1996), pp. 43–55 (Hebrew).

[25] On Ludovico's appointment to the office of Protonotaro in 1507: ASP Tribunale Real Patrimonio, Lettere Viceregie reg. 213 c 108r–110v; on the office of Protonotaro in the kingdom of Sicily see: A. Baviere-Albanese, "Diritto publico e istituzioni amministrativi in Sicilia," *Archivio Storico Siciliano* Ser. III 19 (1969), pp. 478–479.

[26] Marriage contract in Randazzo: Archivio di Stato di Catania, sezione Notai di Randazzo, ND Nicolò de Panhormo reg. 24 cc 73r–74r, discussed in N. Zeldes, *The Former Jews of this Kingdom. Sicilian Converts after the Expulsion (1492–1516)*, Leiden, 2003, p. 97.

family had the most to gain from this match.[27] Although it is risky to draw conclusions when given only two cases, I believe that these contracts are representative of a more general trend, where Old-Christian families married converts to improve their financial situation. It is interesting to note that the question of dowries figures among the complaints addressed to Emperor Charles V by the Sicilian Parliament in 1522.[28] The Sicilians complained that the Spanish Inquisition confiscated the property of accused converts and did not return the dowry of innocent wives (as dictated by law). The complaint suggests that by that time there were enough cases of intermarriage for the confiscation of dowries to cause concern.

Despite certain similarities to the Iberian model, the Sicilian model of "convivenza" has its own peculiarities. Whereas in the Iberian Peninsula some converts reached the highest echelons of the Church hierarchy, such developments were practically non-existent in Sicily. There were almost no former Jews in the Holy Orders, unless they were of Iberian origin. The Sánchez family, related to Gabriel Sánchez, the treasurer of Aragon, is a case in point. The sons of Aloysio Sánchez, the king's treasurer in Sicily, Giovannotto and Antonio, obtained ecclesiastical benefices in Mazara and in Malta, respectively.[29] Otherwise, there were few monks and nuns of Jewish extraction in Sicily. Members of the monastic orders condemned by the Inquisition for heresy were in most cases Old Christians. Inquisitorial records list only two nuns: Francisca Blancolilla of Militello chose to become a nun after she was reconciled by the Holy Office,[30] while Catherine Capitello of Caltagirone asked to retain one *onza* from her confiscated property so that she could put her daughter into a convent.[31] A special case is that of the Franciscan friar, Giorlando de Andrea of Agrigento, who in 1540 was accused of Judaizing: "*Por haver stado siemper judio, y quando dezia la missa no*

---

[27] Archivio di Stato di Sciacca, Notaio Pietro Buscemi, reg. 48 (no page number), 26/12/1513. See: Zeldes, *The Former Jews of this Kingdom*, p. 98.

[28] "Quod uxores et filii orthodoxi neophitorum condemnatorum dotem, dotarium et legitimam consequantur"... F. Testa, *Capitula regni siciliae quae ad hodiernum diem lata sunt*, Palermo 1741, Vol. II, Cap. LXXV, p. 54.

[29] These benefices are mentioned in a series of letters issued in 1495: ASP Conservatoria di Registro reg. 77 c 198r, c 199r c 201r.

[30] Archivio di Stato di Palermo (ASP) Tribunale del Sant'Uffizio (TRSU) Ricevitoria reg. 19 c 175v.

[31] ASP TRSU Ricevitoria reg. 13 c 40v.

consacrava."[32] These are the only cases that I have encountered. They demonstrate, however, that there were no insurmountable obstacles for a convert to enter Holy Orders in Sicily.

The apparent avoidance of religious commitment is also reflected in the material culture. An analysis of the inventories of convert property made by the Inquisition reveals that there were relatively few objects related to Christian practice. Out of 200 inventories, only thirty listed devotional objects such as images of the Virgin, pictures of saints, crosses or prayer books. Although this is by no means conclusive evidence, it signals only limited acculturation and integration into the general society. Some converts may have felt unable to introduce such devotional objects into their homes.

Another peculiarity of the Sicilian Conversos was their absence from political life. Their elite supplied Sicily with skilled artisans, merchants and physicians, but, with the exception of Ludovico Sánchez, mentioned above, were never courtiers or treasurers, and only a few were tax farmers or money-lenders. The converts themselves tended to behave in much the same way as they had as Jews. They continued living in the same neighborhoods as before, pursuing the same trades. The majority of marriages were endogamous and it seems that the strongest personal relationships were those with other members of the same family. An examination of their religious attitudes leads to the same conclusion: most of the surviving evidence suggests that the converts found it difficult to adjust to a Christian way of life and tended to preserve a distance between themselves and the Old-Christian population.

In other words, conversion was for Sicilian Jews a means of retaining more or less the same position that they had occupied in society before the promulgation of the 1492 edict, rather than a way to reach social and economic positions that would have been otherwise inaccessible to them. For Sicily, the Conversos continuing presence ensured the existence of a useful middle class, but one that was not, generally speaking, perceived to be a threat to the fabric of Christian urban society. On the other hand, their integration into the general society was incomplete. Initially, the encouragement of conversion was perceived by Sicilian religious and lay authorities as both a religious aim and an

---

[32] Giorlando de Andrea appears in La Mantia's list: La Mantia, *Origine*, No. 309. Additional information is provided by C. A. Garufi, *Fatti e personaggi dell'Inquisizione in Sicilia*, Palermo 1978, p. 15.

economic necessity. The converts were given promises that they would enjoy the same rights and status as the Old Christians and would be able to keep their property intact. Many converted. But as we have seen, in the years that followed they had to part with 45% of their property. Moreover, all official documents carefully preserved their distinction as a legally separate group, always adding the epithet *neofito* after their name. The population at large also treated them as a group apart, calling them "baptized," or former Jews. On the other hand, while preventing their full integration into Sicilian society, the Sicilians, and not only the elite, tried to protect them from inquisitorial persecution. In 1502 the *jurats* (sworn members of the city council) and judges of Catania denied the Inquisition the right to arrest *neofiti* living in that city. In 1509 an official of the Inquisition who came to arrest converts in the town of Palazzolo was himself arrested by the *capitano* (chief of the local police) because he carried arms without a license.[33] And in 1522 the crowds of Catania expelled the receiver of the Spanish Inquisition that arrested and confiscated the property of *neofiti*, forcing him first to liberate the prisoners.[34]

While, in general, the Old-Christian and New-Christian communities did not maintain close social relations, their separation did not necessarily mean enmity. Violence perpetrated on the Converso community was relatively rare. Most complaints concern the repossession of property and the collection of debts by converts after the expulsion. Collection of debts was a particularly delicate issue. According to the agreements drawn between the royal treasury and Ferrando de Aragona, the representative of the "neofiti" community, property reverted to its original owners or to their heirs, and debtors of Jews had to pay back their debts. The converts as creditors wanted to collect debts, while the authorities had an interest in this matter as well, since it could apply a 45% tax to the recovered money. But angry debtors sometimes attacked their creditors. Most complaints refer to harassment, calling the creditor bad names and the like, but there was also physical violence in certain cases. For instance, Geronimo de Galiono of Sciacca (mentioned above) complained in his petition to the authorities that he had been wounded by debtors. I have, however, encountered only

---

[33] Attitude of the jurats of Catania: La Mantia, *Origine,* pp. 32–33; incident in Palazzolo: P. Burgarella, "Diego de Obregon e i primi anni del Sant'Uffizio in Sicilia," *Archivio Storico Siciliano,* serie III Vol. 20 (1972), p. 294.

[34] *Cronaca siciliana,* pp. 59–60.

one case of actual violence directed at a convert that was unrelated to debt collection. In 1501 Nicolò de Leofante, who may have converted before the expulsion, complained to the authorities that certain persons were accusing his son Giovanni of apostasy (calling him "apostate"), and they had hit him with sticks and whipped him. He was therefore applying for a royal safeguard to prevent further acts of violence. His request was approved.

Discrimination and harassment of a group of converts is apparent in one case only. In 1499 a group of converts from Naro (south-west Sicily) complained to the authorities that they were being treated worse than Jews (*tucti neofati habitaturi ipsius terre asserendo ad ipsi essiri facti multi vexacioni et angarii ac eciam per multi temerrarii essiri iniuriati et distractati peyu assay chi si fussiro iudey*). They claimed that they were constrained to do forced labor (*angaria*) and that certain "rash people" (*temerrarii*) called them "Jewish dogs and sons of dogs." This insult was perceived as particularly offensive in Sicilian society, and since the fourteenth century had been associated with converts (the prohibition to insult converts in this particular way appears already in the legislation of Frederick III of Aragon, 1310). However, the ability to act in concert as a group is more significant than the complaint. It is also important to note that the complaint did not accuse the local leadership, only the "rash" or "irresponsible" elements. In fact, only a few years earlier, the jurats (elected officials) of Naro had offered economic inducement to converts to come and settle there.[35]

Of the factors that led to the formation of this peculiar pattern of "convivenza," perhaps the most important was the Sicilian opposition to the expulsion, and later to the persecution, of the converts. Two petitions, one drawn up and signed by high ranking officials and members of the nobility, and the other from the *jurats* of Palermo (elected city representatives), were addressed to the king, protesting against the expulsion.[36] The arguments brought against the expulsion were several: the Jews played an important part in Sicilian economy and their expulsion would bring economic ruin; the Jews were skilled artisans who

---

[35] Nicolo de Leofante: ASP Conservatoria di Registro reg. 85 c 271r–271v; the neofiti of Naro: ASP Conservatoria di Registro reg. 83 c 424r–424v, Zeldes, *The Former Jews*, Appendix, No. 7, pp. 298–299.

[36] Protests against the expulsion: B. Lagumina, and G. Lagumina, *Codice diplomatico dei Giudei di Sicilia*, Palermo 1884–1890 (Reprint Palermo 1992), III, pp. 46–51 and pp. 86–90; the petition of the *jurats* of Palermo: I. La Lumia, "Gli ebrei siciliani," *Storie Siciliane* II, ed. F. Giunta, Palermo, 1962 (reprint), p. 338. S. Simonsohn, *The Jews in Sicily*, Leiden, 2006, Vol. 8, No. 5497, pp. 4739–4744.

could not be replaced; the country lacked manpower, especially if it were to face a Turkish attack; the Jews did not lead Christians to errors of faith; and when they converted it was always a sincere conversion. The last two arguments were a response to the accusations that appear in the edict of expulsion, in the Aragonese version as well as the Castilian one. These arguments were raised again in the early sixteenth century in the protests brought by the Sicilian Parliament against the Spanish Inquisition. In November 1514 the Parliament convened in Palermo in order to provide the king with new taxes (*donativi*). Sicily's semi-independent status vis à vis the Crown of Aragon required that taxes should be voted by the Parliament, not imposed unilaterally by the sovereign. This was the occasion for Sicilian representatives to present their own demands (*capitoli*) to the king as part of the negotiations.[37] This time, some *capitoli* related to the *neophyti* and the Inquisition:

> In the matter of incarceration as in other procedures, the Office of the Holy Inquisition in this kingdom proceeds much more rigorously than is ordained by Canon Law and [when compared with] other magistrates of this kingdom. In such a manner, that it so happened that after the former inquisitor had condemned some people to death in [front of] the palace (*thalamo*) in the presence of the inquisitor and his officials, before the gathering of almost all the people,[38] some [of the condemned] went back on their words and revoked [their confessions], saying that they confessed only for fear of the tortures or for other reasons. And they died with the greatest signs of devotion, good Christians until the end of their lives, always revoking their confession and saying that they accepted death by torment for committing other sins; in such a manner that the kingdom reacted with vehemence (or fear)[39] and had a feeling that they had died unjustly. This kingdom therefore asks your Majesty to command the Inquisition of this kingdom to observe the order regarding prisons. And in other procedures, that it should act according to Canon Law and not otherwise. And above all, to take into account that in this kingdom it had never been customary to act in this way, even against *neofiti*, miserable persons and foreigners"...and: "Because many [Old Christians] openly and in good faith made contracts with certain *neofiti* or with others who were secret heretics, believing that they were dealing with worthy persons

---

[37] On the constitutional aspects of taxation, see: G. Di Martino, "Il sistema tributario degli Aragonesi in Sicilia (1282–1516)," *Archivio Storico per la Sicilia Orientale* 4–5 (1938–9), pp. 102–145; H. G. Koenigsberger, "The Parliament of Sicily and the Spanish Empire," *Mélanges Antonio Marongiu*, Palermo, 1968, pp. 81–96.

[38] Thalamo (from the Greek—thalamos), palace.

[39] "Rezelo": Trasselli, discussing the Parliament's demands, suggested that the word had the same meaning as the verb "arrizilarisi"—"reacting strongly with harsh and menacing words," C. Trasselli, *Da Ferdinando il Cattolico a Carlo V. L'esperienza siciliana, 1475–1525*, Palermo 1982, vol. I, p. 170. But the word can also be derived from the Spanish verb *recelar*, to fear, distrust.

who had the reputation of being commonly considered good Christians, their credit was questioned when they [the *neofiti*] were condemned as heretics. This kingdom therefore petitions your Majesty to order that all those who in good faith formed a contract with such persons, who at the time of the contract were commonly considered to be good Christians, should have their debts paid back and their contracts honored. Otherwise the trade and commerce of the kingdom will go crazy (*si impachiria lo commercio et negotiationi in lo regno*).[40]

Taken together, these arguments provide an insight into the attitudes of the Sicilian elite toward the convert population. The converts of the first generation were accorded the same role as the Jews, practically retaining the same status; they were encouraged to return and were offered protection in order for Sicily to avoid the economic consequences of the expulsion.

To sum up, high officials, members of the Sicilian Parliament, and governing bodies of the major cities, accepted the presence of the converts as a substitute for the former Jewish population. They consequently supported them and protected them against violence and harassments, according them more or less the same status they had had as Jews. However, this compromise did not last. The problem lay in the different expectations of the king and the Inquisition. Whereas the

---

[40] "Item, perche lo officio di la Sancta Inquisizioni in quisto regno tanto in lo modo di li carceri como in lo resto di lo procediri, si procedi cum plui riguri di quillo ce è statuto di la ligi canonica, et di l'altri Magistrati di lo dicto Regno: di modo, che ha secuto, che essendo per lo Inquisituri passato condemnati alcuni a morti in lo thalamo, in la presentia di lo Inquisituri, et soi officiali, undi era quasi lo populo tucto congregato, alcuni si hanno disdicato et revocato, dicendo haviri confessato per timuri di tormenti, o per altri causi et su stati morti cum grandissimi signi di devotioni, et di boni Christiani, per fina a l'ultimo di loru vita, sempri revocando loro confessioni et dicendo che pigliavano la morti in supplicio di altri loro peccati: di manera, che in lo Regno è restato alcuno rezelo et impressioni, che alcuni di quisti sianu stati morti injustamenti: per quisto lo dicto Regno supplica vostra Majesta voglia ordinari che l'Inquisitori in quisto Regno digiano servari lo ordini in la carceri et in lo resto di lo procediri, secundo ordina et statuixi la ligi Canonica et non altrimenti, et maxime che in lo Regno di tal crimini non si ha processo, ne procedi, si non contra neophiti, vili persuni et exteri"; "Item, perchè multi hanno contracto et contractino cum alcuno neophita o altri che forte occulte fussiro heretici, publicamente et bona fide, contrahiri cum persuni habili, essendo quilli tali reputati communimenti per omni uno per boni Christiani et dapoi essendo stati condemnati per heretici, li hanno miso in disputa loro crediti: per quisto lo dicto Regno supplica Vostra Catholica Majestà, voglia comandar, che quilli che contrahiranno bona fide cum tal persuni, li quali al tempo de lo contracto su reputati communimenti per Christiani, che li siano pagati loro debiti, et servati loro contracti: perchè altramenti si impachiria lo commertio et negotiationi in lo dicto Regno." F. Testa, *Capitula*, Vol. I, pp. 582–584; see also Renda, *L'Inquisizione*, pp. 44–46 (translated into Italian).

majority of the Sicilians were content with preserving the former order of things (objecting even to the expulsion of the Jews), King Ferdinand could not allow Sicily to be an exception to the religious policies that he enforced in his other dominions.[41] The presence of a large number of converts served as a pretext for introducing the Spanish Inquisition in Sicily, thus strengthening the hold of the central government at the expense of the local powers. Ferdinand's insistence on the establishment of the Spanish Inquisition in Sicily was motivated by his wish for religious uniformity throughout his kingdoms, which was connected to his other aim of curbing local autonomy.[42]

[41] On King Ferdinand's religious policies see: M. D. Meyerson, "Religious change, Regionalism, and Royal Power in the Spain of Fernando and Isabel," *Iberia and the Mediterranean World of the Middle Ages, Essays in Honour of Robert I. Burns S.J.*, P. E. Chevedden, D. J. Kagay and P. G. Padilla eds., Leiden, New-York, Köln, 1996, pp. 97–112; Renda, *L'inquisizione*, pp. 41–51.

[42] This is demonstrated by Monter's study of the Aragonese Inquisitions: W. Monter, *Frontiers of Heresy. The Spanish Inquisition from the Basque Lands to Sicily*, Cambridge, 1990.

CHAPTER SEVEN

A THORN IN THE COMMUNITY: POPULAR RELIGIOUS PRACTICE AND CONVERSO DISSIDENCE IN THE DISTRICT OF MOLINA DE ARAGON

Leonor Zozaya Montes*

Introduction

The events described in this essay took place in the district of Molina de Aragón (Guadalajara) from the late fifteenth to the mid sixteenth centuries. This timeframe allows me to examine a number of crypto-Jews and their descendents, focusing particularly on the Rodríguez and Cortés families. In this way I am able to study certain changes in these families' religiosity over a number of generations. It is noteworthy that while the descendents of Molina's crypto-Jews did not appear to follow their parents' religious tendencies, they were far from being sincere Catholics. Indeed, they often attacked Catholic practice, adopting heretical attitudes similar to those manifested by their ancestors. In other words, they maintained a subversive and resistant attitude towards the state religion.[1]

Among the later generations' religious transgressors, of particular interest is Diego López Cortés, who claimed to be in possession of a thorn from Jesus' crown, which he touted as a talisman. While a number of López's neighbors believed in the thorn's powers, others were clearly scandalized by it. After an Inquisitorial investigation, the relic was placed under the guardianship of López's local church of Prados Redondos, which then institutionalized one of the ceremonies

---

* Translated by Kevin Ingram.
[1] This study is based on the analysis of 37 Inquisition trials which are conserved in the Archivo Historico Nacional (AHN), Madrid. All come from the same source: AHN, Inquisición, Legajo 1930. In the following notes I have omitted this legajo (dossier) number, and have limited my references to the name of the trial defendant and the file number. I have used principally the personal confessions of the defendants and deposition statements that are reiterated by a significant number of witnesses and are not contradictory.

that López had practiced: the blessing of the fields in order to protect the harvest. From then until this day the thorn remains in the same church, where it continues to be the center of an annual ceremony of benediction.

The Judeoconversos *of Molina de Aragón and Their Descendents*

The town of Molina de Aragón belongs to what is now the province of Guadalajara (Castilla-La Mancha); however, it is denominated Aragón because it formed part of that Crown's territory for a large part of the Middle Ages. The noble domain of Molina was divided into four districts. One of these was El Pedregal, in which most of the people who figure in this study lived—in the villages of Pradilla, Prados Redondos, Chera, Setiles and Morenilla. All these villages based their economy on livestock and agriculture. In comparison to Molina all were small, slightly populated communities.[2]

From the eleventh to the sixteenth centuries the province of Guadalajara was one of the most important areas for Jewish settlement in the Spanish peninsula, and Molina de Aragón was of particular significance. Its Jewish *aljama* and its synagogues testify to a large and thriving Jewish community. Even today, the Jewish neighborhood maintains its ancient form, as indeed do the town's Muslim quarters. In the fifteenth century the Jewish community of Molina was the largest in the north east of Guadalajara.[3] In the last decades of that century the town was also home to an important concentration of Conversos, a number of whom were crypto-Jews, as Inquisition records reveal.

---

[2] I do not have data on the populations of Molina and the outlying villages for the sixteenth century. However, figures presented in the *Diccionario de Sebastián Miñano* (1826) may serve us as a guide to the size and importance of these communities. In 1826 Molina de Aragón had 805 households (vecinos) and 3616 inhabitants. It also boasted five parish churches, three convents, four hermitages and one hospital. In the same year Prados Redondos had 85 households and 350 inhabitants, a church and a hermitage; and Chera comprised forty households, 158 inhabitants and a church. S. de Miñano, *Diccionario geográfico-estadístico-historico de España y Portugal*, Madrid, 1826. Voces: Molina de Aragón, Chera y Prados Redondos.

[3] See F. Cantera Burgos and C. Carrete Parrondo, *Las juderías medievales en la provincial de Guadalajara*, Madrid, 1975, p. 3 and pp. 45–51; J. Castaño, "Las comunidades judías en el obispado de Sigüenza en la baja Edad Media: transformaciones y disgregación del judaísmo en Castilla a finales del Medievo," Madrid, UCM, 1994, doctoral dissertation. J. Sanz y Díaz, *Historia verdadera del Señorio de Molina*, Guadalajara, 1982, pp. 95–100.

Of the thirty two Judaizers studied that were tried in the last decade of the fifteenth century, all but one were inhabitants of Molina.[4] It seems, however, that many of these people, or their heirs, subsequently left the town for nearby communities, in an attempt to escape Holy Office attention;[5] although they retained close ties to their birthplace. All the descendents of the prosecuted Judaizers studied in the following pages were natives of Molina, although they were residents of a number of communities: Molina,[6] Chera,[7] and Prados Redondos.[8] Almost all were members of the same extended family network. Many had the same surname; others had different surnames but were nevertheless linked by marriage or blood. For example, the brothers Diego López Cortés and Francisco Cortés were grandchildren of Isabel Rodríguez, and were linked through their aunt (Mari Pérez) to the Bernals. In order to facilitate a better understanding of these familial ties, I have included a genealogical tree at the end of this study.[9]

Crypto-Jews in Molina de Aragón at the End of the Fifteenth Century

Judging by the descriptions of the Inquisition trials analyzed for this study, Judaizing was prevalent in the Converso community of Molina in the last decades of the fifteenth century. I have approached these cases with some caution, however, as the majority were presented against deceased people.[10] Nevertheless, a significant number of the accused

---

[4] The exception was Inés Bernal who was a resident of Milmarcos (Proceso against Ines Bernal, no. 2).

[5] The Inquisition's headquarters for the area was situated in Molina de Aragón.

[6] Natives and residents of Molina: Pero Bernal, no. 5, Francisco García Bexís, no. 32 and Pero Bernal, priest at the church of Santa Maria de Pero Gómez. Trial no. 6.

[7] Natives of Molina and residents of Chera: Francisco Cortés, no. 11.

[8] Native of Molina and resident of Prados Redondos: Diego López Cortés, no. 8.

[9] My thanks to Manuel Lamazares and Pablo Pereda for lending me their technical skills for the construction of the genealogical tree.

[10] Constanza Fernández (1494), no. 1; Juan Bernal "el viejo" (1496–1497), no. 3; Pero Bernal (1496–1499), no 4; Isabel Núñez (1496–1497), no. 9; Elvira Rodríguez (1496–1497), no. 12; Juan Fernández "de la puerta del baño" (1496–1497), nº 12; Mari Díaz "la Burgueña" (1496–1497), nº 12; María Fernández (1496–1497), nº 12; García Sánchez de Huerta, clérigo (1496–1497), nº 12; María Álvarez "la Cazorla" (1496–1497), nº 12; Juan Fernández Greson (1493–1495), nº 14; Aldonza Fernández (1493–1495), nº 16; Juan Ramírez "el Ronquillo" (1496), nº 18; Juana Rodríguez (1494–1496), nº 19; Juana Rodríguez, mujer de Ronquillo (1496), nº 20; Constanza Rodríguez (1494–1496),

were alive and able to testify, and many did so voluntarily in a bid to demonstrate their atonement.[11] These declarations describe the same, or similar, Jewish customs outlined in all the other cases mentioned.

The case against Isabel Rodríguez, the maternal grandmother of the Cortés brothers, offers us a glimpse of the religious rites carried out among Molina's crypto Jews in the last years of the fifteenth century. Isabel, a resident of Molina, was married to Garci Gallego from Pradilla. Both husband and wife had been tried and reconciled by the Inquisition previous to 1494. However, in this year Isabel, now deceased, was accused by the Holy Office of having feigned Christian belief during her lifetime, while practicing Jewish ceremonies. This time she was declared a heretic, apostate and heresiarch.[12] Among her Judaizing customs were the following:

> …she often observed the major fast of the Jews, eating nothing until nightfall when the stars appeared, eating meat, using clean table cloths, going barefoot on these days; she rested on these fast days and requested pardon from her seniors and gave pardon to her juniors as in the Jewish custom and way; she lit many branched candles on these Friday nights and she let them burn until they burnt out in the Jewish custom; she enticed others to fast and instructed them in the observance of the Jewish Sabbath, and when someone went on a journey she gave him the Jewish blessing as the Jews were accustomed to give; she bathed women who were menstruating and kept them away from their husbands during this time; she poured away water and required that water was poured away in her house when someone died in her neighborhood; she took out the sciatic nerve from the leg and the veins and the fat; she dressed in clean blouses and garments on Saturdays to honor and celebrate the Sabbath.[13]

---

nº 22; doña Catalina (1492–1493), nº 23; Elvira Núñez (1494–1496), nº 24; Juana Fernández "la Cohena" (1494–1496), nº 25; Pero Fernández Fierro [o Fiero o Hierro, varía según el testimonio] (1496), nº 26; Juan Fernández Morisco (1494–1496), nº 27; Isabel Rodríguez (1497), nº 28; Diego Fernández Morisco (1497), nº 30; Inés García (1497), nº 31.

[11] The accused who testified: Catalina Fernández, mujer de Diego Gigante, zapatero, (1497), nº 10; Catalina García (1493–1495), nº 15; Juan García Bravo, clérigo (1493–1495), nº 17; Juana Fernández "la Brisela" (1496), nº 21; Mari Fernández (1497), nº 29. The accused who testified voluntarily: Inés Bernal (1492–1495), nº 2; Pedro Bernal, hijo de Aldonza Fernández (1492–1496), nº 7; Aldonza Fernández (1492–1494), nº 13.

[12] She was excommunicated and all her property confiscated. Her descendents were declared unfit for titles, ecclesiastical benefices and public office. They ordered her bones to be disinterred and handed over to the secular arm of the Inquisition to be burnt. Trial of Isabel Rodríguez, no. 28, fol. 15r.

[13] See the *proceso* of Isabel Rodríguez, no. 28, fols. 4r–5r.

According to the accusations of the prosecution witnesses and the confessions of the accused themselves, many of the Conversos from Molina practiced Jewish rituals "with the intention of Judaizing."[14] They maintained the Sabbath customs—fasting, lighting candles, wearing clean clothes and using clean table linen; they ignored Catholic ceremonies, gave the Jewish blessing to departing friends and poured water onto the floors of the houses of deceased persons.[15] They also frequently recited Hebraic prayers, ritually bathed and laid out the deceased, celebrated *sukot* and other ceremonies, and met with other crypto-Jewish families on Saturdays.[16]

Among these Judaizers was Aldonza Fernández, a distant relation of the Cortés family. Aldonza was the wife of Pero Fernández, who was

---

[14] The following testified that they observed many Jewish customs: Inés Bernal (1492–1495), no. 22; Catalina Fernández, no. 10; Aldonza Fernández, no. 13; Juana Fernández "la Brisela," no. 21.

[15] This is mentioned a number of times in the proceedings. Other rituals mentioned in the trials: In 1594 Constanza Fernández (deceased) was accused of having cooked *adafinas* (a meat stew associated with the Jews) on Friday to eat on the Saturday and to have baked rye bread (Constanza Fernández, no. 1). File no. 12 contains a number of proceedings against deceased persons. Among other things these people were accused of "storing rye bread in their houses for the Jewish Passover" (no. 12, fol. 3r).

[16] Several of the defendants were accused of praying in Hebrew. For example, Pero Bernal "recited in Hebrew Jewish prayers, raising and lowering his head as Jews did," (Pero Bernal, no. 4, fol. 17r). Inés García, on trial, although deceased, was accused, among other things, of "singing to the dead with Jewish songs and finally saying 'guayas guayas,'" (Inés García, no. 31, fol. 2r). Of Mari Díaz "la Burgueña" it was stated that she "fasted on the major Jewish fast [*ayuno mayor*], not eating until nightfall and reciting Jewish prayers, among which was a prayer that began, "adonay, adonay, cados, cados, orados, orados, hurtos, hurtos," (Mari Díaz, no. 12, fols. 34r–34v). Juana Fernández, "la Brisela," who was sixty-five years old, confessed "that she bathed her husband when he died, the way they did amongst themselves," (Juana Fernández, no. 21, fols. 3r–3v). Regarding funeral rites, Inés Bernal confessed that "she had bathed corpses, shrouding them…with the intention of Judaizing," (Inés Bernal, no. 2, fol. 30r). Juana Fernández, "la Cohena," wife of Juan Fernández Hierro, was condemned because, among other things, "she stayed in a hut during their [the Jews] Easter [a confused reference to the *Sukot* festival] observing their festivities, and hanging lighted lamps in her house, and many Converso heretics went there to observe ceremonies of the Mosaic Law as if it were a synagogue," (Juana Fernández, no., 25, fol. 12r). Juana Fernández "la Brisela" stated that many families (whose names she presented in a long list) observed the major fast (*ayuno mayor*) "because she watched all of them go to pray in the yard of Juan Sánchez del Corral's house, and that her mother went with them, and that she saw all of them rest that day"; and when she was asked how she knew it was the major fast, she said "because it was public knowledge that they did not eat until nightfall and that it was observed every year as a festival in that town…," Juana Fernández, no. 21, fols. 3r–3v.

also accused of Judaizing by the Holy Office.[17] On 18 August 1492, she approached the Inquisition voluntarily to confess. She told the officials that in her infancy her family had encouraged her to observe the Sabbath. Later she continued to observe this day with a friend and that she also induced her daughter-in-law, Juana Rodríguez, to do the same. She lit candles when her husband and children were not in town, or when she could "without them seeing her." She observed the Sabbath with her mother and sisters and very often wore clean clothes on this day. She did not worship on Sunday or on other Catholic festive days, intending instead to Judaize. She also bled meat and took out its sciatic nerve, and ate meat from Jewish and Moorish butchers, although she justified this by stating that this was easily available in Molina.[18] On forbidden days she ate cheese, milk, eggs and meat, even though she was healthy and had no excuse to do so. She never ate bacon or pig fat. She sang Jewish dirges at funerals, especially on the death of her husband, sons and daughters. She emptied out the water pitchers if someone died in her house or in the neighborhood. When her widowed daughter died, she buried her according to Jewish ritual. She also practiced other Jewish rights that were less common in Molina and encouraged others to do likewise.[19]

On 3 October 1494, Aldonza was declared a heretic and a false confessor. However, she stated that she had repented her sins and wished to embrace the Catholic religion. For this reason she was not excommunicated. She was, nevertheless, condemned to perpetual house arrest and to wearing the *sambenito* in order to purge her sins.[20] This was not, however, the end of the Aldonza case. On 26 September 1525, her daughter, Isabel Diaz, reported to the Inquisition that her mother had continued to Judaize after being sentenced.[21] Aldonza was now declared a heretic, apostate and "disseminator and abettor of heresy, a judaizer and false confessor." After the excommunion sentence was passed, her effigy was subjected to a public ridiculing, while her bones

---

[17] He was acused in 1496, sometime after his death. (Pero Fernández Fiero [or Hierro, depending on the testimony], no. 26).

[18] Aldonza Fernández, no. 13, fol. 1r.

[19] For example, she often placed coins in the mouth and hands of the deceased (Aldonza Fernández, no. 13, fol. 1r).

[20] Aldonza Fernández, no. 13, fols. 10v–11r.

[21] Ibid. 14v. The proceedings of Aldonza's second trial are found in the folios 12r to 40r.

were disinterred and burnt at the stake and the inscription on her tombstone erased.[22]

As we have seen, Aldonza did not restrict herself to private Jewish practice, she also made a display of her anti-Catholicism by not observing Sunday religious ceremonies and by instructing others to do the same. Others of Molina's Conversos expressed an even greater anti-Catholic aggression. For example, Pedro Bernal confessed to having conducted business ventures in the church of Milmarcos, offending many of the faithful.[23] In 1496, Pedro Fernández, deceased, was attributed with having stated that he denied the whore-son of God."[24] In the same year, the priest García Sánchez de Huerta, also deceased, was accused of often blaspheming while taking the sacrament, "spitting out the host three times and saying insistently that there was nothing more than to be born and to die…and that for the sins of the body the soul did not receive punishment."[25]

All these demonstrations of anti-Catholicism are of interest because they are similar to those practiced years later by the descendents of Molina's fifteenth-century Judaizers. While the later religious transgressors were not apparently Judaizers, they were, it seems, religious non-conformists, and this non-conformism would appear to betray a lingering identification with the religious plight of their ancestors.

Religious Deviation Among the Descendents of Molina's Judaizers

From the trial records of the descendents of Molina's Judaizers, it is difficult to ascertain their true religious beliefs. While it would seem that they had left Jewish practice behind, they had still not embraced Catholicism. Indeed, they made a point of transgressing or ridiculing orthodox practice. In the following pages I will examine the cases against the Bernal and Cortés families, both linked through endogamous marriage unions.

Pero Bernal, resident of Molina and a man of some means, was accused of heresy and apostasy in 1523. The Inquisition officials believed that these unorthodox practices were the result of a Converso

---

[22] Ibid. fols. 39r to 40r.
[23] Pero Bernal, no. 7, fol. 1r.
[24] Pero Fernández Fiero, no. 26, fol. 2r.
[25] García Sánchez de Huerta, no. 12, fols. 36r–36v.

upbringing in which he was not instructed in the articles and mysteries of the faith.[26] His father, Pascual Bernal, was condemned for Judaizing, as was his grandfather.[27] Although Pero discharged a number of public offices, he was theoretically disqualified from these positions by his Converso ancestry.[28] Among the accusations against him, the following was particularly damaging: during the day of the Passion, when the priest and the town was in procession, he took the cross from the man in charge of it and threw it against a wall, breaking it. Then he threatened those he believed had informed the Inquisition about him, saying that he "swore to God that they would all pay."[29] The Holy Office fined him, and sentenced him to a number of humiliations and to three months exile from the town.[30]

A relative of this Pero Bernal was his namesake, the priest of Santa Maria de Pero Gómez in Molina, who was tried in 1556. According to his own statement, on his father's side he was descended from Old Christians and gentry, the Escobars; however, on his mother's side he was "of Converso background."[31] It appears that on a number of occasions Bernal had insulted and ridiculed officials, ministers and the president of the Inquisition Council. He had also pretended to be

---

[26] Pero Bernal, no. 5, fol. 4r.

[27] Ibid. For his father, see fol. 2v; for his grandfather, fol. 4r.

[28] He was "steward of the Confraternity of Our Lady of the Comillas and another year he was auditor for a knights' chapter and…was appointed *montaraz* or gentleman's squire." He stated that he had gained a licence to hold this honor from the Archbishop of Seville; however, the Inquisition could find no such document in its archives. Ibid., fols. 2v to 4v.

[29] Ibid., fol. 4r.

[30] On 29 July 1524 the Inquisition ruled that "in punishment and penitence for what he has done we must sentence him and do sentence him to walk, next Sunday, in procession…next to the church cemetery…in breeches and doublet and barefooted and without hat and a hemp rope around his neck and a lighted wax candle in his hands and in it [the candle] a *real* coin; and at the end of the procession he should go to the altar where it is said the high mass is given…and when the mass ends offer a *real* and a candle for lighting the Corpus Cristi procession." He was also required to pay fifty ducats for extraordinary expenses, "and moreover that he absents himself from this territory for a period of three months." Ibid., fols 34v–35r.

[31] The parents of the Pero Bernal prosecuted in 1525 were María Nuñez and Pascual Bernal (Pero Bernal, no. 5 fol. 2v). The parents of the Pero Bernal prosecuted in 1556 were Isabel Nuñez and Velasco de Escobar; however, Pero Bernal's maternal grandfather was a Bernal (Mateo Bernal) and many of his family had this surname (Pero Bernal, no. 6, fols. 3v and 4r). According to the prosecutor bachiller Serrano (who also prosecuted Francisco Cortés), this Pero Bernal was "from a great background of Conversos" and many of his family had been "punished and castigated" by the Inquisition (Pero Bernal, no. 6, fol. 8r).

an Inquisition officer himself, arresting people and telling them that they were prisoners. The Holy Office sentenced Pero to two months detention in the Monastery of Saint Francis in Molina and fined him ten ducats.

Related to the Bernal family, Diego López Cortés and Francisco Cortés were tried in Molina in the middle of the sixteenth century.[32] They stated that they were descended from gentry on their father's side and on their mother's side from converts "of Jewish descent."[33] Their maternal grandparents were Garci Gallego and Isabel Rodríguez, whom we have already met. Both grandparents had been investigated by the Inquisition; however the grandmother, Isabel Rodríguez, and her mother—the Cortés brother's great grandmother—were re-tried after their deaths and condemned *en memoria y fama*.[34] Both Francisco and Diego tried to hide information about these and other family members sentenced by the Inquisition, quite understandably, given that these previous family convictions would have been extremely compromising for both men.[35] The two trials are worth studying in some detail.

Diego López Cortés' Trial (1553–1554)

Diego López Cortés was called before the Inquisition when he was sixty years old. This would mean that he was born around 1493, and thus would have had contact with Molina's Judaizers, including his

---

[32] These cases were brought before the Cuenca tribunal in one of its periodic *visitas*, or tours of its jurisdiction. From 1553 to 1554 the inquisitor Enrique de la Cueva headed an itinerant tribunal that visited Molina de Aragón, Sigüenza and Medinaceli, hearing cases against Conversos. See Sara Tilghman Nalle, *Mad for God*, Charlottesville and London, 2001, p. 28.

[33] Diego declared that on his father's side he was an "Old Christian without trace nor mixture of Converso or Morisco," (Diego López Cortés, no. 8, fol. 7v). Diego's brother, Francisco, also stated that his paternal family were descendants of "knights and *hijosdalgo*, without trace or mixture of Converso or Morisco and that his mother descended from Jews." (Francisco Cortés, no. 11, fol. 9v).

[34] Diego López Cortés, no. 8, fol 8v; and Francisco Cortés, no. 11, fol. 9v.

[35] Diego stated that his family had not been prosecuted by the Inquisition (Diego López Cortés, no. 8, fol. 7v). Francisco stated that of his family only his grandparents Garci Cortés (Gallego?) and "Fulana" Rodríguez had been prosecuted (Francisco Cortés, no. 11, fol. 9r). However, among the earlier prosecutions was the Cortés brothers uncle Francisco Bernal. Bernal was married to Mari Pérez, the sister of Diego's father Gil Cortés. However, Diego stated that he did not know "the wife of Francisco Bernal, he did not know her name, nor her business, nor her children," (Diego López Cortés, no. 8, fol. 6v).

maternal grandparents, whom he declared he had known.[36] He was a native and resident of Molina; however, he had lived in the village of Prados Redondos since childhood. Until he was nine or ten years old he lived there with his parents, Constanza Rodríguez and Gil Cortés, who was both a landowner and notary.[37] Later, Diego went to live in Morenilla, where he spent eighteen months in the house of his paternal grandfather, also named Diego López Cortés. He then became a transhumant shepherd, spending his winters in Extremadura and his summers in Prados Redondos. He was married and widowed twice. His first wife was an alderman's daughter from Molina, the second the daughter of a University graduate (*bachiller*).[38] Of his eight children, two had died by the time of his trial.

In charge of Diego López's trial were Andrés González, the prosecutor, and Enrique de la Cueva, the inquisitorial judge for the bishoprics of Sigüenza and Cuenca. The trial began in November 1553 and ended in April 1554. However, the numerous charges against López were for acts perpetrated many years previously. The first prosecution witnesses were two priests (one from Prados Redondos, the other from Anquela), a shoemaker from Molina and Diego's own neice, Juana Cortés. Many others followed suit, offended by Diego Lopéz's conduct.

Diego López was accused by many of the witnesses of having convinced the residents of the area that he had a thorn from the crown of Jesus, which they were required to venerate. For the Inquisition there were two issues to be resolved. First, did López believe the thorn was authentic, or was he fooling everyone? And second, if the thorn was indeed authentic, was it being treated with sufficient respect?[39] In

---

[36] Diego López Cortés, no. 8, fol. 6r to 7v.

[37] The office of public notary in Molina de Aragón had passed to Gil Cortés from his father, Diego López Cortés.

[38] His first marriage was to Catalina González, daughter of Pedro de Ayllón, alderman of Molina de Aragón, to whom he was married fourteen or fifteen years. (It is noteworthy that Diego was denounced by a number of witnesses bearing the surname Ayllón). Two or three years after he was widowed he married Mari Pérez Malo, daughter of *bachiller* Cano, resident of Tordepalos. His second wife had died some six or seven years before Diego's prosecution. Ibid. fol. 6v.

[39] In the words of the fiscal, Andrés González, "[Diego López] has stated to everyone in this area and its residents that he has a thorn from the crown of our savior and redeemer Jesus Christ, and as such he asks all those who see it to revere and respect it, and persuaded by Diego López Cortés they do just that, and if it is true [that it is the holy thorn] he keeps it in a very disgraceful place and that he uses it with such indecency that it is found scandalous by those Christians who know about it; and if it is not [the holy thorn] he is tricking everyone. I ask your worship [the inquisitorial

answer to the second question, the inquisitors were informed that the thorn was kept in a chest in Diego's house, from which it was taken periodically and placed on the breasts of women in childbirth, in order to relieve their pain.[40] Also, when there were hailstones both Diego and his daughters placed the thorn in the window of his house so that these would be transformed into clear rain not to damage the crops.

Before continuing with the other accusations against Diego López, it is important to note that the practice of driving away hailstones by using reliquary was relatively common.[41] It is indeed likely that López had come across a number of these popular religious rites on his transhumant journeys across the country, and that these had inspired him to use the thorn likewise. Given the area's unfavorable climatic conditions, such rituals would have offered a certain psychological security and would thus have gained López a good deal of publicity.

In addition to being attacked for his disrespect for religious reliquary, Diego López was also accused of blasphemy and apostasy. According to some of his detractors, on talking to his brother Francisco about the quality of their lives, Diego stated, "I don't believe in God, nor that Paradise is better than the life that the traitor my brother has at home."[42] Juana Cortés, Diego's niece, stated that the accused had said, "it was impossible to have a better life in heaven." Other witnesses

---

judge] to order him to present the said thorn and his reasons for believing it to be what he says it is." (Diego López Cortés, no. 8, fol. 9r).

[40] There are many testimonies to the fact that the thorn was used to reduce birth pains. The above quote is from the cleric Miguel Cruzado. Ibid., fol. 3r. A similar ceremony to alleviate childbirth pains was that of the *Santa Cinta* ("holy belt"), mentioned by William A. Christian Jr in *Apparitions in Late Medieval and Renaissance Spain*, Princeton, 1981, pp. 53–54.

[41] W. Christian notes that in the sixteenth century "lay professionals circulated through the Castilian countryside selling their services to individuals or communities to ward off disease, locusts, other insect pests, or hailstorms by magical methods. Known variously as necromancers, enpsalmers, or conjurers of clouds, they competed directly with the priests of the parishes… Similarly, the cloud chasers were hired by communities to conjure hail-bearing storm clouds away, or make the hail dissolve into rain." William A. Christian, Jr, *Local Religion in Sixteenth-Century Spain*, Princeton, 1981, pp. 29–31. These and other customs are collected in E. Casas Gaspar, *Ritos agrarios. Folklore campesino español*, Madrid, 1950, pp. 56–71 and 93–95. Some of the ceremonies related to rain have persisted up to the present day. See J. R. Figueras, "Folklore de la lluvia y de las tempestades en el Pirineo catalan," RDTP, 7:2 (1951), pp. 292–326, especially how to combat hailstones and lightning, pp. 309–321. Very often the villagers blame the local priest if hailstones destroy the crop: pp. 310, 311 and 318.

[42] Ibid., fols. 3r and 9r. Often the witnesses differ in their chronology for the same event, as in this case. For some it occurred two years previously; for others just a month previously. This variation in dates was pointed out by Diego in his defense.

accused Diego of stating "that earthly pleasures and pursuits were better than the blessed eternity that the good and Catholic Christians are preparing for."[43]

Another prosecution witness stated that some ten years previously he and a friend had needed bread and thus went to Diego López's house to buy some from two young ladies (probably the daughters). The girls said that they had no bread and thus the two men went to an inn (*posada*) in search of some. Then López turned up and said from the street: "They are scoundrels who come to my house looking for bread…, I deny God if I don't kill them," as well as other bad language.[44] It seems that López had denied God in public on a number of other previous occasions.[45]

Witnesses also reported that eight years previously López had disrupted the procession of the Holy Sacrament during the Corpus Christi celebrations in Prados Redondos. While the other residents followed reverently, López marched "shamelessly and without devotion" among the priests, lance in hand, without humbling himself or paying respect to the Holy Sacrament, without taking off his hat or kneeling down as Christians did, "and he was very disrespectful, acting the fool, scandalizing all the people who saw him." Other witnesses added that Diego created such a scandal that the clergy who took part in the procession did not wish to return to the village.[46]

Diego appeared before the court in November 1553, soon after the proceedings had begun, accused of heresy and apostasy.[47] In December he was ordered to return home to celebrate Christmas, only to be recalled in January, when he was sent to the Inquisition's jail in Molina and told he would not be allowed to leave without a license. Henceforth he was called before the tribunal intermittently to confess his sins and unburden his conscience. The prosecutor, Andrés González, once again accused him of heresy, emphasizing his scandalous manipulation of the thorn, his irreverent behaviour in the Corpus Christi procession and his denial of God and Paradise. González also made much of the

---

[43] This according to prosecuting attorney Andrés González. Ibid., fol. 9r.

[44] Declaration of Martín de Durango, shoemaker, in the trial proceedings of Diego López Cortés, no. 8, fol. 4r.

[45] This was emphasized by the prosecution attorney Andrés González, who accused Diego of "blasphemy, public scandal, heresy and violence," ibid., fol. 9r.

[46] According to the priest Miguel Cruzado, "he caused such a scandal that the priests did not wish to return to take part in the religious festival, seeing how little Christianity and devotion there was there." Ibid., fol. 4v.

[47] Ibid., fol. 5r.

fact that Diego was of Converso lineage and the grandson and great grandson of crypto-Jews.[48]

Throughout his trial, Diego followed the same strategy: he had no idea why he had been denounced; he denied having committed any crime and emphasized that he had many enemies who lied, in particular his brothers-in-law García Rodríguez and García (or Garci, according to his testimony) de Ayllón. As for his statements about an earthy paradise in the village of Chera, this, he said, came from a popular saying, which he exaggerated to emphasise the frugality of his brother's fare.[49]

Regarding the thorn of Christ, he stated that it had belonged to his family since his great grandmother Leonor Vázquez de Barrientos, wife of Gil López Cortés and lady in waiting to Gascón de la Cerda, Count of Medinaceli, received it as a present. According to Diego, the thorn had been venerated "from time immemorial in these parts, and the Bishops of this Bishopric saw and recognized this and presented it to the people as such."[50] His father, Gil Cortés, had stipulated in his will that each year in May, on the day on which the Crown of Jesus was celebrated, the abbot and the canons were to say mass for the deceased in the Church of Saint Martin, in Molina.[51] On the same day the thorn was to be solemnly exhibited in the traditional procession. After the mass, the thorn was to be returned to the eldest member of the Cortés family, in whose possession it would remain.[52] Thus, the thorn passed to Diego, who, according to his confession, wrapped it in silk and placed it in a

---

[48] Ibid., fols. 9r–9v.

[49] Ibid., fol. 15v.

[50] Ibid., fol. 15r. There is no evidence that the thorn was venerated in an earlier period. Other than in the will of Diego's father, Gil Cortés, the thorn appears in no documents prior to the 1553 trial.

[51] Saint Martin was probably Gil López's parish church. Founded in 1182, it is the oldest church in Molina de Aragón. It is situated in a neighborhood on the oppositie side of the city to the *judería* and *morería*.

[52] An authenticated copy of the will appears in Diego López Cortés' trial proceedings. Ibid., fols 37v–38v. Moreover, although not confirmed in the will, Diego stated that his father had asked that a silver grated box be made to contain the thorn and that this be placed next to the host. This box was to be locked by two keys, one in the priest's possession, the other to be held by the eldest male in the Cortés family. However, this box was not made, and this was the reason, according to Diego, that the thorn remained in his house in Prados Redondos. Ibid., 10r–10v. Perhaps this was, in effect, Gil Cortés' wish. In the early modern period not all of the person's wishes were stated in the will. Many were transmitted orally to the executor and the family members. See L. Zozaya and M. Zozaya, "Una fuente archivística inusistada por la historiografía de la muerte en la Edad Moderna: los recibos de las limosnas," *Anexos de la Revista SIGNO*, 2 (1998), pp. 257–267.

silver box, which he kept in his best chest and locked with two keys; one of these was held by himself, the other by his daughter Constanza.[53]

With regard to who exhibited the thorn, the declarations were contradictory. Diego's antagonists stated that both Diego and his daughters, all of whom were laypeople, used it as an aid against storms and the problems of childbirth. However, in his first appearance in front of the Inquisition, Diego stated that the relic was only handled by the clergy. Later he stated that his daughter Constanza took control of it, and then that some women used it for cases of complicated childbirth. Later still, he admitted that if there were hailstones in the village and no member of the Cortés family present, others often took out the chest to combat the storm.[54]

Judging by the above statements, it would seem that the thorn rituals had become a devotional custom in Prados Redondos and that a number of the residents at least were adherents. However, this devotion was quite recent, created by Diego himself. Prior to this the thorn was exhibited only once a year, in a religious procession, in Molina, under the watchful eyes of the local religious dignitaries. Nevertheless, despite this usurpation of religious authority, the Inquisition now appeared to take a much more lenient view of Diego's actions. First it placed him under the custody of his brother, Garci Cortés, a priest in the church of Saint Martin. Next, it granted him licence to move freely in Molina to attend his business. In the meantime the inquisitors asked Diego to exhibit the thorn to the tribunal so that they could determine whether or not it was a relic.

At the beginning of March 1554, Diego chose a *bachiller* Muela to defend his case. Muela's attitude was that the prosecution witnesses were blaming a Christian gentleman whose only crime was to exhibit a relic "for a necessary and just cause." Muela also introduced some new information into the proceedings. He asked the witnesses if they were aware that Diego had suffered some mental problems as a result of falling from a horse in a joust fifteen or so years previously; and he requested that they "be as fair as possible and take into consideration his lack of judgement."[55] For his part, Diego continued to maintain that this was a conspiracy; however, he also began to excuse his actions, stating

---

[53] Diego López Cortés' trial proceedings, fols. 10r, 10v and 15r.
[54] Ibid., fols. 10v and 14r.
[55] For bachiller Muela's declarations, see ibid., 16r to 17v.

that they were the result of "human frailty, as I am a sinner through ignorance or carelessness or too much peevishness and passion, and not through lack of faith or belief."[56]

On 31 March, Diego was acquitted without costs. However, he was still required to present the thorn to the Inquisition officials for examination. Two days later he handed it over to Antón Díaz, the Prados Redondos priest, who, "accompanied by the village residents," presented it to the inquisitor Enrique de la Cueva. The inquisitor then ruled that it was a relic and that it should be kept in the sanctuary of the Prados Redondos' church, next to the Holy Sacrament. Here it was to be stored in a casket locked by two keys, one to be in the possession of Diego, his brothers and legitimate heirs, the other to be kept by the local priest.[57]

It was, thus, the inquisitor Enrique de la Cueva who decided that the thorn was of relic status. However, his decision appears to have been made without access to any apostolic authority, at least none of the sources mention such authentication. Furthermore, none of the residents of Prado, who appear in the case records, refer to any official investigation.[58] Apparently, de la Cueva made his decision on the spot, based on his examination of the thorn and on the oral testimonies of Diego Cortés and the trial witnesses. We should, however, view the decision with a certain amount of circumspection, in view of the fact that the inquisitor was stripped of his office in December of the same year for corrupt practices, among which was the acceptance of bribes.[59]

---

[56] Ibid., 39v.

[57] Ibid., fol. 39v. This decision created a long-term battle between the Prados Redondos church and the Saint Martin parish church in Molina de Aragón, the latter believing that it had a greater claim to the relic by virtue of the fact that it was originally associated with a ceremony held there. See N. Sanz Martínez, *La Santa Espina de Prados Redondos. Su historia, su autenticidad*, Madrid, 1966, introduction.

[58] At least the residents of Prados Redondos could offer no proof of this. Anton Vázquez, a witness in the trial of Francisco Cortés, stated "that he did not know of any authorization by the Pope or by any prelate at all, only the estimation of the Cortés people and later that which don Enrique [de la Cueva] ordered." Francisco Cortés, no. 11, 26r and 28r.

[59] See Sara Tilghman Nalle, *Mad for God. Bartolomé Sánchez, the secret messiah of Cardenete*, Charlottesville and London, 2001, p. 112: "Don Enrique, it turned out, was a corrupt judge who employed a violent young servant, and the *Suprema* began to receive complaints and appeals from aggrieved parties in the towns where he had conducted trials and his servant had committed crimes. Sometime later in the summer [of 1555], Cueva was recalled to Valladolid and placed under arrest, and in December, after an investigation, was stripped of his judgeship in Cuenca and permanently barred from holding any position in the Holy Office."

Is it possible that Diego had paid de la Cueva for an acceptable resolution to his case, and that this included an official recognition of the thorn's relic status, which would also have met with the local community's approval? It does, indeed, seem strange that a case that began with an emphasis on Diego López Cortés' heresy and his suspicious use of the thorn should suddenly end in the exoneration of the accused and the legitimization of a relic, certified by the same institution that had previously questioned its authenticity.

The Trial of Francisco Cortés (1553–1558)

Francisco Cortés, Diego's younger brother, was born in Molina de Aragón in 1505 but raised in Prados Redondos. He was a transhumance shepherd from an early age; at first he looked after his father's herd and later his own. When he was seventeen he spent a year in Molina, followed by nine months in the city of Sigüenza. He then returned to Prado Redondos, where he married Juana Catalán, daughter of Juan Catalán, lord of Valdecabriel and Villa Cadina. Soon after their wedding the young couple took up residence in the village of Chera. Francisco was still residing in the village when, in 1553, he was called before the Inquisition. He was originally denounced by three priests and his niece Juana Cortés; however, other prosecution witnesses soon came forward. Most of the prosecution witnesses were those who had also informed on his brother Diego. The majority of their accusations concerned events that took place ten or more years previously.[60]

Among other things, Francisco was accused of having desecrated Chera's church and cemetery, stabling his and his servants' animals within these sacred places, and causing a great scandal in the village.[61] He had also used the church to lodge his workmen, placing beds there for them to sleep, and had used the baptismal font as a repository for their tools. Furthermore, Francisco's men had used the chest which contained the holy ornaments as a table for eating their food. Both the priest, Miguel Cruzado, and the verger, Antonio Vázquez—Francisco's principal critics—had reprimanded the workers and had thrown them

---

[60] In the following section I refer only to the most reiterated accusations or the most significant.

[61] This occurred five years prior to the trial. Francisco Cortés, no. 11, fol. 3r.

out of the church. However, Francisco had argued with them, stating that the church was "for everyone's use." On another occasion a Morisco plasterer from Granada had lived in the church while he worked on Francisco's house, and had used the dais as a bed. This incident was related by the verger, who also noted that Francisco was the grandson of Garci Gallego, who had been tried by the Holy Office as a Crypto-Jew.[62] It would seem evident that the verger had linked Francisco and the Morisco plaster in an act of New-Christian religious subterfuge.

Francisco had also attacked the village clerics on a number of occasions. During an All Saints Day mass, he accused the priest of offering unconsecrated hosts to the parishioners.[63] On another occasion he had dressed in a dishevelled manner to hear mass in the church of Prados Redondos; and at Christmas he had listened to mass while intermittently covering his eyes with his cape.[64] On yet another occasion, a banquet, he got drunk and "began to sing in a loud voice the response *ne recorderis peccata mea*, scandalizing all those who testified against him, who also pointed out, as the verger had done, that Francisco was a Converso.[65]

Indeed, it would seem that Francisco identified more with his Converso roots than his Old-Christian ones. For example, some years previously he had expressed in public that the law of the Conversos was better than that of the Old Christians, because the former helped each other while the latter would "pull out your eyes" if they could. As far as the prosecuting attorney was concerned this statement was tantamount to a confession that Francisco was an adherent to the Mosaic Law of his ancestors.[66] On another occasion, Francisco had denied God. On yet another, he had stated that God favored those who had money and their fields sown, and not the needy;[67] this was proof, the prosecutor

---

[62] This occurred three or four years before the trial. Ibid., fols. 2v, 7r and 36r.

[63] The priest Pero Jiménez stated that this had occurred two years previously, while Chelo Marco Torrijo, a resident of Chera, stated that it had taken place only three months before the trial. Ibid., 2r and 7v respectively.

[64] According to the deposition of García Rodríguez, taken on 26 February 1554, this took place three or four years previously. Ibid., fol. 5v.

[65] Ibid., fol. 23v.

[66] For example, in a conversation with the priest Domingo Vázquez four years previously, Francisco had stated that a neighbor who was in financial difficulties would not have problems recuperating his debts, "because the law of the Conversos was better than that of the Old Christians, because they help each other, and the Old Christians would pull out each others eyes if they could." Ibid., fol. 3r.

[67] Ibid., fol. 5r.

believed, of the accused's lack of faith in God and His mercy.[68] It was also reported that Francisco tried to avoid paying church taxes, stating that his ancestors had not paid them.[69]

When Francisco found out that his two nieces, the daughters of his brother Diego, had been called to give evidence before the Inquisition, he threatened them, telling them to state that they had no recollection of any of the offences he was accused of. He also threatened some witnesses with a *"dolos al Diablo"* and scared others, stating that he consider them his enemies in both this world and the next.[70] It appears that some of the attacks were the result of the usual village factionalism, although this does not discount the fact that Francisco was regarded as a strange fish in Chera.[71]

On 4 November 1553, Andrés González, the same prosecutor who had taken charge of Diego's trial, accused Francisco of heresy and apostasy, making reference, at the same time, to the defendant's Jewish background. Francisco was then incarcerated in the Inquisition jail in Molina. Four days later he stood before the Inquisition judge, Enrique de la Cueva, to answer the charges against him. He stated that he knew of no reason why he was being tried; he had committed no crimes, nor heretical acts, and he was a good Christian. Nevertheless, with the exception of the non-payment of church taxes,[72] he did not deny that he had comported himself in a manner similar to that described by the prosecution witnesses, although he did attempt to show that in most cases his actions had been exaggerated or misinterpreted.

Thus, Francisco explained that as the Chera church doors had fallen down both his and other residents' animals often entered the temple. As for the response *ne recoderis peccata mea*, he sang it often, but always in the church, with priests present and without malice. When he stated

---

[68] Ibid., fol. 45r.

[69] The reference could have been to his *hidalgo* ancestors who, being considered noble, would not have been required to pay taxes. However, it could equally well have been a reference to his Jewish ancestors who would also not have been required to pay tithes.

[70] Francisco Cortés, fol. 6r.

[71] As Francisco noted in his defence, there were two factions in Chera: one was lead by himself, and the other by the priests Domingo Vázquez, *bachiller* Cruzado, Pero Jiménez and Juan de la Muela. Ibid., fols. 29r–35v.

[72] He stated "that he was not obliged to pay tithes nor *primicias* to the priest of Prados Redondos, but to the priest of Saint Martin's, in Molina de Aragón, where he was a parishioner and where he had always paid." Ibid., fol. 46r. It is noteworthy that Francisco's brother, Garci Cortés, was the priest of Saint Martin's.

that God only looked after the rich, he was addressing a group of idle people, whom he berated so that they would plough and furrow. These people had replied that God would take care of what had been sown and would favor them. He had then stated that "they should not believe that God would work miracles while they remained idle." However, with respect to his remarks on the Conversos, he admitted to having said that they "treated each other better than Old Christians treated each other" because the law of the Jews was better.[73]

On 17 November 1553 the inquisitor Enrique de la Cueva suspended the case, stating that the Christmas festival was near and that the Inquisition officials needed to leave the town; and he placed Francisco in the Inquisition jail to await the trial's resumption. Four months later Francisco applied for a licence to take his flocks to Extremadura. This was granted to him. Then, in August 1554, Enrique de la Cueva pronounced his verdict: Francisco was to pay a fifty ducats fine and to refrain in future from improper utterances.[74] This dramatic turn in the proceedings took place just three months after Diego Cortés' trial had been resolved in a similar arbitrary way. It is thus tempting to conclude that sometime at the beginning of 1554 Enrique de la Cueva had come to an amicable agreement with both brothers.[75]

However, eighteen months later, in February 1556, a new Inquisition prosecutor, *bachiller* Alonso Serrano, reopened the case. Serrano had tried on several occasions to catch Francisco, whom he accused of being a heretic. Now he stated that there had been a number of irregularities in the previous trial, the majority of which were related to the inquisitorial judge, Enrique de la Cueva.[76] Cueva, it will be recalled, had been convicted of corrupt practice in 1554 and stripped of his office, although this information was not included in Francisco's trial records.

In the next months Serrano recalled many of the earlier prosecution witnesses to repeat their testimonies against Francisco. As well as re-examining all the previous accusations, the prosecutor also brought up

---

[73] Ibid., fol. 43r.

[74] Ibid., fols. 19r and 19v.

[75] It is significant that in March 1555, after prosecuting de la Cueva for corruption, the Suprema declared Francisco's case null and void and ordered the fifty ducats in costs to be returned to the defendant.

[76] He declared that Enrique de la Cueva's decision was made without consulting the prosecuting attorney, and that Francisco should be punished for his "scandalous, ugly, disagreeable crimes against the Holy Office…" Ibid., fol. 39r.

the matter of the thorn. Had a clerical authority declared it authentic, or was it merely the assertion of the Cortés family? The witnesses stated that the thorn was officially recognized as a relic when the inquisitor Enrique de la Cueva had ordered it to be kept in the church at Prados Redondos, in a cask locked by two keys.[77] On the recent death of Diego Cortés, one of these keys had passed to Francisco. The thorn was no longer used on an ad hoc basis to combat storms and hailstones but was now the object of an annual procession around the village, when it was venerated by many people, both within the community and outside.[78]

All this information was presented to the Inquisition officials in the Cuenca tribunal, who, unlike Serrano, appeared to be in no hurry to convict Francisco of heresy. Francisco eventually appeared before the court in January 1557, only to be informed that as the officials were very busy there was no time to attend to his case.[79] He next appeared on 13 May, when he asked for permission to postpone the proceedings so that he could look after his livestock. When he finally testified before the tribunal, in June 1558, he maintained the same attitude as during his previous trial, justifying his actions with unconvincing arguments; he also repeated his view that the law of the Conversos was better than that of the Old Christians.

On June 12 the tribunal reached its verdict: Francisco was required to listen, while kneeling, to five masses for the souls in purgatory, all at his own cost; provide five pounds of oil to illuminate his parish church; and pay twenty ducats in fines to the Holy Office. Furthermore, he was ordered to desist in future from making inappropriate remarks and from threatening those who had testified against him.[80]

---

[77] For example, Juan Alonso, "el Mozo," stated that "he did not know if this thorn had been approved by an ecclesiastical authority before Señor Enrique inquisitor ordered it to be placed in the church and ordered a key to be given to the eldest of the Cortés family." Ibid., 28r.

[78] Anton Vázquez stated that "once a year in the month of May, the Day of the Crown, everyone takes [the thorn] out and in procession through the village." Ibid., fol. 26v. Juan Alonso, "el Mozo," stated that "many people have worshipped [the thorn] both from the village and outside, especially when it was returned to Prados Redondos after being seen by señor Enrique inquisitor." Ibid., fol. 28v.

[79] Ibid., 42r.

[80] Ibid., fols. 47v–49r.

The Present Day Festival of the Holy Thorn

Once the López family's relic was safely housed in the Prados Redondos church, an annual Festival of the Holy Thorn was instituted; and in 1583 a Confraternity of the True Cross and Holy Thorn was established, to which most of the families of Prados Redondos and the neighboring villages subscribed. Later the confraternity was fused with the Brotherhood of the Holy Sacrament.[81] Unfortunately, I have found no description of the original event. I have, however, witnessed the current festival, which I believe follows closely the sixteenth-century ceremony, and thus merits a brief description.

Traditionally the festival took place on May 4; however, in recent years the date has been changed to August 14 (the day before the celebration of the Asuncion), when the majority of the villagers, who now live and work outside the area, are present for their summer vacations.[82] The festival begins at midday with a mass in honor of the Holy Thorn, in which biblical passages are read out alluding to the crown of Jesus. At the end of the mass, while the church bells ring, everyone leaves the church to march in procession through the village. At the head of the group are two men who carry enormous flags of the confraternity; these are followed by a group of men who wave banners embroidered with cross and thorn motifs, and, behind them, the priest, who carries the reliquary, covered by an antique canopy whose four poles are held by senior citizens; the rest of the congregation follows, singing songs related to the relic. At the rear of the procession a group of musicians play guitar, mandolin and violin.[83] A few yards outside the church, the procession stops briefly at a simple rustic altar dedicated to the thorn.[84] Here the priest points the relic toward the fields and blesses the crops; the congregation responds with "Long Live the Holy

---

[81] The confraternity members are obligated to attend the ceremonies in honor of the Holy Thorn and Holy Cross. See N. Sanz Martínez, *La Santa Espina...*, pp. 65 and 66.

[82] Nowadays Prados Redondos is almost empty in the winter months. In the summer months another hundred and fifty absentee residents converge on the village. I would like to thank the Prados Redondos community for its generous hospitality they showed me during the 2007 Festival of the Holy Thorn.

[83] The procession is brief and without a doubt follows the same route as it did in the sixteenth century, as the village center has clearly not changed shape in four hundred years. None of the streets carry a formal street name.

[84] Previously this altar was covered with an antique cloth (the oldest preserved in the village) which was decorated with images of the Holy Thorn. Some seven years

Thorn" ("*Viva la Santa Espina*"). In the evening there is a service for the Adoration of the relic. After this ceremony the faithful sing "Verses in Praise of the Holy Thorn" (*Gozos de la Santa Espina*),[85] while they file past the relic to kiss it, first the men and then the women. At the same time they offer donations to the church.

It seems that in an earlier period so many people came to the Festival of the Thorn that they were unable to fit into the church. For this reason at the end of the sixteenth century a small tower was constructed in an adjacent square. This strange construction allowed the priest to show the thorn to all the devotees who gathered to worship the relic. Nowadays barely a few dozen people are present for the ceremony, all of whom fit comfortably into the small church.

Conclusions

At the end of the fifteenth century the town of Molina de Aragón, in the province of Guadalajara, was home to a group of crypto-Jews. Several decades later the descendants of this group no longer Judaized, or at least there is no solid evidence of this; however, in spite of declaring themselves Catholic practitioners, it is clear that their religious tendencies were not orthodox Christian ones. Indeed, the trial records suggest that they rejected not only formal Catholic practice but also the belief that Jesus Christ was the son of God and the conduit to eternal salvation.[86] While there is insufficient evidence to present these Conversos, the majority of whom were related, as a self-conscious socio-religious group, the views expressed by Francisco Cortés on the superiority of

---

ago a resident made a new cover on which the casket holding the relic is portrayed, surrounded by the words: "Viva la/Santa Espina."

[85] According to one of the residents, these verses in praise of the thorn are very old and have been transmitted orally from generation to generation. Many, like himself, know them by heart. I will cite only the first and last verse, as these are most relevant to this study: "If for painful suffering/you want to find medicine,/come to the garden of the thorns/and you will find a garden of roses…If pestilence, if illness/if hunger, if famine/one day afflict you,/come hither pious ones/and cry out to the thorns,/and they will relieve you of all this." ("Si de aflicciones penosas/queréis hallar medicinas,/venid al huerto de espinas/hallaréis huerto de rosas./…Si peste, si enfermedad,/si hambre, si carestía/nos afligiese algún día,/venid devotos llegad,/y a las espinas aclamad,/y os librarán de esas cosas.")

[86] For example, Sánchez de Huerta's statement in 1525, repeated by Diego Lopéz Cortés in 1553.

"Converso law," reveal that at least one of their number believed in a discrete Converso identity.

The descendents of the crypto-Jews expressed their non-conformism mostly in a series of actions that we would now describe as "exceptional normal."[87] These are everyday acts that are recognized as transgressions, but which do not lead immediately to the perpetrator's denunciation. Thus certain heterodox practices are ignored by the community for a number of years until, suddenly, something triggers a group reaction and infractions that were committed years previously are denounced.

Of all the religious transgressions mentioned in this study, the most significant are those associated with Diego López Cortés' "holy thorn." Given the subsequent importance of the thorn to religious practice in the Prados Redondos area, it is important that we examine the birth and legitimization of this religious tradition. First, let us examine it from Diego's perspective. What was his view of the thorn? We know, for example, that his father had stipulated in his will that the thorn was to be exhibited once a year in a religious procession in Molina de Aragón. However, Diego did not follow these instructions; instead he kept the thorn separate from formal religious practice, initiating certain popular rituals which gained many adherents in the Prados Redondos community.

Did Diego himself believe in the authenticity and supernatural properties of the thorn? Given the scant information available on his religious views, this question is impossible to answer with any conviction. It is significant, however, that a number of witnesses reported that Diego believed only in this world and not the hereafter. This belief, referred to often in fifteenth century texts as "Epicurean" or "Sadducean," appears to have evolved originally within a Jewish courtier elite influenced by rationalist (Averroistic) philosophy. It became popular in the fifteenth century among Conversos who rejected Catholicism for a private religiosity based on certain tenets of Judaism.[88] The materialistic view that

---

[87] See, for example, A. Pons and J. Serna, Cómo se escribe la microhistoria. Ensayo sobre Carlo Ginzburg, Madrid, 2000, pp. 258–259 and 268–269.

[88] "Unlike Christianity, Jewish philosophy and rituals give little attention to the idea of individual salvation or to the concept of a physical heaven..." David M. Gitlitz, *Secrecy and Deceit: The Religion of the Crypto-Jews*, University of New Mexico Press, 2002, p. 110. This Saduccean outlook was also expressed by the Garcia Sánchez de Huerta, a Converso priest of Molina de Aragón, who stated that there was nothing more than to be born and to die.

one should focus only on creating prosperity for oneself in this world, expressed by Diego's brother Francisco, is also linked to this "Sadducean" outlook.[89] It would seem unlikely, then, if we give credit to the witnesses' testimony, that Diego believed in the mission of a Christian Messiah or, by extension, the supernatural power of icons associated with Him. However, this does not necessarily mean that Diego was a complete charlatan. He may indeed have believed in the supernatural qualities of the thorn (associated with the Holy Land), without linking them to Jesus. Talismans and amulets were very popular in both Christian and Jewish communities. It is thus possible that Diego used the thorn as a magical object, like, for example, fennel, which Jews sometimes wrapped in silk (as Diego wrapped his thorn) and employed as a phylactery to guard the home against evil.[90]

While it is impossible to determine Diego's religious credo, it seems certain that he felt possessive of the artefact and unenthusiastic about sharing it with the local church. It is also possible, indeed, that he saw it as a means of thumbing his nose at an institutional religion, while acquiring for himself a certain amount of social prestige as the proprietor of an important talisman. However, as his extra-official rituals gained adherents, they began to challenge the role and status of the local priests, who thereupon denounced Diego to the Inquisition. Once the Holy Office began to investigate the issue, others came forward with tales of the Cortés brothers' anticlerical and antisocial attitudes.

What was the local Church's attitude to the popular religious practices that grew up around Diego's thorn? Curiously, they do not appear to have doubted the thorn's authenticity (it was only the Inquisition that posed this question). The priests' major preoccupation was that an important relic was in the wrong hands. Thus, they used the Inquisition to wrest this powerful object away from a member of the lay community and deposit it within the church, where it would no longer pose a challenge to clerical authority. In taking possession of the thorn the church was able to capture popular enthusiasm for an unofficial icon and channel it into official religious practice. Moreover, in incorporating the thorn into the local church reliquary, the Prados Redondos clergy

---

[89] Ibid., pp. 89–90 and 110–115. Francisco Cortés' had stated that God favored those who had money and their fields sown.

[90] Joshua Trachtenberg, *Jewish Magic and Superstition*, 1939, p. 136.

were enhancing the town's religious and social prestige. Thus, church and local community were happy with the arrangement, and have remained so up until the present day. As for the thorn's connection to a tainted Converso family, that has been effectively wiped clean from local memory.[91]

---

[91] The history of the Prados Redondos' holy thorn has already been treated in N. Sanz Martínez, *La Santa Espina. Su historia, su autenticidad*, Madrid, 1966. However, the purpose of this publication, co-published by the Archbishopric of Madrid-Alcala, was to celebrate the fact that the thorn had been re-examined in 1960 by ecclesiastical authorities and authenticated (pp. 31, 32, 61, and 63). For this authentication, the investigating committee had partially studied the Cortés brothers' trial proceedings, citing those parts that confirmed the thorn's relic status, with the view to demonstrating that no one doubted the thorn's authenticity in the sixteenth century. Although Sanz mentions the principal accusations against Diego, he does not mention that he used the thorn to alleviate birth pains. Furthermore, he does not mention the accusations against Francisco Cortés at all. Most important, he makes no mention of the brothers' Converso background.

Genealogical Table of the Cortés Family

Descendents of Old Christians*

Descendents of Jews

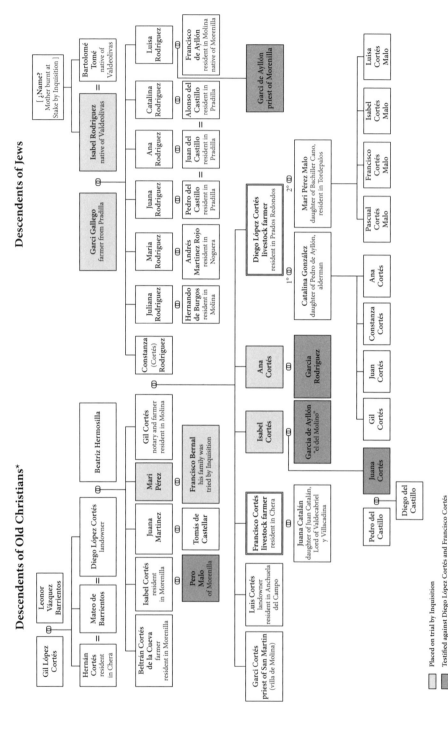

Placed on trial by Inquisition

Testified against Diego López Cortés and Francisco Cortés

Source: AHN, Inquisición, Procesos de fe, Legajo 1930

* Or supposedly of Old Christians

CHAPTER EIGHT

INQUISITION AND CRYPTO-JUDAISM:
THE 'COMPLICITY' OF THE MORA FAMILY OF
QUINTANAR DE LA ORDEN (1588–1592)

Vincent Parello*

Towards the end of the reign of Philip II, between 1588 and 1592, the inquisitors at the Cuenca Tribunal discovered a homogeneous "complicity" of autochtonous Judaisers in Quintanar de la Orden in the region of La Mancha. This was a group whose members had continued to follow the precepts of Mosaic law even at a time when the Holy Office had shifted its focus and was working in aid of the Counter-Reformation, punishing the misdeeds of Old Christians and trying to prevent Protestant thought from entering Spain. I deliberately choose the term 'autochtonous Judaisers' because, at about the same point in time, the Inquisition was in the process of dismantling a number of other "complicities" exclusively involving Portuguese Marranos (the "complicities" of La Roda and Santa María del Campo) or mixed groups of Spanish and Portuguese Marranos (as in the Toledo and Andalucía "complicities").[1] The records of the trials for Judaism against various members of the Mora family, preserved in the Diocesan Archive in Cuenca and the National Historical Archive in Madrid give us a fairly clear picture of this family group, unravelling the different strands of this "complicity."[2]

But what exactly do we understand by the term "complicity"? In everyday language, the word refers to deliberate involvement in an offence, misdeed or crime committed by another and, by extension, to a deep, spontaneous and often unspoken friendship among a number of individuals. As this definition reveals, the term can have both a

---

* Translated by Nicola Stapleton.
[1] Professor Rafael Carrasco studied these "complicities" in "Preludio al siglo de los portugueses. La Inquisición de Cuenca y los judaizantes lusitanos en el siglo XVI," *Hispania* XLVII (1987), pp. 503–559.
[2] In order to keep the text of this article brief, all sources are listed in the appendix.

positive meaning (bond, solidarity) and a negative one (crime, offence). Yet the word "complicity" also ties in with a very precise concept in inquisitorial law, a mixture of common and canonical law. It refers to a group of accomplices who are guilty of a very specific offence—heresy and apostasy—and who must be severely punished by society. By using the statements made by the accused themselves, the inquisitors were able to feed their own repressive activities without the need to resort to external witnesses. This enabled them to break up existing solidarity networks, attack the grassroots of dissidence and destroy whole communities and autonomous cultures.

The unusual nature of the Inquisition's repression of the Mora family of Quintanar de la Orden did not escape the notice of I. S. Revah and his disciple the French Hispanist Charles Amiel.[3] According to this author, the existence of such a "complicity" was evidence that Castilian Judaism had not completely disappeared from the inquisitorial scene at the end of the sixteenth century, as some historians had perhaps been too quick to assert.[4] Indeed, the arrival of Portuguese immigrants in La Mancha and the Cuenca diocese, starting in 1565–1570, gave rise to what is known as the "prelude to the Portuguese century," signalled by the "complicities" of La Roda and Santa María del Campo. The crypto-Jewish heresy continued to be suppressed in these areas until the middle of the sixteenth century. After a brief anti-Morisco interlude, between approximately 1525 and 1530, the inquisitors undertook a new "crusade" against the Conversos in the northern area of the bishopric. The Holy Office paid successive calls on the cities of Sigüenza, Medinaceli, Atienza, Berlanga and Almazán. In theory, this "crusade" should have completed the cycle of anti-Converso repression. In the 1580s, however, a further

---

[3] C. Amiel, *El siglo pitagórico y la vida de don Gabriel Guadaña*, Paris, 1977; Idem, "La mort juive au regard des inquisiteurs ibériques," *Revue de l'Histoire des Religions*, CCVII-4 (1990), pp. 389–412; Idem, "Crypto-judaïsme et Inquisition. La matière juive dans les édits de la foi des Inquisitions ibériques," *Revue de l'Histoire des Religions*, CCX-2 (1993), pp. 145–168; Idem, "El criptojudaísmo castellano en la Mancha a finales del siglo XVI," A. Alcalá (ed.), *Judíos. Sefarditas. Conversos. La expulsión de 1492 y sus consecuencias*, Valladolid, 1995, pp. 503–512; Idem, "Les cent voix de Quintanar. Le modèle castillan du marranisme," *Revue de l'histoire des religions*, CCXVIII (2001), pp. 195–280. The recent publication of the book by I. S. Révah, *Antonio Enríquez Gómez. Un écrivain marrane (v. 1600–1663)*, Carsten L. Wilke ed., Paris, 2003, also deserves mention.

[4] Although the Quintanar de la Orden "complicity" seems atypical, it was by no means the only one that existed at the time in the kingdoms of Castile. The Granada Tribunal heard 221 cases between 1529 and 1595 and the inquisitors of the Murcia district prosecuted over 550 people accused of Judaising between 1550 and 1570.

Jewish "complicity" was discovered in Quintanar de la Orden which breathed new life into a seemingly extinct heresy. This "complicity" is doubly interesting for the historian. Firstly, it allows an assessment of the effects of inquisitorial repression. Secondly, it brings to the fore the kinship, and the economic and religious solidarities that existed among the members of the persecuted collective.

In quantitative terms, the Inquisition's repressive action against the Mora family affected 63 out of 135 individuals, or over 46% of the extended family group. In their investigations against "perfidious and heretical depravity," as it was known at the time, the inquisitors collected 47 external statements by Old Christians from the town of Quintanar de la Orden, with ages ranging between 20 and 40 years. These individuals, who testified between 1579 and 1588, are listed in a 1588 record citing the witnesses appearing at each of the Mora family trials.[5] Among these witnesses we find Old-Christian peasant-farmers, Inquisition familiars, pious ladies, learned gentlemen, two tailors, Alonso Hernández, who was a notary to the authorities, a cleric, an *alguacil* and representatives of the town's main aristocratic families, including the Laras, the Cepedas and the Castañedas. Not content with external witnesses alone, the Holy Office also used the declarations of the victims themselves, casting their nets far and wide to maximise the catch. It was not long before the Moras started informing on one another, thereby fulfilling the dearest wishes of the guardians of the faith. The most conspicuous example is that of Juan López de Armenia, married to Juana de Mora, who, in the course of his first appearance before Dr Francisco de Arganda and *Licenciado* Francisco Velarde de la Concha on August 20, 1590, not only accused his own wife and child, but over sixty members of his family-in-law as well.[6]

Of the 63 people convicted by the Toledo and Cuenca inquisitors, 17 were "*relajado*" or turned over to the secular arm to be burnt at the stake (five in person and twelve post mortem), 35 were "*reconciliado*" or reconciled to the Church and had their assets confiscated, three were "suspended," i.e. neither convicted nor acquitted, and a further three were administered pecuniary penalties and exile sentences. The final sentence for five of the trials is unknown.

---

[5] 'Memoria de los testigos que ha de tener cada uno de los procesos de los Moras del Quintanar,' Diocesan Archive of Cuenca (ADC), legajo (leg) 748B, expediente (exp) 99.

[6] ADC, leg. 283, exp. 3946.

There is evidence that the Holy Office showed a certain leniency towards the victims by pronouncing a greater proportion of "reconciliation" sentences than death penalties. Moreover, the latter were handed out primarily to those who were already dead. We can perhaps infer that the inquisitors did not wish to eliminate the Mora family altogether, but rather to stain its collective honor and reputation. The two auto-de-fes celebrated on August 12, 1590 and August 16, 1592 in front of the Cathedral on Cuenca's Plaza Mayor, can only be explained within the context of the Inquisition's aim to discredit the whole family group. Forty people appeared at the dock, of whom 31 were "reconciled" and nine turned over to the secular arm. The aim was to achieve maximum publicity to ensure that these two Sundays were etched forever in the collective memory of the people of Cuenca and the surrounding district. The sentences were read out aloud in the presence of the inquisitors, the city's mayor, the bishop, the local church dignitaries and members of the council, plus swarms of local people who had gathered in the square to watch the performance.

Such instances of inquisitorial repression fall within the discourse of "complicity" as a misdeed followed by exemplary punishment. The other side of the coin—complicity in the sense of a set of bonds linking individuals together—is well worth a deeper analysis. Most of the Mora family lived in the town of Quintanar de la Orden, within the province of Toledo, in the region known as La Mancha Aragonesa. Since 1375, Quintanar was the administrative center of the district under the jurisdiction of the Order of St James of the Sword.[7] In 1575, it was governed by Don Pérez Manuel, governor and magistrate of the Province of Castile, which comprised the districts of Uclés, Ocaña, Montiel and Quintanar de la Orden. There is nothing unusual about the Mora family settling in this town. Quintanar de la Orden had much to offer. It was a prime geographical location, at the crossroads between the trade routes linking the cities of Valencia, Alicante and Murcia with the heart of Castile on the one hand, and Catalonia, Teruel and the province of Cuenca with Andalucía on the other. Rich in agriculture and an administrative capital, it also offered employment in the tertiary

---

[7] As per the listing *Relaciones topográficas* (*Relaciones de pueblos del obispado de Cuenca*, Cuenca, 1927, p. 158).

sector. This, together with its extremely dynamic demographics, made the city the perfect match for the Moras' socio-professional profile.[8]

When questioned by the inquisitors about their professional activities, many of the members of the Mora family replied that they were smallholders or livestock farmers, making most of their living from agriculture and sheep farming: vineyards, olive groves, merino sheep etc. The trial records abound in statements such as "lives off his estate" and "worked on and improved his estate." In terms of New-Christian communities, such a massive presence in the primary sector is the Moras' first claim to originality. It reflects a very clear will to achieve social integration and to embrace the values of mainstream ideology. Let us remember in passing that, since the first half of the sixteenth century, agricultural activity was at an all-time peak due to the combined effect of population growth and demand from the American colonies. This made investing in land an extremely attractive proposition from a speculative point of view. As farmers the Mora family blended into the general economic life of a town where the majority of the population made a living from the raw materials sector, as we read in *Relaciones topográficas*: "the people of this town live on wheat and barley farming, as well as their wine, olive and saffron crops, plus sheep and some goat farming."[9]

Parallel to their agricultural activities, the Mora family had a presence in the financial sector. As merchants and dealers in textiles, spices and livestock, they combined business and public administration. Quintanar de la Orden was ruled by the military order of St James (*Santiago*), at whose head was the King, as grand master of the military orders of the kingdom of Castile since the times of Ferdinand and Isabella. The order therefore received ecclesiastical taxes, i.e. tithes on bread (wheat, oats, rye and barley), on the use of communal pastures, on the smaller crops (saffron, chickpeas, olives etc.), on livestock and on wine. The order was also entitled to secular taxes, such as the tributes of feudal origin *pedido* and *martiniega*, as well as income from oven rental and from the offices of the notary public. These taxes were managed indirectly through a privatised tax collection system known as "*arrendamiento de*

---

[8] The population of Quintanar grew from 315 to 691 hearths between 1528 and 1591 (A. Molinié-Bertrand, *Au siècle d'or, l'Espagne et ses hommes*, Paris, 1985, p. 251).
[9] *Relaciones de pueblos del obispado de Cuenca*, op. cit., p. 160.

rentas."[10] In this area the Mora family created veritable corporations of merchants and tax collectors. For example, Lope, son of Juan de Mora and Marí López, was simultaneously smallholder, livestock farmer and *arrendador de la renta,* collecting livestock and wine taxes, as well as the "*alcabala del viento*" tax levied on goods sold by travelling merchants. His brother Hernando owned a spice shop, managed the assets of the parish church and was also an *arrendador de la renta* for wine and livestock taxes.[11] In contrast to working the land, which was said to enhance all Christian virtues, mainstream thought at the time considered commercial activity shameful and despicable, with debauched connotations pertaining to a bourgeois way of life, the uncleanness of money and ethnic impurity.

Based on these assumptions, the following points are worthy of note:

1. The primary sector is strongly represented within the Mora family, totalling 24% of their socio-professional activity.
2. The secondary sector is very underdeveloped, with a presence of barely 8%.
3. The tertiary sector is overdeveloped, represented by 67.6%.

The Mora family were therefore members of an urban bourgeoisie that was becoming increasingly integrated into a mixed semi-rural, agricultural and commercial economy. Yet unlike many New Christians elsewhere, they did not gravitate towards the city councils and local authorities. Although they played a key role in the economy of late-sixteenth-century La Mancha, the Mora family never had an important role on the political scene. For this reason, their profile is closer to the Portuguese Jewish-Converso communities of La Roda and Santa María del Campo than to the local, autochtonous Marrano communities of the Campo de Calatrava district.[12]

A study of the Mora family should be approached on four different levels:

---

[10] C. López González, "Un caso de administración territorial de la renta de los maestrazgos: la Mesa Maestral de la Orden de Santiago en el partido de Ocaña en el siglo XVI," J. López-Salazar Pérez ed., *Las órdenes militares en la península ibérica,* t. 2, Cuenca, 2000, pp. 1777–1796.

[11] ADC, leg. 320, exp. 4618.

[12] On the subject of these communities see my study: Vincent Parello, *Les judéo-convers de Tolède (XV–XVᵉ siècles). De l'exclusion à l'intégration,* Paris, 1999.

1. *Macrolineage.* Every member of the family was conscious of being of New-Christian stock and a descendant of the House of Israel. In other words, the Mora family saw themselves as a separate ethno-social group, living apart from mainstream Old-Christian society. This awareness of otherness was essential to the group's identity. Juan de Mora, for example, declared his status as a Converso with a pride and arrogance that irked the inquisitors: "taking pride in his ancestry and bloodline, he did not take offence at being called a Jew, but instead delighted in it."[13] During the first admonition on October 2, 1590, the scrivener Cristóbal Molina de Mora, son of the deceased Juan de Mora, made the following statement before the court, in the same vein as many other witnesses:

> …that he is of Converso descent, and so are all those he has mentioned as far as he is aware, and that he has never been arrested or convicted by the Holy Office and that one of his paternal grandmothers is said to have been sentenced by the Holy Office, and that he does not know her name and that he has not heard of any of the aforementioned ever having been convicted by the Holy Office.[14]

2. *Lineage.* In the course of the trials the Moras kept referring to 'kinsmen' and "relatives." They shared the same patronym, a feeling of belonging to a great, homogeneous family and a common identity. In the society of that period, a person's surname served as an element of social discrimination according to the honor or dishonor ascribed to it. This is why certain patronyms were preferentially associated with others in the sphere of marriage, giving rise to clan-type social structures. As we will see below, the Mora family married mainly into families from Alcázar de Consuegra, such as the Villanueva or Falcón families.

3. *"The house."* The Mora lineage can be subdivided into a number of different houses, each comprising the parents, their children and often other close relatives such as cousins, nephews and nieces. The house of Juan de Mora, Marí López and their twelve children, evoking the twelve tribes of Israel, yielded a futher eleven houses. The accused repeatedly refer to "the house," especially when addressing issues of crypto-Judaic practice.

4. *The individual.* Although the individual only exists as a function of the group, life experiences vary widely from person to person. The

---

[13] ADC, leg. 318, exp. 4587.
[14] ADC, leg. 321, exp. 4621.

life histories told by the accused and recorded at the trials give access to the added dimension of individual originality. Let us look at a specific example. When Cristóbal Mora de Molina was arrested by the Cuenca inquisitors in 1590, he was only about twenty years of age, but his life experiences were worthy of the hero of a picaresque novel or adventure story. After his father's death circa 1569, Cristóbal was taken in and brought up by his uncle, Francisco de Mora the Elder. Aged eleven, he left his native town of Quintanar and moved to Toledo, where he took up residence with a silversmith called Francisco Carrillo. A year later, he moved on to the household of a Gonzalo de Villanueva in Ocaña, a close kinsman of María and Catalina de Villanueva. Four years later he was living in Madrid, in the house of treasurer Luis Vázquez de Acuña. In 1587 he returned to Toledo to work in a commercial venture owned by the merchant Fernando de Torres. In 1589, after a short stay in Quintanar, he travelled to Murcia, where he enrolled as an infantry soldier in Captain Pelicer's army. After eight months at sea, touching port at Oran and Lisbon, he finally returned to Castilla la Nueva through Portugal. In 1590 he was in one of the Inquisition's secret jails.[15]

The Mora family's main claim to originality lies in its exclusively endogamous practices. Every marriage alliance involved New-Christian families, many of whom had been in trouble with the Inquisition. An example from the third generation is Juan, the son of Hernando de Mora, who was turned over to the secular arm on September 25, 1496. He married Mari López, daughter of Pedro López Farín and Catalina López, both of whom were turned over in effigy by the Ciudad Real Inquisition Court on March 15, 1485.[16] In the fourth generation, Elvira de Mora married a peasant-farmer from the town of Alcázar de Consuegra, Alonso de la Vega, who was turned over post-mortem by the Toledo inquisitors in 1494.[17] Juan de Mora's second wife was Isabel Falcón, whose ancestors had been convicted by the Ciudad Real inquisitors between 1483 and 1485.[18] In the fifth generation, María and Francisca de Mora married Pedro and Hernando de Sauca respectively, both of whom appeared before the Holy Office in Cuenca in 1588,

---

[15] ADC, leg. 321, exp. 4622.
[16] Heim Beinart, *Records of the Trials of the Spanish Inquisition in Ciudad Real*, Jérusalem, 1981, vol. 4, p. 477.
[17] Archivo Histórico Nacional (AHN), leg. 187, exp. 840.
[18] Heim Beinart, *Records*, op. cit., p. 444.

accused of perverting the course of justice.[19] In the sixth generation, Ana del Campo and her husband, Francisco de la Vega, were reconciled to the Church by the Toledo Inquisition in 1592.[20]

The Mora family practiced a strict matrimonial policy that only admitted a small number of Converso families from the provinces of Cuenca and Toledo. They thus formed kinship networks with the following families: López de Armenia (four marriages), Vega-Ruiz (three marriages), Villanueva (three marriages), Gómez-Bedoya (three marriages), Moya (three marriages), Navarro (two marriages), Campo (two marriages), Carrillo (two marriages), Falcón (one marriage), Enríquez (one marriage) and Villaescusa (one marriage). On many occasions, the Moras ignored the Church's ban on marriage between relatives up to the fourth degree of consanguinity. In fact, it was quite common for members of the family to marry their first cousins or nephews/nieces. Let us look at some examples of patronymical and parental endogamy among the offspring of Juan de Mora and Mari López. Juana, Diego and María de Mora married Juan, Mari and Alonso López de Armenia respectively, children of Juan López de Armenia and Leonor Díez. Their nephew, Juan de Mora, married a López de Armenia (first name unkown), the niece of Juan, Mari and Alonso. Elvira de Mora married Alonso de la Vega, son of a Vega (first name unknown) and a Carrillo (first name unkown), and had three children: Francisco, Catalina and Leonor Ruiz, who in turn married Mari López, Álvaro and Lope de Mora, niece and nephews of Elvira de Mora. Diego and Francisco de Mora married María and Catalina Villanueva, daughters of Rodrigo de Villanueva and Marí González. Their niece Ana Navarro married Lucas de Villanueva, nephew of María and Catalina.[21]

When we speak about patronymic and parental endogamy, we are necessarily talking about constraints in the field of marriage. Given the limited number of families in the pool of eligible individuals, there comes a point where it becomes difficult to find a spouse. In a 'shortage' situation it is preferrable to remain celibate than to make an unsuitable marriage which might lead to a loss of collective identity. This phenomenon can be seen clearly within the Mora family. Up to the fourth generation every individual marries, whereas from the

---

[19] ADC, leg. 315, exp. 4560.
[20] AHN, leg. 187, exp. 841.
[21] See genealogy in the appendix.

fifth generation onwards a high proportion of maidens and bachelors ("*doncellas*" and "*mancebos*") appear in the records. Out of 55 people of the standard marriagable age, only 20 (36.4%) had started a family and 35 (63.6%) remained single. It is my view that celibacy on such a massive scale is not so much a social integration "strategy," as in the case of the ecclesiastical celibate, but a response to external pressures created by a resolutely endogamous matrimonial policy. Proof of this is that no member of the Mora family ever embraced the clerical o monastic life.

As stated above, religious solidarity played a key role in the life of the extended Mora family, since they persisted in their clandestine practice of Mosaic law. Details of these Marrano practices need not be analysed here, for they have already been thoroughly analysed by Charles Amiel. Let us recall, however, that these Judaic rituals can be divided into three main categories: rituals marking the birth and death of the individual, food and hygiene practices, and the main religious festivals. To these should be added the various prayers, often taken from the Psalms of David ("*Chema*," "*Canto grados*" y "*Somos obligados*"), which the majority of the group knew by heart.

Under questioning by the inquisitors the Moras would confess that they had been brought up under the Old Alliance, that is, the one sealed by God and Moses, as opposed to the New Alliance attributed to the Gospels, the Acts of the Apostles, the Epistles and the Apocalypse. Contrary to Christianity, which believed in a new alliance between God and humanity and therefore considered the Old Alliance, in the words of the inquisitors, "perfidious, obsolete and deadly," Jews asserted that the alliance between God and the people of Israel was valid for all eternity and could never be superseded. Beatriz, daughter of Hernando de Mora, made the following statement before the inquisitors: "...that their relationships, conversations and dwellings were very different from those of Old Christians because all their discussions were based on the Old Testament and on the prophecies of the coming of the Messiah and the time when God had given his law unto Moses."[22]

Crypto-Judaism, also known as the "*Marranic* religion" was unorthodox both from the Christian and the Jewish point of view. It arose out of the rejection of Catholicism combined with a process of acculturation characterised by the loss of the Hebrew language and the impoverish-

---

[22] ADC, leg. 318, exp. 4586.

ment of worship practices. The result was an unofficial religion practiced by its adepts in utter clandestinity. Nevertheless, the different members of the family practiced their religion in different ways, and individual consciences, intractable as ever, conferred different values on such practices. Indeed, some individuals appeared to have had more solid beliefs than others. Juan de Mora's son Cristobal, for instance, appears to have aroused the suspicions of Fernando de Mora's daughters, who took a dim view of his tepid approach to religion. In their own words, transcribed in the third person by the Holy Office's scrivener: "they were guarded and wary towards the accused because he kept the things that Francisco de Mora had shown him without due care."[23]

Transmitted orally down the generations, the Mora family's crypto-Judaism takes on its full meaning in the family context and, more precisely, within individual houses. Every house had its own "dogmatisers" or "teachers" of Mosaic law, generally very old people, whose role was to preserve the collective memory. These religious leaders were both patriarchs and rabbis, and their mission was to educate the younger generations in the Marranic religion. On the Sabbath and the great religious festivals, it fell to them to summon the faithful to gatherings which the inquisitors called "meetings" or "assemblies." Meals could easily turn into large family gatherings and it was not unusual for the Moras to invite Moriscos to their table to share "meat killed according to the law of Moses." In general, disciples were initiated in the religion of their ancestors at the age of thirteen or fourteen.

Although women were often entrusted with the job of transmitting Jewish traditions, it was not exclusively a female activity. In her Inquisition deposition, María de Mora stated:

> Diego de Mora, her father, taught her aforementioned brothers as well as herself and her sisters, and she believes and is certain that they [her brothers] know as much as her and the others [her sisters], and that on Fridays they swept and cleaned the house in honor of the Sabbath and left a lamp lit at night until it died out, everybody staying at her father's house many times, and sometimes her aforementioned brothers were present, approving and allowing it, just like the deponent and her sisters, as something that their father had taught them and they had all kept up the practice and communicated amongst themselves about it.[24]

---

[23] ADC, leg. 321, exp. 4621.
[24] ADC, leg. 313, exp. 4549.

In addition to the oral transmission described, the Moras might also have gained awareness of their own Judaism through the "edicts of faith," detailed catalogues of heretical crypto-Jewish practices proclaimed when the Inquisition visited an area, during *auto de fes* and in pre-Lent sermons. When the inquisitors asked Antonio, son of Juan de Mora, how he knew that the ritual decapitation of birds was an act of heresy, he replied: "because he heard it read aloud from an edict of the Holy Office and that he had done it so few times before that he did not even know whether it was good or bad."[25]

Books and written culture were also an efficient means to propagate Judaism within the Mora family.[26] Although some of the people on trial declared that they could neither read nor write, this did not prevent their being read aloud to, a custom that played a key role at the time in the "different forms of social interaction, be they within the family, cultured, mundane or public."[27] The typical reader in the Spanish Golden Age either read aloud to others or was read to (i.e. a listener). The books owned by the Moras were mainly romances of chivalry—a very fashionable genre at the time at every level of society—the Bible in the vernacular, devotional manuals and religious works, such as the *Flos sanctorum* (1578 and 1591) by Alonso de Villegas, *La conversión de Magdalena* (1588) by Pedro Malón de Chaide, *Horas de Nuestra Señora*, a book of psalms by Saint Jerome, a book on Saint Benedict and his monks, *La torre de David* by Juan de Lemos, *Espejo de consolación* (1543 and 1591) by Juan de Dueñas, dealing with the lives of the Old Testament prophets. Mystic literature was also included with Fray Louis de Granada, whose *Libro de la oración y meditación* (1554) and *Guía de pecadores* (1556) were listed in the Valdés Index of Forbidden Books published on August 17, 1559. Beatriz de Mora had a books on the plagues of Egypt, Leviticus and the prophets.[28] María de Mora, wife of Pedro de Sauca, had learned to observe the three Jewish Passovers from her father Diego de Mora, who had learned them from a book entitled *Las edades del mundo*, whose owner was a so-called Oregón from the town of Miguel Esteban.[29] When Luisa, the daughter of Juan

---

[25] ADC, leg. 324, exp. 4652.
[26] According Charles Amiel, 72.7% of the men in the Mora family were literate ("Les cent voix de Quintanar...," op. cit., p. 511).
[27] Roger Chartier, *Culture écrite et société. L'ordre des livres (XIVe–XVIIIe siècle)*, Paris, 1996, p. 30.
[28] ADC, leg. 318, exp. 4586.
[29] ADC, leg. 322, exp. 4631.

de Mora, was arrested by the Inquisition, "she had an old book that they found on her which they called the Tower of David and another one on Saint Benedict and his monks which was not hers, and when she was at Isabel de Mora's house in Quintanar, her aunt read from *Espejo de Consolación*, a book that had been brought from the house of Alonso del Campo."[30]

We can therefore conclude that, in the late sixteenth century, a group of autochtonous Judaisers lived in Quintanar de la Orden who bore no relation to the Portuguese Marrano communities that settled in Castile for demographic, economic and political reasons. The Mora family were relentlessly persecuted by the Cuenca and Toledo inquisitors between 1588 and 1592. They practiced a form of militant crypto-Judaism that was transmitted orally within the family group by "dogmatisers" and teachers, but also externally through sermons and edicts of faith, and in written forms, including mystic literature and devotional and pious books.

A study of the various kinship and economic bonds that united the Moras reveals the exclusively endogamous marriage policy adopted by the family. Relatives intermarried rather than mixing their blood with that of the Old Christians. This brand of endogamy is shrouded in ambiguity. On the one hand, it reflected adhesion to certain notions of collective identity, memory, work and business that did not exclude combining "dirty" activities like trade and tax collection, with other "honest" activities like agriculture and livestock farming. On the other hand, it is indicative of a general refusal by mainstream society to admit New Christians into the fold. Whatever the case, the identity of this Marrano community revolved around the family.

---

[30] ADC, leg. 331, exp. 4734.

APPENDIX I

GENEALOGY OF THE MORA FAMILY

(A) Descendants of Hernando de Mora (c. 1450–1496, merchant and
trader from Alcázar de Consuegra) and Catalina Gómez:
1) Juana de Mora (Villaharta) = Alvaro de Roja.
2) Juan de Mora (Tembleque) = Mari López.
3) María de Mora (Alcázar de Consuegra) = Juan González (Alcázar de Consuegra, procurator).

(B) Descendants of Juan de Mora and Mari López (A.2 above):
1) Juana de Mora (Quintanar, >1506–>1590) = Juan López de
Armenia (peasant-farmer from Socuéllamos).
2) Inés de Mora (>1506–<1590, born in Quintanar, resident in
Granada) = Francisco Navarro (Granada, c. 1506–<1590, *alguacil*, velvet weaver).
3) Juan de Mora (Quintanar, c. 1517–<1590, peasant-farmer,
arrendador de rentas) = 1) Catalina Carrillo; 2) Isabel Falcón;
3) Luisa Díaz.
4) Hernando de Mora (Quintanar, c. 1495–c. 1577, apothecary,
majordomo of the parish church, tax collector, *arrendador de
rentas*) = Beatriz Gómez.
5) Lope de Mora (Quintanar, c. 1498–<1590, peasant- and
livestock-farmer, majordomo for don Francisco de Aguilera,
arrendador de rentas) = Beatriz Carrillo.
6) Diego de Mora (Quintanar, c. 1510–<1590, peasant-farmer,
esquire, kings' tax collector, *arrendador de rentas*) = 1) María
de Villanueva (Alcázar de Consuegra, c. 1519–>1590); 2) Mari
López de Armenia.
7) Francisco de Mora (Quintanar, c. 1520–>1588, livestock farmer)
= Catalina de Villanueva (Alcázar de Consuegra, c. 1522–
>1588).
8) Isabel de Mora (Quintanar, c. 1520–>1588) = Diego del Campo
(Alcázar, c. 1520–<1590, merchant, trader, hatter).
9) Elvira de Mora (Quintanar, >1516–>1590) = Alonso de la Vega
(Belmonte, >1516–>1590).

10) Pedro de Mora (Quintanar, c. 1496–<1590, peasant- and live-stock-farmer) = ?

11) María de Mora (Quintanar, >1516–>1590) = Alonso López de Armenia (Alcázar, c. 1520–>1590, merchant, spice trader).

12) Catalina de Mora (Quintanar, c. 1510–>1590) = Fernando Navarro (Quintanar, peasant-farmer and merchant).

(C) Descendants of Juana de Mora and Juan López de Armenia (B1 above):

    1) Juan López de Armenia (Alcázar de Consuegra, haber-dasher).

(D) Descendants of Inés de Mora and Francisco Navarro (B2 above):

    1) Francisco Navarro (Quintanar, c. 1539–>1590, *alguacil*, peas-ant-farmer) = Jerónima de León (Belmonte, c. 1540–>1590).

(E) Descendants of Juan de Mora and his first two wives (B3 above):

    1) Lope de Mora (the orphan) (Quintanar, c. 1535–>1590, peas-ant-farmer, "lives off his estate."

    2) Isabel de Mora (Quintanar, ?–>1590).

    3) María de Mora (Quintanar, c. 1560–>1590).

    4) Catalina de Mora (Quintanar, c. 1554–>1590).

    5) Antonio de Mora (Quintanar, c. 1560–>1590, peasant-farmer, "worked on and improved his estate").

    6) Francisco de Mora (Quintanar, c. 1560–>1590, peasant-farmer).

    7) Juan de Mora (Quintanar-Madrid, c. 1560–>1590, builder).

    8) Alonso Martínez de Mora (Quintanar, c. 1565–>1590).

    9) Luisa Martínez de Mora (Quintanar, c. 1561–>1590).

    10) Cristóbal de Mora (Quintanar, c. 1568–>1590, scrivener, notary).

    11) Ana de Mora (Quintanar, ?–>1590).

(F) Descendants of Hernando de Mora and Beatriz Gómez (B4 above):

    1) Juan de Mora (Quintanar-Socuéllamos-Baeza, c. 1561–>1590) = (name unknown) López de Armenia.

    2) Mari López (Quintanar-Alcázar, c. 1562–>1590) = Francisco Ruiz (Alcázar, c. 1562–>1590, soap maker).

3) Catalina Gómez (Quintanar-Alcázar, c. 1563–>1590) = Juan Gómez (Alcázar).
4) Juana de Mora (Quintanar, ?–>1590).
5) Beatriz de Mora (Quintanar, c. 1550–>1590).
6) Alvaro de Mora (Quintanar, c. 1551–>1590) = Catalina Ruiz (Belmonte-Quintanar).

(G) Descendants of Lope de Mora and Beatriz Carrillo (B5 above):
1) Lope de Mora Carrillo (Quintanar, >1540–>1590, peasant-farmer, "lives off his estate") = Leonor Ruiz.
2) Isabel de Mora (Quintanar, >1530–>1590).
3) Diego de Mora (Quintanar, >1530–>1590).
4) Catalina de Mora (Quintanar, >1530–>1590).
5) Francisco de Mora (Quintanar, >1530–>1590).
6) Juan de Mora (Quintanar-Huete, >1530–c. 1570, public and royal scrivener) = Beatriz Gómez (Huete, daughter of *licenciado* Bedoya, physician).

(H) Descendants of Diego de Mora and his two wives (B6 above):
1) Juan de Mora (c. 1565–>1590, peasant- and livestock-farmer).
2) Francisco de Mora (Quintanar, c. 1554–>1590, trader, *arrendador de rentas*, tax collector, King's tithe collector) = Leonor Enríquez.
3) María de Mora (Quintanar, c. 1554–>1590) = Pedro de Sauca (Quintanar, c. 1553, constable in Albacete).
4) Francisca de Mora (Quintanar, c. 1558–>1590) = Hernando de Sauca.
5) Catalina de Mora (Quintanar, c. 1558–>1590).
6) Luisa de Mora (Quintanar, c. 1566–>1590).
7) Isabel de Mora (Quintanar, c. 1568–>1590).
8) Pedro de Mora (Quintanar, ?–<1590, illegitimate son of Diego de Mora).
9) Julián de Mora (Quintanar, >1550–>1590).

(I) Descendants of Francisco de Mora and Catalina de Villanueva (B7 above):

1) Alonso de Mora (Quintanar, c. 1558–>1590, majordomo, rent collector).
2) Luisa de Mora (Quintanar, c. 1567–>1590).
3) Ana de Mora (Quintanar, c. 1564–>1590).
4) María de Mora (Quintanar, c. 1558–>1590).

(J) Descendants of Isabel de Mora and Diego del Campo (B8 above):
1) Alonso del Campo (Quintanar, c. 1540–>1590, merchant) = 1) Isabel de Villaescusa; 2) Isabel Romera.
2) Juan del Campo (Quintanar-Argamasilla, c. 1540–>1590, merchant).
3) Rodrigo del Campo (Quintanar, c. 1545–>1590, notary).
4) Inés del Campo (Quintanar, c. 1545–<1590).
5) María del Campo (Quintanar, c. 1545–>1590).
6) Elvira del Campo (Quintanar, c. 1545–<1590) = Alonso Moya (notary).

(K) Descendants of Elvira de Mora and Alonso de la Vega (B9 above):
1) Juan de la Vega (Quintanar, >1540–>1590).
2) Lope de la Vega (Quintanar, >1540–>1590).
3) Francisco de la Vega (Alcázar de Consuegra, >1540–>1590).
4) Isabel de Vega (Quintanar-Villarrubia, >1540–>1590) = Francisco de Yepes (Villarrubia, swordmaker).
5) María de Vega (Quintanar, >1540–>1590).

(L) Descendants of Catalina de Mora and Fernando Navarro (B12 above):
1) Sancho Navarro (Quintanar, >1540–>1590) = (first name unknown) Valencia.
2) Juana Rodríguez (Alcázar, >1540–>1590) = Pedro de Toledo (rent collector).
3) Mari Navarra (Quintanar, >1540–>1590) = 1) Francisco Gómez; 2) (first name unknown) Moya.
4) Isabel Rodríguez (Quintanar, >1540–>1590) = Cristóbal de Moya (Villarrubia, merchant).
5) Ana Navarro (Quintanar-Alcázar, >1540–>1590) = Lucas de Villanueva.
6) Catalina Navarro (>1540–1587) = Pedro del Campo (Quintanar, apothecary, *regidor*).

(M) Descendants of Francisco Navarro and Jerónima de León (D1 above):
1) Diego Navarro (Quintanar, c. 1581).
2) Jerónima Navarro (Quintanar, c. 1576).

(N) Descendants of Marí López and Francisco Ruiz (F2 above):
1) Beatriz Ruiz (Quintanar, c. 1562) = Cristóbal Ruiz (Robledo-Alcázar, soap maker).

(O) Descendants of Juan de Mora and Beatriz Gómez (G6 above):
1) Luisa de Mora (Quintanar, c. 1566).
2) Luis de Bedoya (Quintanar-Indias, c. 1566, merchant).
3) Antonio de Bedoya (Quintanar, c. 1566, student).
4) Juan Baptista de Bedoya (Quintanar, c. 1566, in the service of Marqués de Poza).
5) Baltazar Carrillo (Quintanar, c. 1566, in the service of the Admiral of Castile).
6) Melchor Gómez (Quintanar, c. 1566).

(P) Descendants of Francisco de Mora and Leonor Enríquez (H2 above):
1) Diego de Mora (Quintanar, c. 1582).
2) Antonio de Mora (Quintanar, c. 1583).

(Q) Descendants of Francisca de Mora and Hernando de Sauca (H4 above):
1) Ana María de Mora (Quintanar, 1588).

(R) Descendants of Alonso del Campo and Isabel Villaescusa (J1 above):
1) Ana del Campo (Quintanar, c. 1568) = Francisco de la Vega.
2) Diego del Campo (Quintanar, c. 1561).
3) Rodrigo del Campo (Quintanar-Indias, c. 1564, notary).
4) Juan del Campo (Quintanar-Argamasilla, c. 1570, apothecary).
5) Leonor del Campo (Quintanar, c. 1562).
6) Alonso del Campo (Quintanar, c. 1573).
7) Pedro del Campo (Quintanar, c. 1575).

8) Jerónimo del Campo (Quintanar, c. 1583).

(S) Descendants of Catalina Navarro and Pedro del Campo (L6 above):
   1) Ana del Campo (Quintanar, 1583).

LIST OF INDIVIDUALS CONVICTED BY THE INQUISITION[31]

- Hernando de Mora, turned over to secular arm on 25/09/1496 (ADC, leg. 331, exp. 4733).
- Mari López (A2), reconciled on 2/02/1516 (ADC, leg. 331, exp. 4733).
- Juan González (A3), turned over in 1496 (AHN, Inq., leg. 154, exp. 365).
- Juana de Mora (B1), case invalidated on 7/05/1565 (ADC, leg. 235, exp. 3010).
- Juan López de Armenia (B1), reconciled on 16/08/1592 (ADC, leg. 283, exp. 3946).
- Inés de Mora (B2), turned over on 3/03/1592 (ADC, leg. 283, exp. 3946).
- Francisco Navarro (B2), reconciled on 12/08/1590 (ADC, leg. 322, exp. 4639).
- Juan de Mora (B3), case invalidated on 5/05/1565, turned over on 18/03/1592 (ADC, leg. 234, exp. 2996).
- Hernando de Mora (B4), minor sentence on 18/04/1565; turned over on 16/08/1592 (ADC, leg. 320, exp. 4618).
- Diego de Mora (B6), case invalidated in 1565; turned over on 16/08/1592 (ADC, leg. 319, exp. 4607).
- María de Villanueva (B6), reconciled on 12/08/1590 (ADC, leg. 319, exp. 4606).
- Francisco de Mora (B7), turned over on 1588 (ADC, leg. 315, exp. 4562).
- Catalina de Villanueva (B7). Incomplete trial.
- Alonso de la Vega (B9), turned over in 1594 (AHN, leg. 187, exp. 841).
- Pedro de Mora (B10), reconciled on 12/08/1590.

---

[31] This listing has been compiled using Inquisition trial records kept in Cuenca and Madrid only, and does not include information from the *Relaciones de causas* (Summaries of Cases).

- Juan López de Armenia (C1), reconciled in 1590–91 (AHN, leg. 182, exp. 506).
- Lope de Mora (E1), reconciled on 16/08/1592 (ADC, leg. 322, exp. 4635).
- Isabel de Mora (E2), reconciled on 16/08/1592 (ADC, leg. 324, exp. 4647).
- María de Mora (E3), reconciled on 16/08/1592 (ADC, leg. 315, exp. 4549).
- Catalina de Mora (E4), reconciled on 16/08/1592 (ADC, leg. 321, exp. 4620 bis).
- Antonio de Mora (E5), reconciled on 16/08/1592 (ADC, leg. 324, exp. 4652).
- Alonso Martínez de Mora (E8), reconciled in 1590 (ADC, leg. 329, exp. 4706).
- Luisa Martínez de Mora (E9), reconciled on 12/08/1590 (ADC, leg. 314, exp. 4553).
- Cristóbal de Mora (E10), reconciled on 16/08/1592 (ADC, leg. 321, exp. 4621).
- Juan de Mora (F1), 'petition by the prosecutor against him' on 5/04/1591 (ADC, leg. 712, exp. 793).
- Mari López de Mora (F2), 'suspended' in 1564 (ADC, leg. 232, exp. 2919).
- Juana de Mora (F4), reconciled on 12/08/1590 (ADC, leg. 235, exp. 3010).
- Beatriz de Mora (F5), turned over on 12/08/1590 (ADC, leg. 318, exp. 4586).
- Alvaro de Mora (F6), turned over on 16/08/1592 (ADC, leg. 281, exp. 3907).
- Lope de Mora (G1), sentenced to exile in 1565 (ADC, leg. 234, exp. 2987).
- Leonor Ruiz (G1'), convicted in 1589 (ADC, leg. 551, exp. 6918).
- Isabel de Mora (G2), reconciled on 12/08/1590 (ADC, leg. 317, exp. 4585 bis).
- Diego de Mora (G3), turned over on 16/08/1592 (ADC, leg. 246, exp. 3288).
- Catalina de Mora (G4), turned over on 13/12/1598 (ADC, leg. 326, exp. 4682).
- Juan de Mora (G6), minor sentence on 13/07/1573; turned over on 8/07/1598 (ADC, leg. 311, exp. 4733).

- Beatriz Gómez de Bedoya (G6'), turned over in 1591 (ADC, leg. 330, exp. 4721).
- Juan de Mora (H1), reconciled on 12/08/1590 (ADC, leg. 322, exp. 4632).
- Francisco de Mora (H2), turned over on 16/08/1592 (ADC, leg. 329, exp. 4703 bis).
- Leonor Enríquez (H2), reconciled on 16/08/1592 (ADC, leg. 327, exp. 4691).
- María de Mora (H3), reconciled on 12/08/1590 (ADC, leg. 322, exp. 4631).
- Pedro de Sauca (H3), acquitted in 1588 (ADC, leg. 315, exp. 4560).
- Francisca de Mora (H4), reconciled on 12/08/1590 (ADC, leg. 314, exp. 4555).
- Hernando de Sauca (H4), acquitted in 1588 (ADC, leg. 315, exp. 4560).
- Luisa de Mora (H6), incomplete trial (ADC, leg. 316, exp. 4572).
- Isabel de Mora (H7), reconciled on 5/07/1589 (ADC, leg. 327, exp. 4689).
- Pedro de Mora (H8), incomplete trial (ADC, leg. 712, exp. 785).
- Julián de Mora (H9), reconciled on 12/08/1590 (ADC, leg. 318, exp. 4587).
- Ana de Mora (I3), reconciled on 16/08/1592 (ADC, leg. 320, exp. 4619).
- Isabel de Villaescusa (J1), turned over on 13/12/1598 (ADC, leg. 330, exp. 4722).
- Rodrigo del Campo (J3), reconciled on 16/08/1592 (ADC, leg. 321, exp. 4627).
- Inés del Campo (J4), reconciled on 16/08/1592 (ADC, leg. 320, exp. 4620).
- Elvira del Campo (J6), reconciled in 1569 (AHN, leg. 138, exp. 125).
- Francisco de Vega and Ana del Campo (K3), reconciled in 1592 (AHN, leg. 187, exp. 841).
- Catalina Navarro (L6), turned over on 16/08/1592 (ADC, leg. 321, exp. 4626).
- Pedro del Campo (L6), minor sentence on 10/04/1593 (ADC, leg. 327, exp. 4690).
- Diego Enríquez (P1), reconciled in 1623 (ADC, leg. 409, exp. 5750).

LIST OF OCCUPATIONS

I) Agriculture, fishing, livestock farming (17).
   – livestock farmer: 5.
   – peasant-farmer: 12.

II) Textiles (2).
   – hatter: 1.
   – velvet weaver: 1.

III) Metalwork (1).
   – sword maker (1).

IV) Other crafts (3).
   – builder: 1.
   – soap maker: 2.

V) Trade: (16).
   – apothecary: 2.
   – spice merchant: 4.
   – merchant: 7.
   – trader: 2.

VI) Services: (11).
   – squire: 1.
   – student: 1.
   – notary/scrivener: 6.
   – procurator: 1.
   – servant in aristocratic house: 2.

VII) Economic and financial management (17).
   – *arrendador de rentas*: 5.
   – majordomo: 3.
   – tax collector: 4.

– rent collector: 3.
– King's tithe collector: 2.

VIII) Civil servants (4).
– *alguacil*: 3.
– *regidor*: 1.

Primary sector: 24%.
Secondary sector: 8.4%.
Tertiary sector: 67.6%.

CHAPTER NINE

BETWEEN RUMOR AND RESISTANCE:
THE ANDALUCÍAN MORISCO "UPRISING" OF 1580

Michel Boeglin*

At the approach of summer 1580, Seville had more Moriscos than any other city in Castile.[1] At the height of war with Portugal and in a period of scarcity in Andalucía, the Morisco population, most of whom had come from the former kingdom of Granada, had become a major cause for concern for the *cabildo* (city council) of Seville. It was in this context of extreme tension that the authorities thought they had uncovered an attempted Morisco rebellion known as "the Morisco uprising in

* Translated by Nicola Stapleton.
[1] Despite the very rich and extensive bibliography on Moriscos in Spain, Seville still lacks a monograph on the community that had settled in the city, even though it had more New Moorish Christians than any other city in Castile at the end of the sixteenth century. Apart from the data contained in general works on Seville's history, one of the first general studies on the city's Morisco community was Ruth Pike's: "An urban minority: the Moriscos of Seville," *International Journal of Middle East Studies*, 2 (1971), pp. 368–375, which provided considerable information about the demographics and social organisation of Moriscos in the city. There is also a section devoted to this group in *Aristocrats and Traders: Sevillian society in the Sixteenth Century*, Ithaca and London, 1972. Aspects of Morisco demographics in Seville can also be found in the study by Juan Aranda Doncel, which analyses population distribution in three Seville parishes, based on a 1589 census: "Estructura de la población morisca en tres parroquias sevillanas: San Julián, San Román y Santa Lucía," *Boletín de la Real Academia de Córdoba de Ciencias, Bellas Letras y Nobles Artes*, 96 (1976), pp. 77–84. Antonio Luis Cortés Peña tackled questions on the integration of the Morisco minority in Seville in his article "Una consecuencia del exilio: los Moriscos granadinos en Sevilla," in E. Berenguer Cebrià, *Felipe II y el Mediterráneo*, Madrid, 1999, pp. 537–552. I have myself analysed the assimilation policy planned and implemented by Seville's authorities in Michel Boeglin, "Conjonction des pouvoirs et désarticulation des réseaux de croyants: les morisques Séville (1560–1610)," *Actes du colloque de Montpellier de Familles, pouvoirs, solidarités*, Montpellier, 2002, pp. 237–263, and the actions of Seville's Inquisition with regard to this part of the population in *L'Inquisition espagnole au lendemain du concile de Trente. Le tribunal du Saint-Office de Séville (1560–1700)*, Montpellier, 2003, pp. 233–279. Finally, statistics for the time of the expulsion can be found in Manuel Serrano y Sanz, "Nuevos datos sobre la expulsión de los Moriscos andaluces," *Revista contemporánea*, volume xc (1893), pp. 113–127.

Andalucía," a plot hatched by a group in Seville, with repercussions in all the major Andalucían cities with large Morisco communities.

In the early twentieth century, Seville historian Celestino López Martínez, described the details of this rebellion in a work based on sources that have apparently disappeared.[2] The presentation of events is well known: a large-scale rebellion was planned for the eve of St Peter's on June 29, the moment when the Moriscos of Seville, Córdoba and Écija were to rise up together, in the hope that the rebellion would then spread to other Andalucían cities, and that support would arrive from Barbary. Without noting the true scope of events or, indeed, quoting his sources, Celestino López Martínez presented an epic description of a would be rebellion, very much in keeping with his view of the Morisco community as a homogeneous, inassimilable group resistant to any form of integration and deeply anti-Christian. He presented it as a community that was keen to rise up as one against the city, when, in fact, the few documents pertaining to the case, subsequently consulted by researchers, (generally brief references in official correspondence),[3] are insufficient for definitive conclusions about its scope. Despite very real doubts about the significance of these events, most historians chose to accept his version,[4] albeit voicing certain reservations about the true basis for the rebellion. This continued until the recent discovery of new sources in the Royal Council in Simancas.[5] In 2002 an article was published

---

[2] Celestino López Martínez, *Mudéjares y moriscos sevillanos*, Seville, 1999 [1935]. Documents on the Moriscos in Seville's Municipal Archive are few and far between and the documentation on this rebellion is virtually non-existent, except for brief references in the *capitular* records (Municipal Archive Seville. Sec. X, volumes 57–59, undated).

[3] A few brief references to the event are made in the inquisitorial archives of the Court of Seville, in the holdings of the Valencia de Don Juan Inventory (IVDJ), at the Spanish National Library (BNE) and in Simancas, quoted below. These did not, however, provide sufficient data to gauge the real seriousness of the situation in 1580, until the Royal Council document was discovered.

[4] Ruth Pike, "An urban minority…"; Antonio Domínguez Ortiz and Bernard Vincent, *Historia de los moriscos*, Madrid, 1993 [1978], p. 62. The first to raise questions about the attempted revolt was Antonio Domínguez Ortiz in "Desventuras de dos Moriscos granadinos," *Homenaje al Profesor Jacinto Vilá*, Granada, 1991, I, pp. 89–93.

[5] General Archive of Simancas, Royal Council (A.G.S. C.R.) leg. 257 exp. 4 f. 8–I to 8–III: a wad of documents on the rebellion of the Moriscos entitled *Cartas para el Consejo del asistente de Sevilla y corregidores del Andaluzía sobre los Moriscos de Sevilla* (C.R. 174–5 old catalogue number).

with the suggestive title, *Les rumeurs de Séville*, which considerably reduced the scope of the uprising.[6]

The Simancas document is formed of a thick wad of letters from *corregidores* and fragments of interrogations that were referred to the Royal Council, showing the gravity of the plot hatched by the Morisco community. Testimonies from Old Christians about the community or some of its members, accusations by Moriscos or confessions—often obtained under torture—by purported conspirators, help to piece together a picture, albeit filtered through distorting intermediaries and contradictions.[7] This valuable document offers information of considerable interest about the everyday life of Moriscos in Seville and throws light on the would-be Morisco uprising, confining it within more precise boundaries and revealing how tensions regarding the New Christians from Granada that had been brewing in the late 1580s, came to a head, not only in Seville, but in other Andalucían cities.

It was not the first rumor about a rebellion attempt among Seville's Morisco community after 1568, nor was it the last;[8] but none of the others had such significance nor generated such concern among local and royal authorities. For fears of such a conspiracy among the New Christians from Granada to have taken on such proportions, a series of factors must have influenced and heightened perceptions of the Morisco question, creating a unique context which enabled this "plot" to provoke the reactions it did, amidst considerable confusion and hysteria. The fact that the revolt was thwarted suggests limited organisational capacity among the deportees, divided as they were after their deportation and as a result of the assimilation policy implemented under royal orders.

* * *

---

[6] Bernard Vincent, "Les rumeurs de Séville," Dionisio Pérez Sánchez (coord.), *Vivir el Siglo de Oro. Poder cultura e historia en la época moderna*, Salamanca, pp. 165–177.

[7] On the limitations of this kind of document, see Carlo Ginzburg, *Le fromage et les vers*, trans. from Italian, pp. 8–13, 18–21, Paris, 2002 [1980].

[8] On agitation in Andalucían communities in 1577, see A. Domínguez Ortiz and B. Vincent, *Historia...*, p. 60. In 1595, Moriscos were forbidden to leave their homes while the English sacked Cádiz, ibid., p. 162; May 16, 1600, "*a warning...said* that *the Moriscos of this city of Seville wanted to rise up together with those of Córdoba...the asistente...had an edict proclaimed that no person should dare to say or to do any harm to the Moriscos*": Francisco de Ariño, *Sucesos de Sevilla*, Seville, 1993, p. 112; for 1602, see Manuel Serrano y Sanz, "Nuevos datos...," p. 119.

There is no shortage of cases of socio-political turmoil that have arisen as the result of rumors in a period of crisis or tension, as was the case in Seville on the eve of war with Portugal.[9] On January 31, 1580, King Henry was dying. The Courts of Almeirim had still not settled the issue of his succession or Philip II's claims to be natural lord and king of Portugal.[10] Given the dynastic crisis and the need to resort to force to impose the rights of the Spanish monarchy, troops had concentrated on the border and in Seville. Philip II had left Madrid on March 4 for Guadalupe and then returned to Badajoz from whence the Duke of Alba's army was preparing to enter Portugal in late spring.[11]

Men had enlisted in Seville; and faced with the prospect of what could be a long war, it had been suggested that the city's Moriscos might also be called to arms, creating some unease among the Granadans who had been deported to the city ten years earlier. According to an account by one of the conspirators, Juan de Palma, some were pleased by the idea because, as they put it, "There they could turn against His Majesty and his army."[12] Fears that they might indeed flee with their arms or go over to the enemy eventually made it preferable to rule out their participation.[13] This was a double victory for one sector of the Morisco community. Not only would they not have to pay with their life and blood but, as Juan de Palma stated, "they would then be

---

[9] On the role of rumors in the socio-political context, see Nicole Pons, "Information et rumeurs: quelques points de vue sur des événements de la guerre civile en France (1407–1420)," *Revue historique*, t. 297/2 (1997, n° 602), pp. 409–443. For sociological studies on the subject, see Pascal Froissart, *La Rumeur. Histoire et fantasmes*, Paris, 2002 and Jean Noel Kapferer, *Rumeurs, le plus vieux média du monde*, Paris, 1987.

[10] See Alfonso Danvila, *Felipe II y la sucesión de Portugal*, Madrid, 1956, pp. 223–241. See also Fernando Bouza, *Portugal en la Monarquía hispánica (1580–1640)*, Unpublished doctoral thesis, Madrid, 1986, pp. 631–642.

[11] Diego Ortiz de Zúñiga, *Anales eclesiásticos y seculares de la Muy Noble y Muy Leal ciudad de Sevilla Metrópolis de la Andalucía que contiene sus más principales memorias desde el año de 1246...hasta el de 1671...*, Seville, facsimile ed. of 1988 [1795], 5 vol., vol. 4, p. 112.

[12] A.G.S. C.R. leg. 257 exp. 4 f. 8–II, Confessions of Juan de Palma of 19/6/1580.

[13] Doubts about whether to enlist Moriscos arose on many occasions. Even in 1602, the Marquis of Montesclaros, *asistente* of Seville, wrote to the King ruling out recruitment among the Moriscos: "*I thought we could make use of the Moriscos of this city, who are many and rich, and as they are no longer physically available for what we had intended at least their money should be. To achieve this is purely a question of skill, and I shall ask them to send what they consider to be an appropriate number of sappers, saying that they are for the service to be rendered and then it will be easy to make them wish to redeem their humiliation by means of some service that could be used to buy soldiers.*" The idea was met with enthusiasm by Philip III and the funds raised were used to pay for clothing for the troops. BNE ms 207, f. 658–9 and 618.

better placed and have more opportunity to rise up."[14] This echoed the oft-repeated and growing public rumor circulating on the streets of Seville, exacerbating fears among the common people.

The Moriscos were seen as a perpetual fifth column that could be mobilised at any time by the enemies of the day, be they Turks, Portuguese, English or French. This gave rise to rumors, concerns and fears of all kinds among the local population.[15] According to the *corregidor* (Crown magistrate) of Málaga in a dispatch sent to the King on June 26, 1580, shortly after the rebellion attempt in Seville was discovered: "The Portuguese are trying to sow disquiet in every way they can, as we have seen in their dealings with the Moriscos of Seville, Córdoba and Écija."[16] However, the Count of Gelves stated that a servant of his, who had taken part in a mission to the neighboring kingdom, had heard Portuguese knights allege that, despite a continual stream of letters received by the Council in Lisbon from Moriscos offering assistance in exchange for arms and men, they would never make use of heretics or Moors to resist the King of Spain.[17] In these circumstances, tension in Andalucía seemed to have reached a climax, although the Count of Gelves did not appear to have found this kind of gossip sufficiently relevant to mention until the plot was actually discovered.[18]

The departure of troops for Portugal was seen by the local population as a dangerous turn of events in a city where, in the second half of the sixteenth century, women were in a decisive majority, owing to the large number of men who had emigrated to the Indies and were participating in the war effort. This could only exacerbate fears among the population and alert the authorities, who were always fearful of any disobedience from those who had been displaced from the kingdom of Granada. Indeed, every enemy attack brought renewed fears of a treacherous uprising among the Morisco population. In 1602, the Archbishop of Valencia was still voicing surprise at how much fear the Moriscos aroused in the area: "No less relevant is what we saw yesterday in Cádiz, when the Armada occupied that square... People were placed in the districts to guard them [the Moriscos] and they were ordered

---

[14] A.G.S. C.R. leg. 257 exp. 4 f. 8–II, Confessions of Juan de Palma of 19/6/1580.

[15] See Bruce Taylor, "The enemy within and without: an anatomy of fear on the Spanish Mediterranean littoral," *Fear in Early Modern Society*, W. G. Naphy and P. Roberts eds., Manchester, 1997, pp. 78–99.

[16] Letter from Don Pedro Zapata y Cardenas of 26/6/1580.

[17] A.G.S. C.R. leg. 257 exp. 4, f. 8–I, f. s/n, Testimony of the Count of Gelves.

[18] Ibid.

not to leave their homes at night, to judge by which there was more to fear from the Moriscos than from the English."[19] But over and above this fear of Morisco treachery, the army's departure in 1580 came at a particularly tense moment, owing to the scarcity and expense of basic products.

The year 1580 was the beginning of a critical episode marked by a production crisis, perhaps one of the severest in the second half of the sixteenth century. The dire situation was to continue into the following years when plague broke out in Seville.[20] The decline in the income of the Archbishopric of Seville is indicative of the decline in the farming sector: in 1577, revenue totalled 39,459,273 maravedis, but by 1584 (no figures are available for the intervening years), once the crisis was over, it had dropped by a quarter to just 28,517,908 maravedis.[21] Other administrative documents recount the terrible sterility of that year.[22] Although persistent popular belief considered the Moriscos rich,[23] most Granadan Moriscos in fact belonged to the lower social strata, the population sectors that were always hardest hit by food shortages and price rises, particularly in periods of war. One of the Moriscos prosecuted is reported as saying, "There was a lack of everything in this city, bread and soap and one of them had said they needed water

---

[19] Letter to Philip III, quoted by Manuel Serrano y Sanz, "Nuevos datos…," p. 119.

[20] I.V.D.J. dispatch 55, f. 34, letter to the king of May 19, 1581. In 1583, the terrible harvests in Castile meant stepping up attempts to get grain. That year, ambassadors were once again sent from Vienna and the Low Countries to get help from the Hanseatic cities: see Carlos Gómez-Centurión Jiménez, *Felipe II, la empresa de Inglaterra y el comercio septentrional (1566–1609)*, Madrid, 1988, p. 225.

[21] A.G.S. Patronato Eclesiástico, leg. 136. Although data on 1580 is missing, the income of the Archbishopric of Seville, based essentially in the production of the primary sector, confirms the decline in agricultural output.

[22] A.H.N. Inquisition, leg. 2947, letter to the Council of the Inquisition received in Madrid on 18.7.1580: *"the sterility of this year is so great in this city and its lands that there will be a need to provide for wheat to feed the prisoners, who, once judgement is passed, will remain in the jails of this Holy Office which, as Your Excellency will see from your lists of cases, will be many, in particular who have already testified, and another ten or twelve Moriscos are to be brought who wanted to go to Barbary from Cadíz. And it is understood that there is a suspected rebellion among the Moriscos who live in this city and its land, and the Law is making its inquiries and many will be sent to this Holy Office who appear to have done and said things against out holy faith."*

[23] On this persistent belief, see *Informe de D. Alonso Gutiérrez acerca de la cuestión morisca* in P. Boronat y Barachina, *Los Moriscos españoles y su expulsión*, Valencia, 1901, p. 637. There were undoubtedly rich merchants, to whom the Marquis of Montesclaros was probably referring (cf. Note 13). But this was not the case for the great majority of displaced persons, as censuses and diverse documents show.

even more than to put an end to the Christian seed."[24] Even if the 1580 Morisco rebellion was nothing like other riots of the Ancien Régime, which sometimes led to anti-aristocratic or anti-governmental reactions, here too physical hardship was instrumental in exacerbating disquiet among a growing displaced population.[25]

Indeed, the growth of the displaced population, combined with these other factors, undoubtedly heightened perceptions of the Morisco issue in Seville. From early 1580 onwards, juries began to echo the feeling of insecurity in Seville, which they attributed to the dramatic increase in the population of Granadan origin and to scant compliance with royal and municipal edicts on control of new arrivals. On January 20, the juries called for a visit to the districts where most Moriscos lived and for a census to abide by royal pragmatics that had not been implemented and which they were to call for again shortly afterwards.[26] In June 1580, Seville's authorities gave in to repeated petitions from the courts and on the 21st of that month a census was finally carried out, probably one of the first since the deportees' arrival ten years earlier.

The results spoke for themselves. According to the 1570 census, on November 27, 4,300 Moriscos had been deported to Seville by galley and many were in an appalling state after the journey.[27] Of these, only 2,159 "sick and healthy" remained in the city, the remainder having been handed over to inhabitants and councils of the surrounding villages which fell under the jurisdiction of Seville. But by June 1580, just ten years later, Seville's Morisco population registered 6,247, even though no other convoys of displaced Granadans had been sent to the city. Of those registered, 1,083 were slaves and captives to whom the residence prohibitions did not apply.[28] Consequently, the scrivener concluded that there were 3,005 Moriscos more than there should have been in Seville, in contravention of all existing edicts. It should be noted that this quick headcount did not take account of the transfer of many Morisco families from coastal areas and certain estates to Seville, imposed by the Council of Castile and War Council in the years after

---

[24] A.G.S. C.R., leg. 257 exp. 4, f. 8–II, hearing of 9/6/1580.

[25] See Pedro L. Lorenzo Cadalso, *Los conflictos populares en Castilla (siglos XVI–XVII)*, Madrid, 1996, pp. 1–20.

[26] Municipal Archive of Seville, Section XVI, Various old documents no. 334, f. 1r–v and 2r–v, petitions of January 20 and April 20, 1580.

[27] Others documents from the same source, the *asistente* of Seville, mention November 29 as the date of the galleys' arrival.

[28] A.G.S. C.R., leg. 257 exp. 4, f. 8–I.

1571; but even so, this could in no way explain such a massive increase of population.

These figures indicated that Seville had become a magnet for Moriscos unable to find work in rural areas or access to land, for deportees trying to earn a living, or for those who simply wished to pass unnoticed in the densely-populated city. Above all it confirmed what the people of Seville could see in their own daily lives: a dense concentration of Moriscos in the municipality of Triana and certain districts like San Bernardo and San Lorenzo, as well as around the outside of the city walls, where they lived in communal yards, contrary to the royal edicts which ordered their dispersal amongst Old Christians, designed to speed up and enforce conversion and integration. It was therefore a community that accounted for between six and eight per cent of the population of Seville, which at that time must have had some one hundred thousand inhabitants.

The local inhabitants lived with the constant preoccupation of being in a city that accommodated a large, vociferous group seen as fiercely anti-Christian and unwilling to assimilate with the dominant society. Moreover, in view of the increased insecurity in the city, measures that had previously not been heeded now had to be applied, and these were taken as affronts by the Morisco population, to whom they caused considerable inconvenience. The jury letters testify to the desire expressed by part of Seville's population that the royal pragmatics on displaced persons be implemented, and in particular the prohibition on using their own language and on carrying weapons. The testimony of the Morisco Hernán Jiménez, which was presented before the *asistente* (Crown magistrate)[29] of Seville at the end of August 1580 as evidence of what he had heard about preparations for an uprising, shows that diverse measures were already being introduced by the end of 1579. He declared:

> About ten months or so ago, the Moriscos of Seville were rather uneasy and, in their conversations, many of the Moriscos residing in this city who had come from the Kingdom of Granada were determined to rise up and go one night through the Mountains of Ronda to the Alpujarras because they had been angered by being imprisoned and by the difficulties caused to them for speaking Arabic or carrying weapons and many other things.[30]

---

[29] In Seville the *corregidor* went by the title *asistente*.
[30] A.G.S. C.R., leg. 257 exp. 4 f. 8–III.

Underlying this rebellious attitude was a profound resentment for the unjust treatment received at deportation, despite the background many of these people came from. They were also upset by the humiliating measures adopted in subsequent years, which sought to destroy the cultural specificities of the Morisco group. For ten years the rigorous pragmatics adopted by the Council of Castile appear not to have been strictly applied, particularly in Seville; but in the late 1570s repressive measures clearly began to predominate. Both the reports of the procurator of the Castilian Moriscos and the letters sent to the Curia of the Archbishop of Seville testify to a growing apprehension towards the Morisco community, requiring more stringent implementation of the regulations on controlling these inhabitants.[31] Meanwhile, the rumors of a Morisco conspiracy gained credence.

* * *

On June 20, the city's highest authorities were convened as a result of a warning issued by Seville's *asistente*. They were to be informed about a plot hatched by Granadan Moriscos, who, it was claimed, planned to rise up the following week in different parts of Andalucía. Their leader was said to be a Granadan of noble origin called Hernando Muley, although the authorities did not find him in Seville when the plot was uncovered. An Uprising Assembly was formed to stifle the Morisco rebellion, presided over by the Court Regent, Doctor Juan Fernández Cogollo.[32] According to the information available to the *asistente* of Seville, Fernando de Torres y Portugal, Count of Villar, the Moriscos had planned to rise up *en masse* with the Moriscos of Córdoba and Écija.

On June 19, 1580, the *alguacil mayor* (High Constable) of Seville had appeared before the *asistente* to inform him that on Friday 17, a cleric called Delgadillo, "*who is the Arabic translator for the Inquisition*," had spied on the city's Moriscos gathered on the steps of the Cathedral, and in particular on a group of four or five of them talking in Arabic who had criticised the situation and lamented the food shortages in

---

[31] *Informe del Doctor Liévana, procurador de los Moriscos, 1583*, Real Academia de la Historia (R.A.H.) Secc. mss, leg. 9/6436, exp. s/n. See also the letter sent to *Doctor Luciano de Negrón canónigo y arc[edian]o de Sevilla, provisor sede vacante*. undated, R.A.H. Jesuitas Volume 104, leg. 9/3677 exp. 22, published in M. Boeglin, "Conjonction des pouvoirs…," p. 262.

[32] Celestino López Martínez, *Mudéjares y Moriscos…*, pp. 69–72.

Seville. Delgadillo had followed one of the Moriscos who had apparently blurted out to one of his companions, "Don't be surprised if the whole Christian seed has soon disappeared." This information appeared to confirm the rumors of preparation for a baneful event, and the man in question—who was later identified as the slave, Juan de Palma—was immediately arrested and roughly interrogated at the *asistente*'s instigation.

Tortured on the rack in a particularly long and violent session on June 19, Juan de Palma eventually confessed to a plan hatched by the Moriscos for St Peter's Eve to rise up and flee to the Alpujarras:

> On St Peter's Eve, at night, during the festivities, the Moriscos plan to rise up at the fair when the Christians go to the Main Church and the Moriscos of Triana and San Bernardo were to go there and place themselves under the orders of their captains. There are a lot of brave Moriscos in this city who took part in the uprising in the Kingdom of Granada and who killed many priests. And with the people in Church commending their souls to God and the festivities underway, all those Moriscos were to go to that place and wage battle on the Christians, who would be caught off guard. And they are determined to place themselves at risk, whoever might die in the process, and it would be like it was in Granada. And the Moriscos of Córdoba and those in the lands of Seville would also join the uprising, and together they would return to the Granada Mountains and in that night do all the damage that they could...[33]

Given the urgency of the situation, exceptional security measures were adopted. An edict was immediately proclaimed in the busiest parts of the city, strictly prohibiting Moriscos, either free or captive, from leaving their homes day or night until further notice; only Morisco women were allowed out between sunrise and sunset to get provisions for their homes.[34] Moriscos were forbidden to enter the city on penalty of death, and the guards at the city gates were authorised to apprehend any who tried to do so. At the same time, about fifteen people mentioned by Juan de Palma were seized in broad daylight, in addition to others who had been imprisoned the day before; the confessions obtained by torture led to new arrests. Given the state of alarm and to prevent any unrest, seven *plazas de armas* were established, where men from the different districts were to assemble at the sound of the alarm, to help the detach-

---

[33] A.G.S. C.R., leg. 257-4 exp. 8-II, f. s/n, interrogation of Juan de Palma.
[34] See the *asistente*'s letter of 21/6/1580, in Appendix 1.

ments of soldiers gathered there.[35] Help was also at hand from the crews of the Sicily and Naples fleet, both moored on the River Guadalquivir, which were to go, if necessary, to the populous municipality of Triana in the port of Seville.

The situation appeared dramatic. The *asistente*'s edict called for the Moriscos to stay indoors, while forbidding other inhabitants to do them any harm. This injunction reveals the reaction expected from the local population. But the announcement of these exceptional measures, coupled with daylight raids, provoked uproar among the people, already unnerved by rumors of an uprising. In the village of Guillena, 20 km distant, on the night of June 20, shortly after warning of the situation was given in Seville, violent acts—even deaths according to some witnesses—were attributed to Moriscos, and some 20 men found roaming the fields were immediately detained. Although it was realized subsequently that these were no more than harvesters on their way back from Badajoz, the hysteria had reached such a pitch that the villagers ran out on to the streets shouting "Moors, Moors."[36] In Seville, the same frenzied climate of irrational fear appears to have prevailed; eye-witness accounts state that children threw stones at Moriscos in the street as a result of the proclamations and arrests. On June 20, to add even further confusion to the disturbances, soldiers from the galleys invaded the Triana and San Bernardo districts and others within Seville's city walls, attacked Moriscos, plundered neighborhoods and seized goods and people to be used as galley slaves.[37] Despite the swift intervention of the city council to re-establish law and order, this sorry episode did not prevent retaliation by the Moriscos, gangs of whom left Seville, pillaging everything in their path. The authorities, however—aware of both the disobedience and the desperation to which they had been driven—ordered that no harm should come to them.[38]

Dispatches were now sent to the major cities to which it was thought the rebellion would spread.[39] In Córdoba, all except four city gates were

---

[35] Ibid.

[36] A.G.S. C.R., leg. 257 exp. 4, f. 8–II, hearings of July 3.

[37] Episode related by Ruth Pike, "An urban minority...," and Antonio Luis Cortés Peña, "Una consecuencia...," pp. 547–549.

[38] A.G.S. C.R., leg. 257–4, f. 8–I, Letter from the *asistente* of 21/6/1580. See Appendix 1.

[39] See the letter from the *asistente* of June 21 in the Appendix 1. The capitular records of Córdoba refer to the arrival of this dispatch, *Colección de documentos inéditos para la Historia de España*, vol. cxii, Madrid, 1895, p. 214.

closed, and these were guarded night and day by knights and aldermen in continuous shifts.[40] Similar bans came into force to the ones in
Seville. These were enforced on Moriscos until July 3, three weeks later,
although the *corregidor* Gómez del Castillo did reduce their rigidity
"as it is clear to me that these Moriscos were suffering from extreme
hunger and want, [I decided] to let them come out to work in the city,"
though only in daylight hours. They were still forbidden to leave the
city or walk together.[41]

In Jaén an inhabitant went to report to the *corregidor* that eight
Moriscos who had been with him in the field reaping the corn had
used suspicious words in an argument, one apparently having said: "I'll
tell you this much, we must place our trust in the departure of King
Philip—God save him for not doing any harm to us—once the bread
is brought in, you'll all go off to war and the Christians will leave their
women alone and then you'll see and hear what we will do." The men
were immediately arrested and tortured "*with the rigor that the matter required, with water and ropes and fire.*" Although his companions
denied it, the one who had uttered the threats eventually confessed
that four Moriscos from Córdoba had come to report on the plan
and ask them to go to the city on the day of the rebellion. According
to his account, fifteen Moriscos had left Jaén with that purpose. The
information was then passed on to the cities of Baeza and Úbeda to
enable them to take precautions.[42]

Fear of the uprising had reached such proportions that even cities
where the rebellion was not supposed to reach adopted precautionary measures. In Murcia uproar resulted from the discovery of the
attempted uprising in Seville and several Moriscos were injured in
the backlash.[43] In Málaga, where the Morisco population was mainly
captive, the same measures were adopted for fear of a conspiracy with
the Portuguese.[44] In Ronda panic spread because "300 Moriscos had
departed, mostly from Seville, [and] were coming round the Bermeja
Mountains," reminding the villagers of the unfortunate events of 1569.
In Jerez, which had few Moriscos, most of whom were slaves, the

---

[40] See Juan Aranda Doncel, *Los Moriscos en tierras de Córdoba*, Córdoba, 1984,
pp. 310–312.
[41] A.G.S. C.R., leg. 257–4, f. 8–II, letter from the *corregidor* of Córdoba of
7/7/1580.
[42] A.G.S. C.R., leg. 257–4, f. 8–I, letter from Jaén from *licenciado* Romero.
[43] Ibid. The *corregidor* of Murcia, 14/7/1580.
[44] Ibid. Letter from the *corregidor* of Málaga, 26/6/1580.

corregidor patrolled the streets linking Seville and Ronda for several days with two regiments of knights, though without apprehending any bands of Moriscos. A warning was given, however, that two gangs of Moriscos had been spotted close to Ubrique, killing a goatherd and injuring another man.[45]

Despite the information coming in from all over Andalucía, after two weeks had elapsed it had to be admitted that the gangs of Moriscos supposed to be rampaging through Andalucían territory had vanished into thin air. In cities affected by the rebellion, such as Écija, many *alguaciles* (constables) had been dispatched to keep watch throughout the district, but "found no Moriscos or any sign that they were doing anything out of order."[46] Indeed, it is hard to imagine how a rebellion could have been plotted in a town where Moriscos accounted for no more than two hundred households. The remaining few were the only ones left after an inquiring judge—dispatched by the Council of War—had deported them to Seville, leaving only a small number "to farm the fields."[47] Of the other localities, no report spoke of unrest among the Morisco population. Indeed, quite to the contrary. In Baeza, the *corregidor* wrote about the Moriscos to the Royal Council on July 12: "Those who are here are peaceful and are not to blame," although they [the townspeople] did torture one who had argued with a Biscayan, saying "If we grabbed hold of our beards, we'd all be Biscayans."[48]

After three weeks, when the main precautionary measures imposed on the Morisco population were lifted, doubts began to grow about exactly how well founded the rumors of a rebellion really were. None of the reports sent by different cities provided any solid evidence to confirm a planned uprising or the presence of Morisco brigands from the cities where the rebellion was supposed to take place. Indeed, Seville, which had put the other cities on the alert in the first place, does not appear to have provided any further information other than what had been sent when the Morisco plot was supposedly discovered. In a letter to the Royal Council, dated July 19, 1580, the President of the Granada Chancellory denounced the excessive zeal applied by the local courts and the way they had allowed themselves to be taken in by a rumor, creating uproar in the highest authorities of Andalucía. In no uncertain

---

[45] Ibid. Letter from the *corregidor* of Jerez, 11/7/1580.
[46] Ibid. Letter from the *corregidor* of Écija, 11/7/1580.
[47] Ibid.
[48] Ibid. Letter from the *corregidor* Baeza, 12/7/1580.

terms, *Licenciado* Pedro de Castro was sharply critical of the *asistente*
of Seville for his inability to gauge the true scale of the situation:

> Your Excellency will be aware of…the clamorings of the *asistente* of
> Seville throughout these kingdoms, announcing that the Moriscos of
> that city planned to rise up together with those of Córdoba and Écija,
> which I had thought was a mockery and that in fact these were no more
> than a few [Moriscos] who wanted to go over to Barbary…the *corregidor*
> and his officials were so disturbed, I was afraid Moriscos would be killed
> or plundered as occurred in Seville and that they would do damage to
> defend themselves or go out and waylay…and I did my utmost to make
> them understand that there was nothing in this and that they should look
> after their peoples and roads without creating any new scandals and so,
> thanks be to God, nobody has been deprived of their rights or subjected
> to extortion as happened in Seville and in Jaén with torture by fire, water
> and other things that could be avoided…They will have told Your Excel-
> lency that here the roads are filled with Moriscos and that they have come
> across so many dead people all over the place and that in Jerez they did
> other damage and that three hundred came around the Ronda Moun-
> tains together: all of this is false. Not a hair has been harmed, thanks be
> to God. Given all of this, I believe the matter in Seville must have been
> no more than individuals who had decided to leave or waylay or travel
> to Barbary as they have done before. I have written to the *asistente* of
> Seville asking him to send a record of his proceedings on this to see if
> there was any need to make provisions here.[49]

Dozens of Moriscos were arrested in Seville in the days after the plot
was supposedly discovered and they were immediately interrogated and
subjected to torture, as the President of the High Court (*chancillería*)
at Granada recalls. Yet the testimonies which the authorities managed
to compile, whilst confirming the existence of a planned rebellion,
were fragmentary and disjointed, or even contradictory. A number of
defendants, accused by their companions, withstood the torture and
denied having taken part in the plot, although overall, faced with the
persistent questioning of the officials in the torture chambers, many
admitted that an uprising had been planned for St Peter's or St John's
night. The information on the organisation of the attack was particularly inadequate. In particular, the authorities were unable to find the
offensive weapons—swords, harquebuses and crossbows, presumably
bought from soldiers departing for Portugal—which the conspirators

---

[49] Ibid., Letter from Don Pedro de Castro, President of the High Court (*chancillería*)
at Granada, to the Council of State and War of July 19, 1580.

were known to have gathered.[50] After hearing about the event, some Morisco inhabitants came to inform on other members of their community who had hidden weapons in their houses or yards and some swords were indeed found. It should be noted that, until the 1580s, the ban on carrying weapons was certainly not imposed. In 1575, the Royal Council had demanded that the *asistente* justify failure to comply with the ban in Seville, but even then the ban was not properly enforced.[51] Despite official efforts, the fifty harquebuses and crossbows in the possession of Hernando Muley were not found, nor the drums, standards and gunpowder that he had accumulated, according to some testimonies, to organise the rebellion.[52]

* * *

Everything seemed to suggest that only the main ringleaders of the thwarted rebellion would be able to provide information about the details, in other words, Don Hernando Muley and his son Álvaro Enríquez Marín, Granadan Moriscos of noble lineage as the title of don used in all the official documents shows. They had been imprisoned in Córdoba, but, as tended to happen in cases of this kind, every *corregidor* wanted to be the one to try the case. Despite the petitions of the Count of Villar and the King's dispatches from Badajoz to have them transferred to Seville, they were not actually sent until late July. This was also because, even after the *asistente* had been granted the prerogative to try them, Don Hernando Muley's extremely fragile state of health prevented him from being moved.[53] Don Hernando Muley finally arrived in Seville with his son on July 29, 1580, more than a month after the plot had been discovered. No sooner had he arrived than he was shut in the *asistente*'s house to prevent any communication with the Royal Jail where the other Morisco defendants were imprisoned. In his testimony, he denied any involvement in organising the rebellion. In response, the Count of Villar immediately condemned "his accomplices in crime to torture, notwithstanding the proof that exists against him, which is as considerable as that which I sent your majesty in the trial."[54]

---

[50] A.G.S. C.R. 257 exp. 4, f. 8–II.
[51] Michel Boeglin, *L'Inquisition espagnole au lendemain…*, pp. 241–243.
[52] A.G.S. C.R. leg. 257 exp. 4, f. 8–II, Testimony of Vicente, 19/6/1580.
[53] See the letter from the *asistente* of August 2, in Appendix 3.
[54] Letter from the *asistente* to the King, 2/8/1580; see Appendix 3.

In Muley's case, the *asistente* was unable to inflict the degree of tor-
ment he wished, as the prisoner remained extremely weak.[55] Most of
the information about the rebellion was thus to come from his son,
Álvaro Enríquez Marín, who, after several weeks of confinement and
on hearing the cries of his tortured father one night, became desperate and resolved to cooperate with the court after trying to commit
suicide in the jail infirmary.[56] At the tender age of sixteen at the time
he was imprisoned and moribund after his suicide attempt, he proved
less resistant to the warnings and threats of torture in particular. As a
result, after a number of disjointed and contradictory testimonies in
the first few days, his statements were gradually consolidated, in particular from the moment a healer was appointed to tend his wounds.
On August 2, the *asistente* wrote the following about Álvaro Enríquez
to the King:

> I went to conduct inquiries at the jail…to understand the truth, which
> although he began by denying, a mild threat made him confess at once
> to the uprising which his father and other Moriscos of this city and
> those of Écija and Córdoba had plotted. So that it appears there is no
> doubt that this was true (although I myself never had any doubts about
> it). After this, he confirmed several times what he had said when threats
> were made against him and the others which I have imprisoned and
> which have been pointed out as culprits. Prior to these rectifications, he
> confessed and took communion which, his confessor states, he did in a
> Christian manner and, having shown him the prisoners in question, he
> declared the names of the ones he knew and their trades and where they
> lived and their specific role in this business, and also stated those that he
> did not know. And from the way he has condemned his father and uncles
> who are prisoners and saying what he does about himself and in the way
> he has declared the above, this appears to be the truth and there can be
> no doubt about it, nor that he does so in the interests of Your Majesty's
> service to remedy matters relating to the Moriscos in the way himself
> indicates of his own free will in one of his rectifications.[57]

---

[55] A.G.S. C.R. leg. 257 exp. 4, f. 8–III, Letter from the *asistente* to the King,
22/8/1580.

[56] A.G.S. C.R. leg. 257 exp. 4, f. 8–III, Testimony of Álvaro Enríquez, "*he stabbed
himself beside the left nipple, injuring himself…as the father of the deponent was a
prisoner, he heard him shouting and thought he was being tortured and the deponent
finding himself a prisoner and imprisoned, the devil tricked him and he wounded himself
in this way.*"

[57] A.G.S. C.R. 257 exp. 4, f. 8–III, letter to the King from the *asistente* of
2/8/1580.

According to the jail confessor, then, shortly before bringing him face to face with the other people accused of the rebellion, Álvaro Enríquez took communion and confessed in Christian manner. Indeed, on several occasions, he declared deep hatred for those of his own people, stating in particular in the plenary demonstration, "Your Majesty would be right to have done with these Moriscos now, because they are people with no scruples. For even though he that is testifying is one of them, he still states what is best to be done with them and that is the truth."[58] These declarations only serve to confirm the profound state of abandonment and solitude into which the young man had been plunged by a month of prison, torture and threats. In his confession, he revealed the details of the information he had on the uprising, although it would appear that owing to his youth he was unaware of the preparatory details.

This valuable testimony confirmed the main information on the rebellion that had been organised, despite the contradictions regarding dates, the exact protagonism of Hernando Muley and the preparations involved. Weakened and disoriented, Álvaro Enríquez provided some idea of the preparation of the uprising, but was to die shortly afterwards, while still serving his prison sentence.[59] The only testimony still missing was that of the main defendant, Hernando Muley. Yet, despite the charges against him, he continued to resist the interrogations and refused to comply for several weeks. After a month, probably realising that the charges against him were by this stage more than compromising and weakened by the torture to which he had been subjected, he asked for an audience with the *asistente*, declaring that he "wanted to speak and confess the truth."[60]

* * *

The testimonies contained in the *asistente*'s letters, as well as the dispatches from the different Andalucían authorities, were to bring to light a number of the aspects of what would come to be known as the "Rebellion of the Moriscos." Firstly, the plan to rebel against the authorities and flee to the lands of their ancestors had been in the offing for more than ten months before the attempted uprising in late June 1580. A number of important members of the displaced Morisco

---

[58] Plenary proof of August 1, 1580.
[59] Grace visit, A.H.N. Councils leg. 4412 exp. 13; see Appendix 4.
[60] A.G.S. C.R. 257 exp. 4, f. 8–III, Letter from the *asistente* to the King, 22/8/1580.

community had been contacted to lead the operation. Don Hernando Muley does not appear to have instigated the uprising, but to have been contacted and "importuned" to be its leader by Moriscos from Seville, according to the testimony of his son.[61] His knowledge of the New Christians of Córdoba and Écija, cities where he had settled for some time, led him to invite them to take part in the rebellion, particularly because he needed former soldiers and men with enough charisma to direct operations. However, there seems to have been a total of no more than forty participants in the operation. There was a group of leaders who had been called on to direct operations, and in particular Don Hernando's brothers, but there were also slaves who had been military chiefs during the Alpujarras Revolt and a man called Garcí González, about whom we only know that he had been entrusted to take letters to Barbary to get help from the King of Fez.[62]

Perhaps the conspirators hoped that, when they revolted, other members of their community would follow suit en masse as had previously occurred in Granada in 1568. But unlike twenty years earlier, the Moriscos were now a minority. In Seville, they were certainly a large minority, but there were also deep divisions between those deportees who continued to resist assimilation and those who had opted to integrate. The very fact that members of the Morisco community informed the authorities about the rumors of an uprising and that a number of notable Moriscos refused to take part in the attempt, reveal important difference in Morisco attitudes towards Old-Christian society. It also reveals the success of Philip II's policy of dissolving strongholds of resistance in his attempt to break down solidarity.

Nonetheless, some sectors of the Morisco community continued to reject Castilian society violently, fed by the memory of the humiliation they had suffered and the segregation policy implemented by the authorities. Many of the ringleaders in Seville were men with great prestige in the Morisco community, but who lived in unenviable social and economic circumstances as a result of the decline they had suffered. The head of the rebellion, Don Hernando—or Fernando in some documents—Muley, was probably related to the Nasrid Muley family, a member of which was the author of a report recording the

---

[61] A.G.S. C.R. 257 exp. 4, f. 8–III.
[62] See Appendix 4.

injustices suffered by the Moriscos shortly before the 1568 uprising.[63] According to the testimony of Juan de Palma, he had a grocer's shop in Seville's *Calle Feria*, where the Moriscos met to prepare the rebellion. It was customary to seek help, favors and advice from the nobility, and Morisco men and women approached Don Hernando in this capacity.[64] He was considered a nobleman and also knew how to write.[65] Vicente, a Morisco and servant of the Count of Gelves, who had taken part in the Granada war as a soldier and who must have been one of the captains of the rebellion, asserted that "they made the said Don Fernando Captain Major because he is a nobleman of good blood from Granada."[66] Other testimonies referred to him as "King of the Moriscos."[67]

Muley enjoyed considerable freedom of movement and he made the most of it to try to help members of his community. Before he settled in Seville, he had lived in Córdoba and Écija, where he had stayed for almost a year and three months, until the *corregidor* of Ecija was warned "that in Seville and in this city and the surrounding region they were seeking collaborators to liberate the Morisco captives of the Kingdom of Granada and thus he [Muley] fled and went to Córdoba where he lived with his household."[68] Undoubtedly, Muley's travels through Andalucía and his subversive activities had permitted him to make contacts and become acquainted with other prominent members of the Morisco communities in major cities in southern Spain.

Captured with him were other members of his family, including brothers who were to have taken part in the same revolt and were to

---

[63] Francisco Nuñez Muley referred in his report to a certain Hernando Muley, *"son of Don Álvaro of Fez, his late father, who was brought by his grandfather, my uncle, the late Don Hernando of Fez,"* as the trustee of the document of Charles V which suspended the ban on certain Morisco cultural specificities in 1518. It is unlikely to be the same person, but he must have been related to this family. For the Muley family, see Bernard Vincent, "Histoire d'une déchéance, la famille des Fez Muley a Grenade au XVIe siècle," *Cahiers du C.R.I.A.R.* 21 (2002), pp. 69–79 and "Les rumeurs de Séville," cited above, pp. 169–171. See also María Jesús Rubiera Mata, "La familia morisca de los Muley-Fez, príncipes meriníes e infantes de Granada," *Sharq Al Andalus*, 13 (1996), pp. 159–167.

[64] A.G.S. C.R. 257 exp. 4, f. 8–III.

[65] A.G.S. C.R. 257 exp. 4, f. 8–I, Testimony of Bernabé of Salazar.

[66] A.G.S. C.R. 257 exp. 4, f. 8–I, Interrogation of the Morisco, Vicente.

[67] See María Jesús Rubiera Mata, "La familia morisca de los Muley-Fez, príncipes meriníes e infantes de Granada," *Sharq Al Andalus*, 1996, 13 (1996), pp. 159–167 (pp. 160–161), and Bernard Vincent, "Et quelques voix de plus: de Francisco Núñez Muley à Fatima Ratal," *Sharq al-Andalus*, 12 (1995), pp. 131–146 (p. 136).

[68] Letter from the corregidor of Écija, of July 7, 1580.

have gone to Seville that day, not forgetting his son Álvaro Enríquez Marín, whom the conspirators considered their prince. Other major conspirators were Lorenzo and Vicente, lackeys to the Count of Gelves, and probably slaves, as no surnames are recorded for them. They were held in considerable esteem by the others. As one of the tortured victims confessed, they were "Moriscos of the Kingdom of Granada and noblemen among the others whom the other Moriscos respected."[69] Don Hernando Muley had appointed them captains for the uprising, as they had gained military experience fighting for Don Fernando de Valor—also known as Abén Humeya, King of the Andalucíans—during the War of Granada and against the Turks.[70] There were also a sizeable number of Moriscos and Berbers from Seville. Another document from the Chamber of Justice reports on another main ringleader, Garcí López, and other stevedores, like Juan Sánchez and various members of his family, who was specifically accused in the testimony of Don Hernando Muley's son.[71]

These Moriscos were proud of their lineage and their military feats. They did not necessarily reject the Catholic religion, but were deeply offended by the severe injustices they had suffered, the unbearable situation and the lack of prospects in their new place of residence more than ten years after deportation. In fact, contrary to Inquisition expectations, the roundups hardly resulted in any trials for heresy before the Seville tribunal.[72] This confirms that the rejection of the values of Castilian society, or what has been presented as a refusal to integrate, was in fact more culturally motivated and a reaction to an assimilating policy that sought to erase any distinctive feature of the Morisco identity, rather than due to religious arguments.[73]

By the end of August it was clear that all the elements had finally been gathered to complete the trial, and the testimony of the main defendant allowed the *asistente* to justify his actions in the matter, which had aroused so many questions and been the source of much

---

[69] A.G.S. C.R. leg. 257 exp. 8–II, Testimony of Juan de Palma.

[70] A.G.S. C.R. leg. 257 exp. 8–I, the Count of Gelves' testimony on the revolt.

[71] A.G.S. C.R. leg. 257 exp. 8–III, Testimony of Álvaro Enríquez.

[72] Only one case is recorded, in a ruling from 1583, namely that of the Berber Hernando Muñoz *"imprisoned by the royal courts of justice when an account was received that he had tried to revolt with the Moriscos"* in 1580: A.H.N. Inq. leg. 2075 exp. 7a, f. 24r–v.

[73] See Mercedes García-Arenal, "El entorno de los plomos: historiografía y linaje," *Al-Qantara*, XXIV, 2 (2003), pp. 295–325, (pp. 307–313).

criticism. Don Hernando Muley's confessions had, according to the Count of Villar, provided new and enlightening evidence on preparations for the revolt and had compromised other members of the plot who were subsequently arrested in Seville and other parts of Andalucía. Events rapidly took their course. On the basis of this information and his personal conviction, the *asistente* condemned Don Hernando Muley and the main ringleaders to be hanged, drawn and quartered, hanging being the shameful punishment reserved for plebeians.[74] The son received a lighter sentence for his active cooperation and escaped capital punishment.

The condemned men, however, appealed to Seville's Court, the *Audiencia de los Grados*, which, far from confirming the ruling, modified and mitigated it quite substantially. Don Hernando and Garcí López were condemned to be whipped and to ten years in the galleys and Alvaro Enríquez to four. As Antonio Domínguez Ortiz muses, bearing in mind the crime of which they were accused and the liberal application of the death penalty at the time, it comes as something of a surprise that they should have been spared capital punishment.[75] This mitigation of the sentence may be due to the insistent recommendations of the Madrid courts that the maximum number of galley sentences should be passed in order to remedy the shortage of galley slaves. It may also be attributed to the permanent rivalry between Seville's two supreme authorities. However, it is quite likely that the appeal judges weighed up the charges brought against the ringleaders with greater equanimity and impartiality than the *Assistente* who had, to some extent, been forced to prove he was right to issue the warnings he did, placing every Andalucían city on alert. Not surprisingly, the sentence did not meet with the *asistente*'s approval: a letter from Mateo Vázquez to the King one year later reports briefly that Villar considered the Moriscos had got off too lightly.[76] Apparently refuting the Count of Villar's actions still further, the galley sentences were not applied for nearly ten years, owing to the state in which two of the sentenced men, Hernando Muley and Garcí López, had been left by the torture sessions.[77] Despite this,

---

[74] José Luis Heras Santos, *La justicia penal de los Austrias en la Corona de Castilla*, Salamanca, 1994, p. 318.

[75] Antonio Domínguez Ortiz, "Desventuras de dos Moriscos...," p. 92.

[76] I.V.D.J., letter 55, f. 43 (1581).

[77] As a result of the request for a change in the sentence, Philip II ordered that Muley must serve on the galleys, even if not working at the oar. See Antonio Domínguez Ortiz, "Desventuras...," p. 93 and Appendix 4.

the *asistente* clung to his version of events to the bitter end. Several years later, at his residency examination (*juicio a residencia*),[78] Villar declared that "the handling of the Morisco uprising in this city, which was very much a reality, was as intricate and as dangerous as is stated in the summary of the case conducted on the orders of His Majesty and sent by the aforesaid Count."[79]

Conclusion

However, despite the *asistente*'s protests, it would seem that the President of the High Court at Granada was closest to the truth when he described the rebellion as a mere attempt by part of Morisco society to return to its own lands. A revolt was undoubtedly planned, but by mid-June Hernando Muley had already abandoned or at least postponed the project,[80] in view of a lack of support both within the Morisco communities in Córdoba and Écija and from abroad. At this point, he was not even in Seville.

Nevertheless, the episode did have repercussions for the Morisco community. First, at the local level, it caused the authorities to discover an uncontrolled increase in the Morisco population, which had trebled in the ten years since the group's arrival in 1570. In the eyes of the authorities, they were, more than ever, a threat to public peace. One report, in 1581, accused the Moriscos of planning an attack on the *Casa de Contratacion* (Trading House) to steal its riches at a time when the streets of the city were deserted due to the plague: "there are so many foreign people in it [Seville] and it is such a short time since the Morisco episode and a time of such great ills—the plague, the hunger and the weakness from which people are suffering from on the streets at this time—that (although I am not at all frightened) I consider it appropriate to send a copy of that episode to the *asistente* of Seville so that he should, very cautiously and cunningly, keep watch on Morisco houses."[81]

---

[78] An examination in which *corregidores* evaluated their time in office.
[79] B.N.E., ms 9372, f. 161, *Relación de las cosas en que el Conde del Villar asistente que fue de Sevilla sirvió a Su Md en cinco años o casi que tubo el oficio.*
[80] B. Vincent, "Les rumeurs…," p. 169.
[81] I.V.D.J. dispatch 55, f. 34, letter to the King of May 19, 1581.

At the same time, the revolt also appeared to confirm the opinion of a section of the population that was particularly hostile to the Morisco group and convinced about its incompatibility with Castilian society. It proved, as they saw it, that only repressive strategies would put an end to the resistance. To some extent, the ten years which separated the arrival en masse of the Granadans and the attempted revolt had been years of relative tolerance, despite the repressive arsenal on paper. But, around 1580, coinciding with a more widespread increase in insecurity in Castile, more openly repressive alternatives began to prevail.[82] It seems undeniable that, owing to the importance attributed to it at the time, the attempted Seville uprising contributed to the growing tension regarding the Morisco issue. It is worth noting that in 1582—less than a year after the verdict had been handed out to the plot's leaders—the Lisbon Council began to back the final solution to the Morisco problem, in other words, their mass expulsion from Castile. They called on the King to get rid of these subjects, but it was a decision he resisted until the day he died.[83]

---

[82] See the *Informe del Doctor Liévana, procurador de los Moriscos* quoted above. The work of the Father León, chaplain at the Royal Prison, reveals the high number of Moriscos executed in Seville: cf. *Grandeza y miseria de Andalucía, testimonio de una encrucijada histórica (1578-1616)*, d. de Pedro Herrero Puga, Granada, Theological Library, 1981.

[83] On the Lisbon Council, see M. Dánvila y Collado, *La expulsión de los Moriscos españoles*, Madrid, 1889, pp. 199-203; P. Boronat y Barachina, *Los Moriscos y su expulsión...*, pp. 300-301.

LETTER FROM THE *ASISTENTE* OF SEVILLE TO THE ROYAL COUNCIL OF JUNE 21, 1580 AGS ROYAL COUNCIL 257 EXP. 4, F° 8-I

SRCM

Habiendo habido algunas pláticas en esta ciudad, de algunos días a esta parte, de que los moriscos que residían en ella trataban de levantarse, hice para la averiguación de ello algunas diligencias que me pareció que convenía de las cuales ha resultado entenderse que tenían determinado de hacerlo la víspera de San Pedro en la noche y que para entonces tenían tratado y concertado con los moriscos que hay en las ciudades de Córdoba y Écija y tierras de ésta, que les acudiesen y juntasen con ellos para hacer todo el mal y daño que pudiesen a los cristianos vecinos de esta ciudad y después de haberlo hecho, los que de ellos quedasen vivos, irse la Sierra de Granada. Y luego di noticia de todo al cabildo de esta ciudad y a la Audiencia y los demás tribunales y tratado y conferido con ellos y juntamente con algunos comisarios del cabildo de esta ciudad con el Regente y Audiencia y, acordando lo que pareció que convenía se hiciese para la seguridad de esta ciudad y su quietud, se ha ido poniendo en efecto y juntamente continuándose la averiguación de este negocio y prisiones de culpados, como de todo constará a Vuestra Majestad en los testimonios y averiguaciones que cerca de esto se han hecho que envío a Vuestra Majestad y suplico a Vuestra Majestad sea servido de mandar se vea. Y he dado aviso a los Duques de Medina Sidonia y de Arcos y Marqués de Villamanrique de este suceso para que estén advertidos de él y prevengan y hagan lo que convenga al servicio de Vuestra Majestad y quietud y recaudo de la tierra y la misma diligencia he hecho con los corregidores de Carmona, Écija Jerez y Córdoba y Jaén, Baeza, Antequera y Ronda y lugares de esta ciudad y su frontera, alcaldes y capitanes algunos de ellos y también he dado este aviso al Marqués de Santa Cruz. Y, aunque hubo diferentes pareceres en lo que se debía hacer con estos moriscos para asegurarnos de ellos y prevenir a todo lo que conviene, tomamos resolución de dejarlos en sus casas mandando no se les hiciese maltratamiento y a ellos que no saliesen de ella ni de esta ciudad hasta otra cosa se les mandase, ni entrasen en ella los que están fuera y que, de noche, rondasemos la ciudad y estuviese la gente de ella apercibida y advertida para acudir a las plazas que se señalaron con sus cabos, para lo que se les ordenara y conviniese hasta tanto que dándose cuenta y avisé a Vuestra Majestad de todo. Vuestra Majestad mandase lo que fuere servido se hiciese con ellos, el cual [sic] no he dado antes a Vuestra Majestad por parecerme no convenía hasta estar tan averiguado, como lo está ahora el trato y determinación de estos moriscos y haberse hecho y proveído lo que he referido, que todo deseo haya sido tan conforme al servicio de Vuestra Majestad cuánto yo lo he deseado y procurado y así se irá continuando, esperando lo que Vuestra Majestad será servido de mandar se haga con estos moriscos de lo cual humilmente [sic] suplico a Vuestra Majestad mande yo sea avisado con la brevedad que Vuestra Majestad se sirviere.

Ayer lunes, habiéndose entendido y publicado este negocio en esta ciudad y hallándose en el río de ella algunas galeras de las de Nápoles y Sicilia y en esta ciudad los generales de ella, sucedió que salió alguna gente de las dichas galeras que, a lo que ha parecido por la información que de ello se hizo, fue toda, o casi, de las de Sicilia y comenzaron a saquear los moriscos de Triana y San Bernardo, arrabales de esta ciudad y a algunos moriscos de los que viven dentro de los muros y tomaron algunos y los entraron en las galeras. Y como yo tuve noticia de ello, fui luego a pedir a don Alonso de Leiva (que estaba en su posada) que lo remediase, el cual, aunque pareció que dudó de pasar esto así, fue a ello y recogió la gente a sus galeras y así cesó aquello; y yo le envié a requerir hoy castigase a los culpados e hiciese restituir el robo que hicieron, pareciéndome que él de su oficio lo haría y yo era obligado para cumplir con el mío a proceder contra los delincuentes, pues el delito fue en tierra y tan grave, o a hacer esta diligencia y enviéle a pedir con un criado mío lo tuviese por bien y el requerimiento con un escribano, y todo por la forma y término y no menos comedimiento que era justo, el cual hallándose visitando las galeras, no se lo dejó notificar y de palabra respondió lo que le pareció con sentimiento de que con él se fuese a hacerla, como todo constará por el testimonio que de ello envío que suplico a Vuestra Majestad humilmente sea servido de mandar se provea y proveer cera de ello lo que Vuestra Majestad fuere servido para que todos sirvamos a Vuestra Majestad con el ministerio de nuestros oficios sin atender a nuestros particulares ni impedirnos unos a otros. El daño que se hizo con este saco a los moriscos fue se entiende de mucha cantidad y consideración y no es poco haber sido a la peor coyuntura que pudo ser porque los moriscos se habrán puesto de más mala intención de la que tenían si es posible y podría resultar de ellos nuevos inconvenientes y así tenemos la obligación de redoblar el recato y cuidado en que nos han puesto, en lo cual [el saqueo] parece haber algunos culpados de esta ciudad, aunque muy pocos. que se juntaron con la gente de las dichas galeras a ayudarles al saco y participar de él, contra los cuales yo procedo.

Por mandado de Vuestra Majestad hice alistar los moriscos de esta ciudad y por el alistamiento y el que se había hecho cuando aquí se trajeron, parece que hay más que los que vinieron como consta por un testimonio de ello que me ha parecido enviar a Vuestra Majestad y tengo para mí por cierto que hay muchos más que los que vinieron sin orden a esta ciudad y sin haberse entendido por la grandeza de ella, los cuales no se han alistado ahora por haberse escondido y estar algunos ausentes y no haberse podido haber para ello. En este punto me han certificado que andan algunas cuadrillas de moriscos por el campo, de los que [los moriscos] fueron saqueados y se salieron de los dichos arrabales de Triana y San Bernardo haciendo delitos y desórdenes y parece que se puede bien creer que hubiesen tomado para ello ocasión para ello del dicho saco y maltratamiento que se les hizo: a los menos, no ha habido otra parte para que lo hiciesen, porque con estar averiguado su trato se ha pregonado que nadie les haga ningún maltratamiento para remedio de lo cual se tratará luego de lo que convenga y se pondrá en efecto. Vuestra Majestad sobre todo mandará lo que más fuere servido. Guarde Nuestro señor la SCR Persona de Vuestra Majestad con aumento de más reinos y señoríos como la cristiandad ha menester y los vasallos de Vuestra Majestad deseamos.

De Sevilla 21 de junio 1580

Los testimonios que he referido que envío a Vuestra Majestad tengo enviados en las reales manos de Vuestra Majestad y así sólo va con ésta el del alistamiento de los moriscos.

LETTER OF JULY 19, 1580 FROM DON PEDRO DE CASTRO, PRESIDENT OF THE HIGH COURT (*CHANCILLERÍA*) AT GRANADA TO THE COUNCIL OF STATE AND WAR AGS ROYAL COUNCIL 257 EXP. 4, F° 8–1

Ilustrísmo Señor

Ya Vuestra Señoría Ilustrísima habrá sabido la grita que el asistente de Sevilla ha dado por este Reino que querían hacer levantamiento los moriscos de aquella ciudad con los de Córdoba y Écija. Yo lo tuve siempre por burla y que había de parar en pocos que se quisiesen pasar a Berbería, por salirse a saltear por los caminos como lo hicieron los de Priego el año pasado. Causó tanta alteración esta nueva en esta ciudad que me dicen que no estuvo más alterada en la rebelión pasada de los moriscos [de 1568] con tenerlos en la Sierra y junto a ésta y estuvo tan alterado el corregidor, y sus alcaldes mayores y oficiales y Regimiento y los vecinos que un muchacho que lo meneara tuviéramos mucho que hacer en sosegarlo y tuve temor no matasen algunos moriscos o los saqueasen como se hizo en Sevilla y que ellos, por se defender, hiciesen algún daño o se fuesen a saltear por los caminos. Todo mi cuidado fue darles a entender que no era nada, y así se sosegó que no fue poco, la misma orden di a los corregidores de este Reino que velasen por sus pueblos y caminos sin causar nuevos escándalos y así, bendito sea Dios, no se ha hecho a nadie desafueros ni extorsión como se ha hecho en Sevilla y en Jaén de tormento de fuego, agua y otras cosas que pudieran excusarse.

Habrán dicho a Vuestra Señoría Ilustrísima que por acá andan los caminos llenos de moriscos y que se han topado [sic] en muchas partes tantos muertos y que en Jerez hicieron otros estragos y que por la Sierra de Ronda pasaron trescientos juntos: todo ha sido fingimiento, no ha parecido ni uno ni ha habido daño de un cabello, bendito sea Dios. Con todo esto creo que lo de Sevilla debió de ser alguna determinación de particulares de salir a saltear o pasarse a Berbería, como lo hacen otras veces. He escrito al asistente de Sevilla que envíe un traslado del proceso que sobre este negocio hizo para ver por él si hay necesidad de proveer acá algo, que ahora que está aquí todo sosegado cualquier cosa se podrá hacer cuerdamente.

Tengo aviso que algunos corregidores como el de Jaén, han pasado en este negocio del pie a la mano por mostrarse muy diligentes. Vuestra Señoría Ilustrísima, si fuere servido, verá si convendrá que el Consejo les pida la razón de lo que han hecho. Nuestro Señor, la Ilustrísima persona y estado de Vuestra Señoría, guarde y prospere. De Granada, 19 de julio 1580.

Ilustrísimo Señor.

Besa las manos de Vuestra Señoría Ilustrísima, su hechura y servidor, El licenciado don Pedro de Castro

LETTER OF AUGUST 2, 1580 FROM THE ASISTENTE OF SEVILLE TO THE KING AGS 257 EXP. 4 F° 8–III

SCRM

Habiendo yo enviado tercera requisitoria al corregidor de Córdoba para que me remitiese a don Hernando Muley y a su hijo, aunque con poca esperanza de que lo haría, respecto de lo pasado, que lo principal era habérselo Vuestra Majestad mandado tantas veces desde Badajoz, me los remitió y llegaron a esta ciudad a 29 del pasado [mes de julio] y yo hice poner aquí en mi posada a recado al dicho don Hernando Muley y luego le tome su confesión y estuvo negativo en ella y condénele a tormento para lo que tocaba a los cómplices en el delito sin perjuicio de la probanza que contra él hay, la cual es tan bastante como en el proceso que envié a Vuestra Majestad se podrá ver (que para con él no era necesario). Por venir flaco de la enfermedad que tuvo y del trabajo del camino y prisiones, no se le dio mas que una conminación con la cual no declaró nada, y así se suspendió el tormento para después.

Y a su hijo, que se dice Álvaro Enríquez, de edad de dieciséis años, le tomé su declaración y no confesó ninguna cosa e hícele enviar a la cárcel de esta ciudad donde estuviese a recado aparte de los otros moriscos que están presos por esta causa. El cual fue puesto en una pieza de la enfermería, pareciendo ser a propósito y otro día por la mañana pidió a un portugués que allí estaba unas tijeras que tenía, diciendo que las quería para cortar un sombrero, el cual se las dio y el dicho Álvaro Enríquez quedando sólo se las entró por el pecho izquierdo y luego comenzó por quejarse de la herida que se dio diciendo que en Córdoba se la había dado con un cuchillo de cierta manera desgraciadamente de que estuvo malo y se había curado y sanado de ella y que entonces se le abrió.

Y luego que lo supe fui a hacer diligencia a la cárcel con él y con el cirujano de ella y otras personas para entender la verdad, el cual aunque la comenzó a negar con una conminación ligera la confesó y siguientemente al levantamiento que su padre y los demás moriscos de esta ciudad y de las de Écija y de Córdoba tenían tratado, con que parece queda sin duda haber sido cierto (aunque para mí nunca tuve duda ninguna de ello), después de lo cual se ha ratificado diversas veces respecto de la dicha conminación que se le hizo para lo que a él toca y para lo tocante a los demás que yo tenía presos y a los que éste señaló por culpados. Precediendo a las dichas rectificaciones, [consta] haberse [sic] confesado y comulgado, lo cual su confesor dice hizo cristianamente, por lo cual y porque habiéndole mostrado los dichos presos, declaró los nombres de los que conocía y sus oficios y dónde vivían y que habían sido particularmente en este trato y a los que no conocía lo declaraba. Y por condenar a su padre y tíos que están presos y decir de sí lo que dice y por su manera de declarar lo referido, parece que lo ha hecho con toda verdad y que no se puede dudar de ello ni deconvenir al servicio de Vuestra Majestad, en lo general para lo que en adelante tocante a moriscos, mandar poner [sic] el remedio que él, de su voluntad apunta en una de las dichas sus rectificaciones, u otro que Vuestra Majestad se sirva, de las cuales envío a Vuestra Majestad testimonio.

Luego envié a Córdoba y Écija con requisitorias para que se prendan y traigan aquí los que ha declarado ser culpados y aquí se hace diligencia para prender a otros y se harán todas las que convengan en este negocio y al don Hernando se dará tormento en estando para ello, si sin él no dijere la verdad. Y dentro de tres o cuatro días entiendo justiciar a algunos de los culpados, que no sea necesario detenerlos más para averiguar la culpa de otros, y así iré procediendo en el negocio hasta acabarlo, no me mandando Vuestra Majestad otra cosa y de todo daré siempre cuenta y aviso a Vuestra Majestad y en su real mano, como ahora lo hago de lo referido en ésta y Vuestra Majestad siempre me lo ha mandado por sus cartas. Guarde Nuestro Señor la SCRP de Vuestra Majestad con aumento de más reinos y señoríos como la Cristiandad ha menester y los vasallos de Vuestra Majestad deseamos.

De Sevilla, 2 de agosto 1580.

PLEA FOR ROYAL GRACE FOR HERNANDO MULEY
AND GARCÍ LÓPEZ
AHN COUNCILS LEG. 4412 EXP. 13. GRACE VISITS

Don Fernando Muley y Garcí López, de los naturales del reino de Granada, dicen que ha más de diez años que están presos en la cárcel de Sevilla y condenados por el asistente de ella en diez años de servicio de galeras cada uno por haber sido acusado que ellos y otros se querían levantar con la dicha ciudad y suplican a Vuestra Majestad que teniendo consideración al trabajo que han padecido y a su larga prisión y que, de los tormentos que se les dieron, quedaron inútiles para el servicio de las dichas galeras, les haga merced de remitirles la dicha pena de galeras. Y por la relación de sus culpas que ha enviado por cédula de Vuestra Majestad el Regente de Sevilla, consta que el dicho Fernando Muley fue preso por decir que se hacía cabeza de los moriscos que residían en Sevilla para levantarse con ella (sic) y que para confirmar su intención había escrito cartas al rey de Fez sobre ello y señaladamente dijo Álvaro Enríquez su hijo (el cual murió ya en la cárcel), que residiendo el dicho su padre en las ciudades de Córdoba y Écija como en la de Sevilla se juntaban muchos moriscos a tratar del dicho levantamiento y que había aceptado ser rey de ellos y en el tormento que se le dio a él lo confiesa. Y el dicho Garcí López, en el que se le dio, declara que el dicho don Fernando le dio una carta para que la encaminase a Berbería para pedir socorro a los moros y que la dio a un morisco de galera para que la enviase a Argel y que por esto fue condenado el dicho don Fernando por sentencia del asistente a arrastrar ahorcar y hacer cuartos, y que habiendo apelado de ella para el Regente y oidores, se revocó y fueron condenados él y el dicho Garcí López en 10 años de galeras y 200 azotes y el hijo del dicho don Fernando en 4 años de galeras y que, por la declaración que los médicos de Sevilla hacen, consta que los susodichos serán cada uno de edad de 50 años y más y que, de los grandes tormentos que les dieron, quedaron ambos mancos de los brazos izquierdos y que al dicho don Fernando se le quebró una de las dos canillas del dicho brazo y que así están inútiles para el servicio de las dichas galeras.

Y el dicho Regente dice que la causa por que no han sido llevados a las galeras éstos es porque habiendo dado noticia a Vuestra Majestad, el conde del Villar siendo asistente de aquella ciudad, que se había moderado la sentencia de muerte en revista Vuestra Majestad mandó por cédula de 9 de junio del año de 1581 enviase el testimonio del proceso y se sobreseyese la ejecución hasta que Vuestra Majestad mandase lo que se había de hacer. Y el alcalde Bravo, a quien se ordenó que lo viese e hiciese justicia conforme a la comisión que tiene de los galeotes, dice que la comisión de los galeotes que él tiene no se extiende a conocer de los que están inútiles, antes Vuestra Majestad ha dado cédula para que los de todo el Reino que no se quisieren recibir por inútiles en las galeras se traigan a la cárcel de esta Corte juntamente con sus culpas para que vistas se les conmuten las dichas galeras en otras penas, y que así se ha hecho muchas veces, y que el dicho Don Fernando Muley no parece haberse llevado a las galeras ni que en ellas se haya querido recibir por inútil y que si esto no parece a Vuestra Majestad de inconveniente, aunque la cédula lo requiere, podría Vuestra Majestad siendo servido mandar que se diese provisión por la Sala de los alcaldes para traer el proceso y conmutársele las penas de las galeras en otras conforme a la calidad de su delito, si constare ser verdaderamente inútil. Y comoquiera que el delito es de mala calidad, todavía visto en la cámara y teniéndose consideración al mucho tiempo que ha que están presos los dichos don Fernando Muley y Garcí López y a ser tan viejos y mancos, según consta por la dicha relación, ha parecido que sirviéndose Vuestra Majestad de ello podría mandar que éstos fuesen llevados a algún lugar de Galicia o de Portugal para que estén allí sin poder salir de él, el dicho don Fernando perpetuamente, y el otro por el tiempo que había de servir en galeras pues no tiene salud para cumplir el dicho servicio y conviene que estén apartados de los moriscos del reino de Granada y también de los de Aragón y Valencia. En Madrid a 3 de febrero 1590.

[respuesta]: envíense a las galeras de España y adviértase al Conde de Santa Gadea de la calidad de la culpa con orden que estando para bogar, remen y si no que estén a la cadena con buena guarda y custodia, en diferentes galeras. Vino esta respuesta en 22 del dicho mes.

CHAPTER TEN

JERÓNIMO ROMÁN DE LA HIGUERA AND THE LEAD BOOKS OF SACROMONTE

Mercedes García-Arenal and Fernando Rodríguez Mediano[*][1]

One of the sources cited by Father Román de la Higuera in his *Historia Eclesiástica de Toledo* is *La Historia verdadera del rey don Rodrigo*, a work authored by the Morisco from Granada Miguel de Luna.[2] In this famous work of falsification Luna claimed to have translated an ancient Arab chronicle housed in the Royal Library of El Escorial, which related a history of the Muslim conquest of the Iberian Peninsula. Luna's history was in fact an absolute fantasy, not that this impeded it from becoming a popular success in both Spain and abroad.[3] As is well known, Miguel de Luna is also one of the protagonists in the "Turpiana Tower parchment" and "Lead Books of Sacromonte" falsifications, both forgeries executed in the city of Granada. Physician, translator and Arabic interpreter, Luna "translated" these texts in collaboration with the celebrated Alonso del Castillo, who, like Luna, was also a Morisco, physician and Arabic interpreter.[4] Supervised by the Archbishop of

---

[*] Translated by Nicola Stapleton and Kevin Ingram.
[1] This text forms part of the project of investigation "Los libros Plúmbeos del Sacromonte. Edición y estudio del texto árabe," (HUM2004-02018/FILO), financed by the Ministry of Education and Science, Spain. The authors are researchers at Spain's Higher Council of Scientific Investigations (CSIC).
[2] Granada, René Rabut, 1592. Facsimile edition with introductory study by Luis Bernabé Pons, Granada, 2001.
[3] There are two basic references on this work: Francisco Márquez Villanueva, "La voluntad de leyenda de Miguel de Luna" in *El problema morisco (desde otras laderas)*, Madrid, 1991, pp. 45–97; and Luis F. Bernabé Pons, in the introductory study quoted above. A more recent addition is Mercedes García-Arenal and Fernando Rodríguez Mediano, "Médico, traductor, inventor: Miguel de Luna, cristiano arábigo de Granada," *Chronica Nova* 36 (2006), pp. 187–231; and Mercedes García-Arenal and Fernando Rodríguez Mediano, "Miguel de Luna, cristiano arábigo de Granada," in Manuel Barrios and Mercedes García-Arenal, *¿La historia inventada? Los libros plúmbeos y el legado sacromontano*, Granada, 2008, pp. 83–136.
[4] Darío Cabanelas, *El morisco granadino Alonso del Castillo*, Granada, 1965, republished 1991 with a study by J. Martínez Ruiz. Bibliography on the Lead Books is extensive: all references, in addition to newer and more recent contributions to the subject can be found in the monographs coordinated by Mercedes García-Arenal in

Granada Pedro de Castro, the Lead Books project became a fascinating process in which linguistic problems were intertwined with doctrinal controversies, intellectual polemics and political machinations.[5]

Like Luna the Jesuit Jerónimo Román de la Higuera was also a famous literary forger who, propelled by the need to rewrite the history of his city, Toledo, and to ennoble its lineage, fabricated a series of "false chronicles." These "chronicles" along with the "Lead Books of Sacramonte" had an enormous impact on late sixteenth- and early seventeenth-century Spain. Furthermore both sets of falsifications had an extraordinary effect on seventeenth-century historiography. Indeed, Spain's proto-Enlightenment scholarship (the work of Nicolás Antonio is an example) developed its critical tools precisely as a result of confronting these falsifications and their implications for Spanish history.[6]

In the present article we will examine in some detail the relationship between Jerónimo Román de la Higuera and Miguel de Luna, a connection which can be traced not only to the famous "Lead Books of Sacramonte" affair but also to the matter of the Caravaca Cross. Indeed, we believe that the forgeries of Román de la Higuera and Luna share a common goal: an interest in establishing the Christian legitimacy of the Moriscos and Conversos by tracing the presence of such converts to Spanish antiquity and dissociating their cultural characteristics from their religious ones. In this way both men aimed to promote the integration of the two minority groups within mainstream, Old-Christian culture.

---

the journal *Al-Qantara*, 23 (2002), pp. 342–543; and 24 (2003), pp. 295–573. These two monographs, which have been duly corrected and significantly expanded, constitute the basis of the volume published by Mercedes García-Arenal and Manuel Barrios, *Los libros plúmbeos del Sacromonte: invención y tesoro*, Valencia-Granada, 2006.

[5] It was M. J. Hagerty who coined the phrase "interested translation" to refer to the complex translation process behind the Lead Books ("La traducción interesada: el caso del Marqués de Estepa y los libros plúmbeos", *Homenaje al prof. Jacinto Bosch Vilá*, vol. II, Granada, 1991, pp. 1179–1186).

[6] See, for example, Odette Gorsse and Robert Jammes, "Nicholas Antonio et le combat pour la vérité (31 lettres de Nicolás Antonio a Vázquez Siruela)," in *Hommage des Hispanistes français à Noël Salomon*, Barcelona, 1979, pp. 411–429. For Nicolás Antonio, who is, as we have mentioned, one of the most influential figures in the Spanish pre-Enlightenment, see, for example, José Cebrián, *Nicolás Antonio y la ilustración española*, Kassel, 1997. For Antonio's attacks on the "fabulous histories" of Dextro, Máximo and company, see Nicolás Antonio, *Censura de historias fabulas. Antecedida de su biografia por d. Gregorio Mayáns y Siscàr. Se añaden cartas de Nicolás Antonio y otros eruditos*, Madrid, 1742, re-edited facsimile, Madrid, 1999.

The Sacromonte Lead Books

In 1588, while demolishing the old minaret of the great mosque of Granada to make way for the new cathedral, a group of workers discovered a box which contained what appeared to be an ancient parchment, written in Latin, Arabic and Spanish and dated in the period of the Emperor Nero's reign. The box also contained human remains and ashes, immediately identified as those of Saint Stephen, and a cloth which was said to have been a scarf belonging to the Virgin Mary. Some time after this discovery, in 1595 and in subsequent years, a number of lead discs were found on the Valparaíso hill, later named Sacromonte (Sacred Mount) in reference to the findings. These discs were covered in an angular Arabic script (referred to as "salomonic") without diacritic points. They made up twenty two books in all, covering a number of topics, including the announcement of a new gospel, transmitted by the Virgin Mary. The books also made reference to a number of relics found in close proximity to them, describing these as the remains of early Christian martyrs, all of whom were Arabs, who had come to Spain with the apostle St James and had been converted and indoctrinated by him before their death in Granada. Among the persons cited were Tesifón and Cecilio, the latter, whose name appears in the Turpiana Tower manuscript as a signatory, was supposedly the first bishop of Granada.

These texts, evidently false, reworked certain legends or traditional stories concerning the Christianization of Andalucía in order to present Arabs as the first Christian missionaries in Spain. They also presented a vision of early Christianity very close to Islam, that is to say, without any reference to the Trinity, to the divine character of Jesus, or to religious icons. At the same time Arabic gained an eschatological and superior status, being the language of the first Arab Christians. However, according to these documents, Castilian was also an ancient language, pre-dating Latin. They also gave weight to the claim that the Virgin was immaculately conceived and that St James had visited the peninsula. Equally important, they established the spiritual pre-eminence of Granada at a time when a number of cities were competing for the privilege of being the primary religious see of Spain. For all these reasons local religious authorities, headed by the archbishop Pedro de Castro, were disposed to regard the Lead Books as authentic and to view the find as a miracle. With this interest in establishing the finds as authentic and miraculous, it was evident that the campaign would be successful. It was not until 1682 that the Vatican declared the books fraudulent.

Sacred History

Even at a very early stage, it was suspected that Alonso del Castillo and Miguel de Luna had actively participated in the Sacromonte forgery and, indeed, that they were physically responsible for it. This, for instance, appears to be the insinuation made by Luis del Mármol, who asserted, when drawing up a report on the authenticity of the Turpiana Tower parchment, that the prophesy it contained was similar to the predictions circulating among the Moriscos during the Alpujarras war, which Alonso del Castillo had translated.[7] Even more explicit on the authorship of the Lead Books was Kurdish Arabist scholar Marcos Dobelio, a fascinating character who, in the early seventeenth century, eventually worked on the translation of the Lead Books himself and who considered Castillo and Luna to have been the "authors of this novelty."[8] Modern historiography has given growing credence to these early suspicions, asserting with considerable conviction that both men were actively involved in the Granada forgeries.

This acknowledgement, however, goes far beyond a simple accusation of fraud. The repercussions of the findings were vast, implicated a large part of Baroque Spanish society and covered a period that can be traced far beyond the papal bull of 1682 which declared the books forgeries.[9] The cultural codes present in the Sacromonte texts are skilfully handled, facilitating their use by the more radical sectors of the counter-reform movement[10] and by followers of Morisco culture in the

---

[7] D. Cabanelas, *El morisco granadino*, p. 250.

[8] Marcos Dobelio, *Nuevo descubrimiento de la falsedad del metal*, Mss. 285 of the Library of Castile—La Mancha in Toledo, ff. 36v–35r. Our grateful thanks to Maylene Cotto Andino who supplied and allowed us to use this manuscript. See Fernando Rodríguez Mediano and Mercedes García-Arenal, "De Diego de Urrea a Marcos Dobelio: intérpretes y traductores de los 'Plomos,'" in Mercedes García-Arenal and Manuel Barrios eds., *Los libros plúmbeos del Sacromonte. Invención y tesoro*, pp. 297–334.

[9] For an example of this resistance, see Manuel Barrios, *Los falsos cronicones contra la historia (o Granada, corona martirial)*, Granada, 2004. Barrios argues, in this and other works, the existence of a counter-reformist Granadan paradigm based largely on the Sacromonte forgeries.

[10] In addition to the work by Manuel Barrios, see also Katie Harris, "The Sacromonte and the Geography of the Sacred in Early Modern Granada," *Al-Qantara*, 23 (2002),

diaspora.[11] As a result, the whole affair relating to the Sacromonte Lead Books is about far more than how successful they were as forgeries. Rather, it enables us to tackle in greater depth the issue of "forgery" as a historiographical problem, leading us to explore the limits of discursive systems, the processes of social construction of truth or, as in the case of Sacromonte, the establishment of collective identities based on complex historiographical investigations.[12]

With this in mind, modern historiography has attached or is beginning to attach more precise historical significance to the figures of Alonso del Castillo and Miguel de Luna, and to their part at the center of a complicated scheme of intellectual controversy, nobility interests and religious fervor, which takes us to the very heart of long and serious historiographical processes involving Spain in its Golden Age. As a fraud that sought to exploit the vestiges of Granada's sacred history, the Lead Books cannot be fully understood unless in the context of a series of similar contemporaneous findings: the remains of saints or churches, the bones of martyrs and ruins of buildings, which appeared in a host of villages and cities linking Spain with sacred history. All of these discoveries must be understood in the context of an acute rivalry between kingdoms and cities, fiercely competing for the supremacy of their Christian pedigree against the backdrop of the preachings of St James (and other apostles) in Spain.[13] This process of constructing a sacred history of Spain and its cities was profoundly linked to an obsession to recover ancient Spanish artefacts and to trace the evolution of

---

pp. 517–543. More recently, by the same author, *From Muslim to Christian Granada. Inventing a City's past in Early Modern Spain*, Baltimore, 2007.

[11] See, for example, the extraordinary text by Ahmad b. Qasim al-Hayari, *Kitab Nasir al-din 'ala 'l-qawm al-kafirin (The Supporter of Religion against the Infidel)*, edited by P. S. van Koningsveld, Q. al-Sammarai and G. A. Wiegers, Madrid, 1997. For his part, Luis F. Bernabé Pons has defended the continuity between the Sacromonte findings and the famous *Gospel of Barnabas*, as part of the same Morisco eschatological cycle (see his introductory study to Miguel de Luna, *Historia verdadera del rey d. Rodrigo*, *passim*). This is a continuity that can be traced through diverse Morisco communities with a dense relationship network along the Mediterranean: see G. Wiegers, "Nueva luz sobre Alonso de Luna, alias Muhammad b. Abu l-Asi y su proceso inquisitorial (1618)," in Mercedes García-Arenal and Manuel Barrios eds., *Los libros plúmbeos del Sacromonte. Invención y tesoro*, pp. 403–417.

[12] See, for example, Anthony Grafton, *Falsarios y críticos. Creatividad e impostura en la tradición occidental*, Barcelona, 2001, Mark Jones ed., *Why Fakes Matter. Essays on Problems of Authenticity*, London, 1992.

[13] This is an issue that has been studied from early times. All references, from Kendrick to O. Rey Castelao, can be consulted in the recent work by F. Márquez Villanueva, *Santiago, trayectoria de un mito*, Barcelona, 2004.

its ancient history. It is common knowledge that, in the course of this antiquarian quest, modern Spanish historiography often allowed itself to be seduced by the forgeries of Annio da Viterbo, which dramatically linked the history of Spain with the mythology of the Great Flood and the genealogy of Noah.[14]

This reconstruction of Spanish antiquity and its sacred history posed a whole series of problematic issues and controversial matters regarding historical, philological and archaeological methodology, which affected the debate about the origins of the Spanish language and the etymologies of towns and villages. One matter which cropped up constantly in historiographical discourse was the position of the Jewish and Muslim cultures in Spanish society, an issue created by Old-Christian Spain's attempt, through its *limpieza de sangre* legislation, to marginalize its two socio-ethnic minorities. Both the Granada Lead Book forgeries and those of Jerónimo de la Higuera are related to this problem. Whereas the Jesuit claimed the existence of documents demonstrating the ancient presence of a Jewish population in Spain who had opposed the death of Christ and were therefore unencumbered by the heavy burden of this sin,[15] the Lead Books appeared to defend the existence of a Spanish Arab culture, represented by Arabs who had converted to Christianity at an early date and who had not taken part in the 1568–1570 Alpujarra war. This war ended not only with the victory of the royal forces, led by don Juan of Austria, but also with the deportation of the greater part of the Morisco population from Granada to Castile. Indeed, as Mercedes García-Arenal has recently shown, the intellectual inspiration of the forgeries could be linked to the Venegas family's literary

---

[14] Annio de Viterbo, o Giovanni Nanni, was a fifteenth-century Italian historian famous for his falsifications of ancient history of mankind and the colonization of the earth after Noah. In order to give substance to his fabrications, Viterbo attributed his views to an ancient Chaldean historian named Beroso, who in fact did exist. Annio's pseudo-Beroso had a great influence on Spanish historiography. A classic review of this series of forgeries and its influence on Spanish historiography can be found in J. Caro Baroja, *Las falsificaciones de la historia (en relación con la de España)*, Barcelona, 1991.

[15] For an account on how this matter regarding Jews and, subsequently, Jewish-Conversos is described in different chronicles, and on their strongly apologetic tone, which are ultimately related to the issue of Toledan lineages and Higuera's own lineage, see the work by Juan Gil, "Judíos y Conversos en los falsos cronicones," in Annie Molinié and Jean-Paul Duviols dirs., *Inquisition d'Espagne*, Paris, 2003, pp. 21–43. We are grateful to Kevin Ingram for this reference.

circle, an aristocratic Morisco elite which was closely integrated into the political system of Granada.[16]

Miguel de Luna

It is now evident that the Granadan Morisco Miguel de Luna not only translated the fraudulent Lead Books of Sacramonte, he also played a part in their fabrication and defense.[17] However, far from being pre-occupied with religious questions, for example promoting an Islamic infiltration of Christianity, as some authors have suggested, Luna's interest was rather in defending and preserving a Moorish cultural identity (the Arab language, medicine and hygienic traditions) while separating it from Islamic religion. Above all he wished to link the origins of Christianity in Spain with an ancient Arab community, with the view to changing the Old-Christian perception of the Morisco population. His aim was not only to prevent the Moriscos from being expelled from Spain as aliens closely connected to the eighth-century Arabo-Muslim invaders, but also to be considered as people worthy of honors and privileges. This strategy was also evident among other members of the Morisco elite (Fernando Núñez Muley is an example),[18] who hoped to link themselves to Old-Christian society and thus enjoy similar privileges, while preserving a cultural identity that they were reluctant to renounce; this did not, however, mean that they continued to be Muslims *in pectore*. In all his works Luna insisted that there were Arabs (or "*arábigos*") who were good Christians, hoping, in this way, to influence the Old-Christian authorities' attitude towards the Moriscos. Like many other New Christians of the time, Luna looked for access into a society which, dominated by *limpieza de sangre* statutes, had denied him the right to positions of power. Like others, he wished to

---

[16] M. García-Arenal, "El entorno de los Plomos: historiografía y linaje," *Al-Qantara*, 24 (2003), pp. 295–326.

[17] Mercedes García-Arenal and Fernando Rodríguez Mediano, "Médico, traductor, inventor: Miguel de Luna, morisco de Granada," *Chronica Nova* 32 (2006), pp. 187–231; and M. Barrios and M. García-Arenal ¿*La historia inventada? Los Libros Plúmbeos y el Legado sacromontano*, pp. 83–136.

[18] The tract written by Fernando Núñez Muley has been edited by Bernard Vincent in his introduction to A. Gallego y Burín and A. Gámir Sandoval, *Los Moriscos del Reino de Granada según el Sínodo de Guadix*, Granada, 1996, XXXVI–LII.

design a new Spanish history in which Christians of Islamic or Jewish origin were included.

This indeed would appear to be Luna's ultimate goal in his *Historia verdadera del rey don Rodrigo*. For some the *Historia* was, as Luna himself stated, an authentic translation of an old Arab chronicle. For others it was clearly a fraud. This was the opinion, for example, of Diego de Urrea, chair of Arabic at the University of Alcalá de Henares, who was familiar with the manuscripts housed at El Escorial library, where Luna stated he had encountered the work.[19] It should be noted, however, that the *Historia* was a well crafted fake, which cleverly used a supposed Arab chronicle as a means to give authority to its invention. This option taken by Luna indicates a reevaluation not only of Arab texts as faithful sources for the writing of the history of Spain, but also of the role of the Arab culture within Spanish culture. The Jesuit Father Jerónimo Román de la Higuera, whom we met briefly at the beginning of this essay, also took advantage of this more favorable reception of Arab culture to write his own creative interpretations of Spanish history.[20]

The Tower of Hercules

As we noted earlier, one of the sources used by Jerónimo Román de la Higuera for his fraudulent history of Toledo was Miguel de Luna's famous *Historia verdadera del rey don Rodrigo*, claimed by Luna to be a translation of the Arab Tarif Abentaric's history of the Islamic conquest of the peninsula in 711 and the defeat of the Visigothic King Rodrigo.[21] As a Toledan, Román de la Higuera was particularly interested

---

[19] F. Rodríguez Mediano y M. García-Arenal, "De Diego de Urrea a Marcos Dobelio, intérpretes y traductores de los 'Plomos'" in M. García-Arenal, Manuel Barrios eds., *Los Plomos del Sacromonte, invención y tesoro*, pp. 297–333.

[20] For example, Román de la Higuera transcribed, with some modifications ("I shall remove some words that the Moors have used that do not make for the true story and which the modesty and purity of our sacred religion would not accept or endure") the translation made by Diego de Urrea of the tombstone of a Muslim king of Toledo (*Historia eclesiástica de la imperial ciudad de Toledo*, III, ff. 398v–399r).

[21] This is not the only time that Jerónimo Román de la Higuera quotes this work; see, for example, *Historia eclesiástica*, III, f. 389r foll., on the civil war between the Moorish kings of Córdoba and Toledo.

in Luna's version of the opening of the Tower, or Cave, of Hercules near Toledo, where King Roderic received a portent of his later defeat at the hands of the Arabs. Father Jerónimo Román de la Higuera recounts an early version of this story, according to which, when Don Rodrigo entered the Toledan cave, "he found a chest and in it a cloth that, when unstitched, revealed many faces whose countenance and garb appeared to represent the Arabs of Africa. The cloth contained letters stating that when unstitched men of that face and form would take over Spain and take away its dominion."[22] This version, the origins of which go back to Arab sources,[23] differs, Román de la Higuera tells us, from the account given by "Tarif Abentaric in the history of the Arabs which was recently translated from Arabic, the original of which they say is in the library of San Lorenzo el Real," (in other words, in the *Verdadera historia del rey don Rodrigo* of Miguel de Luna). Here, the story is much more spectacular: after forcing entry into the enchanted cave, some spirited men are bold enough to enter but immediately flee, "terrified at the sight of some horrific vision they discovered there." Finally, the king himself ventures into the cave, with many torches which manage to hold out against the wind issuing from within. Inside, a tall bronze statue armed with a mace is violently beating the ground and a number of inscriptions on the walls warn the king of his ill fate: "Oh unfortunate king, woe to you for entering this place"; "you shall be dispossessed by strange peoples and your people badly punished"; "I appeal to the Arabs"; "I do my duty." Then, from a boulder at the entrance to the cave "there came a thunderous noise which sounded like the heavy pounding of water."[24] After listing the names of several historians who also allude to this legend but who dispute its authenticity, Father Román de la Higuera states that he himself does not consider it impossible, for in the stories of the Indies "it can be read that the devil had painted the faces of Spaniards on mules, wearing the dress we used then and with long beards, saying that men like those would

---

[22] Jerónimo Román de la Higuera, *Historia eclesiástica*, vol. III, BNM, mss. 8194, f. 363r.

[23] Like Ibn Habib: see, for instance, Julia Hernández Juberías, *La Península imaginaria. Mitos y leyendas sobre al-Andalus*, Madrid, 1996, p. 200.

[24] Miguel de Luna, *Historia verdadera*, p. 24.

subdue the Indies. I saw one of these books in the year 1590 in the College of Madrid."[25]

The Caravaca Cross

The history of the Cave of Hercules' inscriptions brings to mind another matter where Jerónimo Román de la Higuera and Miguel de Luna again coincide (this time much more significantly), namely the apparition of the Holy Cross of Caravaca.[26] The matter can be summarised as follows. Although the cult of Caravaca can be traced back to the Low Middle Ages, in the early seventeenth century the legend took a more complex narrative turn, thanks to a version by the forger Juan de Robles Corbalán, a disciple of Román de la Higuera, from whom he took most of his source material.[27] This material, according to Corbalán, came from a manuscript stored in the Jesuits' house in Toledo, where his master, Román de la Higuera, "renowned for his virtue and intelligence, famous in that period [the late sixteenth century] among intellectuals," found it.[28] Corbalán's version (based on Román de la Higuera) is, in broad strokes, the following: The monk Chirinos, born in Cuenca, had been made captive by the Moorish king of Caravaca, Zeyt Abuceyt. Chirinos wanted to say mass and gained permission from the king to bring all the necessary accessories from Cuenca. But, as the ceremony began, the monk realised that he had forgotten the most important element of all, the cross. At that very moment, angels entered through the window of the room where the mass was about to be said carrying a cross built with a piece of the real Cross of Christ, taken from the chest of the Patriarch of Jerusalem himself. Faced with

---

[25] *Historia eclesiástica de la imperial ciudad de Toledo*, III, f. 364v. For Spanish versions of this legend, see Fernando Ruiz de la Puerta, *La Cueva de Hércules y el Palacio Encantado de Toledo*, Madrid, 1977.

[26] This subject is dealt with in detail in Mercedes García-Arenal and Fernando Rodríguez Mediano, "Miguel de Luna 'cristiano arábigo' de Ganada," in M. Barrios y M. García-Arenal, ¿*La historia inventada? Los Libros plúmbeos y el legado sacromontano*, Granada, 2008, pp. 83–176. See also Emilio Molina, "Fray Darío Cabanelas, historiador de los fraudes del Sacromonte," in Manuel Barrios and Mercedes García-Arenal, ¿*La historia inventada. Los libros plúmbeos y el legado sacromontano*, pp. 438–464, and the references cited there.

[27] *Historia del mysterioso aparecimiento de la Santísima Cruz de Carabaca, e innumerables milagros que Dios N.S. ha obrado y obra por su devoción*, Madrid, 1615.

[28] Ibid. F. 2r.

this miracle, King Zeyt Abuceyt converted to Christianity, followed by his wife, Queen Heyla.

Corbalán's book enlarges on this story and on the miracles resulting from the holy relic in a manner that was to leave its imprint on subsequent literature.[29] The origin of some of the elements of this version can easily be traced, such as the figure of Zeyt Abuceyt, who is reminiscent of the Almohad *sayyid* Abu Zayd Abd al-Rahman, who converted to Christianity in the thirteenth century.[30] But from the perspective of this article, it is not the apparition itself but the inscriptions in the room where the event was said to have taken place that are of interest. These mysterious characters were found inscribed in a circle adorning the window where the Cross-bearing angels appeared (an inscription which still exists) and also on the walls, on frescos representing a Moorish king on horseback, a king fighting, together with his *ulemas*, against a Christian monk, and the baptism of the same king, with his kneeling queen in attendance.[31] Corbalán recounts the attempts to interpret these strange letters: "having taken these years ago to Valencia, Aragón, Portugal, Salamanca and other parts of Spain to intelligent men for translation, and also to places in Barbary, no person could ever be found to explain them until the Lord God revealed the divine treasures hidden in the Holy Mount of Granada, which *Licenciado* Miguel de Luna, doctor and interpreter, interpreted. In two letters, the originals of which are both in my possession and which I am minded to place in the Archive of the Holy Cross, one dated September 29, 1603, and the other March 8, 1604, Luna explained that the figures [relating to the Caravaca Cross] are Arabic figures in a similar style to those we here call Gothic."

[29] See for instance, Martín de Cuenca Fernández, *Historia sagrada de el compendio de las ocho maravillas de el mundo, del non plus ultra de la admiración y de el pasmo, de el emporio donde se hallan los portentos más singulares, de un lignum-crucis que se compone de quatro brazos, de la quintaesencia y más principales partes del sacrosanto madero y dulce leño en que murió el Rey de los cielos y de la tierra y el segundo Adán, nuestro redemptor Jesu Christo, de la santíssima cruz de Caravaca*, Madrid, Viuda de Juan García Infançón, 1722. A summary of local Caravaca historiography which has dealt with this subject and Corbalán's work in posterity can be found in Juan Manuel Villanueva Fernández, *Historia de Caravaca de la Cruz*, Cartagena, 1999, and in the bibliography he refers to.

[30] For more on this Moorish king, see, among others, Emilio Molina López, *Ceyt Abu Ceyt. Novedades y rectificaciones*, Almería, 1977.

[31] Juan de Robles Corbalán, *Historia del mysterioso aparecimiento de la Santíssima Cruz de Carabaca*, ff. 46v–48v and 50v–56r.

Indeed, to go by this account, Corbalán believed that in Miguel de Luna he had found the ideal interpreter of these strange characters which, once finally revealed, merely confirmed in Arabic the story of the apparition of the cross and the conversion of Zeyt Abuceyt and his wife, Heyla. According to Luna, the inscriptions read as follows: "In the year 594 of the Arabs in the time of Mohammed: Abuzeyt, all powerful king, and thirty men in this dwelling were converted to the true law of salvation by the grace of God, by means of a four-armed cross brought by angels, accompanied by many others assisting in the celebration, to the memory of whom these letters were carved here"; "In memory of my conversion, and to the glory of God, I offered these royal vestments to be brought on the day of the Holy Cross given the solemnity of this festival"; "With this horse I extolled the Law of God and conquered his enemies in battle many times"; "I, Queen Hayla (now Elena), wife of King Abuzeyt and my two children were converted to the Holy Faith by Divine Grace, in memory of which I am depicted here."[32]

As can be observed, the wall paintings with their cryptic messages are strongly reminiscent of those in the Cave of Hercules, as narrated in Miguel de Luna's *Historia verdadera del rey don Rodrigo*. The characters in question, reproduced by Corbalán in his book, are not, of course, Arabic at all, and the whole story is once again a forgery which can be attributed to Luna, if we are to believe the version given by Corbalán (who, incidentally, must have destroyed the letters in which Luna sent him his versions of the inscriptions).[33]

Jerónimo Román de la Higuera was interested in the story of the Caravaca Cross for a number of reasons. Firstly, he claimed to have been miraculously cured of a serious illness as a child thanks to a cross that had been in contact with the Caravaca cross.[34] Secondly, the Jesuit appears to have constructed a genealogical link with Chirinos, having traced his ancestry to a group of Toledan Mozarabs,[35] who had left the city and spread to other parts of Castile, including Cuenca. In a rather unclear reference, Higuera appears to assert that one of his ancestors

[32] Ibid.

[33] Agustín Marín de Espinosa, *Memorias para la historia de la ciudad de Caravaca (y del aparecimiento de la Sma. Cruz) desde los tiempos remotos hasta nuestros días, e ilustradas con notas históricas*, Caravaca, 1856, p. 74.

[34] Ibid., f. 11r.

[35] The term Mozarab refers to Christians living in the Islamic zone of Spain, who had adopted the Arabic language and culture.

had married a woman in the Chirinos family,[36] which, according to posterity, "descended from the conquerors of the city."[37]

The connection between the figures of Luna and Román de la Higuera in the Caravaca affair, through Juan de Robles Corbalán, shows not only where their interests coincided, but also where they parted company. The Jesuit undoubtedly investigated and manipulated Spanish sacred history out of pious feeling, but with obvious genealogical interests at heart: in this case, the story of Caravaca is linked, via Cuenca and the priest Chirinos, to the Mozarabs of Toledo, which, as we shall see, was a vital theme in his life and work. It was with good reason that he put a great deal of his scholarly efforts into linking his family history to these early Toledan Mozarabs who, according to his account, were to spread throughout Castile. Luna's contribution to the Caravaca story, on the other hand, had more to do with the attempt to show Arab culture as one that could be integrated into that of Spain. Part of Luna's argumentation on the subject is linked to the historic existence of Arabs who had converted to Christianity prior to the forced conversions of the sixteenth century.

The Cult of Saint Thyrsus

In 1595, when house foundations were being dug up near Toledo's Plaza Mayor to build the new *Hospital del Rey*, the ruins were found of an old temple along with bones and human artefacts. These included the copper cover of a vessel carved with the letters S.C., joined together at the top by a crown. The finding did not greatly impress anyone until Román de la Higuera presented a letter in Latin, stating that a Gothic book had been found in the library of Toledo cathedral. This letter, which was a reply from King Silo to Archbishop Cixila, spoke of Silo's problems with the Moors who dominated the city at the time when he tried to build a temple to the martyred Saint Thyrsus. The letter spoke of a chalice and pitcher with its cover, on which appeared the crown

---

[36] Jerónimo Román de la Higuera, *Tratado del linaje de Higuera*, Real Academia de la Historia, mss. 9–5566, f. 16r.

[37] See Juan Pablo Mártir Rizo, *Historia de la muy noble y leal ciudad de Cuenca*, Madrid, 1629; ed. facsimile, Barcelona, 1979, pp. 55–6. Otherwise, Mártir Rizo repeats Juan de Robles Corbalán's version, with certain additions.

and initials of both the king and the archbishop: S and C.[38] This letter, then, indicated that the ruins found were those of the Temple of Saint Thyrsus and that the city had a new saint among its founders. It also proved the heroic worth of the Mozarabs, the Christian heirs of the Goths who had kept their faith throughout Islamic domination. The *corregidor* (Crown magistrate) of Toledo, Alonso de Cárcamo, was enthused by this finding and its documentary explanation. At Higuera's instigation, he sent an account to Philip II, which the Jesuit father had drawn up himself, along with a copy of the letter. The people of Toledo exploded in ardent devotion at the discovery of this new saintly compatriot, and acclaimed Saint Thyrsus their patron.

But a group also formed which believed the letter a forgery and which printed challenges to it, calling on paladins like Juan Bautista Pérez and the chronicler Esteban de Garibay in their defence. When asked to present the original letter, Román de la Higuera was evasive, defending himself with turns of phrase that might even be read as a confession of fraud: "What possible problem could there be with Saint Thyrsus being from Toledo, what harm could it do to the faith or what detriment to good custom? And should there have been any error in this, it was not a harmful error."[39] Higuera defended his pious forgeries, which created or confirmed equally pious legendary traditions, in the face of challenges from those who had embarked on a determined quest for historical truth. Indeed, unmoved by his critics, he includes the whole Saint Thyrsus episode—together with the transcription of the letter and the details of how it was encountered and with which papers—in his *Historia de Toledo*.[40] In this he includes the connection with his history of the Mozarabs of Toledo, the subject dearest to his heart and to which we shall return below. The fact that Higuera failed to understand the struggle of chroniclers and critical historians to overcome deception does not mean that he did not apply the methodology of true scholars

---

[38] See Godoy Alcántara, *Historia crítica de los falsos cronicones*, Madrid, 1868, re-ed. 1981, pp. 39 and foll. Nicolás Antonio, *Censura de historias fabulosas*, published by G. Mayans y Siscar, Valencia, 1742, p. 525 and foll.

[39] In Godoy Alcántara, *Historia crítica*, p. 42. This would appear to be a response to comments by Nicolás Antonio who, when referring to Higuera's chapter on Saint Thyrsus, urges "that the truth must be sought out and defended, even if, in so doing, other laws of piety are breached, for it cannot be governed as personal property but must be yielded up to public property which is best served by seeking to banish common deception, distinguishing light from darkness, truth from falsehood." Nicolás Antonio, *Censura de historias fabulosas*, p. 524.

[40] *Historia eclesiástica de la imperial ciudad de Toledo*, III, f. 420r foll.

in his attempts at authenticating the chronicles and aged documents which he had forged to support his own histories.

But to return to Saint Thyrsus, the round metal cover with the mysterious letters appeared in Toledo at the same time, namely 1595, as the Lead Books of Sacromonte were appearing in Granada in the midst of the ashes and bones of saints (just as the parchment in its metal cask had appeared amidst the ruins of the Turpiana Tower a few years earlier).[41] The Lead Books, as we have seen, touched on diverse questions of both doctrinal and political interest while establishing a common historical origin for Spanish Christians and Arabs. As well as showing the antiquity of the Castilian language, they made a case for the antiquity of the Arabic language on the peninsula, as practiced by these Christian martyrs, separating it from the Islamic religion. They demonstrated the spiritual pre-eminence of the Church of Granada at a time when a number of Spanish cities were vying for the privilege of being the Primate's see; they consolidated the controversial dogma of the Immaculate Conception and they also proved that St James the apostle had come to the peninsula. Many of these were passionate issues for Higuera, in defence of which he had persisted with the forgery of the chronicles.

The False Chronicles

Jerónimo Román de la Higuera authored numerous falsifications or "false chronicles" in the last decade of the sixteenth century. Among these works was a chronicle attributed to Dextro and Máximo, two Latin authors whose names were known and whose work he claimed to have found in the Monastery of Fulda, along with a work by the Lombard author Liutprand, Bishop of Cremona.[42] All of these authors were supposed to have written histories of the Church in Hispania. Here Higuera continued down the selfsame path taken by Annio de Viterbo, with his forged Beroso, which had proved so successful in Spain. The

---

[41] Jerónimo Román de la Higura refers, for instance, to the discovery of the Turpiana Tower parchment in one of his chronological disquisitions, as an argument to prove the use of the Hispanic era at a very early date; see *Historia eclesiástica de la imperial ciudad de Toledo*, vol. II, BNE, Mss. 8193, f. 127v.

[42] Juan Bautista Pérez, also an opponent of the Granada Lead Books, was the first to denounce the forgery in a declaration against Román de la Higuera, written in 1594. See G. Mayans y Ciscar, *Obras completas*, Valencia, 1983, vol. I, p. 355.

invention and writing of these supposed Latin chronicles was intended to demonstrate that certain pious traditions of the utmost importance for the religious history of Spain were grounded in absolute truth. They made it possible to establish ancient and holy origins for specific places in the peninsula based on their long lines of bishops (uninterrupted, despite the Arab conquest). The intention was very similar to that of the Sacromonte Lead Books, that is to say, the desire to present Spain and, in particular, the author's home town (in this case Toledo), as of central importance to early Christianity.

One of Higuera's invented chroniclers was a so-called Julián Pérez, Mozarab of Toledo, Archpriest of its St Justa Church and Vicar of the Archbishopric of Toledo in the time of the reconquest of the city in 1085. Higuera used Julián Pérez—an eye-witness of the reconquest—to talk about the city's Mozarab population and the conservation of its liturgy, which had consoled it through four hundred years of captivity. It was important to emphasise the Mozarab's mass—the so called Mozarab rite[43]—because it followed the principles established by St James. However, above all the chronicle of Julián Pérez allowed Higuera to indulge his genealogical obsession, by presenting the history of the foremost Mozarab families, including the one which he claimed to belong to himself. It is a significant comment on the society in which he lived, that Román de la Higuera, who appears to have been of Converso background,[44] was so keen to demonstrate that he came from a Mozarab line. This demonstration is also the purpose of his *Tratado del linaje de Higuera*. In this opuscule, he again pays special attention to the way in which the Mozarabs adopted the Arab language: "they adopted Moorish ways, they took from here the use of surnames which is the name of the father given to the son as a sobriquet, which the Moors took from the Hebrews and these in turn from the Egyptians..."[45] This again helps us to understand the multiple interests which Higuera shared with Miguel de Luna and other Moriscos determined to rewrite the origins of Granada so that their Arab and Morisco lineage would acquire Christian legitimacy, in spite of their Morisco dress, surnames

---

[43] The so-called Mozarab rite refers to the liturgy practiced in the Visigotic kingdon of Toledo and continued by those Christians (the Mozarabs) who later lived under Islamic rule. It is thus a liturgy strongly linked to Hispanic "identity."

[44] J. Caro Baroja, *Las falsificaciones de la Historia (en relación con la de España)*, Barcelona, 1992, p. 162.

[45] *Tratado del linaje de Higuera*, f. 13r.

and use of Arabic. It was in this same vein that the noble Morisco Fernando Núñez Muley, the author of the famous *Memorial* of 1567, claimed that Christian Moors were not only free from blemish, but were also entitled to honors and privileges. In 1598, a number of the members of the Higuera family, including Jerónimo, had requested that information should be established on the purity and antiquity of their blood.[46]

Like the Lead Books in Granada, the work of Román de la Higuera had an immense effect on religious and patriotic enthusiasm and local pride. As Caro Baroja puts it, Higuera "had a tendency, that might even be considered sentimental and Romantic, to turn 'pious traditions' into truths which were better able to attract the people."[47] However, in writing his false chronicles, Román de la Higuera had, as we have already noted, another, somewhat more delicate, task in mind: to convince his readers that there were Jews in Toledo before the death of Christ, thus exempting Spanish Jews from the crime of deicide. The Toledan Jesuit, who was himself, it seems, from a Converso background, cited documents according to which the Spanish Jews dispatched legates to the Apostles so that the latter would send evangelists to instruct them in the new teachings. He also stated, through his invented chronicler Dextro, that the Jews of Spain were overjoyed to receive the teachings of St James, for whose arrival they were responsible. Higuera's forgery was clearly designed to "cleanse" and ennoble the genealogy of the Toledan Conversos at a time when the *limpieza de sangre* or "purity of blood" laws were being imposed in the city. It was in 1556, at the request of Cardinal Silíceo, that Philip II ratified these laws, placing his royal seal on the established custom of investigating the blood purity of candidates for the city's benefices. This rigorous implementation of the limpieza law in the See of the Spanish Primate was a decisive step in the process of prohibiting the Conversos from occupying public office.[48]

---

[46] Caro Baroja, *Falsificaciones*, p. 173.
[47] Ibid., p. 164.
[48] A. Sicroff, *Los estatutos de limpieza de sangre. Controversias entre los siglos XV y XVII*, Madrid, 1985, p. 170 foll.

Higuera and the Lead Books

Román de la Higuera was interested in everything related to the Lead Books, whose authenticity he ardently defended. We know that Higuera was perfectly in touch with what was happening in Granada. Again in 1595, the same year as the appearance of the "temple" of Saint Thyrsus and the first Lead Books, he was in contact with Alonso del Castillo. Higuera himself refers to his correspondence with the Morisco from Granada in his *Historia de Toledo* (L. III, c.1), considering him "a man of great learning." Referring to a number of Arabic manuscripts that Castillo stated he had found in El Escorial in 1584, Higuera wrote, "you may be certain that a man of such virtue would not affirm anything he had not seen." In his *Historia* Higuera notes that he spoke with Castillo on a number of matters, although he refrains from stating what these were.[49] We do know, however, that in 1594 and 1595, respectively, the Bishop of Segorbe, Juan Bautista Pérez, had written declarations to his correspondents disputing the work of Román de la Higuera and the Lead Books. This may have been the common link between the two men.

But if the defence of the "pious traditions" were governed, as Nicolás Antonio claimed, by private interest, it is true that, in principle at least, the defence of Toledo as the See of the Spanish primate, which was one of Higuera's aims, would compete rather than coincide with the intentions of the Granada Lead Books. However, first and foremost the content of the Lead Books was used as evidence of St James's arrival in Spain, a tradition which Higuera fervently supported and which had reached a particular low point at that time. The supposed arrival in Spain of St James affected rivalries between a number of Spanish cities, all vying for the privilege of being declared See of the Primate, a title disputed by Toledo, Santiago, Seville, Tarragona and Braga (the latter was also home to a number of famous forgeries). While Toledo acquired papal bulls confirming its primacy, these denied the arrival of St James in Spain and his participation in the battle of Clavijo.

At the same time as the discoveries in Sacramonte, in Rome Cardinal Cesar Baronio—whom Pope Clement VIII had placed at the head of Pius V's *Breviario Romano* review commission in 1592—accepted

---

[49] J. Martínez de la Escalera, "Jerónimo de la Higuera, S.J.: falsos cronicones, historia de Toledo, culto de San Tirso," *Tolède et l'expansion urbaine en Espagne (1450–1650)*, Madrid, 1991, pp. 69–97.

García de Loaysa's reasoning in *Collectio conciliorum* (1593) and expressed his scepticism regarding St James's arrival in Spain, as did the Jesuit, Cardinal Roberto Belarmino (1542–1621). Official denial from Rome of the Jacobean myth was received in Spain as an affront and even led to the personal intervention, in February 1600, of Philip III.[50] At an opportune moment, the Lead Books provided the Compostela myth with just the kind of "historical" foundations that, in view of the attitude of Rome, were desperately needed. They provided the longed-for documentary proof of the Apostle's preaching: St James had said the first mass held in Spain in Granada and did so surrounded by future Arab martyrs who, in the Sacromonte iconography, are wearing ostentatious turbans.[51] Various authors, not just Higuera, were quick to exploit such necessary support. What rite was used in St James's first mass in Granada, surrounded by Arab disciples? This, as we shall see, was another of Higuera's favorite topics. However, given that there could be no question of casting doubt on the miraculous nature and authenticity of a "discovery" that was useful for so many purposes, a new answer had to be found to a number of questions: how could they have been using Castilian on the Iberian peninsula such a short time after it was turned into a Roman province? Why would Cecilio and his companions have been preaching in Arabic on the Iberian peninsula? Who would have understood them?

Román de la Higuera used all his efforts to defend the Lead Books. Indeed, we know that in a letter dated December 7, 1595, the Jesuit offered the Archbishop of Granada, Pedro de Castro, "an *Apología y Antiapología* in defence of the relics," and that in a subsequent letter of January 7, 1596, he informed him that he had completed "the discourse offered" that addressed "55 difficulties."[52] In a long letter, dated July 27, 1596, Higuera offers yet another passionate defence of the Lead Books, which, he states, prove that "this province [Hispania] was the first after that of Jerusalem to be bathed in the blood of as many martyrs as these tablets proclaim."[53] Román de la Higuera was writing to provide Castro

---

[50] F. Márquez Villanueva, *Santiago*, p. 315 foll.

[51] J. M. Pita Andrade "La iconografía de Santiago en el Sacro Monte," p. 893 foll., quoted by Márquez, *Santiago*, p. 313.

[52] Pedro de Valencia, *Obras Completas. IV.—Escritos sociales. 2.—Escritos políticos*, León, 2000, in the "Comment" to a letter from Arias Montano to the Archbishop of Granada, p. 384.

[53] BNM, mss. 5953. The Biblioteca Nacional in Madrid holds the *Diario de viaje desde Valencia a Andalucía hecho por Don Francisco Pérez Bayer en este año de 1782*, which

with arguments in favor of the Lead Books, refuting the arguments of those who proclaimed their fraudulent nature, for, "so great is the love I have towards the saints that I would gladly buy with my own blood their honor and exaltation and so anything that can help in this cause, even though it may not be much, I humbly place before Your Excellence." But if saints, martyrs and relics impassion Higuera, it is Jews and Mozarabs which are of most interest to him.

In his letter to Castro, Higuera maintains that, in the age of Christ, the Arabian Peninsula was made up almost totally of Jews, as well as Nabataeans and the Arab-speaking Jewish Idumeans. At the same time, he shows that the Arabic language is most closely related to Hebrew. Hence the saints of Granada are of the "Arab nation and Hebrew profession." The "Phoenicians were of the same stock as the Arabs and in their language and garb were one people and one folk"; "Now the Jews are the most detested people but in ancient times they were the most honored because God gave them the treasures of His writings from which He became flesh."[54] He quotes Strabo and Pliny and resorts to the Nabataeans and Idumeans to prove, as he did in his Liutprand chronicle, that there can be saints from the Arab nation and of Hebrew profession. Some of his arguments are clearly aimed at Juan Bautista Pérez: faced with the latter's denial that the "Salomonic characters" of the Lead Books could be genuine, given that Solomon wrote in Hebrew, he alleges that the Arab language comes from Hebrew, an issue to which he devotes many pages, explaining, amongst other things, its vocalization system using lines and dots or over or under consonants. The language issue is one that takes up a substantial part of his writings to Castro, because he wishes to respond to the charge that that Arabic could not have been spoken on the Peninsula before the Muslim Conquest.[55] Higuera once again uses Pliny, Strabo and Herodotus to demonstrate, with authoritative arguments, that the Arabic language spread across the peninsula to

---

includes extracts and copies of letters, papers and documents belonging to Granada's Sacromonte and preserved in the city's Chancery.

[54] Archive of Sacromonte Abbey, Leg. 2, p. 47.

[55] See B. Ehlers, "Juan Bautista Pérez and the Plomos de Granada: Spanish Humanism in the Late Sixteenth Century," *Al-Qantara* XXIV (2003), pp. 427–448: "And if he was writing his book for Spaniards, it would have been a mockery to have written it in a language which nobody in Spain understood." This same argument, the impossibility of preaching in Spain in a language that would not appear until the Muslim Conquest is also used by Gonzalo de Valcárcel, in R. Benítez Sánchez-Blanco "El *Discurso* del licenciado Gonzalo de Valcárcel sobre las reliquias del Sacromonte," *Estudis*, 28 (2002), pp. 137–165, p. 161.

become as common as Castilian, "and as such a commonplace language in Andalucía, scholars used it to write on the Tablets."[56] Higuera also makes a connection that was very important to Granadan sentiment and that was to link those who were martyred during the 1499 uprising in the Alpujarras at the hands of Muslim insurgents with martyrs whose relics had appeared on the Holy Mount. To do so, he wrote a *Historia del levantamiento y marcha de los nuevamente convertidos en el Reino de Granada y algunos ilustres martirios que en ella padecieron algunas personas por la confesión de su Fe Católica*, which is preserved, hand-written like all his work (Higuera never published anything in his lifetime), in the Real Academia de la Historia.[57] In this work, Higuera once again reveals his special sensitivity towards capturing the religious sentiment of those for whom he was writing and making links with some of the best-loved traditions which had most symbolic power. It also comes as no surprise to find in them references to the works of "the *Licenciado* Luna."[58]

Pedro de Castro took his time in responding to Higuera's barrage of letters. When he did reply, in a letter dated June 15, 1597, he was respectful, although reserved. It is as if Castro were perhaps not keen to have Higuera among his supporters.[59] He begins by saying that his reply is to the many letters sent by Higuera last July (in other words, almost a year previously) and he states that he is "most obliged" for the amount of work Higuera has done, but appears to suggest that these matters are too serious for dubious speculation: "Your Grace will see in the account I am now sending you, how serious is the matter about which you write to me; and if you were to see the books, you would realise that there has been no greater finding since the time of the Apostles; although the relics are sacred and so significant, the most significant are the books themselves, the honor of Spain and of Granada, and for which the whole world should envy us." Castro refuses to accept Higuera's

---

[56] When the wars between Caesar and Pompey brought soldiers from Arabia, the Arabs were great merchants and reached every part of the Mediterranean, including Spain, where many were to stay. Moreover, the Phoenicians were already there, and had built Cádiz and spread throughout the Kingdom of Granada. The relationship between Arabs and Phoenicians was a close one (as shown by Ptolemy and Homer). The language of the Phoenicians is as similar to Arabic as Galician to Portuguese, etc., etc.

[57] RAH. Salazar y Castro, 9–749, especially, f. 114 r.

[58] RAH. Salazar y Castro, 9–749, f. 117r.

[59] Archive of Sacromonte Abbey, Leg. III, fol. 298 (copy of the one sent). Reproduced in *Epistolario español. Colección de cartas de españoles ilustres antiguos y modernos*. II, BAE, 62, Madrid, 1965, pp. 46–47.

assertion that the Saints were Hebrews, "This cannot be disputed, sir, neither were they Hebrews nor did they ever receive the Law of Moses, nor were they circumcised." He replies succinctly to the different points Higuera had dealt with in his letters, including Saint Thyrsus ("I do not feel what was found in Toledo to be well founded [...] I did not give this much credit") and the Mozarab rite: "The Mozarab mass which you wished to send me I already saw years ago; because in Salamanca, as a boy, I sometimes heard it in Doctor Talavera's chapel, in the Main Church; but that is not what we have found in Granada, and nor was it composed by these saints."

Furthermore, Castro does not show much enthusiasm about Higuera coming to Granada, which the latter suggests in some of his letters. Nor does he show much interest in an ancient tablet Higuera claims to have found: "You tell me an ancient tablet which counts in dots has come into your possession. I should be very pleased for Doctor Herrera to see it and bring it to me. I have nothing further to write as I shall leave it to the papers and the messenger. May God keep you for many years." The messenger Castro referred to was his secretary, Doctor Herrera, who, in the summer of 1597, was going to Madrid with a whole series of documents which attested to the findings. These documents, as well as a "print" of the Lead Tablets, Herrera was to present to Philip II's confessor Friar Diego de Yepes, Prince Philip's confessor Friar Gaspar de Córdoba, Friar Martín de Villanueva, of the order of St Jerome, Francisco de Aguilar Terrones and Cardinal Fernando Niño de Guevara, whose help he had enlisted for classification of the relics. Letters are preserved from all of these men acknowledging both Herrera's visit and reception of the documents he showed them in support of Castro's cause.[60]

It would seem apparent that Castro did not trust Higuera, whose reputation must already have been in question. However, others were less sceptical. A group of writers responsible for some of Granada's early histories did appear to accept some of Higueras bolder assertions. One of these writers was Pedro Guerra de Lorca, who authored *Memorias eclesiásticas de la ciudad de Granada*, the manuscript of which is undated, although internal evidence would suggest that it was written

---

[60] Conserved in the Archive of Sacromonte Abbey, Legs. III and IV and reproduced in *Epistolario español*, pp. 45–49.

between 1595 and 1597.[61] In this work, Guerra maintains that Granada
was founded by the Jews expelled by Nabucodonosor, in other words, by
Jews who belonged to one of the lost tribes of Israel, otherwise known as
the Ten Tribes. Another writer, Luis de la Cueva, *Diálogos de las cosas
notables de Granada y lengua española*, insists on the antiquity of the
Spanish language, a vital premise for the authenticity of the Turpiana
parchment and Lead Books, and in so doing defends the antiquity and
Christianity of the Moriscos, descendents of the primitive Christians
who spoke Arabic and for whom St Cecilio wrote. Like Guerra, Cueva
maintains that "Granada has the oldest Castilian writing in the world,"
namely the Turpiana Tower parchment. According to this, rather than
Castilian coming from Latin, the opposite is true: Castilian is considered the mother of Latin, because Spaniards colonised Italy centuries
before the Roman Empire arose.[62] For Cueva, Granada is the ancient
Iliberis, a Christian city, but a Christian city inhabited by Arab-speaking Phoenicians.

In his *Historia eclesiástica del monte santo*,[63] dedicated to Philip III,
Pedro Velarde de Ribera, a canon of the collegiate church of St Salva-
dor of Granada, explains how many Jews of Gad and others belonging
to the Ten Lost Tribes were banished from Granada, which they had
reached long before the coming of Christ: "these glorious saints who
wrote in the Arabic language and in the characters of Solomon were
of the Hebrews sent to Samaria, or from the tribes of Gad and Ruben
[the lost tribes], who were in Spain where they were converted by our
Lord St James the Apostle."[64] According to Velarde these lost tribes
spoke in Arabic, and as evidence he cites Saint Thomas, who stated
that "St Paul went to the Arabias because it was the land of infidels
and likewise it would seem that he went to the Arabias, inspired by
the Holy Spirit, to communicate in the language of the Arabs that was
so necessary for the conversion of the ten tribes which were spread
throughout different provinces in the world and to try to converse
with our blessed Saints Cecilio and Tesifón."[65] According to Velarde

---

[61] AGS, C48. Various, fols. 166–377. The manuscript is preserved in the Sacromonte
Archive. Guerra also wrote *Catecheses mystagogae pro aduenis ex secta Mahometana.
Ad Parochos et Potestates*, Madrid, 1586.

[62] Luis de la Cueva, *Diálogos de las cosas notables de Granada y Lengua española y
algunas cosas curiosas*, Seville, 1603.

[63] BNM, mss. 1583.

[64] Ibid., f. 90 v.

[65] Ibid., f. 11r–11v.

de Ribera, before his conversion Tesifón was known as Aben Hatar and acknowledged being "of the Hebrew nation, of the lineage and descendents of Aaron."[66]

Meanwhile the false chronicles of Dextro and Máximo were copied and circulated around the Peninsula at the request of bishops, cathedral chapters and other interested parties, thereby acting, to some extent, as accomplices to Roman de la Higuera's invention. Inevitably suspicion began to emerge as to their authenticity as soon as parallels were drawn between the chronicles and the Lead Books. In 1630 the rumor circulated that Rome was about to prohibit both. One of the chronicles most fervent advocates was Cardinal Baltasar de Moscoso y Sandoval, Bishop of Jaén, in whose diocese, like that of Pedro de Castro, a mine of saints had been discovered. Moscoso went to Rome to defend the chronicles precisely because they contained information that authenticated the newly discovered Jaén relics.[67] It was feared that the cause of the prohibition was a reference to the festival of the Immaculate Conception as having been instituted during the time of the Apostles, as well as the reproduction of stories which had obviously originated in apocryphal gospels. It will be recalled that in the seventeenth century the Virgin's Immaculate Conception had not been recognized by Rome as dogma, and that its defence by the Church and Crown of Spain created a certain tension with the Holy See.[68] However, despite the rumors, the Lead Books were not proscribed for yet another fifty years (in 1682), and continued to have wide repercussions for Spanish historiography, much wider, indeed, than the false chronicles of Román de la Higuera. It would seem that the Granadan archbishop Pedro de Castro had been right to distance himself from the Toledan Jesuit's histories.

A different matter, however, is the connection—perhaps even friendship—between Higuera and Luna. Both forgers were convinced they were doing a great deal of good and certainly no harm with their falsi-

---

[66] Ibid., f. 163r.

[67] Godoy y Alcántara, *Historia crítica*, pp. 227 foll. In fact, the discovery of the relics of the saints of Arjona, occurred as a result of Dr. Francisco Háñez Herrera, chair at the University of Baena, reading in Dextro that the saints Bonoso and Maximilian had been martyred in Urgabona. See, for example, *Memorial del pleito sobre el reconocimiento, aprobación y calificación de los Milagros, veneración y colocación de las reliquias de los santuarios que se descubrieron en la villa de Arjona desde el año de mil y seiscientos y veinte y ocho hasta el de quarenta y dos*, sl, s.a, *passim*.

[68] A. Prosperi, "L'Immacolata a Siviglia e la fondazione sacra de la Monarchia espagnola," *Studi Storici*, 2 (2006), pp. 481–510.

fications. Thanks to them, their respective cities could swell with native pride and define an ancient and sacred identity for themselves (which could be converted into privileges). At the same time, it included sectors of the Spanish population who had been left out of honors and glory as a result of the blood purity laws, creating Arabs who were separate from Islam and Jews who were cleared of any responsibility for the death of Christ. Both of these original inhabitants of the Peninsula linked it to times when Humanity was closer to its Creator; thus the two authors shared a major personal objective which speaks volumes about the society in which they lived, a society in which not having "pure blood" was painful, shameful and dangerous. That their inventions should have generated interpretations and readings that did not wholly suit the forger's original motivations is another matter. The Count of Mora, for instance, was an ardent follower and apologist of Jerónimo Román de la Higuera, but was more intent on proving the primacy of Toledo. Consequently, he appeared to treat the Sacromonte findings with the slight disdain one might feel for a competitor: "for although it may provide news of holy men who suffered martyrdom in Granada, whose ashes were found in its Holy Mount, with books and tablets of the year one thousand five hundred and ninety five, these are now in Rome where the truth will be determined. Let us leave them to that, and turn to the history of a city [Toledo] which was worthy enough for St James to have seated within it the primacy of the churches of all Spain [...]."[69] In the context of this crude clash between Spanish cities all claiming sacred genealogy, the struggle of Higuera, Luna and other fellow fraudsters on behalf of certain aspects of their own dubious genealogy appears to have been relegated, at least in part, to the sidelines.

To conclude, we would like to cite the views of the eighteenth-century scholar Gregorio Mayáns y Siscar and propose a hypothesis. Despite the fact that the Lead Books were declared falsifications by the Vatican in 1682, they remained a source of debate within Spain. In 1744 Mayáns, a critic of Román de la Higuera, found himself involved in a polemic with the Jesuit father Andrés Burriel on the views he had put forward

---

[69] Pedro de Rojas, Conde de Mora, *Historia de la nobilísima, ínclita y esclarecida ciudad de Toledo*, Madrid, 1654.

in his work *Vida de Don Nicolás Antonio* (Valencia, 1742).[70] Burriel was aggrieved by Mayáns veiled claim that Román de la Higuera was the author or at least a fellow conspirator in the Lead Books affair. In his correspondence with Burriel, Mayáns justified his accusation thus: "if the Lead Books were discovered in 1595 and the false chronicles a year earlier and if Father Higuera was the creator of these, as the world's most erudite men believe, and if we find in these works the same novelties that are also present in the the Lead Books, novelties that only the forgers and their accomplices could have known, how can we not believe that Father Higuera was involved in the [Lead Books] deception or knew about it, or emended his chronicles in light of the Lead Books find? I will leave your reverence to judge which is the correct scenario, comparing the Lead Books with the first and last sections of Dextro."[71]

Regarding Mayáns hypothesis, it should be noted that Lead Books were discovered in Granada in 1595 and in subsequent years up to 1598, during which time Higuera and Luna were in contact. It would thus seem reasonable, as Mayáns recommended, to compare the two works for signs of similar authorship. In this regard, it is noteworthy that a number of scholars (Godoy Alcántara, Cabanelas y Hagerty) have pointed out that the various Lead Books exhibited differences in style and content, leading to the conclusion that they were authored by several people. Was it possible that Higueras was one of these authors? Once these books have been edited and studied, perhaps we will be able to find closer connections between Higuera and Luna than the ones we have presented in this article.

---

[70] Sobre este asunto véase Rafael Benítez Sánchez-Blanco, "Gregorio Mayans y las Láminas y libros de Plomo de Granada. Los límites de la crítica ilustrada" en M. Barrios y M. García-Arenal eds. *¿La historia inventada?* pp. 375–393.

[71] G. Mayans y Siscar, *Epistolario*, vol. II, ed. Antonio Mestre, Valencia, 1987, pp. 14–24.

CHAPTER ELEVEN

MAUROPHILIA AND THE MORISCO SUBJECT

Barbara Fuchs

This essay is part of a larger project on the negotiation of the Andalusi cultural heritage within Spain after the fall of Granada.* My goal is to challenge the sense of 1492 as an absolute dividing line for Hispanic culture. I want to argue that the fiction of *supersession*, which imagines a present that replaces and improves upon a past left behind, involves a deliberate effort of rhetorical and historiographical construction, in order to tell one calculated story of how the nation came to be. For early modern Spain, the signal event is the fall of Granada in 1492, and the story of supersession proposes an avidly Christian, "Gothic" Spain that replaces the Semitic hybridity of earlier times. This is the story promoted in the new monarchical histories of a unified Spain and in the Counter-Reformation construction of Spain as Defender of the Faith.

Any simple narrative of supersession, however, immediately raises our suspicions. Cultural transformations do not align themselves neatly even with such major events as the end of the *Reconquista*. The gradual nature of Christian advances meant that Christian and so-called "Moorish" practices coexisted more or less uneasily for centuries, even where the Christians had triumphed. In terms of everyday life, the fall of Granada was far from decisive: as is well known, the *Capitulaciones de Santa Fe*, which detailed the terms of the Nasrid's surrender, included significant protections for Andalucían culture and religious practices. Although these terms were not respected for long, Moorish cultural forms nonetheless survived for decades in a variety of guises.

Moreover—as my use of the term "Moorish" rather than "Muslim" is intended to suggest—those practices that were not directly related to Islam and its attendant apparatus, including purification and dietary restrictions, seem to have been integrated to a greater or lesser degree into so-called "Christian" Spain. Language, architecture,

---

* A more extensive version of this argument appears in my book, *Exotic Nation: Maurophilia and the Construction of Early Modern Spain*, Philadelphia, 2009.

domestic practices, dress, aristocratic deportment: all of these aspects of the culture were profoundly hybridized by the late fifteenth century. What seems obvious from an ethnographic point of view—that the "Christian" culture of 1492 could never be the "Christian" culture of 711—is often discounted when historians stress the fall of Granada as a definitive rupture. The model of supersession thus appears as a powerful historiographical fiction designed to consolidate an emerging sense of national identity. And yet, for all that, it has been extraordinarily powerful: Spain's self-fashioning has for centuries been predicated on the strict boundary between then and now, mapped onto Moors vs. Christians. Even from our own more sophisticated historiographical purview, we tend to assume that everything changed in 1492. I want to argue instead that a hybrid, Moorish-influenced culture survives in sixteenth-century Spain, long after the fall of Granada, and that it represents an often unacknowledged challenge to the official narratives of a new national identity. Thus I propose that we imagine, however counter-intuitively, a *mudéjar* Spain for the sixteenth century, long after the official historiography would have us believe all such hybridizations disappeared. Although Spaniards themselves might have had trouble recognizing this aspect of their culture, foreigners and travelers certainly did not. And while these outsiders can hardly be considered objective, invested as they were in their own construction of Spain, it at least helps to remind us of how profoundly different Spain appeared to other Europeans.

Maurophilia and maurophobia are inextricably intertwined with central strands of Spanish history in the sixteenth century: not just the obvious questions of religious assimilation vs. the racialization of minorities, but also the problem of local vs. national cultures, the tension between a centralizing monarchy and regional aristocracies, and the struggles between political exigency and religious policy. While the official discourse is generally anti-Morisco, there is a large body of evidence that suggests an alternative stance. I would like to propose that we consider the corpus of maurophilia—the many texts across a variety of genres that idealize Moors and Moriscos, or at least present them favorably, as the literary tip of a cultural iceberg. Far from being a mere literary fashion, maurophilia is the legible incarnation of a much broader cultural phenomenon, one that often goes unremarked for its ordinariness. The maurophile texts represent the explicit embrace of Moors and Moriscos within Spain; in some cases, as with the anonymous *Abencerraje* or the much-postponed second part of Pérez de

Hita's *Guerras civiles de Granada*, with a clear political purpose. In other cases, as with the *romancero morisco*, the political affiliations are perhaps less self-conscious, but no less significant for that.

Romances à clef

I turn now to the ideological significance of the *romancero morisco*, the corpus of incredibly popular ballads whose maurophilia is most often dismissed as mere literary fashion.[1] And a spectacular fashion it was: in the first part of the *Flor de varios romances nuevos*, a collection of "modern" ballads published in nine parts between 1589 and 1597, fully forty percent of the poems dealt with Moorish topics, although the proportion gradually diminishes after that.[2] The late sixteenth-century *romancero* seems to me a kind of extreme case: if one can show a political charge in these highly stylized, generically determined, and self-conscious fictions, then no maurophilia can really be considered purely literary.

These ballads have a complex relationship to their predecessors, the *romances fronterizos* of the late fifteenth century. Whereas the *fronterizos* are generally recognized as historical, topical, and epic, the *romances moriscos* are dismissed as lyrical trifles, showcases for Moorish regalia and chivalric pomp with no connection to the great national enterprise of the *Reconquista*. This critical commonplace is of course basically true—the Moors of the latter corpus are much more concerned with love and panoply than with war—but I take issue with the ideological weightlessness assigned to the "lighter" fare. As I will suggest, the *romances morisco* need not deal explicitly with the *Reconquista* to make its political point; in fact, the avoidance of the subject may itself constitute its most striking ideological feature, one abundantly noted by its contemporary critics.

Before discussing the reception of the *romanceros moriscos*, however, I would like to explore the problem of their personae. While

---

[1] See the series of essays by Georges Cirot on "Maurophilie littéraire," in *Bulletin Hispanique* 40 (1938) to 46 (1944).

[2] Ramón Menéndez Pidal, *España y su historia*, 2 vols., Madrid, 1957, vol. 2, p. 255. Menéndez Pidal notes that the collection was printed and reprinted several times in Huesca, Valencia, Burgos, Toledo, Lisbon, Madrid, Barcelona, Perpiñán, Zaragoza, and Alcalá de Henares.

these ballads were generally anonymous, it is well known that Lope de Vega, in particular, was responsible for several of the most famous examples, including "Mira, Zaide," and "Ensíllenme el potro ruzio." The assumption is that when Lope writes in the voice of a Moor in these *romances à clef*, widely acknowledged to describe his own erotic misfortunes, he is simply in a kind of Moorish drag that has no ideological significance, and that functions in exactly the same way as the pastoral guise he adopts elsewhere. Yet the question of why he and other poets would so frequently choose a Moorish voice, a mere generation after the extraordinarily violent War of the Alpujarras (1568–70) against the Moriscos, goes begging. There are several possible explanations, all of which have political implications. First, there seems to be a particularly Spanish connection between Moorishness and aristocratic, chivalric culture—the culture of the *juegos de cañas*, of falconry, and of all the practices that Christians learned from their Muslim invaders. Some critics speak of the idealization of Moors in these poems as post-facto praise of a defeated foe, aimed primarily at glorifying their Christian Spanish conquerors by association, but this seems to me to evade the very real Spanish indebtedness to Moorish culture. Second, and perhaps more importantly, there seems to be, for authors as for readers, a real *jouissance* in consuming Moorish bodies. Rather than emphasizing bodily difference, these ballads foreground the pleasure to be found in the Moors. The genre suggests the possibility of a highly enjoyable, idealizing identification that is very different from the staging of otherness in European representations of an Islamic East, outside of the Spanish context. Although often it is the *mora* as love object who is highly eroticized, the male lover is also depicted in a highly aestheticized fashion. The multiple encounters and subject-positions suggest that there is no easy distinction to be made across the corpus between a "European" self and an "Oriental" other, as in the theories of forsaken *jouissance* proposed by Mladen Dolar and Alain Grosrichard.[3] Instead, this *romancero* forces us to recognize how different the situation is for Spain than for the rest of Europe—what Josiah Blackmore and Gregory

---

[3] See Mladen Dolar, "Introduction: The Subject Supposed to Enjoy," in Alain Grosrichard, *The Sultan's Court: European Fantasies of the East*, trans. Liz Heron, London, 1998. They argue that the Western subject's *jouissance* in the fantasy of an erotic East comes from the renunciation of the erotic pleasure ascribed to the Other, and the subsequent difference of the Self. However, there is no such distancing in the *romanceros*.

Hutcheson have called the *queerness* of Iberia—given the pervasiveness and familiarity of Moorish culture. Neither the Saidian version of Orientalism, in which the distance between self and Other is crucial for the construction of European superiority, nor the Lacanian version of Dolar and Grosrichard fully accounts for the intimacy of these texts. While the *romances* may be orientalizing in some respects, particularly in the heightened eroticism and luxury of the more conventional representations, they often undermine the Foucauldian ordering that seems so central to our usual understanding of Orientalism. It would be naïve to assume that this *jouissance* has no political ramifications, in that so much of the anti-Morisco rhetoric of the period depends on the crassest othering, emphasizing the filth and contagious rot of the ostracized group.

I offer these rationales to suggest that Lope's maurophilia, or that of his contemporaries, is certainly not unmotivated. (Clearly, the tremendous popularity of the first poems immediately reinforces their maurophile tendencies.) Yet there are also political effects that do not necessarily depend on authorial motivation and that have an impact regardless of the basic apolitical stance of the post-adolescent, lovelorn balladeer into which critics have transformed the maurophile Lope. In part, these unwitting ideological effects depend on the resonance of the Morisco problem in the period. Thus, in "Mira, Zaide que te aviso," Lope describes the hero's banishment from the presence of his beloved, with a highly conventional "que no pases por mi calle" [I warn you, Zaide, do not come by my street].[4] The immediate autobiographical referent, as is well known, is Lope's exile from Castile in 1588 for his poison-pen attacks on Elena Osorio, the lover who had spurned him, and her family. As Menéndez Pidal noted long ago, Lope's judicial sentence specified "que de aquí adelante *no pase por la calle* donde viven las dichas mujeres" [that he no longer go by the street where the said women live].[5] But in the satirical ballad "Háganme vuestras mercedes," a mordant response to Lope's inordinately popular poem, the lover's punishment is more clearly recognizable as exile, and thus echoes more closely the position of the historical Morisco subject ostracized by maurophobia. The poem begins by listing all the tradesmen who repeat

---

[4] Agustín Durán, ed. *Romancero general*, vol. 10, n. 56, p. 27. Durán does not attribute the ballad to Lope, but critics since then have generally done so. The force of my argument here does not depend on the specific authorship of Lope de Vega.
[5] Ramón Menéndez Pidal, *Romancero hispánico*, Madrid, 1953, vol. 2, p. 128.

Lope's verse: the apothecary, the tailor, the sailor, all tell Zaide "que no pase por su calle."⁶ Even the *buñoleros* (doughnut-sellers) "aunque son de su linaje" [although they are of his own lineage—i.e. Moriscos like him], send him away. The *romancero's* very popularity, its geographical and social ubiquity, thus transforms the beloved's interdiction into a more general banishment for the Moor. The poem then voices a plaintive complaint about his displacement:

> ¿Qué tiene este triste moro?
> ¿Está tocado de landre,
> que así desterralle quieren
> de todas las vecindades?
> ....
> ¿Adónde ha de ir el cuitado
> pues en el mundo no cabe?
> Que tengo sospecha y miedo
> no vaya a desesperarse.
> Merezca el humilde moro
> que su destierro se acabe,
> que quien de humilde se venga,
> humilde venganza hace.

> [What is wrong with this sorry Moor?
> Does he have a touch of plague,
> That he is banished thus
> From all neighborhoods?
> ....
> Where is this afflicted one to go,
> Since he does not fit in the world?
> For I suspect and fear
> That he may despair.
> May the humble Moor
> Deserve an end to his banishment,
> For he who takes revenge on the lowly
> Takes a lowly revenge.]

In 1609, of course, exile would be Spain's violent solution to the problem of acculturating the Moriscos. Long before the general banishment, however, the Crown punished Morisco uprisings with forcible relocation within Spain. In the most widespread occurrence, as a result of the war in the Alpujarras, the Moriscos of Granada had been expelled from their homes and dispersed throughout Castile. In this apparently

---

⁶ *Romancero general*, vol. 10, no. 257, p. 136.

light-hearted ballad, Lope's metaphorics of exile thus reverberate with concurrent political debates about how to solve the Morisco question, and what claim, if any, these subjects had on a Spanish identity.

An even darker subtext appears in the exchange between the highly conventional *romanceros* that peddle Moorish trappings to their audiences, and the satirical ballads that literalize the "trade" in Moors. In "Quién compra diez y seis moros," the *madrileño* Gabriel Lasso de la Vega offers the fine Moors of the *romancero* for sale as slaves, with the added advantage that their owner may also sell their ornate clothes, as depicted in the ballads, for a tidy sum. To make the irony more acute, the slaves will entertain their master with the romancero material:

> Contaránme del invierno
> las noches prolijas, largas,
> los asaltos de Jaén
> y los combates de Baza,
> la muerte de Reduán
> y los amores de Audalla,
> con el destierro de Muza,
> porque el Rey quiso a su dama,
> y tras esto dormirán
> en el pajar con dos mantas.

> [They will narrate to me
> On long, lingering winter nights,
> The assault on Jaén
> And the battles of Baza,
> The death of Reduán,
> And the loves of Audalla,
> Along with the banishment of Muza,
> Because the King loved his lady,
> And after this they will sleep
> In the hayloft with two blankets.][7]

The literary value of the Moors as fashionable maurophile product is thus gradually transformed into the crassest economic good: the persons of the Moors as slaves, who tell fabulous stories by night but labor by day, ultimately to be sold "a galera/cuando monedas no haya" [to the galleys, when I'm out of money].[8] Again, the historical context makes this ostensibly literary satire much more resonant: slavery was the

---

[7] Gabriel Lasso de la Vega, *Manojuelo de romances* [1601] Madrid, 1942, pp. 102–103.

[8] Lasso de la Vega, p. 103.

fate of thousands of captured Moriscos after the Alpujarras, and the population of Morisco slaves in Spain rose considerably in the latter part of the century. Thus, while it is certainly true, as critics suggest, that ballads such as "Quién compra diez y seis moros," point out the vast difference between the Moors of the *romancero* and the historical condition of the Moriscos, it is also important to emphasize that this distance itself becomes part of the debate about how to resolve the Morisco question. If the diminished Moriscos were once the heroic, beloved Moors of the *romancero*, does their decadence reflect well on Spain? And how is the stubborn popular attachment to their past incarnation to be negotiated?

I offer these discussions of exile and of the traffic in Moors as examples of how the literary phenomenon of the *romances moriscos*—and the sometimes virulent responses they elicited—became part of a broader cultural conversation on the Moriscos, from the "inconsequential" popular attachment to the ballads catalogued in "Háganme vuestras mercedes," to a more profound questioning about the place of the Moors in a hostile society. As I will argue, it is precisely in the responses to *romancero* that the most interesting aspects of this conversation can be observed.

"Renegade" Poetry

As the above examples have suggested, the *romancero* is particularly interesting as a corpus of maurophilia in that we have striking textual evidence of its contemporary reception, including what one might call the maurophobic ripostes. Critics have long noted the subgenre of responses to the *romancero morisco*, which chart a variety of accusations against them.[9] Many of these dialogic poems register not only aesthetic ennui at the repetition of so much Moorish lore, but, more importantly, political outrage at the choice of topic. The responses also confirm the extraordinary popularity of the genre: as in the response to "Mira, Zaide," above, they provide evidence of an avid readership, and satirize both the texts themselves and their popular reception. It seems important to consider this well documented readership (and

---

[9] Durán edits them as their own class, which somewhat erases the connection between them and specific *romances*, as in the Lope case above.

subsequent oral reproduction) across social classes when assessing the contestatory force of the genre. While its authors might not have set out to rehabilitate the Moors or mount them on a pedestal of national poetry, there is evidence that some readers thought they came dangerously close to doing just that. And while, as the satirical responses never cease to remind us, the idealizing corpus bears little relation to the experience of the average Morisco at the end of the century, its very popularity does lead us to wonder what kind of conceptual spaces, at least, the *romancero* offered a Morisco subject. Thus many of the satirical ballads, such as Lasso de la Vega's, mock the chasm of difference between the chivalric Moors of the texts and the Morisco muleteers, water-carriers, or agricultural laborers of contemporary Spain. Critics concur, arguing, as for *El Abencerraje*, that the representation of noble Moors, essentially white knights in disguise, bears little relation to the actual marginalized Morisco population of the sixteenth century.[10] But for the Moriscos who were not quite as abject—and even for those who were—could this corpus have represented an idealizing alternative to everyday ostracism? The satire focuses in particular on the material trappings of the chivalric fantasy: liveries, costumes, and arms, all of which are abundantly described in the *romances*.[11] These descriptions are clearly an imperfect form of cultural survival: accidental, ephemeral, and, more importantly, refracted through a Christian sensibility that carefully selected the more harmless elements of Moorishness. Yet while these superficial survivals might not offer any solace to Muslims who desperately held on to their own religion and culture, their popularity would seem to suggest that there was nothing inherently abhorrent about Moorishness or about inhabiting such an identity—a powerful point to make in the 1590s.

There is good evidence that this literary Moorish drag, which constructs a sympathetic other, however fictive, was received with suspicion in some quarters. Critics responded with poems calling for Lope and his imitators to give up their Moorish impersonations and write instead about Spanish glories. One particularly striking example actually tags the

---

[10] See Claudio Guillén, "Literature as Historical Contradiction: *El Abencerraje*, the Moorish Novel, and the Eclogue," in his *Literature As System: Essays toward the Theory of Literary History*, Princeton, 1971, p. 170.

[11] María Soledad Carrasco Urgoiti notes the prevalence of these material details, in "Vituperio y parodia del romance morisco en el romancero nuevo," in *Culturas populares: diferencias, divergencias, conflictos*, Madrid, 1986, pp. 115–137. Also note that these were the elements actually "borrowed" for *juegos de cañas*, etc.

maurophiles as renegades—a particularly loaded term of abuse in this
historical context—who shower glory on Mohammed while neglecting
Spanish heroes of the *Reconquista*:

> Renegaron de su ley
> los romancistas de España
> y ofrecieron a Mahoma
> las primicias de sus gracias…
> Los Ordoños, los Bermudos,
> los Rasuras y Mudarras,
> los Alfonsos, los Enricos,
> los Sanchos y los de Lara,
> qué es dellos y qué es del Cid?
> ¡Tanto olvido en glorias tantas!

> [The balladeers of Spain
> Reneged from their law
> And offered to Mohammed
> The first fruit of their talents…
> The Ordóñez, Bermudos,
> Resuras and Mudarras
> The Alfonsos, Enricos,
> The Sanchos and the Laras—
> What of them, and of the Cid?
> So much forgetting of so many glories![12]

In the eyes of these critics, the fascination with Moors implies a concomitant abandonment of a "proper" Spanish tradition; that is, of Spain
as a Visigoth remnant that heroically triumphs over an encroaching
Islam. While the neglect of this "gothic," Christian Spain is a central
problem, the poets' impersonation of Moors seems particularly threatening. One response specifically attacks the Moorish drag, and suggests
other forms of literary artifice, such as the pastoral, as a more decorous
disguise for authorial identities:

> ¡Ah! Mis señores poetas,
> descúbranse ya esas caras,
> desnúdense aquesos moros
> y acábense ya esas zambras;
> váyase con Dios Gazul,
> lleve el diablo a Celindaja,
> y vuelvan esas marlotas
> a quien se las dio prestadas.

---

[12] Durán 244, p. 128.

Dejáis un fuerte Bernardo,
vivo honor de nuestra España;
dejáis un Cid Campeador,
un Diego Ordóñez de Lara.
¡Celebran chusmas moriscas
vuestros cantos de chicharra!
Si importa celar los nombres,
porque lo piden las causas,
¿por qué no vais a buscarlos
a las selvas y cabañas?

[Oh, my poet lords,
Uncover your faces
Let those Moors disrobe
And those *zambras* [Moorish dances] end;
Let Gazul go with God,
And the devil take Celindaja,
Return those cloaks
To those who loaned them to you.
You leave behind a strong Bernardo,
Live glory of our Spain,
You leave a warring Cid,
A Diego Ordóñez de Lara.
Your cicada songs
Celebrate the Moorish rabble!
If names must be hidden,
Because the circumstances demand it,
Why do you not go seek them
In woods and huts?][13]

Presumably, a conventional shepherd or peasant would prove a far less discomfiting persona than a sympathetic Moor. Yet the *romancero morisco* was, for its authors, a more effective and powerful voice than the proposed alternatives. Part of the reason, I would hazard, is that the identification is more proximate: the *marlota*, or loose cloak, singled out in the ballad as the mark of a borrowed Moorish identity, for example, had in fact been adopted not just by the poets of the *romancero* but by Christian Iberian aristocrats at large as part of the hybridization of costume.[14] The poets dressed as Moors are wearing perfectly recognizable Christian aristocratic costume.

---

[13] Durán 245, p. 129.
[14] In her *Hispanic Costume 1480–1530*, New York, 1979, Ruth Anderson describes the *marlota* as a "Hispano-Moresque" garment (p. 93).

The unease with which the literary Moorish drag is received suggests that, despite its frequent appearances, the figure of the romance Moor has not become inert through its conventionality. Its status as a vehicle for the *romance à clef* challenges its readers' notions of what is properly Spanish. The maurophile fashion coexists, however uneasily, with the maurophobic discourse of Spain's vulnerability to, and definition *against*, Moorish culture. This is perhaps clearest in a fascinating meta-ballad, "¿Por qué, señores poetas/no volvéis por vuestra fama,"[15] itself a response to the satirical protests, and in particular to the question of whether Spanish and Moorish elements can be reconciled. The poem begins by decrying the poetic censure of other poets by a "Judas" figure, thus summarily including one and all in the Christian "cuerpo":

> Un miembro de vuestro cuerpo
> quiere romper vuestras galas,
> un Iudas de vuestro gremio,
> que jamás un Iudas falta.

> [A member of your body
> Wants to ruin your fineries
> A Judas of your trade,
> For never is a Judas lacking.]

There follows a reflection on the tension between Renaissance and Moorish themes, which anticipates the more serious question of Moorish claims on Spain:

> ¿Qué le aprovecha a Gazul
> tirar al otro la lança,
> si hoy un ninfo de Leteo
> quiere deshacer sus zambras?
> Como si fuera don Pedro
> más honrado que Amenábar,
> y mejor doña María
> que la hermosa Celindaxa.
> Si es español don Rodrigo,
> español el fuerte Audalla,
> y sepa el señor Alcalde
> que también lo es Guadalara.
> Si una gallarda española
> Quiere bailar doña Iuana,

---

15 Durán 246, p. 130.

las zambras también lo son,
pues es España Granada.

[What good is it for Gazul
To throw his lance at the other,
When today a nymph of Lethe
Wants to undo his *zambras*?
As though Don Pedro were
More honorable than Amenábar,
Or Doña María better
Than the beautiful Celindaxa.
If Don Rodrigo is Spanish,
Spanish is the strong Audalla,
And the lord Mayor should know
That so is Guadalara.
If Doña Juana wants to dance,
A Spanish *gallarda*,
The *zambras* are that too,
For Granada is Spain.]

In this context, the "ninfo de Leteo" suggests the willful forgetting of Spain's Moorish past, a deliberate erasure of anything but the high Gothic mode. Instead, as the poet suggests, the Moors are part of Spain—not as an alternative, Other, history, but inherent in the nation's past.[16] Moreover, the historical problem here connects to the contemporary relation of the regional to the national: Granada and her *zambras* are not relics of a colorful past, but actual, present-day, variations on a national theme. The ballad thus takes up the terms of the long-standing debate over the survival of Moorish—or is it Granadan?—culture, perhaps most eloquently defended by the Morisco notable Francisco Núñez Muley.[17] In his petition to the Audiencia of Granada, against the repression of Morisco culture by the 1567 decrees, Núñez Muley had invoked precisely the same arguments as does the ballad: regional variations should be allowed to exist within the nation; what appears Moorish is actually Granadan; and finally, the greatness of the *Reconquista* can only be appreciated if the culture of the Christians' enemies is acknowledged and preserved.[18] As "¿Por qué, señores poetas" puts this last point:

---

[16] Carrasco Urgoiti, p. 32.
[17] Carrasco Urgoiti, p. 129.
[18] See my *Mimesis and Empire: The New World, Islam, and European Identities*, Cambridge, 2001, ch. 4.

No es culpa, si de los moros
los valientes hechos cantan,
pues cuanto más resplandecen
nuestras célebres hazañas.
Que el encarecer los hechos
del vencido en la batalla,
engrandece al vencedor,
aunque no hablen dél palabra.

[It is not a fault, if they sing
Valiant deeds of Moors,
For our famous feats
Thus shine all the more.
For praising the deeds
Of the loser in battle,
Ennobles the victor,
Even if not a word is said about him.]

The last line grudgingly acknowledges that it is hard to argue that the *romanceros moriscos* reflect glory on the Christians, when these often fail even to put in an appearance. The poet then moves to a less honorable justification: Moors should be the protagonists of all these love affairs and games, because true men—i.e. the Roman conquerors of Iberia, or its defenders—cannot be bothered with such trifles. Yet even at this apparently Orientalist moment, the alternative to the Moor isn't the Christian hero of the *Reconquista*, but instead a much earlier figure from before the Muslim invasion.

Nevertheless, what stands between Núñez Muley and the anonymous balladeer, in historical terms, is nothing less than the failure of the last-minute petition, the subsequent uprising by the oppressed Moriscos in the Alpujarras, the bloody conflict, and the forced transport and relocation of the Granadine Moriscos to Castile. (The ballad alludes to this in its last lines, a surprisingly realistic and contemporary curse: "en conclusión te apedreen/los moros del Alpujarra.") This huge histori-cal distance is what makes the claims in the ballad—and the general maurophile fashion—particularly striking. One would not imagine that this historical trajectory would leave such arguments, or proclivities, intact. And yet there does seem to be an odd stubbornness to mau-rophilia, at this very late point in the century. In fact, while critics have been quick to associate the disappearance of the Moorish themes within the *romancero* with the increasingly hostile political climate of years leading to the expulsion, they offer no similar motivations for its original rise.

Moriscos in Our Midst

I would like to conclude, on a more speculative note, by discussing the Moriscos in between; that is, the subjects who match neither the idealized version of the *romancero* nor the debased version of the satirical responses. The particular challenge when considering this population, as Francisco Márquez Villanueva has usefully noted, is that many of them would have been intent on leaving no trace. Imagine, if you will, classes of Moriscos intent on assimilating into Spain, and whose response to persecution may well have been to make themselves invisible. Their existence, I would suggest, may account for some of the anxiety in the responses to the *romancero morisco*. If, in the poems, Spaniards essentially pass as Moors, could not historical Moriscos pass as Spaniards?

Although we do not have the kind of historical evidence for this population that does exist for Conversos, there are certain powerful literary representations of the problem. One is Lope de Vega's play, *La villana de Getafe*, which has been astutely analyzed by Márquez Villanueva.[19] This critic is primarily interested in demonstrating the connections between Lope's *comedia* (1613–14), written towards the end of the Morisco expulsions, and the Moorish persona that the author had adopted earlier in his inordinately popular *romanceros moriscos*. The play features a noble suitor, the none-too-faithful Don Félix, whose intended marriage to Doña Ana is derailed by the peasant girl Inés, the *villana* of the title. Inés's brilliant scheme (the first of many) to thwart a proper aristocratic union and keep Félix for herself involves planting a libel, to the effect that he is actually a Morisco, as is his servant, significantly named Lope. In fact, the libel states, the two are under investigation: "ya se les hace la información para echallos de España" [they are being investigated in order to throw them out of Spain].[20] Márquez convincingly shows how Lope de Vega thus cannily stages his own suspicious "Moorishness," only to dispel all qualms as calumnies. Just as the characters Don Félix and Lope are actually above reproach, whatever may be said about them, the historical Lope de Vega is not a Morisco, despite his literary proclivities. Márquez argues that Lope is

---

[19] Francisco Márquez Villanueva, "Lope, infamado de Morisco: *La Villana de Getafe*," *Anuario de letras* 21 (1983), pp. 147–182.

[20] Lope de Vega, *La villana de Getafe*, José María Díez Borque ed., Madrid, 1990, p. 165.

not satirizing the preoccupation with *limpieza de sangre*, but rather the particularly urban sin of *murmuración*, gossiping or rumor-mongering. Yet even though the satire against *limpieza* may be contained by Félix's indignant appeal to both a magically smooth judicial process and a duel in order definitively to clear his name, the *comedia* does have ideological implications beyond the injured author/protagonist. The humor of the scene immediately following the accusation is quite devastating: suddenly everyone in Doña Ana's household recalls having suspected all along that there was something not quite right about the "dark" Lope. When Don Félix, unsuspecting, walks in, he too is promptly confirmed as a Morisco:

> Ana: Más de espacio le miré,
> no en balde la fama suena.
> Morisco me ha parecido,
> y aun en el habla también.
>
> [I looked at him more carefully.
> Fame does not proclaim in vain.
> He seems Morisco to me,
> And in the way he speaks, too.]

Beyond this sharp satire of suspicion, the play suggests that genealogy is opaque and malleable, even if there are social mechanisms that purport to render it transparent. And while the *comedia* dispels the possible libel of Morisco ancestry, it tells us nothing about the opposite situation: the actual Moriscos' ability to pass, constructing themselves as fully Old-Christian subjects. It is left to the reader to imagine, in the heated political climate of the expulsions, a Morisco Félix, (or a Lope) less prone to romantic complications, perhaps, and thus better able to remain undetected.

Another striking literary manifestation of this problem is the well-known story of the Morisco Ricote and his daughter Ana Félix, in the second part of *Don Quijote* (1615), written soon after the expulsion decrees. Ricote and his family are neither chivalric fantasies nor abject laborers, but instead prosperous farmers. Father and daughter have an uncanny ability to pass, moving not only in and out of Spain, but also in and out of religious, national, and even gender identities. Yet in this context what I find most striking about the protracted narrative of their adventures is the inconclusive ending: after a famously ironic debate about the merits of the Morisco expulsion, Ricote and his daughter are left waiting in Barcelona to see whether their aristocratic patrons can intercede for them at court, to arrange their exemption from banishment. And there they remain, eternally waiting, long-term houseguests of the Catalan noble Don Antonio and of the Viceroy himself, availing themselves of Christian hospitality for now almost four hundred years. Surely this inconclusive ending is itself a conclusion of sorts: it suggests that no great harm proceeds from the inclusion within Spain of Moriscos who want nothing more than to assimilate. De facto, Ricote and Ana Félix quietly remain, not only benignly overlooked but actively welcomed by the regional aristocracy.

Literary evidence aside, the historical ironies here are profound: an individual's success in challenging the racialized accounts of essential Morisco difference in order to assimilate and pass within Spain paradoxically seems to require the disappearance of any cultural distinctions, or at least so it would appear. Yet perhaps this is simply a matter of what the historical record has yielded to this point, and analogies to long-term Converso practices might be useful in escaping the dispiriting paradox. But there is another way to think about the ostensible disappearance of these subjects into the Spanish population. Instead of imagining their cultural dissolution, we might recall the argument with which I began: rather than accept the ostensible disappearance of Moorish culture in 1492, I urged us to reconstruct the hybrid, *mudéjar* Spain that lasts long after the fall of Granada. Perhaps this is the culture that might most easily assimilate Morisco subjects over the course of the cruel sixteenth century—a culture already marked not only by the high aristocratic borrowings charted in the *romancero* but by a multitude of quotidian habits that render Moorishness quintessentially Spanish.

CHAPTER TWELVE

MANZANARES, 1600: MORISCOS FROM GRANADA ORGANIZE A FESTIVAL OF "MOORS AND CHRISTIANS"

William Childers

On August 16, 1600, St. Roque's Day, the Moriscos of the town of Manzanares, in La Mancha, were the protagonists of a festival in honor of the Virgin Mary, to raise funds for gilding the recently completed altarpiece (*retablo*) of the local church. All were members of families from the Kingdom of Granada, redistributed in New Castile as a result of the War of the Alpujarras (1568–1570). All were armed; in fact, for six weeks they had held military exercises and parades through the town square every Sunday, in preparation for the simulacrum of a battle, or *zuiza*.[1] Here is how the local pharmacist, Bartolomé de Herrera, describes it:

> During the month of August and some days before, this witness saw them march through the streets of town, to the beat of a drum and with a flag with towers and an insignia with half moons on it. Luis Pérez was their captain, with Juan Pérez, son of Diego Pérez, and many others the witness did not recognize, but he knew they were all from Granada, except for Melchor Díaz, who was the sergeant of the company, and they all had swords in their belts and halberds, and he does not know how many harquebuses they had or who carried them, just that he heard them going off. And he has heard that during one of these parades they got into a fight among themselves, and with the weapons they carried some were injured, which he heard talked about publicly in the main square of the town, but he does not remember who told him of it. And this witness saw that in the public square the day of the festival the soldiers and their captain and the other officials took captives and brought them to the castle they had erected there, shouting "li, li" as a battle cry when they took a captive. And this witness was one of the captives and he gave four *reales* ransom, which this witness paid because the ransom was for gilding the altarpiece of the parish church. And he heard they raised one hundred

---

[1] The term *zuiza*, nowadays seldom used, refers to a public celebration involving mock military exercises. The chief contemporary example of its continued use is in reference to the annual commemoration of the Battle of Clavijo in Astorga (León).

ducats. And this witness saw there, keeping track of the money, Juan de Canuto, chief bailiff (*alguacil mayor*), Blas de Quesada, alderman (*regidor*), and Juan de Bolaños, steward (*mayordomo*) of the church. And he has heard it said publicly in the town that it was proclaimed that all of those from the Kingdom [of Granada] between eighteen and forty years of age had to present themselves for the festival and mock battle (*zuiza*), but this witness does not know nor has he heard said who it was that ordered that proclamation. And he did not see that there was any public scandal or controversy as a result of their carrying the said weapons, rather everyone enjoyed it, considering that the money raised was to be used for gilding the altarpiece. Moreover, he said no harm could come from this, neither in the town [of Manzanares] nor in any neighboring towns, considering the fact that there were many people in that town and the others, but they only did it to make a more enjoyable fair and for the other reasons already mentioned.[2]

There were forty-three 'soldiers' altogether, four of them armed with harquebuses. The festival was a noteworthy success; people came from neighboring towns to enjoy the spectacle, similar in many respects—though not in all, as we will see—to a modern festival of Moors and Christians. Of course the most interesting thing about this case is that the Moriscos themselves played the role of Moors from Granada.[3]

What for many was a fascinating simulacrum, all the more enjoyable because of the element of authenticity, others considered a case

---

[2] Archivo Histórico Nacional, Órdenes Militares, Archivo Histórico de Toledo 36.658, "Proceso causado a pedimento del licenciado Pedro Cortés, fiscal del Real Consejo de Órdenes y por su mando por el alcalde de la villa de Almagro en la villa de Manzanares," folios 14–15. For the original of this and other quotations from this document, see the Appendix, below. The foliation of this document only continues through folio 25, though the document contains 68 folios. All translations from this and other archival sources are my own. Hereafter, documents from the judicial archive of the Consejo de Órdenes will be abbreviated thus: "AHN, OO MM, AHT," followed by the document number.

[3] To my knowledge the only previous discussion of this event is in Miguel Fernando Gómez Vozmediano, *Mudéjares y moriscos en el Campo de Calatrava. Reductos de convivencia, tiempos de intolerancia (Siglos XV–XVII)*, Ciudad Real: Diputación Provincial de Ciudad Real, 2000, pp. 130–31. Gómez Vozmediano assumes, mistakenly in my view, that the festival must have involved two opposing sides, though the document makes no mention of there being a Christian band. He has a tendency to exaggerate the "explosive" nature of the situation, somewhat sarcastically ridiculing the decision to allow the Moriscos to participate ("was it not possible for the townspeople to have chosen anything more inappropriate than to celebrate the traditional Moors and Christians *suizas* using real Muslims," p. 130, my translation) Yet even he has to admit that, "in any case, the fact that the Christian community would call on the Moriscos to celebrate this religious festival could lead us to think there were spaces emerging for integrating the Moorish quarters [*morerías*] in La Mancha" (p. 131, my translation). He includes a transcription of Gutiérrez de Villegas' final report as Appendix 8, pp. 224–26.

of flagrant disregard for public safety and civic order. Although all the witnesses on record agree with Bartolomé de Herrera that there was neither scandal nor danger, *someone* in Manzanares—we do not know who—was seriously alarmed to see an armed squadron of Moriscos marching every weekend with swords, daggers, halberds, and firearms, training themselves, as it were, in the use of weapons and military maneuvers. Seeing that the local authorities supported and even encouraged this *zuiza*, this person, acting alone or on behalf of some faction within the town, alerted the Consejo de Órdenes Militares in Madrid, and their prosecuting attorney lodged a formal complaint against the local officials for having authorized the Moriscos to carry weapons, despite a royal ban. In October, the Consejo sent an official, the *licenciado* Gutiérrez de Villegas, *alcalde mayor* of the Campo de Calatrava, to investigate. His sixty-eight folio report documents the events in full detail, culminating in a recommendation of modest punishment against the local government of Manzanares and none at all against the Moriscos themselves, who had prudently requested written permission before agreeing to prepare the *zuiza*. The report does not have the decision of the Consejo attached to it, in the absence of which we do not know whether the punishments he recommended were carried out or not.

Given what we do know—or think we know—about the situation of the Moriscos around 1600, it is hardly surprising that somebody was alarmed. Rather, more surprising is the complacent tranquility of most of the residents of Manzanares whose opinions are preserved in the report. After all, the town's Moriscos were the vestige of a group that had rebelled against the king in a brutal and bloody civil war. They lived under constant suspicion of continuing to be disloyal subjects, Christians in name only, as is amply demonstrated in the documentation preserved in inquisitorial archives, the papers of the Junta de Población del Reino de Granada in Simancas, and the judicial archive of Órdenes Militares. Rumors spread about their conspiring with the Turks, and all banditry in the area around Toledo was attributed to their greed and their hatred of all Christians. The general impression the archival record provides is of a closely watched minority.[4] And

---

[4] Among the many studies that could be cited, the best for the Inquisition in La Mancha are Mercedes García-Arenal's magnificent *Inquisición y moriscos. Los procesos del tribunal de Cuenca*, Madrid, 1978, and the chapter she co-wrote with Jean-Pierre Dedieu, "Les tribunaux de Nouvelle-Castile," in Louis Cardaillac, ed., *Les morisques et l'Inquisition*, Paris, 1990, pp. 276–95. Full-fledged studies of the vigilance of the

yet in Manzanares we have a company of forty-three men, aged between eighteen and forty, marching in the streets with daggers, swords, halberds, and harquebuses! The Moriscos themselves saw how problematic this could be, so when they were invited to dress as Moors and prepare the *zuiza*, they insisted on having written authorization, which the magistrates (*alcaldes*) did not hesitate to issue. In fact, when the turnout was weak the first Sunday, the magistrates proclaimed a fine of one thousand *maravedis* for any Moriscos between eighteen and forty who failed to come out and march, to be applied to the gilding of the altarpiece. So not only did they *allow* the Moriscos to carry arms, they actually *ordered* them to do so.

Considered in its immediate context, this event throws into relief the ambiguities of the Moriscos' situation at the end of the sixteenth century. Both the Moriscos and their host communities found themselves at a crossroads with a number of alternative outcomes, and what happened in Manzanares dramatizes the multiple possibilities open to participants on both sides. On the one hand, the *zuiza*, a collaboration between the Moriscos and local authorities, represents a model of integration that preserves a distinct identity for the Granadans. A place for this community is reserved within the social and cultural configuration of Manzanares, implying recognition of the valuable contributions this new socio-ethnic group can make. On the other, the alarmist attitude of whoever denounced the indiscretion of arming the Moriscos represents the rejection of the recent arrivals as a foreign presence, emphasizing the importance of keeping a close eye on them. Implicitly, this point of view projects their separation from the rest of society into an indefinite future, anticipating the expulsion as the only solution, in the long run, to an intolerable situation.

Like their Old-Christian neighbors, the Moriscos themselves did not form a solid block, but exhibited, rather, a range of attitudes. Just like the rest of the population, they engaged in a struggle for relative status, driven by public representations of genealogy. (This struggle was the underlying cause of an isolated outbreak of violence associated with the *zuiza*, to which I will return later). Moreover, among the elite of this marginalized community, the possibility of full assimilation to

---

Morisco minority in New Castile reflected in the documents of the Junta de Población or the Consejo de Órdenes do not yet exist. For the latter, until a more theoretically sophisticated exploration becomes available, see Gómez Vozmediano, op. cit., especially pp. 71–124.

the dominant group emerged as a means for consolidating their social superiority over the rest of the Moriscos. Around the same time as the festival, several of those who participated, including the captain, Luis Pérez and his brother Diego, whose son Juan Pérez acted as *alférez* (lieutenant), as well as Pedro de Ayala, another soldier, initiated proceedings to be formally recognized as Old Christians by means of lawsuits in which they demanded their names be removed from the official list of the Moriscos residing in the town. On the other extreme, there were also some Morisco families that preferred to abandon Manzanares for a more familiar landscape, moving to a place closer geographically to the Granada they had left behind years before. Despite what we might imagine, both those who sought Old-Christian status and those who desired to relocate to Andalucía found sufficient support among local citizens of influence to be able to achieve these goals in a perfectly legal fashion.

Of course the most dramatic element in this document is the clash between the attitude of those who supported the *zuiza*, who appear to have been the vast majority, to judge by the written record, and those who found the event alarming, from whom no testimony is preserved in the report itself, but without whom it would never have been generated. The attitude of the denunciators is indirectly reflected in the prosecutor's formal complaint that heads the report:

> I hereby criminally accuse Gonzalo Ruiz de Bolaños and Juan Díaz Hidalgo, magistrates (*alcaldes ordinarios*) and Alonso Díaz Ibáñez and Blas de Quesada and other aldermen (*regidores*), along with any other residents of the town of Manzanares who turn out to be implicated. And referring to the case at hand, the aforesaid, with little fear of God or of the justice of your grace, have allowed the Moriscos of the town of Manzanares, over two hundred in number, and those of Membrilla, around as many, to gather, and have even called upon them to do so, and with the pretext of preparing a *zuiza* they have been carrying weapons for about three months now, including swords and daggers, and they have appointed a captain and a sergeant, and every Sunday and on holidays they march and train in the middle of town, firing off many harquebuses. The squadron flies a flag with five half moons as its insignia, and they end their training sessions by gathering together to make battle cries in Arabic, all of which has produced great scandal and controversy in Manzanares.[5]

---

[5] AHN, OO MM, AHT, 36.658, folio 1.

When compared with the declarations of the various witnesses, this statement reflects a tendency to exaggerate: it describes an army of four hundred Moriscos, whereas the official list gives only forty-three names; and they are said to have been preparing for three months, as opposed to a month and a half. It may not be out of place to remark that a similar Islamophobia exists in our own time, and that a politics based on exaggeration of the threat and manipulation of citizens' fear is practiced today as well, above all in the United States. In New Castile, however, practically on the eve of the expulsion, when Gutiérrez de Villegas asked some of the Manchegans he interviewed whether they were afraid, they responded that, on the one hand, the Moriscos were few in number, and, on the other, that the spectacle was both entertaining and had a pious motivation. And they pointed out that people came from nearby towns to see it. Thus, Juan Díaz Abad, for example, denied categorically that there was any danger:

> The witness was asked whether it seemed to him that allowing the forty-three on the list, and those who came from the town of Membrilla, a quarter of a league from Manzanares, to train with weapons, learning to handle them effectively, could cause trouble insofar as it would give the Moriscos from the Kingdom of Granada a chance to form squadrons in Manzanares and Membrilla, becoming powerful and threatening the many smaller towns and villages nearby. He said they could do nothing of the sort, considering that Manzanares is a large town with many residents and the other towns in the area were also large, and even all the Moriscos in Campo de Calatrava would not be enough to do any real damage, let alone just the ones in Manzanares and Membrilla.[6]

To this explanation can be added the comment by the twenty-eight year old Juan de Velasco: "He did not see any scandal or controversy as a result of the Moriscos' training with weapons. Actually the people in the town of Manzanares and other nearby localities who came to see the festival enjoyed watching them, in view of the fact that the festival was prepared to make an offering to help pay for the gilding of the altarpiece, which was very much needed."[7]

The approval comes, then, from a combination of factors. First, the sense of security derived from the fact the Moriscos were too few in number to attempt rebellion. It is worth mentioning that this reasoning process presupposes that the Moriscos' hostility would not extend

---

[6] Ibid., folio 13.
[7] Ibid., folio 19.

beyond the limits of their own self interest, and that the dominant group and the minority shared a similar understanding of their real situation. Second, the awareness, also shared, that the purpose was to gild the altarpiece not just to honor the Virgin Mary, but to enhance the reputation of the town itself, so that it could compete in Baroque splendor with its neighbors. And finally, the enthusiasm for watching the Moriscos perform, a crucial factor without which it would not even have occurred to the town's leaders to invite them to organize such a festival in the first place. I do not hesitate to term this enthusiasm "popular maurophilia," as a counterpart to the literary fad that was sweeping through Spain at the time.[8] In this last sense, it is noteworthy that people came from nearby towns to watch, constituting a further enhancement of the town's prestige. Thus, the residents of Manzanares appear to have recognized and accepted the festival as a means for the Moriscos to participate and contribute in a positive way to local cultural life. This gave them a certain dignity, a role to play, making them protagonists of something. Perhaps, then, the anonymous denouncer was not worried so much about security, but by the fact that the Moriscos were receiving such recognition.

It is important to mention that this was not just an isolated event, but a trend, a fashion. In Membrilla, a neighboring village, they had celebrated just such a *zuiza* three years earlier. At the end of his report, moreover, Gutiérrez de Villegas mentions that "for many years in this

---

[8] "Maurophile literature" is the most widely accepted term for the novels, poems, and plays celebrating the noble Moor that swept through Spain during the most intense moment of the crisis that led to the expulsion of 1609–1614. Márquez Villanueva (*El problema morisco (desde otras laderas)*. Madrid, 1991) and María Soledad Carrasco Urgoiti (for example in *El moro retador y el moro amigo (Estudios sobre fiestas y comedias de moros y cristianos)*, Granada, 1996) have been the two most eloquent voices articulating the interpretation of this literary trend as a defense of the Moriscos. Others, most notably Israel Burshatin in "Power, Discourse, and Metaphor in the *Abencerraje*," MLN 99.2 (1984) pp. 195–213, have drawn attention to its inherent Orientalism, thus questioning the depth of its commitment to helping flesh-and-blood Moriscos. By referring to "popular maurophilia," I do not mean to imply that there was a consistently pro-Morisco position implied in the enjoyment of performances of exotic otherness such as the *zuiza* in Manzanares, or the eagerly attended Morisco weddings. I only intend to draw attention to a parallel phenomenon to the literary trend, for which I assume an equally complex array of contradictory attitudes and motivations as critics have found for the works of literature termed "maurophile." Though the maurophile attitude, in literary manifestations or as part of popular cultural practices, often appears to indicate a certain acceptance of the Morisco minority, at times it also coexists with Islamophobia, as well as with indifference to or even hostility toward real-life Moriscos.

province these *zuizas* have been extremely common (*usadísimas*), performed, as here, by the folks from the Kingdom [of Granada], in almost all of the towns of Calatrava, at the head of which is the town of Almagro."[9] It appears, then, that during the Morisco period a custom was established of organizing festivals that in some aspects resemble festivals of Moors and Christians of the sort that are widely performed in Spain to this day, but rather than two rival bands, in sixteenth-century La Mancha they were celebrated with just one, the Moors, using the descendants of the Moors of Granada to play the role of their own ancestors. And this took place during the last decade of the Morisco period, even as the moment of their expulsion approached. They could not know that, of course, nor could the Old Christians who found it so entertaining to watch them imitate the Moors they knew about from reading *El Abencerraje* and Pérez de Hita, or from listening to Morisco ballads that were at the height of their popularity in that moment.

To begin to situate this *zuiza* in some way, I have called it a festival of "Moors and Christians" in my title. But at least as described in the report, which is our only source of information about it, this does not really correspond to the festivals of Moors and Christians as we know them today. According to María Soledad Carrasco Urgoiti's definition, a festival of Moors and Christians is "a representation with a dual and parallel structure in which two bands, symbolically representing the Islamic and Christian past, confront one another, first verbally and subsequently in a simulacrum of battle."[10] These festivals are "dual and parallel" in structure insofar as they successively represent first the triumph of the Moors and then their defeat, which in the national myth correspond to the Muslim Conquest and the Christian "Reconquest" of the Peninsula. Here, on the contrary, we have only the first half of this sequence, the triumph of the "Moors" and the captivity of the "Christians," which is resolved in the end by the payment of a ransom. This is how Pedro Cuellocarrillo, chief bailiff (*alguacil mayor*), described the festive atmosphere and collaboration between the disguised Moriscos and the leading residents of Manzanares:

> This witness saw how, the day after the Day of Our Lady, the New Christians took captives in the town square and brought them to a platform they had constructed there as a sort of castle, where Juan Ruiz de Bolaños,

---

[9] AHN, OO MM, AHT, 36.658, without foliation.
[10] Carrasco Urgoiti, op. cit., pp. 67–68 (my translation).

steward [*mayordomo*] of the town church, and Juan Díaz Abad, and other important personages were receiving the ransom paid by those who the Moriscos took captive in order to gild the altarpiece of the main church of the town, which was why they had organized the festival. And this witness understands that was the reason why the magistrates allowed the New Christians to perform the *zuiza* with weapons, swords, daggers, halberds, and the aforesaid harquebuses, and he has heard that they raised more than 1,300 *reales*, and to the people who were taken as captives to the 'castle' they gave them some refreshments, and when they captured them they danced and cried elatedly, "li, li," showing their delight as they took them away to the castle...In addition to which this witness knows for a fact that the Granadans themselves gave, of their own property, three hundred *reales*.[11]

Another difference between the Manzanares celebration and the typical Moors and Christians festivals is that the latter offer the public a representation intended to commemorate "historical" events supposed to have occurred in the very place where they were reenacted. These events relate to the Reconquest, and as such dramatize and legitimate the current residents' claim to possess the territory. Here, though, this dimension linking the actual place and its inhabitants with the fictional setting and participants in the events is entirely lacking. The castle set up in the town square does not represent a castle supposed to have ever existed in Manzanares or any location in the region. Nor do the events belong to a sequential process of Christianization. Rather, they appear to evoke a frontier zone along the long-standing border between Granada and Christian Andalucía, and the ongoing practice of taking, exchanging, and ransoming captives, regularly engaged in by both sides. Unlike Moors and Christians festivals, then, the *zuiza* does not commemorate the establishment and legitimacy of Christian hegemony on the Peninsula, but simply takes advantage, in an improvised way, of the opportunity created by the presence of a group of newcomers associated in the popular imagination with a glorious and exotic past. But it takes advantage of their presence for the purpose of constructing something for the future, a gilded altarpiece that will remain in the church as a testimony to this new group's contribution to the common good, thus converting their cultural difference into an additional resource. In the remainder of this essay, I would like to sketch an interpretation of these contrasts between the *zuiza* in Manzanares and the later development of

---

[11] AHN, OO MM, AHT, 36.658, folio 23.

the Moors and Christians tradition. I hope this interpretation will allow us to begin to see in popular maurophilia the possibility of constructing a cultural identity that could have integrated the Moriscos, rather than excluding them. This is in keeping with a line of research on the dynamic of social interaction between Moriscos and Old Christians in New Castile which began with Mercedes García-Arenal's seminal study of the Inquisition records of Cuenca, and has continued in the work of Francisco Márquez Villanueva, and, more recently, Trevor Dadson.[12]

The difficulties posed by the origin and meaning of Moors and Christians celebrations in Spain are far from resolved. Barbara Fuchs has pioneered an approach that relates them directly to the forging of a national identity based on the militant Christianity of the Counter-Reformation.[13] The festival facilitates the incorporation into this new identity of the local *patria chica* where it is celebrated, through the semi-mythic commemoration of the "Reconquest." Thus for Carrasco Urgoiti, the commemorative *comedias* of the sixteenth century are an important antecedent to the festivals. Similar to the *auto sacramental*, these dramatic pieces, represented in Spanish towns in honor of their patron saints, participated in "the generalized consciousness that Spain had taken on the mission of protecting Catholic orthodoxy."[14] The foundational myth of the Spanish nation as having always been free of the 'taint' of Islam, which was forged during the Hapsburg dynasty as part of the process of consolidating the absolutist monarchy, finds a localized manifestation in these festivals. According to Max Harris, truly popular examples of Moors and Christians as we know it today do not begin to appear until well into the seventeenth century, which is to say several decades after the events in Manzanares. But *zuizas* such as the one under study, which really ought to be called just plain *Moorish* festivals, may have been more common than is generally supposed. In which case spectacles of Moors and Christians could turn out to be a subsequent modification, implanted after the expulsion of the Moriscos, to substitute for the earlier custom.

---

[12] Mercedes García-Arenal, *Inquisición y moriscos*, Francisco Márquez Villanueva, *El problema morisco (desde otras laderas)*, Trevor J. Dadson, *Los moriscos de Villarrubia de los Ojos (siglos XV–XVIII)*, Madrid, 2007.

[13] Barbara Fuchs, *Mimesis and Empire. The New World, Islam, and European Identities*, Cambridge, 2001, pp. 99–117.

[14] María Soledad Carrasco Urgoiti, op. cit., p. 87 (my translation).

In this regard, it is useful to consider Daniel Flesler and Adrián Pérez Melgosa's discussion of Moors and Christians. In their view, these festivals have as their purpose the legitimation on the symbolic plane of the occupation of the territory on the part of its current occupants.[15] In any territory, these authors affirm, following Jacques Derrida, the roles of host and guest are arbitrarily interchangeable. I would add that these celebrations are especially common in areas of Spain, such as Alicante, Valencia, and the Alpujarras, where the current population consists primarily of the descendants of *repobladores* who came to occupy the lands that had once belonged to the expelled Moors. These areas could be said to have posed a special necessity of self-legitimation for their new inhabitants. Flesler and Pérez Melgosa insist that the simulacrum has the ultimate purpose of excluding the Moor, and for that reason it is unimaginable for Moroccan immigrants, who currently number 582,923[16] ever to play that role. The hyper-visibility of the Moor in the fiesta has its basis precisely in his invisibility outside the spectacle. And now we can also add that in the foundation of Moors and Christians lies the reconfiguration—indeed, it is not too much to speak even of repression, at least in the Freudian sense—of a previously existing practice that had the opposite meaning, that of recognizing the Moriscos in their otherness, and inviting them to participate, starting from that distinct identity, in the construction of a new society that would include them.[17]

Returning to the *zuiza* in Manzanares, we can now see the importance of the fact that, as opposed to festivals based on the *conquest of territory*, which appear to have as their goal the legitimation of the victors' domination over the land, the Manzanares *fiesta* is based on a dynamic of taking and ransoming captives. And once taken, the ransom money

---

[15] Daniela Flesler and Adrián Pérez Melgosa, "Battles of Identity, or Playing 'Guest' and 'Host': the Festivals of Moors and Christians in the Context of Moroccan Immigration to Spain," *Journal of Spanish Cultural Studies* 4:2 (2003), pp. 151–168.

[16] *España en cifras 2008*, p. 10.

[17] In her recent book, *The Return of the Moor, North African Immigration in Contemporary Spain*, Purdue UP, 2008, Flesler extends these observations on the absence of participation on the part of Moroccan immigrants, arguing finally that "the logic of the excessive visibility of the exotic Moor on which the festivals are predicated betrays the desire to relegate Moorish presence to a remote past and to distant lands, thus predetermining the invisibility of the real Moroccan immigrant of today. But the immigrants exist, and their mere presence dismantles the carefully constructed complex of rituals woven over centuries in order to erase all possible doubts about the Christian Spaniards' status as owners of their national territory." (114).

is voluntarily relinquished, as it were, to the Virgin Mary, by the very Moriscos who collected it. It is relevant here to evoke the widespread custom, in the sixteenth century, for captives returning from Muslim lands to make a pilgrimage of thanks to one of the major Marian shrines on the Peninsula. Especially common were the visits of freed captives to the Basilica of the Virgin of Guadalupe in Extremadura, where they would leave their chains as an offering and a testament. In the *zuiza*, then, by having the "Moors" themselves donate the ransom taken from their captives directly for the purpose of gilding the altarpiece, what is represented is not the triumph of a Christian community, as a political entity bent on augmenting its worldly power, but rather the triumph of Marianism, which here comes to serve as a bridge between the Muslim and Christian traditions on the Peninsula. This idea, that veneration of the Virgin Mary could facilitate the reconciliation between Old Christians and Moriscos, appears increasingly as the crisis nears its cataclysmic *finale*. The argument is explicitly made in Pérez de Chinchón's *Antialcorano*, a collection of sermons for converting crypto-Muslims, first published in 1532 (or possibly even 1528), but reissued in 1595.[18] One of the primary strategies of maurophile literature generally is the assimilation of the Hispano-Arabic tradition to Christianity by means of conversion. Veneration of the Virgin Mary is the principal motivation for Zoraida's conversion in *Don Quixote*, I.40. The most thorough attempt, however, at using the Virgin Mary's powerful hold on the Iberian imagination to create a synthesis between Christianity and Islam were the *Libros Plúmbeos* of Granada. This aspect of the extraordinary late sixteenth-century hoax is discussed by Francisco J. Martínez Medina in his contribution to Barrios Aguilera and García-Arenal's important new collection, *Los plomos de Sacromonte*.[19]

In my view, the phenomenon of popular maurophilia should lead us to question the often repeated idea of a generalized rejection of the Moriscos on the part of the population at large. The receptive attitude toward the Granadans' participation in public life is one of the clearest demonstrations I have seen of the possibility in early modern Spain of

---

[18] Bernardo Pérez de Chinchón, *Antialcorano. Diálogos christianos*, Francisco Pons Fuster, ed., Alicante, 2000, pp. 61–63 and 357–366.

[19] Martínez Medina, Francisco J. "Los hallazgos del Sacromonte a la luz de la historia de la Iglesia y de la teología católica," in Manuel Barrios Aguilera and Mercedes García-Arenal, eds., *Los plomos del Sacromonte. Invención y tesoro*, Valencia, Granada, Zaragoza, 2006, pp. 79–111.

constructing cultural identities that did not have their starting point in religion as a principle of exclusion. Here the Moriscos could belong as members of a new social configuration, without necessarily renouncing their Hispano-Arabic cultural legacy. Yet the practical and political consequences of this receptivity were capable of being shaped by a public discourse that was turning increasingly hostile to the Moriscos from around the turn of the century onward.[20] More than anyone, it has been Francisco Márquez Villanueva who has revealed the intense public debate that existed in these years surrounding the "Morisco question." His research has restored this debate to the prominent place it held at the time. What is at stake, ultimately, is nothing more or less than the emerging sense of national identity that was being forged across Spain during the Baroque. The central issue raised by the Morisco question was, ultimately, whether or not they belonged to the Spanish nation. From the perspective of those trying to define Spain in terms of militant Counter-Reformation Catholicism, the Moriscos were the perfect scapegoat. Nor should we allow ourselves to be distracted by the religious issue *per se*; it served, rather, as a pretext for the exclusion of an element represented in the new national narrative as not "Spanish." Indeed, it is by means of this exclusion that "Spanishness" comes into being, projecting its own origin back into the past in the pre-existing distinction between the religious groups on the Peninsula.

But this miniscule example from Manzanares shows an opposite tendency, a spontaneous, localized effort to construct inclusive identities in which all could participate. And this was not a unique case, as is now well known as a result of Trevor Dadson's monumental study of the Moriscos of Villarrubia de los Ojos, 34 kms northwest of Manzanares.[21] It is still too soon to determine in how many places and by

---

[20] Morisco weddings offer a simple yet quite effective example of how easy it could be to shape the attitude of a population at best ambivalent toward the newcomers. In 1590 the Inquisitor Velarde de la Concha, of the Tribunal of Cuenca, visited Quintanar de la Orden. In the Edicto de Fe he mentioned the 'crime' of celebrating weddings with "*zambras y ritos mahometanos.*" Many residents of Quintanar came forward to denounce their Morisco neighbors for celebrating such weddings, and several told the Inquisitor they had been to seven or eight of them. Obviously, they had enjoyed the music and dancing at the Morisco weddings without necessarily thinking there was anything wrong, anything sinful, about them. But the moment the Inquisitor informed them that such celebrations were a crime, they did not hesitate to come forward and accuse those whose dancing they had so often enjoyed in the past (Archivo Diocesano de Cuenca, Inquisición, Libro 326, folios 166r–248v).

[21] Trevor J. Dadson, op. cit.

what means the project of integrating Morisco communities into local social organization was moving forward, despite official pressures in the opposite direction emanating from within the monarchy. Scholars have long failed to see the signs of this project, since they have simply assumed it did not exist. As the evidence accumulates, as it undoubtedly will over the next few years, we would do well to consider the possibility, however unlikely it may now appear to us, that what really motivated the expulsion of the Moriscos was not the *impossibility* of their integration, but rather *just the opposite*. It had become all too obvious to some that their integration was quite possible, was in fact already beginning to take place, but into a Spain that was *not* the one the intellectual proponents of the Counter-Reformation sought to construct.

If the festival in Manzanares and the subsequent report generated by the alarm it caused dramatically reveal divisions within the Old-Christian population, the same can also be said for the Moriscos. On August 10, six days before the *zuiza*, a street fight (*reyerta*) took place in front of Juan Pérez' house, as the participants were gathering after that afternoon's rehearsal. Several members of the Castillo family, who were from the city of Granada, were offended by comments made by some of those from Benamaurel, who considered themselves superior because their village converted to Christianity before those from Granada itself. Gutiérrez de Villegas gives the following description in his report:

> And on one of their rehearsal days, five or six with the surname Castillo got into an argument with some of the company over the fact that some said those who came from towns that had converted before the Conquest of Granada had more honor than those were from Granada itself, over which they [the Castillos] drew their weapons and wounded one or more.[22]

Those whose families had been Christian the longest claimed higher status, and in the resulting confrontation one of the Moriscos from Benamaurel, Juan Díaz, was seriously injured by blows to his head, hand, and arm. This was the only outbreak of violence of any sort mentioned in the entire report, but since Gutiérrez de Villegas decided to include a complete transcript of the trial against the Castillos, it takes up nearly two thirds of the document. In the trial, the Castillos reported that Moriscos from Benamaurel had been going around saying they were going to use their weapons to kill some of the Granadans, and at least

---

[22] AHN, OO MM, AHT, 36.658, without foliation.

some witnesses to the fight claimed that the shotguns (*escopetas*) they were using just for noise and show were loaded with lead (not just gunpowder) and pointed at the Castillos. Interrogated on the subject, several witnesses acknowledged the animosity between the Moriscos from Granada and those from Benamaurel, who were the majority in Manzanares.

In Ginés Pérez de Hita's *Historia de los bandos de Zegríes y Abencerrajes*, better known as the First Part of the *Guerras civiles de Granada* (1595), the noblest and most virtuous warriors of the Nasrid kingdom of Granada are all represented as having converted to Christianity before the conquest, that is to say, before the end of 1491. This notion of a hierarchy of lineage based on the date of conversion, which the *reyerta* in Manzanares shows had been fully internalized in Morisco communities, is an indication that, in their new circumstances, they were assuming values of the dominant culture, though adapted to their own traditions in such a way as to force us to speak of cultural hybridity.

It is quite revealing to discover that some of the same families that proudly displayed their Moorish heritage by participating in the *zuiza* were engaged around the same time in a legal battle to gain the rights of Old Christians, demanding that their names be stricken from the list of Morisco residents altogether. Specifically, on December 9, 1600, Pedro de Ayala, from Benamaurel, initiated formal proceedings to prove he should be considered an Old Christian and not a Morisco. The record of this lawsuit, which ended in the Spring of 1602 in a failed appeal to the Consejo de Órdenes, contains partial transcriptions from two others: Mateo Ruiz' successful bid for old Christian status, with a favorable decision in Manzanares dated June 3, 1600; and Luis and Diego Pérez' attempt, whose outcome is not given, and may even have still been pending in early 1602, since it contains *probanzas* from May 1601.[23] A full exploration of the fascinating topic of the *pleitos de cristiano viejo*, lawsuits brought by Moriscos claiming Old-Christian status, is beyond the scope of this essay.[24] Briefly, though, these are claims brought by Granadans who presented credentials and testimony from witnesses to show that they belonged to a category exempting

---

[23] The document in which all of this can be found is catalogued as AHN, OO MM, AHT 36.662.

[24] I am currently working on just such a study, mainly focused on the corpus of documentation preserved in the papers of the Junta de Población y Hacienda del Reino de Granada, in the Cámara de Castilla section of the Archivo General de Simancas.

them from the restrictions applied to Moriscos from the Kingdom of Granada, especially the prohibition against carrying weapons and the requirement that they not leave the town or village where they were listed as residents without a passport. The two most frequent bases for their claims were either descent from *cristianos viejos de moros* ("Old Christians descended from Moors"), i.e. from Muslims who converted prior to the final conquest of Granada, or from Old-Christian *repobladores* who married Moriscas. But many other legal justifications for the claim were employed, and in fact each of the three cases in Manzanares used a different argument. Mateo Ruiz presented documentation that his parents were *repobladores* from Blanca (Murcia) along with a copy of a royal decree granting them the privileges of Old Christians. Luis Pérez, who was the captain of the *zuiza*, claimed to descend from a royal line of Arabs, the Calis of Baza; his father, he stated, was Gonzalo Pérez Abengaliz, of Benamaurel, wealthy, respected, and privileged with the right to bear arms.[25] His brother, Diego Pérez, who was over forty years old, was represented in the *zuiza* by his son, Juan Pérez, who was the *alférez* of the squadron. Given the prominent status of uncle and nephew as captain and second in command of the *zuiza*, it seems fair to say that this was the leading Morisco family of Manzanares, and that their high status in the community was a result of their royal ancestry. The third supplicant, Pedro de Ayala based his *cristiano viejo* status on the fact that his grandfather, Juan de Ayala, was named by Don Enrique Enríquez de Guzmán *alcaide* of Cortes, some ten kilometers from Benamaurel. He rode a horse, carried arms, and had the keys to the castle. Unfortunately for Pedro de Ayala's case, however, several witnesses expressed uncertainty as to whether only Old Christians who already had the right to bear arms were named as *alcaides*, or if Juan de Ayala had acquired that right as a result of his being made *alcaide* by Don Enrique.

---

[25] A suggestive detail concerning Gonzalo Pérez Abengaliz comes out in the testimony of the witnesses from Benamaurel, who explain that there were two men named Gonzalo Pérez living there when the War of the Alpujarras broke out. One was an ordinary Morisco, a butcher with no particular social distinction (one witness calls him "un morisco hombre vil y bajo," literally "vile and low"), while the other was a descendant of the noble Abengaliz family, an honored landowner, much respected in Benamaurel, who had permission to bear arms. In one witness' description, the vulgar Morisco is tall and robust, and *whiter* ("más blanco") than the Moorish prince. This is actually quite logical, since the Calis would have been Arabs, whereas most Moriscos probably descended from local Iberians who converted to Islam sometime after the Muslim invasion. AHN, OO MM, AHT 36.662, without foliation.

The Moriscos of Manzanares collectively hired a lawyer, the licentiate Villaescusa, with an annual salary of three hundred *reales*, to manage their cases for them. It is likely that he had initiated other claims. Comparison between the lists of soldiers in the *zuiza* and the claimants and relatives named in these lawsuits shows that several families were implicated in each case. Luis Pérez had three nephews in the *zuiza*, and Pedro de Ayala's nephew was also listed as a soldier in the squadron. Since the partial transcripts of the other two lawsuits contained in Pedro de Ayala's are too incomplete to judge for certain the relative merits of the three cases, it is difficult to know the reasons for the different outcome in Mateo Ruiz' case. It is true that of the three plaintiffs he was the only one who had a transcription of a royal decree (*provisión real*) granting his ancestors the privilege of bearing arms. But it is also true that interesting changes occurred in local politics between the pronouncement of that sentence, in June of 1600, and Pedro de Ayala's losing his case in 1602. The magistrate (*alcalde ordinario*) who found in favor of Mateo Ruiz was none other than Juan Díaz Hidalgo, who was one of the local officials who encouraged the Moriscos to organize the *zuiza* less than two months later. Moreover, when Pedro de Ayala initiated his claim, the magistrate who received his petition was Bartolomé de Herrera, the pharmacist whose testimony presented the festival in such a positive light. But the unfavorable sentence, which Pedro de Ayala appealed to the Consejo de Órdenes, was issued in February 1602 by Diego de Salcedo, a *newly elected* magistrate who was obviously less favorable to the Morisco cause than either Juan Díaz Hidalgo or Bartolomé de Herrera. It seems there was a political change in Manzanares, and that the pro-Morisco faction lost influence, precisely around the end of 1600. The denunciation against the magistrates and aldermen who supported the *zuiza*, which led to Gutiérrez de Villegas' visit may have been a political maneuver, part of a larger strategy to gain power. Only a more thorough study of local rivalries than can be undertaken here would ultimately shed light on the question of whether the Moriscos found themselves embroiled in a struggle for power among rival factions within the governing elite of the town.

The fact that several of the Morisco families involved in the *zuiza* were simultaneously soliciting Old-Christian status, although seemingly contradictory, was, in fact, consistent with the overall project to enhance the status of their community. The right to bear arms was the degree zero of masculinity in late sixteenth-century New Castile. Participation in the *zuiza* at least gave the Morisco protagonists a temporary, provisional opportunity to walk the streets with swords on their belts; but these men aspired to permanent authorization to wear one. By the same token, we should not too readily assume that the anti-Morisco faction was scandalized by the festival simply because they believed the squadron represented a real military threat. They understood as well as the Moriscos that gaining the right to carry weapons meant achieving a certain minimum status, and it was that attainment that rankled them. Denouncing the local officials who had authorized it was a way of blocking any progress, however slight, for a group they were determined to keep "in their place."

Despite constituting a fairly large minority within a prosperous Manchegan town, the Morisco community of Manzanares does not appear to have left a wide trail in the documents of the Consejo de Órdenes. In addition to Gutiérrez de Villegas' report, Miguel Fernando Gómez Vozmediano mentions a few relatively early documents concerning the establishment of the Morisco minority, and little more.[26] Besides what he mentions, I have thus far come across only Pedro de Ayala's lawsuit, and one other document that discusses two Morisco families from Manzanares. It is from twenty years earlier, but it is still worth considering for the light it sheds on the attitude of the town's governing elite. The document is a transcript of the measures taken in the Sierra de Segura when they received a royal provision of 1579 admonishing local authorities to better enforce controls on Moriscos. The Moriscos in Beas de Segura were fined, unjustly they claim, and this transcript was produced in response to their complaint.[27] It shows how magistrates in Segura checked every village in their jurisdiction, no matter how small or remote, uncovering many interesting instances of Moriscos living without royal authorization, sometimes within a day's walk of the Kingdom of Granada. Two families from Manzanares were living in the village of Hornos. Both of the men, Gonzalo de Buendía and Luis de Ribera, were originally from Benamaurel. They came to Hornos

---

[26] Among the documents Gómez Vozmediano discusses are several lawsuits concerning the newcomers right to sell their goods without renting the expensive stalls in the central market (104); a document from shortly after their arrival dealing with control over their religious practices (109), and a minor incident from 1606 in which a mother and daughter complain to the Consejo de Órdenes about the abusive attitude of a magistrate (167). This last document, though quite brief, seems to confirm the hypothesis sketched above, according to which a political change sometime during 1601–02 led to a less favorable attitude toward the Moriscos on the part of local authorities.

[27] AHN OO MM AHT 51.575.

because a priest from there who was visiting Manzanares requested two families of Moriscos to tend his garden. The agents from Segura interviewed a number of residents in Hornos, all of whom were quite happy with the hard-working pair, who seemed well integrated into the village. They received direct authorization from the magistrate in Manzanares at the time, Francisco de Sandoval Negrete, to live anywhere they chose in Andalucía, as long as they did not enter the Kingdom of Granada. Though technically he should have sought the permission of the Junta de Población in Madrid, Sandoval Negrete did not feel the need. This relatively minor example shows a similar willingness on the part of local authorities to help the Moriscos under their supervision integrate in whatever way they could, and a similar disregard for the prohibitions and restrictions imposed by the Crown.

Of course, this support for Morisco integration was of little avail when faced with the draconian "final solution" of 1610. The protagonists of the festival that raised 1,300 *reales* to pay for the gilding of the altarpiece in Manzanares were irremediably expelled, but the town continued to enjoy the beauty of the *retablo* for several centuries. Ironically, however, the funds they raised were not actually used for the purpose for which they were intended. In a lawsuit from 1613, Cristóbal and Pedro Ruiz de Elvira, two brothers belonging to the family of sculptors who built and gilded the altarpiece, demanded to be paid for their work. They pointed out that the parish church had received funds specifically earmarked to pay for the gold leaf and gold sheets needed to *dorar el retablo*, "and not to be used for anything else," but that now the town council and the parish were seeking permission to use the money for some other purpose.[28] With the Moriscos who raised the funds out of the way, it was that much easier to forget the pious goal for which the money was originally amassed. As late as 1622 the Ruiz de Elvira clan was still trying to get the town to pay up.[29] These corrupt dealings are more than just an ironic footnote, for they force us to question the original motives of the officials who organized the festivities. Were they cynically exploiting both popular maurophilia and Marianism, taking advantage of the Moriscos and the sculptors to raise funds with a view to lining their own pockets? Such hypocritical manipulation, one could argue, is

[28] Ibid. 36.420.
[29] Ibid. 39.879.

always a danger when religious sentiments are pressed into the service of political aims, as they so often were in the Spanish Baroque.

Today, the visitor to Manzanares who inquires of the town's beautifully gilded sixteenth-century altarpiece will be told that it was destroyed by fire several decades ago. Thus the work no longer stands as mute testimony to the cooperative spirit between the towns Old-Christian and Morisco communities. We do, however, have Gutiérrez de Villegas' report, housed in Madrid's *Archivo Historico Nacional*, to provide us with a glimpse into the history of Manzanares' Morisco minority, who four hundred years ago, on the eve of their expulsion from Spain, helped to gild a Christian shrine.

TRANSCRIPTIONS FROM GUTIÉRREZ
DE VILLEGAS' REPORT

These passages from the original Spanish text correspond to the principal quotations given above in the body of the article.

Bartolomé de Herrera, pharmicist (*boticario*), folios 14–15:

Por el mes de agosto y algunos días antes, este testigo vido andar por las calles de la dicha villa en paseo, al son de un tambor y con bandera que parescían almaizares y en ella por insi[g]nia traían unas medias lunas, a Luis Pérez capitán y Juan Pérez hijo de Diego Pérez de los naturales del Reino de Granada y otros munchos qu'este testigo no conoció más de que sabe que todos ellos eran de los naturales del Reino de Granada exento Melchor Díaz que era sargento de la dicha compañía, los cuales traían espadas en las cintas y alabardas y que no tiene noticia de los arcabuces que llevaban más de que oyó disparar, ni se acuerda quién eran los que los llevaban. Y que ha oído decir que andando en el dicho paseo se habíen arrebuelto los unos con los otros y que con las armas que llevaban se habíen herido, lo cual oyó decir públicamente en la plaza pública de la dicha villa [15r] que no se acuerda a qué personas. Y vio este testigo que, estando en la plaza el día de la fiesta los dichos soldados y capitán y los demás oficiales, llegaban a cautivar para los elevar al castillo que estaba en la plaza, haciendo 'li li' a modo de algazara cuando hacían la presa. Y este testigo fue uno de los cautivos y dio de limosna cuatro reales, los cuales este testigo dio porque la limosna que allí se llegaba era para ayuda a dorar el retablo de la iglesia parroquial de la dicha villa. Y oyó decir que se habien llegado cien ducados. Y este testigo vio qu'estaban allí para la cobra Juan Canuto, alguacil mayor y Blas de Quesada regidor y Juan de Bolaños mayordomo de la dicha iglesia. Y que ha oído decir públicamente en esta dicha villa en la plaza della que se pregonó que todos los del dicho Reino de diez y ocho años hasta cuarenta saliesen a la dicha fiesta y zuiza, pero este testigo no sabe ni a oído decir por cuyo mandado se dio el dicho pregón y que no vio que por razón de traer las dichas armas los susodichos hubiese escándalo [15v] ni murmuración, antes se holgaban de vello respeto que la limosna se había de convertir en dorar el retablo. Y que ansimesmo dijo que de haber fecho los dichos naturales lo susodicho por ello no pudo venir daño alguno a la dicha villa ni a los pueblos circunvecinos por ser muncha la gente de la dicha villa y de los demás pueblos, sino que lo hicieron por regocijar la fiesta por las demás razones que ha declarado. Y qu'esto es la verdad para el juramento que tiene fecho, que es de edad de cincuenta años. Y lo firmó y el dicho señor alcalde mayor leyósele su dicho. Ratificóse en él. El licenciado Gutierre de Villegas. Bartolomé de Herrera. Ante mí, Alonso de Bados, escribano.

The formal accusation that heads the report, folio 1:

Acuso criminalmente a Gonzalo Ruiz de Bolaños e Juan Díaz Hidalgo, alcaldes ordinarios y Alonso Díaz Ibáñez y a Blas de Quesada y a los demás regidores que parescieren culpados, [1v] vecinos de la villa de Manzanares, y contando el caso digo que los susodichos con poco temor de Dios y menosprecio de la justicia de Vuestra Alteza, han dejado juntar y se han convocado todos los moriscos de la dicha villa de Manzanares que son mas de doscientos y de la Membrilla otros tantos, y so color que hacen una zuiza habrá tres meses poco mas o menos que traen armas que son espada e daga y han levantado capitán alférez y sargento e todos los domingos e fiestas se ejercitan en el campo en la dicha villa, tirando e disparando munchos arcabuces y enarbolando bandera con cinco medias lunas por insignia y al tiempo de recoger su escuadrón hablan en algarabía haciendo algazara de lo cual hay gran murmuración y escándalo en la dicha villa de Manzanares.

Juan Díaz Abad, folio 13:

Preguntado si le paresce que habiendo salido en esta dicha villa los cuarenta y tres moriscos contenidos en la dicha lista y los que salieron en la villa de la Membrilla qu'está a un cuarto de legua de la dicha villa con armas y ejercitados en la destreza dellas será tan de inconviniente para que munchos mas de los del dicho reino de Granada en las dichas dos villas de Manzanares y la Membrilla a los cuales podrían ejercitar en el uso de las dichas armas e hacerse poderosos para los que quisieren en los lugares circunvecinos y comarcanos que son munchos y pequeños, dijo que no pueden hacer cosa alguna respeto de ser la dicha villa de Manzanares grande y de muncha [13v] vecindad y los lugares circun-vecinos buenos pueblos grandes y que no bastaran para hacer daño todos los moriscos que ay en el Campo de Calatrava, cuanto y más los de las dichas dos villas de Manzanares y la Membrilla.

Juan de Velasco, 28 años, folio 19:

[Dijo que] no a vido escándalo de lo susodicho ni murmuración dello entre los vecinos de la dicha villa por ver los dichos moriscos con las dichas armas y uso y ejercicio dellas, antes la gente de la dicha villa [19v] de Manzanares y de los lugares circunvecinos que vinieron a la dicha fiesta se alegraron de vellos, atento que la dicha fiesta se hacía para hacer el ofrecimiento que hicieron para ayuda a dorar el retablo desta villa, que tiene grande necesidad d'ello.

Pedro Cuellocarrillo, chief bailiff (*alguacil mayor*), folio 23:

Este testigo vido que el día de nuestra señora otro día siguiente los dichos cristianos nuevos cautivaban en la plaza y llevaban a un tablado que estaba hecho en la plaza a modo de castillo, dentro del cual estaba Juan Ruiz de Bolaños, mayordomo de la iglesia de la dicha villa y Juan Díaz Abad y otras personas principales que recibían las limosnas que daban las personas que llevaban los dichos moriscos para dorar el retablo de la iglesia mayor de la dicha villa, para cuyo efe[c]to e fin se hizo la dicha fiesta y a esta causa entiende este testigo que los dichos alcaldes [23v] permitieron que hiciesen los dichos cristianos nuevos la dicha zuiza con armas espadas y dagas y alabardas y los dichos arcabuces y que a oído decir que se dejaron mas de mil y trescientos reales y las personas que ansí llevaban les daban en el dicho castillo colación y al tiempo que cautivaban bailaban y gritaban diciendo 'li, li' y llevándolos con este regocijo al dicho castillo para dicho efe[c]to … Que más de lo susodicho tiene por cierto este testigo que de sus haciendas los dichos naturales para la dicha obra dieron trescientos reales.

CHAPTER THIRTEEN

SANCHO PANZA AND THE MIMESIS OF SOLOMON:
MEDIEVAL JEWISH TRADITIONS IN *DON QUIJOTE*[1]

Francisco Peña Fernández

> *Then he ordered the cane to be broken open in the
> presence of everyone; and when this was done they
> found ten gold crowns incide. Whereupon everyone
> expressed astonishment, and hailed the governor as
> a New Solomon.*[2]

The above quote, in which the people of the Island of Barataria liken
Don Quijote's squire Sancho Panza to the figure of King Solomon,
constitutes the only explicit mention of the legendary Biblical monarch
in Cervantes' entire masterpiece. This paper seeks to show that this
allusion to the figure of Solomon is actually the culmination of a series
of intertextual echoes of Hebrew legends in *Don Quijote*. Although the
association between the squire Sancho Panza and King Solomon is
evident in different ways throughout the novel, I will focus especially
on a series of events linked to the episode of Sancho's governorship
in Barataria. The shadow of King Solomon in *Don Quijote* is not only
that of the monarch described in several books of the Bible, but also
the mythical Solomon popularized in diverse Hebrew and specifically
Judeo-Spanish legends that circulated throughout Spain in the Middle
Ages.

Carmen Vega Carney, bringing to light the "meticulous" study by
R. M. Flores, has summarized the main critical approaches to the character of Don Quijote's squire. Sancho has been considered—among other
things—a madman, a fool, a carnivalesque buffoon, an instrument for

---

[1] Parts of this paper appeared in a previous article: Francisco Peña Fernández.
"Medieval Traditions of Jewish Origin in the Episode of Sancho Panza and the Island
of Barataria" *South Atlantic Review* 72 (Special Issue: *Cultural Studies in the Spanish
Golden Age*) 2007, pp. 212–229.
[2] Miguel Cervantes, *Don Quixote*, trans. J. M. Cohen, Harmondsworth, Middlesex,
1950, II, XLV, p. 758.

satire, and the symbolic mother or wife of Don Quijote.[3] Specifically, Sancho's role as governor of the Island of Barataria has been regarded either as a touch of historical realism or as a manifestation of the concept of the "world upside down." According to the latter interpretation, Sancho, in becoming the ruler of an island, would be transformed into the exact opposite of his servile role as a knight's squire. Nonetheless, as we shall see, such an affirmation is not entirely true.

According to the concept of kingship characteristic of the Ancient Near East, all monarchs were at the same time servants. This is evident in various cycles of myths. For example, in the Canaanite pantheon, the god Baal—king of mankind—is at the same time the servant or "amusement" of the god Ilu—the heavenly monarch and universal ruler. This idea will later influence the concept of kingship among the Israelites. It becomes especially evident in the images of the early Jewish kings David and Solomon. David and Solomon both appear with the name Jedidiah, "beloved of Elohim." Such favor or predilection in Near Eastern courtly scenarios is also related to the fact of being "at the right hand" of the Master. The humble origins and servanthood of David, the founder of this royal dynasty, are evident in his double role as a shepherd in Bethlehem and the musician who entertains King Saul. This dual aspect of Israelite kings, which is described in the Bible, demonstrates that the roles of "squire" and "monarch" can be perfectly compatible, rather than contradictory. Although it is very possible that Cervantes did not necessarily take into account this concept, it is essential to remember that this idea reaches Christianity through the Messianic image of the Suffering Servant, the servant-king described by the prophet Isaiah. Later, in the Gospels, it will become identified with the figure of Christ as both king and servant of humankind. Nevertheless, it is clear that there are great differences between Don Quijote's faithful squire and the great monarch described in Biblical tradition. Sancho Panza is completely different from Solomon, especially with regard to his socioeconomic status and physical appearance. Let us remember that, unlike Solomon, Sancho is not tall, attractive, immensely wealthy, or irresistible to women.[4] In spite of this, in the episode of the Island of Barataria, certain similarities between the character of the

---

[3] Vega Carney,Carmen. "Justice in Barataria", *Romance Languages Annual* 2 (1990), pp. 586–597 (p. 586).

[4] Pablo Torijano, Solomon, the Esoteric King: from King to Magus, Development of a Tradition, Leiden, 2002, p. 28.

Cervantine squire and that of the Biblical monarch—such as wisdom and the search for justice—will bridge the gap that separates them. An analysis of the dynamic of opposition and likeness that links these two characters reveals a rich spectrum of intertextual allusions, and thus, a new perspective from which we can approach not only Sancho Panza but also the very process of Cervantes' literary construction.

Sancho as Hameléj or Ruler

An aspect that captures the attention not only of the readers of *Don Quijote* but also of the inhabitants of the invented Island of Barataria is Sancho Panza's ability to govern the people with justice. Everyone is struck by the squire's wisdom in his role as judge of the various legal cases brought before him. Likewise, all are amazed by Sancho's eloquence, made all the more striking since both the readers of the novel and those who live in the supposed kingdom know that his opportunity to govern is nothing but a prank. Thus, the speechless witnesses of Sancho's "good government" find a double explanation for this amazing phenomenon: the peasant-governor's wisdom must be the result either of divine favor or of magic.

Let us look first, for a moment, at the element of "divine favor." The concept of wisdom inspired by God serves to connect the figures of Sancho Panza and Solomon if we take into account the observations made by Augustin Redondo in his well-known study on carnivalesque elements in the episode of Barataria Island. This expert on Cervantes establishes an interesting connection between the squire's "good government" and the figure of the madman associated with Carnival:

> To be a *madman* or a *fool* is to have one's head sufficiently empty, and one's mind sufficiently distanced from ordinary worries and from worldly concerns to be able to receive the breath of the Holy Spirit, so that the *pneuma* can fill the head and exit through the channel of speech. Therein lies the importance of carnivalesque rituals designed to allow the freeing of the head and the circulation of the Breath of the Holy Spirit.[5]

---

[5] "Ser *loco* o *tonto* es tener la cabeza lo bastante vacía, la mente lo bastante apartada de las preocupaciones ordinarias, de las solicitudes del mundo, para poder recibir el soplo del Espíritu Santo, para que el *pneuma* pueda llenar la cabeza y salir por el canal del habla. De ahí la importancia de los ritos carnavalescos destinados a permitir la liberación de la cabeza y la circulación del Soplo del Espíritu Santo." See "Tradición

King Solomon, just as he is described in the First Book of Kings, receives his wisdom by means of God's action. After experiencing a dream, or *incubatio*, the monarch asks God to grant him that gift above all others. Therefore, Solomon's wisdom is a knowledge induced by the action of Yahweh, not acquired through study or learning. The legendary tradition not only preserves this element in the description of Solomon's intelligence and prudent actions, but also extends and enhances it: Solomon's good judgements occur thanks to the support and inspiration provided by the *Ruaj hakodesh* ("the Sacred Spirit"). Likewise, all misfortune occurs when this holy force is absent. In this respect, both Sancho's intelligence and his popular wisdom are related to the wisdom of Solomon. In contrast to the supposed erudition of other characters such as Sansón Carrasco, the wisdom of Sancho Panza, like that of King Solomon, does not come from the halls of a university.

Cervantine criticism has dedicated much effort to understanding the possible double reading of Sancho's apparent stupidity and at the same time clear intelligence. Some experts admit that Sancho, in his role as judge, behaves in a Solomonic manner.[6] However, the fact that this observation is presented as quite obvious could indicate that the critics themselves have not focused on the reasons for or the nature of the connections between Sancho and King Solomon. As we shall see, these need to be explored further as a means of illuminating the coexistence of ignorance and intelligence in Sancho Panza and understanding his evolution as a character as the novel unfolds.

Both Don Quijote's squire and King Solomon, in their respective positions of leadership, are examples of justice, equanimity, defense of the weak, support of the oppressed, and, in general, righteous action. In addition, their personalities are composed of a combination of Epicurean and Dionysiac elements. According to Pilar Romeu Ferré: "Solomon had a great aesthetic sense of life. He enjoyed wine, women, music and conversation."[7] Thus, the concept of a good monarch is not associated with a sober, Apollinean ideal. Rather, it is linked to closeness to the people and enjoyment of life.

---

carnavelesca y creación literaria: El personaje de Sancho Panza" in Agustin Redondo, *Otra manera de leer El Quijote*, Madrid, 1997, pp. 191–203 (p. 200). My translation.

[6] Ludovik Osterc, "Actualidad del gobierno de Sancho Panza," in Ludovik Osterc, Dulcinea y otros ensayos cervantinos, Mexico, 1987, p. 83.

[7] Pilar Romeu Ferré, *Leyendas del Rey Salomón en textos sefardíes*. Barcelona, 1999, p. 11: "Salomón tenía un gran sentido estético de la vida. Gozaba con el vino, las mujeres, la música y la conversación."

A second parallel between the two rulers is the location of their respective "kingdoms." In this case, it is necessary to refer exclusively to legendary sources. In narratives about Solomon that circulated in medieval times, his kingdom is not confined to the geographical borders of Ancient Israel. Rather, it gets transformed into a universal realm that acquires elements of fantasy and also rich symbolism: "Selomó hamélec was a great king who ruled the Holy Land, by the grace of God, from one end of the world to the other."[8] The kingdom of Barataria is not only an imaginary place, but also an indefinite one. The governing monarch does not know where it begins or ends, how he got there, and not even whether it really is an island or not. Nevertheless, and in spite of the fact that certain experts have attempted to specify the exact geographical location of Barataria, what remains clear is that Cervantes does not consider this spatial detail important. The lack of a specific location and the universality of the "kingdoms" of Sancho and Solomon give both of them an exemplary character.

Sancho's Judgements

The first three of Sancho's "judgments" clearly take their inspiration from the Biblical figure of Solomon as the ideal monarch. Nevertheless, legendary or folk elements are also present in all of them. The popular, folk nature of the Solomon legends makes it more difficult to defend the hypothesis of a single origin of the stories that may have served as Cervantes' source of inspiration. Maxime Chevalier, summarizing the different critical opinions with regard to Sancho's first three judgments, asserts that the first of these is more directly linked to the Biblical tradition than the others. This is because the solution to the case involves splitting the disputed object between the two parties, just like the case of the baby described in the Book of Kings.[9] Without disputing Chevalier's observations, if we return for a moment to the quote with which this paper began, one can ask a rather intriguing question: Why is it that Sancho's courtiers identify him explicitly with King Solomon after the second of his judgments rather than the first? This would imply that

---

[8] Hesec-Selomo, p. 9: "Selomó hamélej hue un rey grande que lo enreinó el Santo, bendicho Él, de cabo de el mundo hasta su cabo."

[9] Maxime Chevalier. "Sancho Panza y la cultura escrita", *Studies in Honor of Bruce W. Wardropper.* D. Fox, H. Sieber and R. Ter Horst eds., Newark, 1989, pp. 67–73.

the popular legends regarding Solomon circulated more widely than the information available in the Biblical text. This, in turn, provides evidence for assuming an oral tradition much more widespread than the "official" or scriptural tradition.

In identifying these traditions within the different judgments, one can see that the connection with Solomon is not limited to the first of these, but rather is present in all three. The brief episodes of Sancho's judgments all possess a series of characteristics in common with those of Solomon. First, the objective of both sets of stories is to prove the king's wisdom as a judge. Secondly, both in the popular legends of Jewish origin regarding Solomon that circulated in the Middle Ages and in the episodes of Sancho as judge in Barataria, the disputing parties are mainly poor people that appear in the governor's court seeking his help. Lastly, the cases are solved with amazing speed and efficiency. The characters that play the role of the tricksters are discovered and punished, while the innocent are freed and rewarded.

In the first of Sancho's judgements, the case of the caps, these characteristics are easy to find. It is interesting to note that the third aspect—the efficiency of the judge—is explicitly mentioned by a very self-confident Sancho: "There seems to me no need for long delays in this suit; it can be decided on the spot by a wise man's judgement."[10] Nonetheless, the opposition between trickster and victim is not as evident as in the other two judicial cases. As we will see, Sancho's second and third cases have more elements in common with the typology of the legends about Solomon than the first.

The second of Sancho's judgements is the one that has the clearest Hebrew roots. The legend of the Hidden Coins, one of the tales of Solomon's judgements in the *Exempla of the Rabbis* (*Exemplum* 121a) appears also in *Levitico Rabba* 6, 3, *Nedarin* 25a and the *Pesikta Rabbati* 22, 6. On the other hand, this case presents a characteristic that is strongly emphasized in the episodes of the legendary Solomon as judge: there are no witnesses and, in fact, witnesses are unnecessary. This factor, which is strongly rooted in popular tradition, is intimately linked to the figure of Solomon[11] and serves to accentuate the exceptional quality of the judge. In the legend of The Disinherited One, which is

---

[10] *Don Quixote*, II, XLV, p. 756.
[11] Stith Thompson, *Motif Index of Folk Literature*, Bloomington, Indiana, 1989, J11140.1.

part of the *Sipure maasiyot*, Solomon's greatness and brilliance stand out against those of his own father, David, since Solomon needs no witnesses to resolve a case. Other elements present in Sancho's second case that mirror those of Solomon's judgements are the false oath, and above all, the hidden coins. For example, in a popular medieval legend, Solomon is able to successfully identify a fraud when he finds some ducats hidden in the bottom of jars of honey by the man who plays the role of the trickster. A final detail is the source of "inspiration" for the verdict given by Sancho: "it had occurred to him" ["le vino a la imaginación"][12]

The third of Sancho's judicial cases includes the appearance of a character that is a recurring motif in the Solomon legends: the manipulative or deceitful woman. This role, which is inspired in that of the wicked prostitute recorded in the Book of Kings, appears in different legendary stories such as "Women's Infidelity" and "The Dishonest Wife and the Bandit". While in the legends about Solomon it is not common to find the image of the virtuous woman, we do find it in the episodes related to the Island of Barataria as well as in the entire *Don Quijote*.

The Impersonated King and the Enthroned Squire

Of all the medieval legends regarding King Solomon, the one that is most interestingly connected to the story of Sancho Panza's governorship of Barataria Island is a set of stories that revolve around the theme of Solomon's exile, or the usurpation of Solomon on the throne by the demon Asmodeus. The relationship between this set of legends and the story of Sancho's experiences as governor of the island is deeper and more complex than the episodes of the verdicts, since it involves a system of parallels in terms of structure, characters, and plot.

The legend of the king's supplantation tells how Solomon, after being deceived by Asmodeus, prince of demons, is dethroned and forced to live as a wandering beggar for three years. Whether it is because the king is able to find the ring that grants him his power, or due to the people's complaints to those living in the palace, or thanks to the fact that Solomon's mother, Bathsheeba, recognizes the trickster, the king returns to his throne and thus learns an important lesson. All the

---

[12] *Don Quijote*, II, XLV, p. 758.

versions of the legend exhibit a clear ethical or moralizing purpose with respect to the king's sins. In some of these variants, this characteristic is emphasized so much that, although Asmodeus is the perpetrator of Solomon's exile, it appears as God's decision.

The connection between these medieval Jewish stories and Sancho's experiences on the Island of Barataria is structured like a set of two parallel mirrors; since both narratives correspond to each other, but their reflection shows an inverse image. Solomon and Sancho, in spite of appearing like opposites, are not at all antagonists. The parallels between the brief interlude in the reign of the legendary Solomon and the equally brief, and about as legendary, governorship of Sancho Panza granted him by the Duke are most evident in terms of structure. The schematic list below summarizes the parallel but inverse main events that make up both stories.

1. Ascent of Solomon to the heavens followed by descent.	1. Ascent of Sancho to the heavens and descent after the flight of Clavileño.
2. Deception by Asmodeus.	2. Deception by the Duke.
3. Development of story of the usurped throne and the enthroned demon.	3. Development of the story of the squire turned governor and of the Duke turned squire.
4. Return to the initial condition after a process of anagnorisis.	4. Return to the initial condition after a process of anagnorisis.

Flight and Immediate Descent

The main parallel between the stories is that both include a rite of passage of their respective protagonists, Solomon and Sancho, which will cause a radical change in their behavior. Solomon is described at the beginning of most of the versions and variants of the legend as a character that, in spite of being wise and generous, often brags about his power. Likewise, many critics have labeled Sancho Panza's initial attitude as "immediately prior to his Quixotization." Although Sancho exhibits a much more developed imagination than he had when he first became a squire, his behavior before the ascent with the aid of the flying horse Clavileño and his subsequent arrival on the Island of Barataria is reminiscent of the Sancho of Part One. Victor Oeschlager affirms that: "During the gradual *Quixotization* of Sancho the hardest lessons that he has to learn are his own limitations, a more intellectual-spiritual and less materialistic perspective of relative values, the necessity for perseverance, and the virtue of altruistic self-sacrifice."[13] Even just before beginning his ascent, Sancho has to be threatened constantly by the Duke so that he will perform this feat. As Oeschlager points out, Sancho exhibits no spirit of renunciation and sacrifice. Likewise, this episode also emphasizes the issue of cowardice versus the spirit of chivalry.

The dethronement of Solomon and his sudden "descent" from the heavenly spheres constitutes a complete transformation of the king, since not only does he turn into a vagrant, but it is impossible for anyone to identify him as Solomon. From being the possessor of uncountable riches, he immediately becomes a poor man, and his power turns into dispossession. Curiously, in the case of Sancho, the events have opposite effects; but the character's attitude is parallel to that of King Solomon.

According to Franklin O. Brantley, "Sancho's remarkable change of character occurs directly as a consequence of the Clavileño trick."[14] This change infuses Sancho with self-confidence. His materialistic interests begin to disappear as they start to "become a reality." Brantley cites different sources that could have inspired the description of the flight, including descriptions of the cosmos by Ptolemy, Cicero, Lucan, Boetius, Luis de León, Boccaccio, and, lastly, *Christophoro Gnophoso* (40*ff*). Likewise, it is interesting to note certain parallels with the flight described in the Solomon narratives. One of the most curious elements is the fact that both squire and king engage in play with heavenly bodies. In Sancho's case, the seven little goats [the Pleiades] are mentioned, while Solomon refers to the *malayin* or angels. Another aspect in which the Solomon legend is intertwined with the story of Clavileño's flight is the squire's fear of meeting demons. Sancho, riding on the magic horse, asks Don Quijote, "is it surprising that I'm afraid there may be some region of devils hereabouts, who will bear us off to Peralvillo."[15] In Ephesians 6:12 and some other references from the Bible we find

---

[13] Victor R. B. Oelschlager, "Sancho's Zest for the Quest", *Hispania* 35.1 (1952), pp. 18–24 (p. 21).

[14] Franklin O. Brantley, "Sancho's Ascent into the Spheres," *Hispania* 53 (1970), pp. 37–45 (p. 39).

[15] *Don Quixote*, II, XLI, p. 730.

the possibility of finding "spiritual wickedness in high places."[16] This Second Temple Jewish tradition is not as easy to find in later Christian iconography, in which demons inhabit hell or travel to the earth where they tempt mortals. They never live in Heaven. However, the possibility of finding demons in the heavens does exist in the medieval Jewish tradition, specifically in *Merkabah* mystic narratives. In fact, in the stories regarding Solomon's exile, Asmodeus and his legions of devils do not necessarily live in hell, but rather in the heavenly spheres, where they can deceive Solomon.

One of the recurring qualities attributed to the figure of the legendary Solomon is the possibility of flying, which is strongly linked to his magical powers. This characteristic is evident in various forms. A very common element in numerous Near Eastern tales is the ability to cast spells on rugs to turn them into air transportation. Another is the possibility of flying on a horse.

Franklin Brantley, while analyzing the possible meaning of the flight of the horse Clavileño, observes the following:

> The Clavileño trick, then, was an event of great importance in the life of Sancho Panza. As he recalled the experience, it was much like the legendary flights: he rose to the heavens and saw their grandeur, looked down to the earth and saw how insignificant it actually was. His ascent was an illusion, of course; but this illusion provoked an act of will…[17]

This experience marks a true turning point between the character of Sancho in the previous chapters and the one that appears after the Clavileño episode. In the context of this paper, the shift is once again linked to the figure of the legendary Solomon. Sancho's flight constitutes a rite of passage that inversely reflects the dethronement of Solomon. It also brings to mind two other aspects of the Solomon legends: the

---

[16] Ephesians 6:12 specifies the location of spiritual forces of evil in the heavenly realms; see also Ephesians 1:20*ff.* and 3:10; Philippians 2:10. Ephesians 2:2 mentions the "kingdom of the air", between earth and the divine abode. These spirits coincide, in part, with what Paul elsewhere calls the "basic principles" of the world. See Galatians 4:3.

"Satan and the other fallen angels are confined in a prison (= *pit*) that is located in the firmament, according to the Ascension of Isaiah, and in the second heaven, according to II Enoch. The idea that Satan's current dwelling place is in the lower heavens is the common representation found in the New Testament. Thus, Christ '…saw Satan fall like lightning from heaven' (Luke 10:18). Paul locates the 'spiritual forces of evil in *epouranois* [heavenly realms]" (Ephesians 6:12) and Michael hurls Satan to the earth (Revelation 12:8–9)…" J. Daniélou, "Teología del judeocristianismo," p. 123 (my translation).

[17] Brantley, p. 43.

motif of the magic flight on horseback and the explicit mention of seeing people as ants. The latter is directly connected to the lesson in humility that Sancho must learn. In another Solomon legend, a queen ant reminds the king that human beings must not allow themselves to be controlled by the vanity of their power.

> On one occasion he strayed into the valley of the ants in the course of his wanderings. He heard one ant order all the others to withdraw, to avoid being crushed by the armies of Solomon. The king halted and summoned the ant that had spoken. She told him that she was the queen of the ants, and she gave her reasons for the order of withdrawal. Solomon wanted to put a question to the ant queen, but she refused to answer unless the king took her up and placed her on his hand. He acquiesced, and then he put his question: "Is there any one greater than I am in all the world?" "Yes," said the ant.
> Solomon: "Who?"
> Ant: "I am."
> Solomon: "How is that possible?"
> Ant: "Were I not greater than thou, God would not have led thee hither to put me on thy hand."
> Exasperated, Solomon threw her to the ground, and said: "Thou knowest who I am? I am Solomon, the son of David."[18]

Moreover, it is essential to note the role of Sancho's imagination in the Clavileño episode, since the flight makes him connect his fantasy with the legends of Solomon. Likewise, the flying horse episode in Part II of the novel has an interesting parallel in Part I. The squire, aided by his master's imagination, justifies his rapid return from El Toboso by choosing the mode of transportation that most closely resembles that of the legendary Solomon:

> But do you know what does astonish me, Sancho? You must have gone and returned through the air. For you have only taken three days travelling to El Toboso and back, and it is a good ninety miles. For which I conclude that the sage necromancer, who is my friend and looks after my affairs—for I certainly have such a friend, or I should not be a true knight errant—I say that this necromancer must have have assisted you on your journey without you knowing it…
> "That may be so," said Sancho, "for certainly Rocinante went like a gipsy's ass with quicksilver in its ears.[19]

---

[18] Louis Ginzberg, *The legends of the Jews*, volume IV. Philadelphia, 2003, p. 7.
[19] Don Quixote, I, XXXI, pp. 270–271.

Lastly, the flight of Clavileño can be interpreted as an independent "rite," or as a symbol of one.[20] However, from the perspective of this study, the episode of the flying horse constitutes the introductory phase of Sancho's rite of passage on the Island of Barataria, an episode parallel to the legends of Solomon's exile. In the rite of passage, the neophyte finds himself in a place radically disassociated from his previous existence. As we will see, the stages of the initiation rites of both Sancho and Solomon generally conform to the sequence that Anthony Wallace has termed "ritual learning process":[21] The *prelearning* or *anticipation* phase is the flight into the heavens. The *separation* phase corresponds to Sancho's arrival in Barataria and Solomon's transformation into a wandering beggar. The *suggestion* phase involves Solomon's renunciation of his wealth and Sancho's fast. The *execution* stage refers to Sancho's judgements and Solomon's adventures as a wanderer, while *maintenance* occurs with the repetition or succession of such episodes. The final stage, *anagnorisis* or *recognition*, occurs when both characters go through a *liminal* situation that signifies rebirth.

The Antagonists: Asmodeus and the Duke

The relationship between Sancho and Solomon, as mentioned before, can best be described with the analogy of parallel mirrors. While one loses his power, the other acquires it. While one is stripped of his role as monarch, the other is "dressed" as such. Apparently, one occupies the position of the other. As discussed in the previous section, Sancho becomes a second Solomon, but he behaves like him rather than as his opposite. At the same time, the squire-turned-ruler will learn a similar moral lesson to that of the legendary monarch during his exile. In the narratives regarding the dethronement of Solomon, the antagonist is Asmodeus, the most highly developed trickster figure in medieval Jewish tradition. Asmodeus also represents some of Solomon's flaws taken to the extreme. These include lust, vanity, and greed. On the other hand, he represents the image of the bad ruler: He does not take care of his subjects; he does not reign with justice; he does not worry about the

---

[20] Agustin Redondo, "De Don Clavijo a Clavileño: Algunos aspectos de la tradición carnavalesca y cazurra en El Quijote (II, 38–41)," *Edad de Oro* 3 (1984), pp. 181–199 (p. 186).

[21] Anthony F. C. Wallace, *Religion: An Anthropological View*, New York, 1966.

oppressed. In short, he is the idle king whose only preoccupation is satisfying his own vices and whims.

One of the most outstanding tricksters in *Don Quijote* is the Duke, a character that in many ways resembles that of Asmodeus in the Solomon legend. He is undoubtedly a deceiver who, at the beginning of Don Quijote and Sancho's stay in the palace, conceives and facilitates the squire's "exile" as governor. Then, as part of his duty as a host, the Duke adopts Sancho's previous role. When Sancho goes off to the island and is separated from his master, the Duke becomes a surrogate companion-servant of Don Quijote. However, just as Asmodeus is a bad ruler because he only pays attention to his own desires and interests, the Duke turns out to be a bad companion for the knight of La Mancha, since he is unable to mitigate the extreme loneliness that Don Quijote experiences in the ducal palace. In the same way that Asmodeus is a false king, the Duke proves to be a false host and a false friend. In addition, Asmodeus—as a "fallen angel"—is the worst of all servants, and he will likewise become the worst of kings. This legendary prince of demons—who is characterized by idleness, lust, and lack of concern—is responsible for the misfortunes that befall humankind. In *Don Quijote*, the Duke is presented as the worst ruler of the people of Barataria, since we can infer that he does not pay any attention to the needs of his subjects. The demonization of the Duke clearly points to the possibility of a sociohistorical reading: The idle aristocrat is symbolic of the social class that is largely responsible for the evils that plague Spain, since its members do not worry about the well-being of their subjects. In a sense, the aristocracy turns the world upside down. Ironically, during the Duke's "rule" of the inhabitants of Barataria, there is an absence of government; while the squire proves to be the best of rulers. Sancho Panza's ideal government of Barataria is a direct reflection of that of King Solomon. Like the legendary Jewish monarch, the Cervantine squire remains close to the poor, solves real disputes, and governs efficiently. Thus, it is important to realize that, in this game of parallel mirrors, Sancho is not the opposite of Solomon but rather of the Duke.

The Purification Phase: Rule and Exile

The figure of the Biblical Solomon possesses two contradictory facets that were later taken up and amplified by the legendary tradition: On the one hand, Solomon is an ideal king. However, at the end of his reign, he brings about the ruin and separation of the people of Israel. He is accused of not knowing how to curb his "constant desire" and of letting it control him. In addition, he is said to have accumulated too many riches, horses, and women. His sin is the most common one in the Old Testament, that of excess or *hubris*. In the narratives concerning the rule of Asmodeus, King Solomon is given the opportunity to redeem himself and be purified by means of a rite of passage. For an interval of three years, he must descend to the position of a wandering beggar. As such, the king loses his power and wealth, thus learning to recognize his greed.

In Don Quijote's advice to Sancho Panza, we see a foreshadowing of the misfortunes that will befall the squire during his term as governor of Barataria. Don Quijote advises Sancho, "Eat little at dinner and less at supper…"[22] The diet to which Sancho is subjected turns his experience as governor into a veritable season of Lent. On the other hand, in having to refrain from food—one of the things he desires most—Sancho begins to doubt what his original dreams and aspirations were. Likewise, in the legends regarding the exile of King Solomon, there is explicit mention of the hunger that the dethroned monarch-turned-beggar must endure. The association of Solomon with food takes a somewhat contradictory turn in one of the variants of the exile legend. In that particular version, the monarch is transformed into a governor's cook, and it is by means of his great talent in the kitchen that he is able to win the heart of a princess and the favor of a king. Both the Solomon-as-beggar story and governor Sancho Panza's diet highlight the hero's need to prove his excellence in the face of adversity. They also emphasize the actual process of purification, by means of the adventure itself. Fasting is a key element in this process, in both the Jewish legend and Cervantes' novel.

Return to the Initial Situation: Anagnorisis

One of the characteristics that makes Sancho Panza most likeable to the readers of *Don Quijote* is the squire's constant humility during his

---

[22] *Don Quixote*, II, XLIII, p. 741.

rule as governor of the Island of Barataria. In contrast to the arrogance
and material interest that his wife and daughter exhibit when they learn
of his new position, the peasant Sancho continues to feel proud of his
humble origins. This attitude, in turn, is what allows him to judge with
fairness all the cases put before him. His closeness to the common
people is his secret for being a good governor. In a similar fashion, the
legends of Solomon's transformation into a wandering beggar describe
his constant contact with the poor and those who live a simple life, far
away from the luxury of the palace. Yet, living as a beggar helps Solomon get closer to his subjects; whereas for Sancho, life in "the palace"
makes him never want to desire power and wealth.

Sancho's fall into the pit, which is parallel to Don Quijote's descent
into the Cave of Montesinos, constitutes the last stage of Sancho's rite
of passage. Just as in one of the legends of Solomon's exile, before the
hero can make a complete return to his initial situation there must be
a moment of recognition, either of his own origins or by those who
are closest to him. In Solomon's case, this anagnorisis is linked to his
mother, Bathsheeba, and to Benayahu, the chief of the army. The former
represents Solomon's return to his origins, and the latter, a return to
his obligations.

> "Do you have any proof that you are Solomon?"
> He said: "Yes, and the proof is that at the beginning of my rule, my father
> took my hand and clasped it in his and the other hand he gave to Natán
> Manabí and then my mother held the head of my father."
> [...]
> At that moment they placed the seal in Solomon's hand and his face
> changed to its former likeness.[23]

The hero must show who he is, but those who should recognize him
cannot do so. In the case of Sancho in the pit, Don Quijote cannot
even see him.

> "Who is that down there? Who is it crying out?"
> "Who else could it be crying out," came the answer, "but the forlorn
> Sancho Panza, Governor, for his sins and misfortune, of the Isle Barataria,
> once squire to that famous knight, Don Quixote de la Mancha?"
> (...)

---

[23] Romeu Ferré, p. 60.

> "I conjure you by all that is holy to tell me as a Catholic Christian who you are. And if you are a soul in purgatory tell me what you wish me to do for you."
>
> (…)
>
> "A famous witness!" cried Don Quixote. "I recognize that bray as if it were my own child, and I know your voice, dear Sancho. Wait for me. I will go to the Duke's castle, which is nearby, and bring someone to get you out of that pit, where your sins must have cast you."[24]

A series of interesting parallels is evident in the final stage of the rite of passage of each hero. In the first place, we see the importance of recognition: it is essential for the hero to prove that he is who he says he is because he cannot be recognized or even seen. Although in Cervantes' novel the comic tone is maintained in the detail of the braying, there is a clear reference to the process of birth, with Don Quijote taking on a maternal role. After this adventure, Sancho will be reborn, having been reconciled with his true origins, and return to the place that is his own.

The final, and essential, element is the actual moment of anagnorisis. King Solomon asks himself:

> Where is my reign? Where are my concubines? Nothing has helped me at this time. Except that all who humble themselves in this world, the Holy One, blessed be He, exalts them.[25]

Sancho Panza's awakening to a new life is very similar. From the depths of the pit, the squire exclaims:

> [W]hat unexpected accidents do happen at every turn to those that live in this miserable world! Who would have said that the man who saw himself yesterday enthroned as the Governor of an isle, commanding his servants and his vassals, would find himself to-day buried in a pit without a soul to relieve him, or a servant or vassal too come to his aid?[26]

Thus, the squire is liberated from the material burden that stood between him and his master and friend, Don Quijote. The process of anagnorisis leads to catharsis. However, as Aristotle points out in his description of tragedy, it is a catharsis by means of mimesis. In the case of Sancho Panza, the model for mimesis or imitation is Solomon.

---

[24] *Don Quixote*, II, LV, p. 826.
[25] Romeo Ferré, p. 61. My translation.
[26] *Don Quixote*, II, LV, p. 823.

The rule of Sancho finally disappears, as if by magic: the spell, as happens in the case of Solomon, is broken and comes to an end: "…Sancho's governorship vanished into shadows and smoke.…"[27]

Outside Barataria

> Don Quixote, in Cervantes' novel, is a typical example of the victim of triangular desire, but is far from being the only one. Next to him the most affected is his squire, Sancho Panza. Some of Sancho's desires are not imitated: for example, those aroused by the sight of cheese or a goatskin of wine. But Sancho has other ambitions besides filling his stomach. Ever since he has been with Don Quixote he has been dreaming of an "island" of which he would be governor, and he wants the title of duchess for his daughter. These desires do not come spontaneously to a simple man like Sancho. It is Don Quixote who has put them into his head.[28]

In his landmark study, *Deceit, Desire, and the Novel*, Rene Girard proposes an extremely important structural model that serves to illuminate Cervantes' masterpiece: the triangular configuration governing the force of desire in the characters of *Don Quijote*. As the French scholar indicates, the protagonist's mimetic desire, which is mediated by the figure of the literary knight Amadís of Gaul, is the axis and driving force of the novel. Likewise, the concept of triangular desire applies to Sancho Panza in that Don Quijote functions as mediator between the squire's desires and the possibility of fulfilling them. However, keeping in mind that the motivations of knight and squire are different, we will see that Sancho's desires are not governed by the mere imitation of his master, but are mediated by another—implicit and explicit—role model: the figure of King Solomon.

Let us remember that Sancho Panza's greatest aspiration, which is undoubtedly suggested and fueled by Don Quijote's promises, is that of becoming the governor of an island. As has been demonstrated in the analysis of certain episodes from Part II that culminate in the squire's brief rule of Barataria, the recurring and quite direct role model that mediates Sancho's desire is the Jewish monarch, both in his Biblical and especially his legendary facets. Nonetheless, one may ask if the Barataria

---

[27] Burton Raffel trans. *Don Quijote by Miguel de Cervantes*, New York, 1995, p. 628.
[28] Rene Girard, "'Triangular' desire in Don Quixote," in *Don Quixote: The Ormsby Translation, Revised. Backgrounds and Sources. Criticism*, Joseph R. Jones and Kenneth Douglas, eds., New York, 1981, pp. 945–955 (p. 946).

episode alone provide sufficient evidence to prove that Sancho Panza's object of mimesis is King Solomon. To what extent can one perceive the influence of the Biblical and legendary king as the squire's role model in episodes prior to the chapter in which Sancho finally obtains his much-yearned governorship of the island?

In order to answer this question, we must return to certain episodes in which Sancho expresses his desires with a vehemence akin to that of his yearning for the island. In one of the more significant instances, the squire, driven by purely materialistic motivations, appears willing to exchange the possibility of fulfilling his dream of becoming a governor for another prospect that could prove to generate even greater wealth: obtaining the recipe for the famed magic Balm of Fierabrás. The importance of Sancho's desire for this potion lies in the fact that the power to perform magic spells and charms is a characteristic of the extra-biblical King Solomon which proves to be even more important and recurrent than his status as ruler. In this sense, Sancho's desire to manufacture magic potions mirrors that of his legendary role model. Another aspect of Solomon's magic powers is reflected in the squire's flight on the wooden steed Clavileño, since, as mentioned previously, King Solomon was endowed with the supernatural ability to make horses take flight. Likewise, a parodic reference to this power appears in Part I, when Sancho—shortly after the theft of his donkey—manages to travel to El Toboso and back in record speed on Rocinante, thus emulating the legendary Hebrew monarch.

Sancho's imagination and vehement desire also link him to the Solomon of the Old Testament and of popular legend in the area of relationships with the female sex. In contrast to the Jewish king, Don Quijote's squire is anything but a seducer. Nevertheless, it is helpful to bear in mind that the interest in women which is evident both in Solomon and Sancho Panza is motivated by a similar desire, for material gain. King Solomon's numerous marriages to foreign princesses—while considered scandalous by traditional Jewish standards—constitute political alliances that serve to increase his wealth and power. Likewise, Sancho Panza exhibits his materialistic desires as well as other details of Solomonic mimesis in his praise of two beautiful women: Dorotea, as transformed into the fictitious Princess Micomicona (I. 29–30); and Quiteria, bride of the wealthy farmer Camacho (II. 20–21).

According to the narrator, a first glimpse of Dorotea/Micomicona produces in Sancho an even stronger reaction than in the priest and in

Cardenio. Sancho, upon seeing her, springs into action immediately: he must learn more about this exotic lady.

> But most admiring of all was Sancho Panza, who thought that he had never seen so lovely a creature in all the days of his life—and indeed he had not. He asked the priest most insistently to tell him who this beautiful lady was, and what she was looking for in those wild parts.
> "This beautiful lady, brother Sancho," replied the priest, "is, to be very brief, heiress in the direct male line of the great Kingdom of Micomicón. She has come to your master to beg of him a boon…For thanks to your master's reputation as a brave knight throughout all the known world, this princess has come from Guinea in quest of him."[29]

Let us remember that Dorotea—in order to successfully hunt down her seducer—had reinvented herself by dressing as a man. Then the priest transformed her into a princess. Finally Sancho reinvents her once more, putting into practice his peculiar powers of imagination: "And the lady herself is the high and mighty princess Micomicona, Queen of the great Kingdom of Micomicón in Ethiopia."[30]

Sancho's transformation of a princess from Guinea into one from Ethiopia is not casual, since according to medieval tradition, Ethiopia was believed to be the location of the kingdom governed by the Queen of Sheba.[31] Once again, Don Quijote's squire locates the object of his Sancho's "confusion" of these two women leads desire within the legendary world of King Solomon. In fact, we can speak, to a certain degree, of a recognition. Not only is Princess Micomicona seen as a new Queen of Sheba, but also to a deeper typological identification that links the figure of the African queen to that of the invented princess. In the *Targum Sheni* of the Book of Esther, the Ethiopian Queen of Sheba presents a group of six thousand youths—male and female—to King Solomon. All of these were born the same day and at the same hour,

---

[29] *Don Quixote*, I, XXIX, p. 251.
[30] Ibid., p. 253.
[31] The identification of the fictitious Princess Micomicona with the legendary Queen of Sheba is already suggested by the priest's description of Micomicona as the heiress, in a direct male line, to the throne of the Kingdom of Micomicón. An Ethiopian legend about the Queen of Sheba preserved in a pictorial sequence depicts the moment when her father, King Agabos, presents his little daughter, known as Azieb, to the people and names her his direct successor. The pictures show the adult Queen Azieb learning of Solomon's fame from a Jewish merchant and illustrate her famed visit to Solomon. They also depict the Ethiopian queen's relationship with the king, which produced a son, Menelik, founder of the Abyssinian Dynasty (Sölle 196–197).

are of the same height, and are in identical royal purple attire. The king is unable to distinguish the females from the males. According to Jacob Lassner, the nature of the test is to prove that women are equal to men when it comes to fulfilling certain roles. The legendary king despises not only the stratagem of the Queen of Sheba, but also the idea that a woman dare disguise herself as a man. The thematic parallels between the legends surrounding the Queen of Sheba and the Dorotea episodes in *Don Quijote* are not limited to the motif of women cross-dressing as men. Both Cervantes' Dorotea and the legendary Queen of Sheba, as depicted in the *Pseudo Ben Sira*, are involved in stories of men who abuse their power over women and of women who attempt to overcome such abuse. Both Dorotea and the Queen of Sheba fit into the model of the determined woman who fights against the traditional roles assigned to her and, as far as possible, tries to subvert them. Thus, in numerous Jewish legends, the figure of the Queen of Sheba becomes demonized and linked to that of Lilith. This female demon, which was identified by rabbis as Adam's first wife, was punished for rebelling against male domination of women.

Rene Girard, in his specific analysis of "Triangular" Desire in *Don Quixote*', points out that the social class difference that separates the squire from the knight keeps them from entering into conflict with each other, even though they share the same desire. This is true regarding Sancho's interest in Princess Micomicona, since a mere squire cannot hope to fulfill his desire for a princess. Thus, Sancho's desire, which, let us recall, is purely materialistic, must be obtained by means of Don Quijote. Let us recall also that Sancho urges his master to aid the distressed Princess Micomicona and then marry her. Thus, Sancho hopes to "possess" Micomicona's wealth and power through Don Quijote, but using King Solomon as the role model of his desire.

In the chapter dealing with the wedding of Camacho the Rich, the references to the world of Solomon are even clearer than in the previously discussed episode, since the story leads us to an Old Testament text rather than to legendary or extra-biblical sources. The facet of Solomon as poet, both as author of wisdom literature as well as love poetry, is evident in several books of the Bible. The latter genre is exemplified in the Song of Solomon. Although the king is not a character in this book of the Bible, he is presented as its author, and tradition has also granted him the lead role in this song of two lovers. The important issue here is that in the Biblical poem, the depiction of the king is that of a ruler that excels more for his wealth and splendor than for his wisdom. The figure of King Solomon constitutes the principal illustration of excess and exhuberance in the Bible. That same excess is praised by Sancho Panza in the Cervantine episode of Camacho's wedding. In spite of the countless theological readings to which the Song of Solomon has been subjected throughout history, the connection between this poem and the wedding celebration described in Part II of *Don Quijote* is to be found at a much more secular level. One of the most obvious sources of the Song of Solomon, or Song of Songs, is the orally-transmitted popular love poetry sung at banquets and festivals. It is in a very similar rural festive atmosphere that Camacho's wedding banquet takes place. Also, just as in the episode of the rich farmer's nuptials in Song of Solomon 5:1, there is an invitation to drink and to celebrate, since the poem bears direct relation to festivals commemorating the return of spring.

In order to better understand the particular reading of the Song of Solomon that is reflected in the episode of Camacho's wedding, it is essential to point out certain parallels between the Cervantine text and its Solomonic intertext. The first of these concerns the appeal to the senses, with a special emphasis on taste and touch as well as the association between drinking and kissing. The eagerness and passion with which Sulamith in the Song of Solomon awaits the imminent arrival of her lover and the prospect of erotic pleasure are mirrored in the impatience and expectation of Sancho Panza as he beholds and smells the upcoming sumptuous banquet. However, it is important to note that in the case of Don Quijote's squire, such rich foods are not a metaphor for sexual desire but rather the very object of his desire.

The arrival of the bride, Quiteria, prompts Sancho to break into his own "song" in praise of her beauty—and her material wealth.

> Well I never! She isn't dressed like a farmer's daughter, but like a fine palace lady! Heavens alive! That necklace of hers looks like fine coral, and she isn't wearing Cuenca cloth but thirty pile velvet! And her trimmings aren't white linen, but I swear they're satin! Then look at her hands! Is it jet rings she's wearing? No, I'll be blowed if they're not gold, and very much so, set with pearls as white as curds, each one of them worth the eye out of my head. Oh, the little whore! And what hair! If it isn't false, I've never seen longer or redder in my life! Then can you find fault with her air or her figure? *Wouldn't you say she is like a palm-tree loaded with bunches of dates?* For that is what they look like, those jewels she's got hanging from her hair and at her throat. My Lord, she's a fine strapping girl, and could sail through the shoals of Flanders.[32] (my emphasis)

---

[32] Ibid., II, XXI, p. 602.

With the entry of Camacho's bride in Chapter 21 of Part II, Sancho undoubtedly adopts the same attitude as the bridegroom in the Song of Solomon (4:6), who publicly praises and proclaims the beauty and worth of his bride. The "Song of Sancho" turns out to be much shorter than its Biblical counterpart, as well as evidently humorous. Nonetheless, it follows a similar structural pattern: Sancho systematically describes the different parts of the woman's body. While in the Song of Solomon the bride is praised by likening her to different aspects of nature, don Quijote's squire, in his praise of the wealthy farmer's bride, emphasizes her material beauty: the finery and jewelry that Quiteria is wearing. However, certain elements of Sancho's description directly mirror the Biblical text, such as the allusion to the date-filled palm tree (Song of Solomon 5:11), which is a recurring image in the Old Testament poem. Likewise, the affirmation that the bride is "the most beautiful of women" is repeatedly proclaimed by the chorus of the Song of Solomon.

Nevertheless, what stands out the most in the Cervantine wedding episode is, once again, Sancho Panza's materialism. Let us remember that in this very episode Sancho sides with the wealthy groom Camacho, intead of with the spurned and poor lover Basilio, and also takes the side of Money, as opposed to Love, in the allegorical dispute staged as part of the wedding festivities. This episode, in the light of Solomonic imagery as applied to Don Quijote's squire, becomes extremely important since it shows Sancho Panza's materialistic tendencies at their greatest. It is because of this flaw that both Sancho and his legendary Jewish role model will have to be transformed, respectively, into governor of an "island" and wandering beggar in order to undergo purification and renewal.

Conclusion

As has been demonstrated by specialists such as Pablo Torijano, the figure of Solomon belongs to the world of the novels of chivalry, due to the spread of numerous medieval legends that emphasize his magical powers.[33] During the Middle Ages, the image of the legendary King Solomon, both as a model ruler and as a magician, became widely

---

[33] Pablo Torijano, *Solomon, the Esoteric King: from King to Magus, Development of a Tradition*, Leiden, 2002.

known because of the dissemination of these popular stories of Jewish origin. It is curious to note that in a work such as *Don Quijote*, in which magic spells and enchanters are a recurring motif, the name of the legendary magician Solomon is never mentioned, although the echo of this popular figure can be heard throughout the novel.

For Sancho Panza, King Solomon is a model that, in contrast to Don Quijote's imitation of Amadís of Gaul, is presented to the reader in a much less explicit manner. It is possible that the desire to keep this element of Jewish popular culture "hidden" may have been the result of a conscious effort by Cervantes. The Semitic element in *Don Quijote* needs to disguise itself, like Prince Clavijo, in order to revindicate its legacy, its heritage, and its imprint on Spanish culture. That is something the knight Amadís need not do. However, while Don Quijote's "imitation" of the Western model of chivalry ends in disaster, Sancho's emulation of a Semitic model purifies him and saves him from the grasp of materialism. The echo of King Solomon, whether he be the Biblical monarch or, more notably, the medieval figure of popular legend, helps Sancho Panza open himself up to the spirit of his Master. Although this transformation will eventually result in his abandonment of Solomon as a model, it will have left its mark on Sancho's character. While Solomon's *hubris* drove his kingdom to a tragic end, Sancho's materialism ends up buried in the cemetery on the famous Island of Barataria.

CHAPTER FOURTEEN

HISTORIOGRAPHY, HISTORICITY AND THE CONVERSOS

Kevin Ingram

The Colombina archive in Seville houses a copy of a *memoria* (discourse) written by Fray Agustin Salucio, at the end of the sixteenth century, in which the Dominican friar examines, with a good measure of irony, the question, "Who is an Old Christian?"[1] While there were no studies available on the subject, Salucio observed, the obvious answer to the question was that an "Old Christian" was the person who converted to Christianity before the "New Christian." However, to fully appreciate the term "Old Christian," he tells us, it was necessary to understand that Spaniards of his own day stemmed from four different social groups: the conquerors, the conquered, those who were neither conquerors or conquered, and a mixture of some or all of the above.

The first group, the conquerors, were those people who initially fled north during the Islamic invasion of Spain, in 711, preferring to live in the Asturian and Vizcayan mountains than to exist under the yoke of Muslim rule. From their mountain retreat, these courageous (*valiente*) Christians waged war on the Muslims and, in the first wave of the *Reconquista*, wrested Spanish territory from the invaders.

---

[1] *Tratado del origen de los villanos, a quienes llaman cristianos viejos en Castilla.* Biblioteca Capitular y Colombina (Sevilla) Ms. 28-7-33. A number of studies exist on Fr. Agustín Salucio. See, for example, Hipolito Sancho, "El Maestro Fr. Agustín Salucio, O.P. Contribución a la Historia Literaria Sevillana del siglo XVI," in *Archivo Hispalense*, XVI (1952), pp. 9–47; and Alvaro Huerga's introduction to Fray Agustín Salucio, *Avisos para los predicadores del santo evangelio*, Barcelona, 1956. All of these studies skirt the issue of Salucio's heterodox views and his Converso background. It is likely, however, that the maternal side of the friar's family were Conversos. In 1570 the Bishop of Córdoba, Bernardo de Fresneda, wrote to the king informing him of a widespread *alumbrado* (heretical) movement in his diocese that was centered on the Converso community; and he linked Salucio, "hijo de Genoves y no de buena [i.e. conversa] madre," to the movement (Instituto Valencia de Don Juan no. 89 leg. 61–393). Salucio was a close friend of Juan de Avila and Fr. Luis de Granada, and shared their views on spiritual reform. He also maintained close ties with the Seville group of humanists which was formed in the 1570s and 1580s around Fernando de Herrera and the Licentiate Francisco Pacheco.

The second group of Spaniards, "the conquered," were those Moors and Jews who, reluctant to abandon their farms and businesses after the northern Christian forces had re-conquered the southern territory (from the twelfth century onward), remained in Christian Spain. These base (*vil*) individuals later converted to Christianity, preferring apostasy to the constant attacks from their Christian neighbors. These were known as "New Christians."

The third group of Spaniards consisted of those Christians—the vast majority—who remained in Moorish territory after the Muslim invasion. Resisting the call of their co-religionists in the north, these Christians—*Mozarabs* as they became known—preferred to cohabit with the Moor, whom they found much more acceptable than the tyrannical Visigoth king deposed by the Muslim invaders. Like the New Christians, these were base (*vil*) people, who were referred to by their Arab hosts as *Marranos*, a term, Salucio tells us, meaning apostate or deserter (an obvious jibe by the author at sixteenth-century Old-Christian society, who used the derogatory term *marrano*, which they associated with swine, to refer to New Christians). The northern resistance movement referred to these Mozarabs as *mixtos*, in reference to their religion, which was mixed with that of the Moors. For their part, the Mozarabs (collaborationists) labeled the northern Christians "rebels," and depicted their king, Don Pelayo, as a charlatan who took up arms against the Moors not for the Christian faith, but for his own political interests.

According to Salucio, then, at the end of the first wave of the *Reconquista*, Christian Spain was made up of converts from Judaism and Islam (New Christians), Mozarabs, who had for centuries practiced an ersatz or tainted form of Christianity, and a small group of Christian conquerors from the north. This last group of Spaniards were not only pure Christians, Salucio tells us, they were also Spain's true nobility (here the author seemingly panders to the Spanish *hidalgos*' conceit that their ancestors were Biscayan nobles who moved south with the armies of Reconquest); however, Salucio goes on to inform us that the names of these noble northerners had been lost to history; the current Old-Christian society, nobles and commoners alike, had no idea who their distant ancestors were. It was highly probable, indeed, that the majority of people who labeled themselves Old Christian came from one of two groups: base Jewish and Muslim converts to Christianity, or base Mozarabs. Regrettably, Salucio writes, in recent times laws had been legislated (*limpieza de sangre* statutes) banning recent converts to Christianity from positions in the Church and other institutions on the grounds that they were of an inferior status. These laws were illogical; there was only one difference between these people and the rest of the Spanish population: the latter group had no clear idea who its ancestors were.

No doubt a more prudent Converso apologist than Fr. Salucio would have written a study indicating how the New Christian could be the equal to his Old-Christian neighbor in moral probity and in the sincerity of his Christian beliefs. However, in Salucio's account the Old and the New Christians are united not in virtue but in self-interest and moral turpitude. The author also notes—in a seemingly gratuitous aside—that the Moors were able to conquer Spain so easily because they were considered an improvement on Visigoth rule (Old Christians, as Salucio well knew, lauded the "virtuous, Christian" Visigoths, whom they regarded as their ancestors). Furthermore, he notes, the head of the Christian resistance movement, King Pelayo (an Old Christian icon), may well have been motivated more by political ambition than by Christian fervor.

Allowing for a certain Converso combativeness, Salucio's *memoria* is an honest attempt to present Spanish history in its less than glorious reality, and a bold challenge to the anti-Converso legislation that was undermining Spanish society. Unfortunately, Old-Christian Spain was in no mood to countenance either historical realism or attacks on its *limpieza de sangre* legislation; Salucio's discourse on the *limpieza de sangre* statutes, in which the above views were incorporated, was withdrawn from circulation soon after its publication, on the orders of Philip III.[2]

---

[2] *Discurso hecho por fray Agustín de Salucio, Maestro en santa Teología, de la Orden de Santo Domingo, acerca de la justicia y buen gobierno de España en los Estatutos de limpieza de sangre: y si conviene, o no, alguna limitación de ellos.* B.N. sig. R/29.688. In his *discurso* Salucio proposed a one hundred year moratorium on the *limpieza* statutes, at which point everyone would be an Old Christian (that is to say all Conversos would be at least four generations advanced from their ancestors' conversion, which most (not all) *limpieza de sangre* statutes used as the guideline for clean blood). In this way Spanish society could avoid the "scandals and nightmares" that the *limpieza* laws caused. See Antonio Domínguez Ortiz, *Los Judeoconversos en España y América*, Madrid, 1978, pp. 89–90. Salucio's was one of many attacks on the *limpieza de sangre* statutes by Converso letrados. These began in the fifteenth century with Alonso de Cartagena's *Defensorium unitatis christianae* and Fernan Diaz de Toledo's *Instrucción del Relator*, both written in response to the 1449 *sentencia-estatuto* of Toledo, considered to be the first *limpieza de sangre* statute. For a history of the *limpieza de sangre* statutes see Albert Sicroff, *Los estatutos de limpieza de sangre*, Madrid, 1985. For an examination of Fr. Agustin Salucio's anti-*limpieza* discourse see ibid., pp. 222–253.

For three centuries after Salucio wrote the above study, Spain continued to subordinate historical reality to national myth. In the popular
view, the Spaniard remained a pure-blooded product of the Cantabrian
mountains, a member of a warrior band who swept south to rid the
peninsula of the infidel in the Middle Ages and reestablish Spain's purity
of race and religious purpose. From this warrior caste there sprang
magically, like Athena from Zeus's head, the brilliant literary works of
the Spanish Golden Age: melancholic and mystical testaments to the
Spaniard's intensity of faith and his singularity of religious vision. In
this historical interpretation, the Jews and Muslims became a nefari-
ous miasma that was purged from Spain in 1492, leaving no cultural
legacy of any importance. As for the Converso, after being exposed by
the Inquisition for his Judaizing ways, he headed for Spain's historical
backwoods, rarely to show his face.

Of course, it was easy to write a jaundiced version of history when
many of Spain's great sixteenth-century Converso figures had, so to
speak, collaborated in the deception by fabricating for themselves false
genealogies. As these bogus documents told later investigators exactly
what they wanted to hear (i.e. that their subjects were Old Christians),
there was little interest in corroborating them against other sources. In
the event that no genealogical study existed, then the tendency was to
link the Golden-Age figure cavalierly to a northern *hidalgo* clan that
bore the same name.

The first serious attempt to examine the Jewish contribution to
Spanish history in any detail came in 1848, with *Estudios historícos,
politicos y literarios sobre los judios en España*, in which the author,
José Amador de los Ríos, lamented his country's ignorance of the
Sephardic culture.

> It would be easy [wrote Amador] to produce here a long catalogue of
> works in which characters of that race have been presented, at times
> real at times false, and in which they have been attributed acts more or
> less true, more or less hateful. But with difficulty will you be able to find
> among us a work that attempts to study the descendents of the prophet
> king [King David] during their long passage in Spain, examining their
> laws, their customs and their relations with Christian society.[3]

---

[3] Amador de los Rios, *Estudios historicos, politicos y literarios sobre los judios de
España*, Madrid, 1848, x. All the translated quotations from the Spanish texts in this
essay are my own.

In contrast to the many prejudicial myths circulating in Spanish society about its Sephardic community, Amador's study presented a picture of an enormously important minority group who in the late Middle Ages became the most ardent cultivators of science and literature in the peninsula. Thirty years after publishing *Estudios historicos*, Amador returned to the same theme in his three-volume *Historia social, política y religiosa de los judíos de España y Portugal* (1875–1876). This time he wrote, "Up until recently a work of this nature could not have been attempted without its author attracting universal opprobrium..." Nevertheless, it is curious, given his professed belief in his country's new-found liberality towards its Jewish past, that Amador had almost nothing to say on Converso involvement in modern (post-1492) Spanish society. True, he makes a passing attack on the Inquisition for unjustly accusing Converso men of science and learning of Judaizing; but, save for one occasion, he does not refer to any of these intellectuals by name, and even then he is sufficiently ambiguous to leave the reader wondering whether he is referring to New-Christian or Old-Christian victims of Inquisition intolerance. Amador writes:

> The century denominated "Golden" by students of the Renaissance, is nevertheless stained at each step with the defamation of the Sambenito; there are thus many illustrious cultivators of science, letters and arts who attracted the terrible suspicions and insatiable ire of the Holy Office. Neither the most refined virtues nor the highest merits were respected; next to a Hernando de Talavera and a Bartolomé Carranza, clear geniuses of the Church and of learning; next to an Arias Montano and a Francisco Sánchez de las Brozas, everlasting glories of classical and oriental philology; next to a Pablo de Céspedes and a Fr. Luis de León, envied ornaments of arqueological science and the divine arts of painting and poetry, the inexorable hand of the inquisitors placed, with more than a little extravagance, the names of another thousand eminent geniuses on whose foreheads it attached the stigma of Judaizer.[4]

The implication here is that Hernando de Talavera, Bartolomé Carranza, Arias Montano, El Brocense, Pablo de Céspedes, and Luis de León, like the "other thousand eminent geniuses" unjustly accused of Judaizing, were Conversos; however, the author avoids stating this directly. It would seem, despite his protests, that Amador was not at all

---

[4] José Amador de los Rios, *Historia Social, Politica y Religiosa de los Judios de España y Portugal*, Madrid, 1960, p. 842.

sure his readers were ready to admit New Christians into the Golden-Age literary pantheon.[5]

Amador de los Rios published his *magnum opus* on Sephardic Spain in the early years of the Restoration regime, at a time when Spanish intellectuals were beginning to reflect upon the origins of their country's decline from a world power to an underdeveloped and politically unstable state, overshadowed by its Western European neighbors. In 1876, the year in which the last volume of Amador's *Historia Social* appeared in print, Gumersindo de Azcárate published an article on Spain's political situation in which he singled out intolerance as the villain behind his country's political and economic stasis. This article soon gave rise to a heated debate among a number of conservative and liberal scholars on Spain's intellectual insularity. For the liberal group, Spain's decline in fortune was the direct result of an obscurantist Church and its reactionary watchdog, the Inquisition. For the group of Catholic apologists, led by Marcelino Menéndez y Pelayo, the Inquisition was blame-free; the country had declined not through closed-mindedness, but through embracing, on certain occasions in its history, foreign pagan views. There was some disagreement among the Catholic apologists as to when the rot had set in. Some believed that it had arrived with the Renaissance, while others, including Menéndez y Pelayo, laid the blame at the Enlightenment's door. All agreed on one thing, however: Spain needed to recover its unique spiritual identity before it could once again triumph in the world.[6]

Spanish spiritual regeneration increasingly preoccupied Spain's late nineteenth-century intellectuals. For Miguel de Unamuno, writing at the turn of the century, his country's spiritual essence was a subterranean stream moving stealthily through history, surfacing occasionally to leave its mark on an age.[7] This intrahistoric spiritual force, according to Unamuno, had emerged in the Golden Age, achieving its greatest

---

[5] As the paragraph comes directly after a section in which Amador criticizes the Inquisition for its attacks on Converso intellectuals, I am led to believe that he is intimating that Arias Montano etc were Converso victims of Inquisition aggression.

[6] For an examination of the debate see Antonio Santoveña Setién, "Una alternativa cultural católica para la España de la Restauracion." *IH* 12 (1992), pp. 237–253.

[7] Unamuno's views on Spain's intrahistoric spiritual force, which he termed "la tradición eternal" were put forward in his work *En torno al casticismo* (1895). The theory is mostly an amalgam of Hegel's *volkgeist* and William James' "stream of con-

visibility in Cervantes' knight; in the Spanish mystics: Juan de la Cruz, Teresa de Jesús, and Juan de Avila; and in the pictorial reveries of El Greco.[8] We now know, of course, that four of Unamuno's emblems of Spanish essentialism were Conversos, and the fifth was a Greek ex-patriate whose mystical vision mostly conformed to that of his Converso clerical patrons.[9] Those characteristics that Unamuno had attributed to atavistic Iberian spiritual traits were, more likely, the result of New-Christian disquiet.

Spain's spiritual regenerationists had resorted to facile pseudo-scientific and quasi-philosophical notions to explain the Spanish character. This folly was attacked by the philologist and historian Américo Castro in his 1965 work, *La Realidad de España*. According to Castro, the regenerationists—he singled out Unamuno and Ortega y Gasset—had taken refuge in fables in which a *Celtoíbero* race, pure in blood and spirit, had traversed the ages, affected only by certain Roman and Visigothic cultural influences. In these fairy tales Spain's Muslim and Jewish cultures had no place.[10] The reality, according to Castro, was

---

sciousness." See Guyana Jurkevich, *The Elusive Self: Archetypal Approaches to the Novel of Miguel de Unamuno*, University of Missouri Press, 1991.

[8] "[El Greco] came to Spain," Unamuno wrote in 1914, "to give us, better than anyone else, the pictorial and graphic expression of the Castillian soul; and he revealed, with his brushes, our spiritual naturalism. I say spiritual nationalism and not idealist realism, because the Castillian soul of Don Quijote and the mystics is not, in effect, idealist, but spiritualist…Idealism is of this world, it is pagan, platonic, of the Renaissance. Our Castillian spiritualism is mystical, of another world, medieval." Quoted from José Alvarez Lopera, *De Cean a Cossio: La Fortuna Critica del Greco en El Siglo XIX*, Madrid, 1987, p. 98.

[9] Don Quijote's epithet "de la Mancha" is almost certainly a play on words, presenting the discerning sixteenth-century reader with both the knight's geographical and genetic provenance, for *mancha* ("stain") was applied to those Castilians (the Conversos) whose blood was not clean. El Greco's close association with Toledo's Converso community and his heterodox religious views are examined by David Davies in his article "The Ascent of the Mind to God: El Greco's Religious Imagery and Spiritual Reform in Spain," in José Alvarez Lopera ed., *El Greco: Identity and Transformation. Crete. Italy. Spain*, Madrid, 1999, pp. 187–215.

[10] "[Ortega y Gasset] has stated that the Arabs were not an 'ingrediant' in the history of the Spanish people; and not even obliquely are the Spanish Jews present. Such an important error in so eminent a person should not be censured but understood. The best Spaniards, without whom many of us would not think as we do, look for refuge in remote and murky "*españolismos*," or in deep and silent strata of Spanish humanity, in the '*intrahistoria*' of Unamuno, in the latencies of life which flow and subsist—according to him—without 'being expressed in books and papers and monuments.'" *La Realidad Historica de España*. 9th edition, México, 1987, vi (my translation). For Castro, a philologist and literary historian, the Spanish character was intimately linked to its language. It was thus impossible to describe a Latin speaking Hispano-Roman as a Spaniard. In

quite different; in his own view the cultural entity known as Spain was formed in the Middle Ages, and was the product of the confrontation of three groups: Christians, Jews, and Muslims. Furthermore, during the medieval period the peninsula's intellectual life was confined mostly to Muslim and Jewish communities; when intellectual pursuits entered Christian courts, they did so, very often, through Jewish and Converso advisors. As for Spain's Golden Age of Letters, that was, by and large, the product of Converso talent. Old-Christian society had reacted to this Converso threat by introducing the *limpieza de sangre* laws, creating a society so sensitive to Jewish taint that its members distanced themselves from everything that might suggest a Jewish background, and this included intellectual pursuits. It was this neurosis, born of fear and hatred, that was behind Spain's decline and not the loss of some intra-historic spiritual force.

Castro had first presented his views on Spain's three-caste culture in *España en su Historia*, published in 1948. On that occasion he was much less abrasive towards Spain's old-guard intellectuals than he later became; not that this made his opinions any more palatable to many of his colleagues. One of Castro's earliest and most vitriolic critics was the medievalist Claudio Sánchez-Albornoz. A historian whose historical vision, like that of Menéndez y Pelayo, was informed by his fervent Catholicism, Sánchez-Albornoz regarded Castro as a Spanish apostate, willfully, perversely intent on undermining Spain's true culture, and he set out, in his *España, un enigma historico*, to expose the treachery.[11] The Jews, he opined, had no visible influence on Spanish ("Hispano") culture. The Spanish people had graciously allowed this minority group into their country, but instead of showing their appreciation, they had continually plotted to overthrow their hosts. They had become money lenders, tax farmers and merchants in order to finance their revolution, which would be signaled, they believed, by the arrival of their Messiah. Unable to tolerate the Jewish subterfuge any longer, the Spanish had expelled them from the country in 1492. As far as Sánchez-Albornoz

---

Castro's view the Spanish character emerged, like its language, in the High Middle Ages, and was forged in an environment in which Christian Spain was in constant contact with two other cultures, those of the Jews and the Muslims.

[11] Claudio Sánchez Albornoz, *España, un enigma histórico*, 2 vols, Buenos Aires, 1956.

was concerned, there was a Jewish mentality and a Christian mentality, and these remained separate throughout Spain's history.[12]

As a corrective to Castro's vision of Spanish cultural development, Sánchez-Albornoz offered his own interpretation—a theory that harkened back to Unamuno's intra-historic Spanish spirit. In Sánchez-Albornoz's opinion the Spanish character was strongly influenced by its *herencia temperamental*, a *volkgeist* which evolved in prehistoric times and traversed history in an all but pristine state of preservation. This prehistoric genetic force was particularly visible in Spain's heroes: those men and women who had appeared at propitious moments to inspire the nation.[13] Spanish history (that is to say the history of the "Hispanos," as opposed to the Moors and Jews) was formed by its heroes, the *herencia temperamental* of the people, and the nation's destiny, or "as believers would see it, the marvelous projection of the supreme will of God whose infinite mysteries cannot be captured by our human reason, both slow and miserable."[14]

Despite his clear ideological prejudice for a Spanish (Hispanic) culture free from Jewish and Muslim influence, Sánchez-Albornoz presented *España, un enigma historico* as the work of a rigorous scholar who, unlike his rival Américo Castro, would not allow himself to be carried away by an "ungainly eagerness to dazzle his readers with clever but

---

[12] For Sánchez-Albornoz's anti-semitic views, see his chapter "Lo judaico en la forja de lo hispanico," in *España, un enigma historica*. Benzion Netanyahu examines these pages in, "Una visión española de la historia judía en España: Sánchez Albornoz," in Ángel Alcalá ed. *Judíos. Sefarditas. Conversos: La expulsion de 1492 y sus consecuencias*, Madrid, 1995, pp. 89–121.

[13] Claudio Sánchez Albornoz, *España, un enigma historica*, 2 vols, 2nd edition, Buenos Aires, 1962, p. 57. Sánchez-Albornoz believed that both the Roman and Visigothic cultures influenced Spanish culture; however, the influence was always tempered or guided by the Hispanic *herencia temperamental*. As for the Muslim influence on the Spanish character, he took the view that this, like that of the Jews, was negligible. According to the medievalist, Islamic culture, that is to say the culture of the East, did not begin to penetrate al-Andalus before the eleventh century, at the time when Christian Spain's forces began to overtake much of the peninsula. The majority of Muslims, that is to say the Neo-Muslims of Hispano Roman descent, and all of the Mozarabs who later found themselves subjects in a Christian realm, were thus immunized against Arab acculturation through their temperamental inheritance as well as through their physical separation from the real Arab world. See ibid., pp. 157–175. The view that Arab culture barely penetrated the Iberian peninsula during the first three centuries of Islamic occupation is described by the Islamist and Hispanist Thomas F. Glick as "simply and clearly wrong." See the introduction to Thomas F. Glick, *Islamic and Christian Spain in the Early Middle Ages*, Princeton University Press, 1979.

[14] *España, un enigma...*, p. 61.

frail fantasies."[15] This image of Sánchez-Albornoz as the professional, dispassionate historian contesting Américo Castro, the *littérateur* out of his element, was readily embraced by a Francoist academy, who shared the medievalist's historical vision.[16] For although Sánchez-Albornoz was, like Castro, a Republican exile, his views on Spanish historiography conformed, in many ways, to those of the Franco regime. Both the exiled historian and Franco's ideologues propounded an essentialist vision of Spain, in which a pure Hispanic race had honed its unique character while triumphing over alien cultures. For Sánchez-Albornoz this character refinement had taken place during the *Reconquista*, when Christian Spain had confronted the Arab interloper. For the ideologues, the *Reconquista* and the Spanish Civil War were engagements in the

---

[15] Ibid., prologue.

[16] This facile comparison has been perpetuated up until the present day by a group of conservative Spanish scholars whose works have purposely obfuscated Sánchez-Albornoz's ideological bias for a *castizo* Spain. This is the case of Jose Luis Gómez-Martínez's *Américo Castro y el origen de los Españoles: historia de una polémica*. Writing in 1975, at the beginning of the Transition period, Gómez-Martínez purports to present a disinterested essay on the Castro Sánchez-Albornoz debate, while egregiously situating the medievalist on the moral and academic high ground. Gómez-Martínez writes: "Sánchez-Albornoz, *in some ways representing historians* [my emphasis], made it a personal issue to challenge Castro's theories, not only refuting those that seemed erroneous, but also presenting his own version of the Spanish past." (p. 52); and several pages later he notes, "The most systematic and most comprehensive attack on Castro's work was without a doubt that of Sánchez-Albornoz. His work, and in particular the two voluminous tomes of *España, un enigma histórica* should have been sufficient, given the intensity and acuteness with which they were written, to end a polemic that was barely started. The result, however, was quite different. *España, un enigma histórico* gave rise to an energetic and determined counteroffensive by Castro [and his disciples]...who taking sides with Castro, began to publish numerous articles, the great majority of which were of a strong polemic character...The disciples of Sánchez-Albornoz, as was to be expected, took it upon themselves to defend their master, who in general remained faithful to his maxime: 'only engage in combat with worthy opponents ['*No toreo sino miuras*']" See José Luis Gómez-Martínez, *Américo Castro y el origin de los Españoles: historia de una polemica*, Madrid, 1975. More recently José Andrés-Gallego dismisses Castro's *España en su historia* by citing a note written in a copy of the work by a certain Rafael Altamira. Andrés-Gallego writes: "Striking are the lines written by Rafael Altamira in the front of his personal copy of Castro's work: "A book full of prejudices against Spain, clearly defeatist, and an exaggerated tribute to his new friends, who are also defeatists, because they proclaim themselves the most worthy Spaniards'" And Andrés-Gallego continues: "In 1957 [sic], Claudio Sánchez-Albornoz, also an academic chair in the Central University and a radical republican—in reality Azañista—minister of state in 1933, ambassador to Portugal in 1936 and president of the Republican Government in exile since 1939, replied to Américo Castro with *España, un enigma histórico*, in which he demonstrated documentarily the primordial weight of Christian Rome [on Spain]." See José Andrés-Gallego, *Historia de la historiografía española*, Madrid, 2003, pp. 344–345.

same conflict against anti-Hispanic forces, in the latter case represented by communists, freemasons, and an international Jewish conspiracy. According to their version of recent history, the Nationalist forces, like the Catholic Monarchs, had liberated Spain of divisive elements, and were now in the process of creating a new society based on "those virtues of our great captains and politicians of the Golden Age, educated in the Catholic Theology of Trent…"[17] However, in order to carry out this counter-reformation, it was first necessary to purge the University system of non-conformist elements. By 1944, 155 of Spain's 278 departmental chairs had changed hands. The majority of the new men, like their colleagues who had managed to hold on to their positions, subscribed to a conservative, Catholic ideology.[18]

Obviously, this cleansed environment was not conducive to a historiographical account that assigned the Jews and Conversos a central place in medieval and early-modern Spanish culture. Nonetheless, a number of studies did begin to appear, albeit by Spanish scholars on the margins of the Francoist academy, which leant support to Castro's views on the importance of the Converso to sixteenth-century Spanish society.[19] These studies indicated that Conversos were prominent in artisanal occupations, especially textile and leather production, and silver-smithing; they were conspicuous as merchants, doctors, printers, notaries and lawyers; they were university professors, civil and clerical bureaucrats, and advisors to royal and noble courts. Indeed, Conversos predominated in all those positions that called for intellectual formation—the administrative office for trade with the Indies, the *Casa de Contratacion*, was, for example, controlled by men from Converso backgrounds. Conversos may have been a social minority, but they held a prominent place in the professional and economic life of Spain's most important urban centers, as studies on a number of early modern Spanish cities began to attest. José Carlos Gomez-Menor's study of sixteenth-century Toledo indicated a large population of Conversos who

---

[17] Cited from the 1938 *Ley de Reforma de la Enseñanza Secundaria*. See Rafael Valls Montes, "El bachillerato universitario de 1938," in *La universidad española bajo el régimen de Franco. Actas del Congreso celebrado en Zaragoza el 8 y 11 noviembre de 1989*, dirigido por Juan José Carreras Ares, Zaragoza, 1991, p. 198.

[18] Alicia Alted Vigil, "Bases politico-ideológicos y juridicas de la universidad franquista," ibid., p. 117.

[19] I am referring, in particular, to Antonio Domínguez Ortiz, *La clase social de los conversos de la edad moderna*, Madrid, 1955; and Julio Caro Baroja, *Los judios en la España moderna y contemporánea*, 3 vols, Madrid, 1961.

controlled the city's commerce.[20] Many of these New Christians had
used their wealth to enter into marriage alliances with members of the
lower nobility, forming what Gomez-Menor termed a "*mestizo*" urban
elite, with a powerful presence in Toledo's cathedral chapter and city
council. Ruth Pike's studies of sixteenth-century Seville also emphasized
the importance of the city's Conversos as artisans, merchants and professionals. Like their Toledo counterparts, Seville's wealthy Conversos
also used their money to gain access to the nobility, either through
marriage alliances or through the purchase of those positions on the
city council that conferred an *hidalgo* status. Seville's Conversos also
formed important endogamous alliances, strengthening their position
in the commercial and political life of the city.[21]

---

[20] José Carlos Gomez-Menor Fuentes, "La sociedad conversa toledana en la primera
mitad del siglo XVI," in *Simposio Toledano Judaico* (Toledo 20–22 Abril, 1972), Toledo,
1972. Gomez-Menor believes it was the Converso community's size that made Toledo's
Old-Christian society fearful of it, and that this fear led to the bloody uprising against the
Conversos in 1457. In a more recent study, Linda Martz cites a contemporary document
which reveals that 2,300 of Toledo's Conversos were reconciled by the Inquisition in
1486. As these figures were taken from only 17 of the city's 21 parishes, Martz estimates
that the true number of reconciled Conversos was around 3,000, or 17% to 20% of
the city's population, estimated to be between 15,000 and 18,000 in the late fifteenth
century. Linda Martz, "Converso Families in Fifteenth- and Sixteenth-Century Toledo:
The Significance of Lineage," *Sefarad* XLVIII 1, (1988). It is evident, therefore, that the
total number of Conversos—both reconciled and non-reconciled—represented more
than 20% of the Toledo population. A census for Talavera de la Reina, taken between
1477 and 1487, reveals that Jews made up 20% of the town's population. See
Maria Jesús Suárez, *La Villa de Talavera y Su Tierra en la Edad Media (1369–1504)*,
University of Oviedo, 1982, p. 118. It is thus very likely, given the fact that by the late
fifteenth-century urban Conversos were more numerous than the Jews, that around
forty percent of the population of Talavera was of Sephardic origin. Cuenca, Segovia,
Trujillo, Ocaña, Soría, Avila, Zamora and Murcia were also home to large Converso
communities. Seville's Converso community was also very visible up until the arrival
of the Inquisition in 1480, when many fled the city. This community recovered rapidly
in the early sixteenth century, dominating commerce and the city guilds. See Antonio
Domínguez Ortiz, *La clase social de los conversos en Castilla en la Edad Moderna*,
University of Granada, 1991, p. 14.
[21] See Ruth Pike, *Aristocrats and Traders*, Ithaca, New York, 1972. A number of
important studies have appeared subsequent to the works by Gomez-Menor and Ruth
Pike, examining the Converso presence in other Spanish cities. See, for example, Haim
Beinart, *Conversos on Trial: The Inquisition in Ciudad Real*, Jerusalem, 1981; Stephen
Haliczer, *Inquisition and Society in the Kingdom of Valencia 1479–1834*, Berkeley, 1990;
Máximo Diago Hernando, "Los judeoconversos en Soria despues de 1492," *Sefarad* LI
2, 1991, pp. 259–97; Pilar Huerga Criado, *En la raya de Portugal: Solidaridad y ten-
siones en la comunidad judeoconverso*, Salamanca, 1993; Pedro Luis Lorenzo Cadalso,
"Esplendor y decadencia de las oligarquias conversas de Cuenca y Guadalajara (Siglos
XV y XVI)," *Hispania*, LIV/1, no. 186 (1994) pp. 53–94.

Meanwhile other studies appeared by Francisco Márquez Villanueva and Stephen Gilman which, in examining the Converso backgrounds of important early modern literary figures, also presented a picture of an intellectual environment dominated by New Christians.[22] The Conversos had, at last, entered Spanish Golden-Age history as important protagonists; however, not everyone chose to recognize the extent of their presence, as Stephen Gilman stated in his 1972 biography of Fernando de Rojas:

> The Jewish origins of many important Spaniards of the past are first of all denied (in the case of Rojas, as recently as 1967); and then, if the denial cannot stand up in the face of the evidence, they are ignored [...] The belief that only the caste of Old Christians was truly Spanish and truly honorable was so in-rooted that it has endured over four centuries. There even seems to prevail among some of our colleagues, peninsular and otherwise, the tacit notion that to bring to light the background of a Rojas or a Diego de San Pedro (not to speak of a Saint Teresa of Avila) is an unpatriotic act, a virtual deletion of their works from the national Honor Roll.[23]

Writing in 1967, after several of the above works had been published, Eugenio Asensio was unable to deny that a number of Golden-Age figures were from Converso backgrounds; however, these figures, he asserted, were few; moreover, it was they who had been influenced by Spanish Old-Christian culture, and not vice versa.[24] St Teresa's mysticism, Luis Vives' pacifism and Luis de León's stoicism were the products not of their Converso condition but of the intellectual milieux (Old-Christian, according to Asensio) in which they moved. Fray Luis, for example, may have been technically speaking a Converso, but it was not unusual for the people in the world in which he moved—Salamanca University and the Augustinian religious order—to have a drop of Jewish blood in their veins; Fray Luis's own drop of Jewish blood did not

---

[22] Francisco Márquez Villanueva, *Investigaciones sobre Juan Alvarez Gato*, Madrid, 1960. Stephen Gilman, *The Spain of Fernando de Rojas*, Princeton, 1972. See also the more recent biographies, Y. H. Yerushalmi, *From Spanish Court to Italian Ghetto: Isaac Cardoso, a Study in Seventeenth-Century Marranism and Jewish Apologetics*, London, 1971; and Y. Kaplan, *From Christianity to Judaism: Isaac Orobio de Castro*, Oxford, 1989.

[23] Stephen Gilman, *The Spain of Fernando de Rojas*, op. cit., (1972) p. 27.

[24] Eugenio Asensio, "La peculiaridad literaria de los Conversos," *Anuario de Estudios Medievales*, no. 4, (1967), pp. 327–351.

affect his religious writings, which, in fact, revealed a man every bit as orthodox as that "sublime Old Christian" Arias Montano.[25]

Asensio's comparison of Luis de León with Arias Montano is an apt one, but not for Old-Christian orthodoxy. For although Arias Montano's family roots remain somewhat opaque, everything about the Spanish humanist points to a Converso background: his birthplace, Fregenal de la Sierra, renowned for its large Converso community;[26] his adoptive Converso parents, Antonio de Alcocer and Isabel Vélez; his close friendship with the Converso merchant Diego Núñez Pérez, whom he referred to as his cousin;[27] his equally close relationship with the Antwerp Converso merchant-banker Luis Pérez; his choice of academic studies—Hebrew—in a period in which Old-Christian Spain was careful to avoid any intimation of Jewish roots; his interest in Old-Testament exegesis and his indifference to the works of the Church Fathers—most unusual for a Catholic theologian. These characteristics may not have impressed Eugenio Asensio; they did, however, impress Montano's famous contemporary Lope de Vega who, in a much cited poem, made a clear allusion to Montano's Jewish roots.[28] Arias Montano and his

---

[25] "Su biblismo, si le hace blanco de malsines, también le vincula a excelsos cristianos viejos, como Arias Montano." Ibid., p. 331.

[26] "The people of the town," writes Henry Lea, "were mostly descendants of Conversos, resorting to perjury and every other means to conceal their origin." Lea notes that in this small town, between 1491 and 1495, 162 people were executed for Judaizing and a further 409 were given lighter sentences. By the end of the fifteenth century 599 *sambenitos* (the cloak worn by Conversos convicted of Judaizing) hung in the town's churches. H. C. Lea, *A History of the Inquisition in Spain*, New York, 1906, vol. III, pp. 167–168.

[27] For Montano's relationship with the Nuñez Pérez family, see Juan Gil, *Arias Montano en su entorno*, Merida, 1998, pp. 130–141.

[28] ...jamón presunto de español marrano
de la sierra famosa de Aracena
adonde huyó de la vida Arias Montano

See "Epistola a don Gaspar de Barrionuevo," in *Biblioteca de Autores Españoles*, 36, p. 427. This is clearly a play on words, based on the fact that *presunto* ("presumed"), also means "ham" in Portuguese; and *marrano* means both pig and Judaizing Converso, a type that was particularly associated with the Portuguese Converso community. Furthermore the area around Aracena, in the Sierra Morena, close to the Portuguese border, was associated with these backsliding Conversos. It was here, as Lope notes, that Arias Montano built his country villa. Thus we can read Lope's poem in two ways. First:

...ham it is presumed from the Spanish pig
of the famous mountains of Aracena
where Arias Montano fled from life.

And second:

...Portuguese ham from the Spanish Jew
of the famous mountains of Aracena
where Arias Montano hid from view.

friend Fray Luis de León certainly shared certain characteristics, but Old-Christian orthodoxy was not among them. Both men were, to use their Old-Christian antagonist León de Castro's term, "*hebreazantes*," that is to say scholars interested in emphasizing the importance of the Hebrew Bible and Jewish culture to Christianity. This interest led to León's imprisonment, from 1570 to 1575. Arias Montano was luckier: certain friends in high places were able to protect him, on a number of occasions, from the Inquisition's grasp.

Although Franco's death in 1975 was followed by a rapid return to a democratic system of government, the new liberal tendencies, manifest in politics, were slow to permeate Spain's university system, where many departmental chairs, loyal to the values of the old dictatorship, continued to influence the tenor of their junior colleagues' scholarship. Resistance to change was particularly evident among historians of early modern Spanish history, who continued to treat the Golden Age as the creation of Old-Christian talent. As Gómez-Menor wrote in 1994, "I am aware that normally Converso roots are hidden in the biographies of well-known people: this is the case of Juan Luis Vives, Juan de Avila, Teresa de Jesús (de Ahumada), Fr. Luis de León and many others."[29] But not only did scholars continue to circumvent the backgrounds of those writers whose Jewish roots were incontrovertible; they also often protested the Old-Christian character of figures whose social identities were, to say the least, ambiguous. In my own investigations into a group of Andalucían scholars I have come across a number of these protestations. One of my favorites concerns the fifteenth-century Córdoban poet Juan de Mena, in the publication *Córdoba y Su Provincia*. Here the author writes, "Although for some time critics have speculated on [Mena's] possible descent from a family of Conversos, this hypothesis has been definitively dismissed by Professor Eugenio Asencio. It seems to the contrary, according to the study (*memoria*) of a number of ancient and noble Castilian lineages—a work attributed to Mena—that his family was from the mountains."[30] Evidently, the local writer felt that Mena's Converso background was an impediment to his entry into

[29] José-Carlos Gómez-Menor, "Linaje Judío de Escritores Religios y Místicos Españoles del Siglo XVI," in Ángel Alcalá ed. *Judios. Sefarditas, Conversos*, Valladolid, 1995, p. 596.

[30] *Cordoba y su provincial*, Seville, 1986, p. 34.

Córdoba's mausoleum of celebrities, and thus he cited Eugene Asensio, an academic of similar sensibilities, in an effort to clean up the poet's image. However, in their eagerness to create an Old-Christian Mena, both men fell for a typical piece of Converso double entendre. For Mena (if indeed it was Mena who wrote the *memoria*) states only that he was from the mountains. The implication, of course, is that he was from Asturias, a region associated (erroneously) with an unadulterated Old-Christian population. In fact the mountains referred to by Mena could well have been the Sierra Morena, to the west of Córdoba, home to many Converso communities. This type of ambiguity was popular among Converso writers, who wished to disguise their origins without, strictly speaking, lying about them. The humanist Arias Montano, whom we have met above, and who Eugene Asensio described as "a sublime Old Christian," adopted "Mountain" as a surname possibly with a similar deception in mind. In fact, the humanist was born in Fregenal de la Sierra, on the foothills of the Sierra Morena, renowned for its large Converso population.[31]

It would seem that some biographers of Golden-Age figures believe that they have a patriotic duty to maintain their subjects free from Jewish taint, and thus they assert Old-Christian provenance on the slimmest of evidence. The editors of the Castalia and Catedra editions of Golden-Age literary works appear to be particularly prone to this "sanitization" process. In the introduction to Luis de Granada's *Introducción del símbolo de la fe*, José María de Balcells writes, "In 1504, the same year that Isabel the Catholic died in Medina del Campo,

---

[31] See note 29. Another example, one of many, is found in the picaresque novel *La pícara Justina*. In book one of the work, the author, Francisco López de Úbeda, describes his heroine as "la pícara montañesa," even though her parents were clearly from Jewish backgrounds. Converso writers often took similar liberties with the term "clean," describing their forebears as *limpios*. This could mean that they were claiming pure, Old-Christian, roots; it could also mean that they were stating that their ancestors were physically clean, an allusion to a Converso background, for Jews, unlike Christians, believed physical cleanliness was necessary for attaining spiritual purity. The Spanish humanist Ambrosio Morales (from Córdoba, like Juan de Mena) wrote the following epitaph to his father: "Here it is stated, with much truth, everything that the deceased was: that is of noble lineage and in all parts very clean." (Aqui se dice, con mucha verdad, todo lo que del difunto hubo: que fue de noble linaje y por todos partes muy limpia."), Ambrosio Morales, *Antigüedades*. The term "parts" could mean the four branches of his family or, simply, bodily parts.

Luis de Sarría was born in Granada, into a very poor family of Old Christians, or of 'pure' blood."[32] And several lines later he returns to Luis's Old-Christian background, pointing out that the monk graduated from the Dominican college of San Gregorio in 1529 "not without having substantiated, with maximum rigor, his *limpieza de sangre*."[33] Why, one wonders, is Bacells so intent on underlining his subject's Old-Christian roots? Is it perhaps because Fray Luis's *limpieza* is by no means certain? Indeed, the only evidence we have that Fray Luis was Old-Christian comes from a seventeenth-century hagiography, in which the author states formulaically: "The parents of Fray Luis were not wealthy or landed, nor of illustrious lineage, but poor and humble although Old Christians, clean and free of all trace of Jews and Moors, and without mixture of bad blood."[34] Fray Luis himself wrote almost nothing about his family background; we do know, however, that the family surname was taken from a Spanish town (Sarria, in Galicia), which is suggestive of Converso roots.[35] As for the fact that Fray Luis passed the *limpieza de sangre* tests for the Dominican college, this, as Balcells must surely know, is no proof of Old-Christian origins; sixteenth-century *limpieza de sangre* statutes were often sidestepped by Conversos, who were prominent among church intellectuals. One of the most celebrated Dominicans of the early sixteenth century was

---

[32] Fray Luis de Granada, *Introducción del símbolo de la Fe*, edición de José María Balcells, Catedra, Madrid, 1989, pp. 13–14: "En 1504, el mismo año de la muerte de Isabel la Católica en Medina del Campo, nació Luis de Sarriá en Granada, en el escenario de una familia modestísima de cristianos viejos, o de sangre pura."

[33] Ibid., p. 16: "no sin haber sido atestiguada, con el máximo rigor, su limpieza de sangre."

[34] Ibid., p. 14, note 3: "Los padres de Fray Luis no fueron ricos o hazendados, ni de esclarecido linage, sino pobres y humildes aunque Christianos viejos, limpios y libres de toda raça de Judios como Moros, y sin mezcla de mala sangre."

[35] Conversos often took their surnames from the town in which they converted to Christianity. For example, an examination of the census taken in 1510 of Conversos in Seville reveals numerous surnames taken from towns of substantial medieval Jewish communities: Sevilla, Jerez, Toledo, Córdoba, Carmona, Llerena, Marchena, Gibraleón, Zafra, Tarifa, Sanlúcar, Palencia, Palma, Aguilar, Burgos, Écija. See Claudio Guillén, "Un padrón de Conversos sevillanos (1510)," *Bulletin Hispanique*, LXXXV (1963), pp. 49–98. In his *Libro de Oración* (III parte, Tratado Segundo, II, I) having recommended a frugal diet, Fr. Luis de Granada makes the comment that in his experience New Christians live longer than Old Christians because they eat less. It seems to me that Granada is not only making a subtle allusion here to Old-Christian greed; he is also linking himself to a more spiritually correct Converso population.

the Converso Francisco de Vitoria (his name taken from the northern Spanish town), who between 1529 and 1546 occupied the prime chair in theology at Salamanca University; another was Fray Agustin Salucio, author of the famous *limpieza de sangre* treatise, whom we met at the beginning of this essay.

   Another Golden-Age figure who continues to be portrayed as Old-Christian despite important circumstantial evidence to the contrary is the sixteenth-century Seville humanist Pedro Mexía. In the introduction to the Catedra edition of Mexía's *Silva de varia leccion*, Antonio Castro writes:

> The Sevillian humanist Pedro Mexía came, according to all the references of his contemporaries, from a lineage originating in Galicia, which uprooted and expanded through all of Andalucía, especially in the zones of Córdoba and Seville, from the time that these two capitals were reconquered in the thirteenth century by King Fernando III, the Saint.
>   Among the remote ancestors of Pedro Mexía we find high ranking knights and clergy who participated with Fernando III in the conquest of Córdoba and Seville (like don Juan de Arias Mexía and don Juan Arias, archbishop of Santiago), important representatives of the military orders (like don Gonzalo Mexía, master of the order of St James, who was actively involved in the civil war between Pedro I and Enrique II of Castile) and titled nobility (like don Gonzalo Mexía, Lord of La Guardia and Marquis of Santofamia).[36]

Antonio Castro's assertion that Mexía came from a northern (and by implication Old-Christian) *hidalgo* family is, in fact, based on the genealogical studies by Mexía's Seville contemporary, Gonzalo Argote de Molina, who used his *Nobleza de Andalucía* to fabricate a noble lineage for the paternal and maternal (Mexía) branches of his own family.[37] Pedro Mexía belonged to no noble clan. He was, like Argote, the son of a successful *letrado*, and like Argote he used his family wealth to buy himself noble status (in Mexía's case this was conferred through his position as city councilor). In Mexía's *Silva de Varia Leccion* the reader is made fully aware of the author's lack of noble lineage by his insistence that nobility is achieved through merit. In the *Silva* IV, 3 of

---

[36] Pedro Mexía, *Silva de varia lección*, vol. I, ed. Antonio Castro, Catedra, Madrid, 1989, p. 9.
[37] Conversos very often fabricated false genealogies, claiming descendants in Vizcaya or Galicia, which Old-Christian Spain chose to believe were zones which Jews had not infiltrated. See note 26.

the work, Mexía takes Cicero (a man he clearly identifies with) as an example of true nobility:

> [I]n his *Oration on the agrarian law* [Mexía writes], Cicero confessed that he himself had no coat of arms as he was a man of new lineage; however, through his personal excellence (that is to say through his eminence in letters, as well as his discretion and extreme eloquence), he occupied a high position in Rome of that time and merited these and other noble and patrician privileges. Thus in his final *Oratory against Berres*, he states that for his work and services when he was a Roman magistrate, they awarded him a coat of arms...[38]

Whether or not a Galician nobleman named Mexía took part in the first Reconquest drive is a moot point; it is, however, a fact that the name Mexía was prominent among sixteenth-century Seville's Converso-dominated merchant and professional groups, as an examination of that city's notarial records attests. Indeed, a Pedro Mexía figures among a group of Converso tax collectors who fled Seville in 1481, on the arrival of the Inquisition, creating a grave financial crisis in the city.[39] Mexía's intellectual formation, both humanist and scientific (he was employed as a cosmographer in the *Casa de Contratacion*) also points to a Converso background, as does his interest in an Erasmian clerical reform program.[40] Furthermore, in his works Mexía not only demonstrates a much greater interest in the Old Testament than the New Testament, he also presents the Jewish culture as the intellectual equal of the Greek and Roman cultures—a prominent concern among Converso humanists.[41] In other words, we have no reason to take Mexía's Old-Christian provenance as an established fact.

---

[38] Pedro Mexía, *Silva de varia lección*, vol. II, Catedra, Madrid, 1990, p. 329.

[39] Juan Gil, *Los Conversos y la Inquisición Sevillana*, Vol. 1, Sevilla, p. 134. The maternal grandmother of the great Golden-Age Seville painter Diego Velázquez was also a Mexía.

[40] For an indication of the predominance of Conversos among Erasmus' early Spanish adherents, see chapters 7–9 of Marcel Bataillon's *Erasmo y España*.

[41] For example, in Silva III, 3, Mexía writes, "The first books and libraries in the world it would seem were those of the Jews; thus as they were first to have writing and the use of it, they also took care to save what they wrote." In associating the first written words with the Jews Mexía was, I believe, giving them a central place in his humanist credo. In both his *Silva de varia leccion* and in his *Coloquios*, Mexía demonstrates a much greater interest in the Old Testament than New Testament. Of the *Coloquios*, Antonio Castro notes "a strong inequality in the citations of the Old and New Testaments, with numerous references to the first and very few to the second,"

The predilection for a Converso-free Golden-Age pantheon has led many Spanish scholars into what would appear to be a naïve acceptance of all sources affirming the Old-Christian roots of Spain's great artistic and literary figures. Curiously, however, this ingenuousness is often transformed into rigid skepticism when sources indicate Jewish origins. In her articles examining the Converso backgrounds of the playwright Diego Jiménez de Enciso and the poet Juan de Jáuregui, both from Seville, Ruth Pike calls our attention to this phenomenon. Pike notes that in his 1914 study of Enciso, the eminent Spanish scholar Emilio Cotarelo y Mori presented the Enciso family as Old-Christian and noble, "despite evidence to the contrary in the documents that he [Cotarelo] utilized, namely, the inquiries conducted in 1624 and 1626 into the qualifications of two of the dramatist's nephews for entrance into the Order of Santiago. Cotarelo dismissed the seventeenth-century charges against the writer's family as vicious attempts at slander by jealous enemies." Pike further notes that: "Cotarelo's description of the noble and Old-Christian ancestry of the Encisos has been generally accepted, even though it was based on a purely subjective interpretation of the facts." Pike's own investigation into the playwright's background reveals that members of his family appeared in early sixteenth-century *composiciones*, or contracts drawn up between the Crown and groups of Conversos, under the terms of which the king returned to those condemned by the Inquisition, or their heirs, all confiscated property, in return for a large contribution to the royal treasury.[42]

In her article on the Converso lineage of Juan de Jáuregui, Ruth Pike notes that Jáuregui's biographer, José Jordan de Urries y Azara, concluded, "despite substantial information to the contrary, that the poet's family, on all sides, was of Old-Christian and Hidalgo origin." In fact, as Pike points out, Jáuregui's mother, Isabel Hurtado de Sal, was a member of a wealthy and influential Sevillian Converso clan.[43] Unfortunately, the editor of the 1993 Catedra edition of Juan de Jáuregui's collected poems, Juan Matas Caballero, appears not to have been aware of Pike's

---

without commenting on why this was so. See Castro's introduction to the *Silva de varia leccion*, vol. I, p. 52.

[42] Ruth Pike, "The Converso Origins of the Sevillian Dramatist Diego Jiménez de Enciso," *Bulletin of Hispanic Studies*, vol. LXVII, no. 2, (April 1990), pp. 129–35.

[43] Ruth Pike, "Converso Lineage and the Tribulations of the Sevillian Poet Juan de Jáurequi," *Romance Quarterly* XXXVIII (1991), pp. 423–29. The paternal side of Jáuregui's family came from Nájera, Logroño, where they were involved in the iron trade.

article; thus his introduction to the compilation perpetuates Jordan de Urries' bias for an Old-Christian Jáuregui. Matas writes:

> His [Jáuregui's] distinguished origins are endorsed by the rank of his parents, the *riojano* don Miguel Martínez de Jáuregui—who was an alderman in Seville from 1586, and whose noble origins go back to the middle of the fifteenth century in the jurisdiction of Vergara, where the estate of the Lizarralde and Jáuregui was situated—and the *sevillana* doña Isabel de Sal—of elevated Seville lineage, among whose ancestors was Pedro González de la Sal, who in 1472 was the "Judge" of Seville, and among whose close family was her cousin, the famous physician and poet Juan de Salinas y Castro. However, neither was his paternal family free of problems concerning its [claim to] noble status, nor the maternal branch free of accusations of [lack of] *limpieza de sangre*; serious questions which finally were resolved in favor of both families.[44]

The implication is that Jáuregui's *limpieza de sangre* examination successfully resolved the matter in favor of an Old-Christian lineage. In fact, the poet underwent a long, expensive and enormously painful *probanza*, which ended in 1628 with a humiliating rejection by the council of the military orders. Nine years later a new committee reversed the earlier decision, for reasons that are not altogether clear, although it appears that Jáuregui, like his friend Diego Velázquez, received his noble insignia only through the intervention of a benevolent Philip IV.[45]

It seems to me that Spanish academics of the post-Franco period have often been reluctant to explore the extent and implications of the Converso presence in early modern Spanish culture. I do not mean to suggest that they have always avoided this exploration wilfully, as adherents to a "*castizo*" outlook promoted earlier by Claudio Sánchez-Albornoz or Eugenio Asensio. I would, however, suggest that they have been formed in environments in which these "*castizo*" views have often prevailed and in which variant ideas have not been encouraged. It is thus not surprising that they have been somewhat sluggish in challenging old shibboleths. Happily, this situation has now begun to change,

---

[44] Juan de Jáuregui, *Poesia*, Catedra, Madrid, 1993, pp. 11–12 (my translation).
[45] Ruth Pike, "Converso Lineage..." p. 427. For my investigations into the Converso roots of Diego Velázquez, see "Diego Velázquez's Secret History," *Boletin del Museo del Prado*, num. 35, (1999) pp. 69–85.

although this is still not reflected in mainstream history texts, which focus on little more than the Converso as Judaizer, or alleged Judaizer, the target of Inquisition aggression. Occasionally an important figure's Converso background is acknowledged, but this only serves to create the erroneous view that all the other figures mentioned in the work are Old Christians. Outside the confines of specialist journals, the Conversos' importance to early modern Spanish culture remains understated.

INDEX

STUDIES IN MEDIEVAL AND REFORMATION TRADITIONS

(Formerly Studies in Medieval and Reformation Thought)

Edited by Andrew Colin Gow
Founded by Heiko A. Oberman†

Recent volumes in the series:

120. BUCER, M. *Briefwechsel/Correspondance*. Band VI (Mai-Oktober 1531). Herausgegeben und bearbeitet von R. Friedrich, B. Hamm, W. Simon und M. Arnold. 2006
121. POLLMANN, J. and SPICER, A. (eds.). *Public Opinion and Changing Identities in the Early Modern Netherlands*. Essays in Honour of Alastair Duke. 2007
122. BECKER, J. *Gemeindeordnung und Kirchenzucht*. Johannes a Lascos Kirchenordnung für London (1555) und die reformierte Konfessionsbildung. 2007
123. NEWHAUSER, R. (ed.) *The Seven Deadly Sins*. From Communities to Individuals. 2007
124. DURRANT, J.B. *Witchcraft, Gender and Society in Early Modern Germany*. 2007
125. ZAMBELLI, P. *White Magic, Black Magic in the European Renaissance*. From Ficino and Della Porta to Trithemius, Agrippa, Bruno. 2007
126. SCHMIDT, A. *Vaterlandsliebe und Religionskonflikt*. Politische Diskurse im Alten Reich (1555-1648). 2007
127. OCKER, C., PRINTY, M., STARENKO, P. and WALLACE, P. (eds.). *Politics and Reformations: Histories and Reformations*. Essays in Honor of Thomas A. Brady, Jr. 2007
128. OCKER, C., PRINTY, M., STARENKO, P. and WALLACE, P. (eds.). *Politics and Reformations: Communities, Polities, Nations, and Empires*. Essays in Honor of Thomas A. Brady, Jr. 2007
129. BROWN, S. *Women, Gender and Radical Religion in Early Modern Europe*. 2007
130. VAINIO, O.-P. *Justification and Participation in Christ*. The Development of the Lutheran Doctrine of Justification from Luther to the Formula of Concord (1580). 2008
131. NEWTON, J. and BATH , J. (eds.). *Witchcraft and the Act of 1604*. 2008
132. TWOMEY, L.K. *The Serpent and the Rose: The Immaculate Conception and Hispanic Poetry in the Late Medieval Period*. 2008
133. SHANTZ, D. *Between Sardis and Philadelphia*. The Life and World of Pietist Court Preacher Conrad Bröske. 2008
134. SYROS, V. *Die Rezeption der aristotelischen politischen Philosophie bei Marsilius von Padua*. Eine Untersuchung zur ersten Diktion des *Defensor pacis*. 2008
135. GENT, J. VAN. *Magic, Body and the Self in Eighteenth-Century Sweden*. 2008
136. BUCER, M. *Briefwechsel/Correspondance*. Band VII (Oktober 1531-März 1532). Herausgegeben und bearbeitet von B. Hamm, R. Friedrich, W. Simon. In Zusammenarbeit mit M. Arnold. 2008
137. ESPINOSA, A. *The Empire of the Cities*. Emperor Charles V, the *Comunero* Revolt, and the Transformation of the Spanish System. 2009
138. CRAIG, L.A. *Wandering Women and Holy Matrons*. Women as Pilgrims in the Later Middle Ages. 2009
139. REID, J.A. *King's Sister – Queen of Dissent*. Marguerite of Navarre (1492-1549) and her Evangelical Network. 2009
140. BRUMMETT, P. (ed.). *The 'Book' of Travels*: Genre, Ethnology, and Pilgrimage, 1250-1700. 2009
141. INGRAM, K. (ed.). *The Conversos and Moriscos in Late Medieval Spain and Beyond*. Volume One: Departures and Change. 2009
142. MACDONALD, A.A., VON MARTELS, Z.R.W.M. and VEENSTRA, J.R. (eds.). *Christian Humanism*. Essays in Honour of Arjo Vanderjagt. 2009
143. KEUL, I. *Early Modern Religious Communities in East-Central Europe*. Ethnic Diversity, Denominational Plurality, and Corporative Politics in the Principality of Transylvania (1526-1691). 2009
144. BAUMANN, D. *Stephen Langton: Erzbischof von Canterbury im England der Magna Carta (1207-1228)*. 2009